AF830784

Extraterritoriality and International Bribery

The book presents a collective action perspective to explain how extraterritoriality functions and assess when, and to what extent, extraterritoriality is effective. A collective action perspective provides a new account of foreign anti-bribery laws and their extraterritorial enforcement that draws on theories discussed in the field of economic governance. Within this framework, the book offers an intensive analysis of US foreign anti-bribery law such as the Foreign Corrupt Practices Act (FCPA), international law as it emanates from the OECD Anti-Bribery Convention, and comparative insights into UK law and German law. To test the theory in practice, the book provides a unique data set of more than 40 foreign anti-bribery enforcement actions conducted by the US Department of Justice (DOJ) and the Securities and Exchange Commission (SEC), and other examples from comparative jurisdictions.

Extraterritoriality and International Bribery is ideal reading for academics and students with an interest in global governance, economic crime, criminology, and law and economics, as well as practitioners concerned with foreign anti-bribery enforcement, including compliance officers, lawyers, investigating and prosecuting authorities, and business leaders. The book also discusses governance alternatives existing outside international anti-bribery law and offers policy and legal reforms proposals. The book suggests a decentralized enforcement model with the delegation of some enforcement tasks to an external body as the most appropriate governance alternative.

Branislav Hock, Ph.D., is a Lecturer in Counter Fraud Studies at the Institute of Criminal Justice Studies, University of Portsmouth. He has research expertise in the area of transnational economic crime such as corruption and bribery along with interests in corporate compliance and economic governance. Dr Hock is a member of the Tilburg Law and Economics Center (TILEC), where he worked as a researcher and completed Ph.D. in anti-corruption law. He worked in the Private Office of the Dutch Member of the European Court of Auditors and for a law firm advising on various compliance issues. Dr Hock is a co-founder of the European Compliance Center.

The Economics of Legal Relationships

Sponsored by Michigan State University College of Law

Series Editors:

Nicholas Mercuro, Michigan State University College of Law

Michael D. Kaplowitz, Michigan State University

20 Predatory Pricing in Antitrust Law and Economics
Nicola Giocoli

21 The Role of Law in Sustaining Financial Markets
Edited by Niels Philipsen and Guangdong Xu

22 Law and Economics
Philosophical issues and fundamental questions
Edited by Aristides N. Hatzis and Nicholas Mercuro

23 Public Procurement Policy
Edited by Gustavo Piga and Tünde Tatrai

24 Legal Origins and the Efficiency Dilemma
Nuno Garoupa, Carlos Gómez Ligüerre and Lela Mélon

25 Law and Economics of Public Procurement Reforms
Edited by Gustavo Piga and Tünde Tátrai

26 Law and Economics as Interdisciplinary Practice
Philosophical, Methodological and Historical Perspectives
Péter Cserne and Magdalena Malecka

27 Extraterritoriality and International Bribery
A Collective Action Perspective
Branislav Hock

*The first three volumes listed above are published by and available from Elsevier

For a full list of titles in this series please visit https://www.routledge.com/The-Economics-of-Legal-Relationships/book-series/ELR

Extraterritoriality and International Bribery

A Collective Action Perspective

Branislav Hock

Routledge
Taylor & Francis Group
LONDON AND NEW YORK

First published 2020
by Routledge
2 Park Square, Milton Park, Abingdon, Oxon OX14 4RN

and by Routledge
605 Third Avenue, New York, NY 10017

Routledge is an imprint of the Taylor & Francis Group, an informa business

© 2020 Branislav Hock

The right of Branislav Hock to be identified as author of this work has been asserted by him in accordance with sections 77 and 78 of the Copyright, Designs and Patents Act 1988.

All rights reserved. No part of this book may be reprinted or reproduced or utilised in any form or by any electronic, mechanical, or other means, now known or hereafter invented, including photocopying and recording, or in any information storage or retrieval system, without permission in writing from the publishers.

Trademark notice: Product or corporate names may be trademarks or registered trademarks, and are used only for identification and explanation without intent to infringe.

British Library Cataloguing-in-Publication Data
A catalogue record for this book is available from the British Library

Library of Congress Cataloging-in-Publication Data
A catalog record has been requested for this book

ISBN: 978-0-367-08607-7 (hbk)
ISBN: 978-0-429-02334-7 (ebk)

Typeset in Bembo
by codeMantra

To my parents Eva and Branislav for all love, support, understanding, and patience.

Contents

Preface xi
List of abbreviations xiii
Acknowledgements xv

1 Introduction 1
1.1 Foreign anti-bribery enforcement and competitive disadvantage 1
1.2 Extraterritoriality and international bribery 4
1.3 Extraterritorial enforcement and collective action 8
1.4 The outline and focus 9
References 11

2 International bribery and collective action problems 13
2.1 Introduction 13
2.2 The theory of collective action 14
2.3 Why the regulation of international bribery is a collective action problem 19
2.4 How extraterritoriality relates to the collective action problem 30
2.5 Conclusion 34
References 35

3 The evolution of foreign anti-bribery legislation 39
3.1 Introduction 39
3.2 The regulation of foreign bribery in historical context 40
3.3 The OECD Convention and functional equivalence 46
3.4 Excursion to national foreign anti-bribery laws 52
3.5 Conclusion 55
References 56

4 The OECD Anti-Bribery Convention and national foreign anti-bribery laws 58

4.1 Introduction 58

4.2 The offense of bribery of foreign public officials 59

4.3 The briber: "any person" 60

4.4 Indirect bribery: intermediaries and complicity 61

4.5 The bribed party: "foreign public official" 70

4.6 The bribe: "any undue advantage" 75

4.7 Jurisdiction 79

4.8 Enforcement 86

4.9 Cooperation and coordination 96

4.10 Conclusion 105

References 106

5 Foreign anti-bribery enforcement schemes 109

5.1 Introduction 109

5.2 Foreign bribery resolution: formal and functional understanding 110

5.3 Enforcement in the US, the UK, and Germany 113

5.4 Qualitative study – analytical framework 118

5.5 Endemic bribery: Siemens *121*

5.6 We will catch them all: Bonny Island *130*

5.7 International bribery and alternative laws: BAE 140

5.8 Conclusion 144

References 146

6 Patterns of foreign anti-bribery enforcement 147

6.1 Introduction 147

6.2 Foreign bribery and territorial nexus with the US 148

6.3 Foreign bribery and concurrence of substantive laws 151

6.4 Indirect bribery: parent–subsidiary liability and agency relationship 161

6.5 Successor's liability 168

6.6 US enforcement and conspiracy charges 169

6.7 Cooperation and coordination 174

6.8 Conclusion 187

References 189

7 The effectiveness of extraterritorial anti-bribery enforcement 191

7.1 Introduction 191

7.2 The effectiveness of international regimes 192

7.3 The effectiveness of the OECD "unilateral" anti-bribery regime in practice 195

7.4 An evolution to a shaky multilateral enforcement regime 203
7.5 Conclusion 213
References 213

8 How should the OECD anti-bribery enforcement regime foster collective action? 215
8.1 Introduction 215
8.2 Desirable and undesirable heterogeneity: when external governance is just effective 215
8.3 Addressing credibility problems 217
8.4 Addressing clarity problems 217
8.5 Conclusion 225
References 226

9 Beyond the OECD: international court and other alternatives 227
9.1 Introduction 227
9.2 International anti-corruption court 228
9.3 WTO model: a body deciding state disputes 229
9.4 Decentralized enforcement models: eCommunication 230
9.5 Transnational regulatory networks 234
9.6 Self-regulation and corporate compliance 239
9.7 Conclusion 242
References 243

10 Conclusion 246
10.1 Foreign anti-bribery enforcement as a collective action problem 247
10.2 More collective action: who else is coming on board? 247
10.3 External governance as a response to new collective action problems 249
10.4 Transnational law: effectiveness and the rule of law – public and private 250
References 252

Table of cases and settlements 255
International Agreements 259
Statutes 261
Recommendations, guidelines, and reports of public authorities and international organizations 263
Index 267

Preface

When I started thinking about the topic of this book in 2012, international anti-corruption law was still a marginal issue in Europe. Ever since then, the interest in this topic has been growing. This is not a surprise given how American, and increasingly also non-American, enforcers are harshly sanctioning firms from all around the world for actions undertaken in far-away jurisdictions. I can say with confidence that at the end of 2019, international anti-corruption law has emerged as a specialized legal and research field that is recognized all around the world.

The global increase in the enforcement of foreign anti-bribery laws leads us naturally to a more sophisticated discussion about the desirability, effectiveness, and fairness of the foreign anti-bribery enforcement regime. In this new era, a large number of specialized corporate bribery-related conferences, business workshops, podcasts, policy events, and research group meetings are taking part every month. Increasingly, these discussions recognize the specificity of this legal field, especially that certain jurisdictional, substantive, and procedural elements of national legal orders function very differently from other legal fields.

In this book, I tried to conceptualize this complexity by introducing a collective action perspective. The perspective will help readers distinguish between foreign anti-bribery law in books and these legal provision and enforcement processes that matter in practice. Moreover, the perspective allows readers to see the function of quasi-legal processes that makes this legal field so complex. You will learn, for example, about patterns of tough negotiations between multiple enforcement authorities and corporations, and how these modify legal institutions and determine enforcement outcomes. This should be appealing to academics and students with an interest in global governance, economic crime, criminology, and law and economics, as well as prove useful to practitioners concerned with foreign anti-bribery enforcement, including compliance officers, lawyers, investigating and prosecuting authorities, and business leaders. Moreover, my aspiration is to allude a vision for the future by engaging in a normative discussion about the desirability of extraterritoriality and about an appropriate anti-bribery enforcement model.

Branislav Hock
Portsmouth
May 2019

Abbreviations

1997	Recommendation Revised Recommendation of the Council on Combating Bribery in International Business Transactions
2000	MLA Convention European Union Convention on Mutual Legal Assistance
2009	Recommendation for Further Combating Bribery of Foreign Public Officials
2013	Act Crime and Courts Act 2013
ACWG	G20 Anti-Corruption Working Group
ADM	Archer Daniels Midland Company
Alba	Aluminum Bahrain B.S.C.
AON	AON Limited
AWAC	Alcoa World Alumina and Chemicals
BGB	Bürgerliches Gesetzbuch
Bribery Act	Bribery Act 2010
Bundeskriminalamt	German Federal Criminal Police Office
CBF	Brazilian Football Confederation
CoE	Council of Europe
CONCACAF	Confederation of North Central American and Caribbean Association Football
CONMEBOL	Confederación Sudamericana de Fútbol
DOJ	United States Department of Justice
DOS	United States Department of State
DPA	Deferred Prosecution Agreement
DT	Deutsche Telekom
EU	European Union
FATF	The Financial Action Task Force
FBI	Federal Bureau of Investigation
FCA	Financial Conduct Authority
FCPA	United States Foreign Corrupt Practices Act
FIFA	Fédération Internationale de Football Association
FIUs	Financial Intelligence Units

FSA	Financial Services Authority
GAO	United States Government Accountability Office
GDP	Gross Domestic Product
Grundgesetz	German Constitution
HP	Hewlett-Packard Bribery Scheme
ICBC	ICBC Standard Bank
ICC	International Criminal Court
ICSID	Convention on the Settlement of Investment Disputes
IntBestG	Gesetz zur Bekämpfung Internationaler Bestechung
ITAR	International Traffic in Arms Regulation
JGC	JGC Corporation
JIT	Joint Investigation Team
J&J	Johnson & Johnson
KBR	Kellogg Brown & Root, LLC
KBR	Kellogg Brown & Root Inc.
MLA	Mutual Legal Assistance
MNCs	Multinational Corporations
MWKL	M.W. Kellogg Limited
Nabisco	RJR Nabisco Inc. v. European Community
NGOs	Non-Governmental Organizations
NNPC	Nigerian National Petroleum Corporation
NPA	Non-Prosecution Agreement
NRAs	National Regulatory Authorities
NYSE	New York Stock Exchange
OAS	Organization of American States
OECD	Organization for Economic Cooperation and Development
OECD Convention	Convention on Combating Bribery of Foreign Public Officials in International Business Transactions
OWiG	Gesetz über Ordnungswidrigkeiten
Petrobras	Petróleo Brasileiro S.A.
Resource Guide	A Resource Guide to the U.S. Foreign Corrupt Practices Act
RICO	Racketeer Influenced and Corrupt Organization Act
SBM	SBM Offshore N.V.
SEC	Securities and Exchange Commission
SFO	Serious Fraud Office
StGB	Strafgesetzbuch
StPO	Strafprozeßordnung
UNCAC	United Nations Convention Against Corruption
UK	United Kingdom
UN	United Nations
US	United States
WGB	Working Group on Bribery
WTO	World Trade Organization

Acknowledgements

This book is based on my doctoral thesis, written during my time at the Tilburg Law and Economics Center in the Netherlands, and re-worked from my current location at the University of Portsmouth in the United Kingdom. This book could not have been written without the help of many colleagues and friends.

Particular thanks must go to my doctoral thesis supervisor Prof. Dr. Pierre Larouche for recognizing my research potential and for giving me the necessary freedom and academic support during my Ph.D. studies. I would like to express my gratitude to my doctoral thesis supervisor Dr. Angelos Dimopoulos not only for his valuable and constructive suggestions during the planning and development of this research work, but also for his empathy and emotional support. His willingness to give his time so generously has been very much appreciated. I would also like to thank the members of my Ph.D. Committee, Prof. Dr. Leigh Hancher, Prof. Dr. Eric Talley, Prof. Dr. Kevin Davis, Dr. Cecily Rose, and Dr. Jens Prüfer for their willingness to read the manuscript and provide comments.

I would like to express my deep gratitude to Prof. Dr. Leigh Hancher for her trust in me, her personal guidance, and for her encouraging words. My grateful thanks to Prof. Dr. Alex Brenninkmeier, Gaston Moonen, and Raphal Debets for giving me the opportunity to work in their team at the European Court of Auditors, teaching me how to deal efficiently with important policy issues, and for many other skills they helped me to develop.

Many thanks also due to Dr. David Shepherd, Dr. Elina Karpacheva, Chris Lewis, Prof. Andrew Spalding, Prof. Dr. Mark Button, Olia Kanevskaia, Dr. Suren Gomtsyan, Prof. Dr. Panos Delimatsis, Dr. Costantino Grasso, Dr. Lorenzo Pasculli, and Prof. Dr. Francis Pakes for their comments and suggestions on earlier drafts of this book.

I wish to thank Tilburg Law School for selecting my research proposal and awarding me a fully funded Ph.D. position, all the members of TILEC, colleagues at the University of Portsmouth and the ICJS, and all other colleagues and friends for their help and support. I am grateful to Fordham Law School where I spent time working on the book as a visiting researcher. I am also grateful to the staff at Routledge for their guidance and support in bringing the book to press.

Finally, I am thankful to my parents Eva and Branislav, my wife Elina, my sister Eva, and whole my family for all love, support, understanding, and patience.

1 Introduction

This book attempts to come to grips with extraterritorial enforcement in the area of international bribery. Extraterritoriality is the key driver of foreign anti-bribery enforcement: national enforcement authorities can sanction subjects, both domestic and foreign, acting beyond the borders of a given country. While extraterritoriality stems from international treaties such as the Convention on Combating Bribery of Foreign Public Officials in International Business Transactions (the OECD Convention),[1] each national enforcement authority has its own perception regarding whether, how, and why a specific case of bribery should be prosecuted. It leads to a wide array of enforcement responses accompanied by legal and political uncertainty and a controversy over the desirability of extraterritoriality.

This study introduces the framework of collective action to analyze and evaluate extraterritoriality. The book argues that extraterritoriality has initiated collective action to fight international bribery. This gives extraterritoriality a price because it has been an alternative to regulatory failures and markets in which corruption and bribery are in practice not sanctioned. The ultimate question, therefore, is not whether extraterritoriality has a price. It is whether, and when, that price is worth paying. Then, how much public good extraterritoriality can produce? And, conversely, what are the limits of extraterritorial enforcement in initiating and sustaining collective action?

1.1 Foreign anti-bribery enforcement and competitive disadvantage

Businesses generally disfavor heavy regulation. More than anything else, however, businesses hate laws that provide their competitors with an edge. The same is true in the field of international anti-bribery law in which businesses have lobbied hard for the level playing field rather than for a lighter

1 OECD Convention on Combating Bribery of Foreign Public Officials in International Business Transactions. Paris, 17 December 1997, in force 15 February 1999, 37 ILM 1 (hereinafter OECD Convention). Available in OECD (2011).

regulation. Paradoxically, the effect of business lobby has been the establishment of an international anti-bribery regime and global increase in catching and punishing companies for international bribery.

Even the advent of the Trump's administration associated with the rise of trade protectionism has not weakened international anti-bribery law. President Trump called the Foreign Corrupt Practices Act (FCPA)[2] a "horrible law." This view of US foreign anti-bribery law has been common among many business people since the adoption of the FCPA in 1977. What they see as "horrible" is that American firms that bribe in far-away jurisdictions face potentially harsh sanctions in the US.[3] In *Bonny Island* bribery scheme, for example, KBR LLC and its parent companies Halliburton and KBR Inc. secured four contracts to design and build natural gas plants in Nigeria worth more than $6 billion. In order to do so, they bribed Nigerian government officials. The United States Department of Justice (DOJ) and the Securities and Exchange Commission (SEC) sanctioned these American businesses with criminal charges and civil penalties of $579 million. One could say: if they did not bribe, other businesses would bribe and secure the contracts.

Nonetheless, such view of the US foreign anti-bribery law is becoming out of step with the times. One does not need to lighten strict national standard to level the playing field. Powerful states can impose such standard on foreigners: 27 out of the 40 largest enforcement actions between the years 2008 and 2018 were directed against non-US corporations (see Chapter 7). What President Trump underestimated is that Halliburton and other US firms are not the only corporations sanctioned by the US authorities. In *Bonny Island,* French, Italian, Dutch, and Japanese firms were also charged with violations of the FCPA alongside the US firms and paid approximately $1 billion in sanctions to the US treasury.[4] In March 2019, the US authorities have started sanctioning even Russian national champions. Consider MTS, the largest telecommunication company in

2 Foreign Corrupt Practices Act of 1977, 15 U.S.C. §78dd-1 et seq. (hereinafter FCPA).

3 "They [the U.S.] prosecute for going over to China and Mexico and other countries and getting business and creating jobs in this country. […] Now, every other country goes into these places and they do what they have to do. […] We are like a policeman of the world it is ridiculous. Every other country in the world is doing it, we're not allowed to. It puts us at a huge disadvantage." CNBC, Trump: Dimon's Woes & Zuckerberg's Prenuptial (15th May 2012) < https://www.cnbc.com/video/2012/05/15/trump-dimons-woes-zuckerbergs-prenuptial.html?play=1> accessed 25 February 2019.

4 The FCPA makes it an offense to provide anything of value to a foreign official for the purposes of securing any improper advantage in order to assist the actor in obtaining or retaining business. 15 U.S.C. §§78dd-1(a), 78dd-2(a), 78dd-3(a). United States Department of Justice and United States Securities and Exchange Commission, 'A Resource Guide to the U.S. Foreign Corrupt Practices Act' (2012) 10 < https://www.justice.gov/sites/default/files/criminal-fraud/legacy/2015/01/16/guide.pdf> accessed 27 February 2019.

Russia that was charged with $850 million for paying bribes in Uzbekistan.[5] Therefore, the US foreign anti-bribery enforcement is not an action directed exclusively against US businesses that bribe but also against non-US businesses.

Moreover, the American businesses lobby worked hard to establish an international anti-bribery regime in order to subject non-American businesses to an anti-bribery standard similar to the US standard (Rose, 2015: 1). They were successful. Besides the introduction of extraterritorial jurisdiction under the 1998 amendments to the FCPA, also other countries introduced foreign anti-bribery laws.[6] More recently, non-US enforcement authorities have started enforcing their own anti-bribery laws. Consider Rolls-Royce, Telia Company, and SBM Offshore, global companies which all entered into global foreign bribery settlements, and agreed to pay fortunes to the US, UK, Brazilian and Dutch authorities because of their bribing. These global settlements indicate that the time when the US was the only enforcer of foreign anti-bribery laws has passed. The foreign anti-bribery regulatory landscape is undeniably becoming global.

In this context, the view that every non-US country in the world is tolerating foreign bribery is misleading. It is true that the extraterritorial enforcement of foreign anti-bribery laws was a unilateral effort of the US. Recently, however, non-US jurisdictions have stepped forward with their own regulatory responses and the enforcement has become a multilateral effort. At the same time, it would be misleading to argue that US extraterritoriality is without limits. Especially companies from China and India have not been sanctioned for international bribery. This is partly because many Chinese and Indian companies are not subject to the FCPA and other anti-bribery laws. Yet, this is partly also because the US enforcement authorities did not treat Chinese and Indian corporations in the same way as other non-US corporations that are subject to the FCPA (see Section 7.3.2). This dynamic may well change soon as the DOJ has recently established the Initiative to Combat Chinese Economic Espionage. One priority of the initiative is to prioritize international bribery cases that include Chinese companies and individuals (Section 10.2.1).[7]

5 United States Department of Justice, Mobile TeleSystems PJSC and Its Uzbek Subsidiary Enter into Resolutions of $850 Million with the Department of Justice for Paying Bribes in Uzbekistan (Press Release 7 March 2019) <https://www.justice.gov/opa/pr/mobile-telesystems-pjsc-and-its-uzbek-subsidiary-enter-resolutions-850-million-department> accessed 18 April 2019.

6 The International Anti-Bribery and Fair Competition Act 1998. Prior to the 1998 amendment of the FCPA, the US approach was based only on territorial jurisdiction.

7 United States (2018) Attorney General Jeff Session's China Initiative Fact Sheet <https://www.justice.gov/opa/speech/file/1107256/download> accessed 28 April 2019.

1.2 Extraterritoriality and international bribery

A collective action perspective introduced in this book highlights two crucial advantages that extraterritoriality offers. The first one is that extraterritoriality can offset failures of some states to regulate international bribery. The second is that extraterritoriality can incentivize non-US jurisdictions to step forward with their own anti-bribery enforcement. This potential gives extraterritoriality a price that should be analyzed and evaluated (see Section 1.3 and Chapter 2). The collective action perspective should inform a broader discussion about the desirability of extraterritoriality, in general, and in the specific context of international bribery. This section summarizes the broader discussion about the desirability of extraterritoriality.

1.2.1 Extraterritorial legislation as a response to global problems

More generally, extraterritoriality of national laws can be seen as the states' response to the rising economic and regulatory powers of multinational corporations (MNCs). While MNCs create jobs, wealth, and innovate, MNCs act mostly in their private interest, in order to maximize profits (Danielsen, 2005). The pursuit of private interest, without good governance, however, results in financial breakdowns, infringements on human rights, and other global problems (Leisinger, 2009).

To address global problems in both the US and the European Union (EU), national states and the EU have increasingly subject MNCs to extraterritorial forms of legislation. In areas such as cybersecurity, environment, and human rights, they have unilaterally, or under the auspices of international law, adopted statutes allowing them to extend their jurisdiction to both domestic and foreign firms (Parrish, 2009: 852–856; Zerk, 2010; Coffee, 2014; Scott, 2014). International bribery is one global problem that has been tackled by extraterritoriality.

International bribery is a hard nut to crack. There is a universal agreement that bribery in international business transactions is undesirable because it undermines overall productivity and public welfare (Shleifer and Vishny, 1993; Méon and Khalid, 2005). Yet, most of the states have struggled to regulate international bribery effectively. They have struggled because they do not have sufficient laws, expertise, political will, and resources to address the transnational character of bribery. Bribery is based on the use of complicated systems of corporate veils to bribe globally public and private officials. In addition, international bribery includes third parties that are controlled by or act on behalf of the main parties: bribe-giver and bribe-taker, and complicated transnational communication channels and payment systems.[8] This struggle to regulate international bribery features a collective action problem (see Section 1.3 and Chapter 2).

8 See the discussion about complexity of foreign bribery in Chapter 2.

Global bribery schemes can hardly be regulated effectively by legislation that is strictly limited by state borders. Without extraterritorial legislation, MNCs could hide themselves from the investigation in secure jurisdictions or be shielded from liability by their intermediaries. The need to overcome these problems is the reason why we see the rise of extraterritoriality in the area of international anti-bribery law. This rise is closely tied with the adoption of the OECD Convention at the end of 1997. The OECD Convention has directly facilitated the adoption of specific foreign anti-bribery legislation, strongly inspired by the FCPA, by countries such as the UK and Germany, and facilitated the cooperation between the US and these countries.[9] Yet the rise of extraterritoriality is not without controversy.

1.2.2 Extraterritorial enforcement is controversial

The higher the expansion of extraterritoriality, the more concern these interested in democratic sovereignty, stable international relations, allocative efficiency, and the rule of law will show. To some extent, these concerns are mitigated by international law because extraterritoriality is envisaged and supported by a number of international treaties. In some cases, these treaties may increase the clarity of measures, the trust between involved actors and their cooperation and coordination. In other cases, however, international law does not prevent various legal, political, and economic conflicts associated with extraterritorial enforcement.[10]

In the area of foreign anti-bribery law, the OECD Convention provides legal basis for extraterritoriality. The OECD Convention provides that states should interpret the territorial basis for jurisdiction broadly.[11] Being it because of moral concerns, good governance issues, negative effects on economic development, and because bribery distorts international competitive conditions, the wide jurisdiction is deemed necessary to oppose negative effects of international bribery. More specifically, the broad application is an attempt to oppose the power of MNCs in order to make markets more competitive (see Keohane, 2005: 1–5). In other words, foreign anti-bribery law and its extraterritoriality, similarly as in competition law and other fields of law, are to a large extent an issue of economic governance and market regulation.

9 The OECD Convention operates in conjunction with many other important international anti-corruption treaties such as the United Nations Convention against Corruption. The UNCAC is still in the review stage that focuses on its implementation, rather than on the enforcement of its provisions. United Nations, Convention against Corruption, New York, 31 October 2003, in force 14 December 2005, 2349 U.N.T.S. 41 43 I.L.M. 37 (hereinafter UNCAC). In this context, see Zagaris (2015: 137–138).

10 Consider, for example, an international conflict between the EU and the US over EU passenger sensitive data sharing with US authorities (see Ryngaert, 2015).

11 Article 4 of the OECD Convention provides that a Signatory shall establish jurisdiction when the offense is committed in whole or in part in its territory. Paragraph 25 of the Official Commentaries to the OECD Convention (OECD, 2011) further explains that "the territorial basis for jurisdiction should be interpreted broadly so that an extensive physical connection to the bribery act is not required."

1.2.2.1 Moral imperialism critique

Economic governance and market regulation, however, compete with other policy rationales. This is why extraterritoriality is the source of intellectual and practical conflicts. Historically, the first efforts to regulate international bribery were largely based on a neoliberal ideology that supported privatization, internationalization, deregulation, and free trade (Kennedy, 1999). Negative economic effects assigned to corruption and bribery were claimed to be universal and presented as the justification for the application of foreign anti-bribery legislation to conduct occurring in other jurisdictions. A number of scholars argue that this is moral imperialism, i.e. the imposition of western anti-corruption standards onto regions with different values.[12] For example, US foreign anti-bribery enforcement in Nigeria might be seen as the imposition of foreign standards on Nigerian markets without involving Nigerian citizens thereby threatening democratic sovereignty.

1.2.2.2 Double measure: domestic vs. foreign corruption

Moral imperialism may be accompanied by hypocrisy in the form of ignoring corruption problems at home. While the US enforcement authorities set a very strong anti-bribery standard in far-away jurisdictions, the US Supreme Court has been narrowing the definition of domestic corruption since the 1970s. In *Citizens United v Federal Election Commission*, the US Supreme Court confirmed the right of corporations to spend de facto unlimited resources to influence elections.[13]

Furthermore, legal gaps in US anti-corruption laws make it difficult to sanction cases of domestic corruption. For example, in 2014, former Virginia governor was sentenced to two years in prison for setting up meetings for a businessman with state health officials. In exchange, he and his wife enjoyed gifts and sweetheart loans worth $175,000.[14] However, this was not enough for the US Supreme Court that overturned the ruling because the government did not show a connection between these gifts and an "official act."[15] In other words, giving expensive gifts to a public official in exchange for setting up meetings with other public officials in order to lobby them was not considered as an official act, hence legal. These domestic limitations can make it hard to justify the enforcement of US foreign anti-bribery law in far-away jurisdictions.

12 The centrum of the discussion was between Nichols (2000), who supports the extraterritorial enforcement, and Salbu (1999) who criticizes it.

13 Citizens United v. FEC (558 U.S. 310). For further discussion about the implications of the decision, see Teachout (2016).

14 Smith, D. (27 June 2016) Supreme Court Overturns Bribery Conviction for Former Virginia Governor. *Guardian* <https://www.theguardian.com/law/2016/jun/27/bob-mcdonnell-supreme-court-ruling-bribery-overturned> accessed 25 February 2019.

15 McDonnell v. United States, June 27, 2016 at 14.

1.2.2.3 Negative effects of foreign anti-bribery enforcement

Furthermore, the extraterritorial application of law has important economic consequences. Spalding (2010) claims that overseas anti-bribery enforcement is, de facto, the imposition of economic sanctions against emerging markets. In effect, if enforcement becomes too demanding, the economy of some countries will struggle, for instance, because relatively more corrupt countries will tend to attract investments from firms based in relatively more corrupt countries and deter investments from firms based in relatively less corrupt countries (Cuervo-Cazurra, 2006). Therefore, despite the fact that foreign anti-bribery enforcement may limit some bribery, it can also negatively influence economic growth and the inflow of foreign direct investment in developing countries (see Koehler, 2010; Westbrook, 2011).

1.2.2.4 Extraterritoriality and the conflict of interests

Besides the mitigation of global problems such as corruption and bribery, the politico-economic interests are a crucial driver of extraterritoriality. These interests, however, may be in conflict with what is needed to address the global problems. Sanctioning of perpetrators in the US may be similarly important as compensating victims that suffered because of the sanctioned perpetrators. While firms from all around the world are being harshly sanctioned in the US for actions undertaken in far-away jurisdictions, the US justice system does not focus so much on injured parties. For example, US law either does not recognize a private right of action for injuries suffered outside the US or the US courts have been increasingly foreclosing this opportunity.[16] Yet, more focus on foreign victims could help justify expansive forms of extraterritoriality.

We can go on and criticize extraterritoriality from much more angles. International lawyers might see some forms of extraterritoriality violating statutory constructions or even as unconstitutional (Colangelo, 2014). MNCs that have to comply with extraterritorial laws might, for instance, be calling for more legal certainty and their right not to be punished by multiple disorganized enforcement authorities for the same offense.[17] Russian hackers might argue that the US Department of the Treasury's Office of Foreign Assets Control (OFAC) lacks legitimacy to sanction them for cyber-attacks.[18] Citizens of Nigeria and Papua New Guinea that suffered from pollution linked to operations of MNCs might find it unfair that monetary sanctions related to extraterritorial enforcement are transferred to a foreign treasury. The criticisms cast a shadow of doubt over whether extraterritoriality has any merit at all. This book introduces a collective action perspective in order to contribute to this broader discussion about the desirability of extraterritoriality.

16 See, for example, Morrison vs. Nat'l Austl. Bank, 561 U.S. 247 (2010).

17 See the discussion about the *ne bis in idem* principle in Chapter 4.

18 US Department of Treasury (11 June 2018), Treasury Sanctions Russian Federal Service Enablers <https://home.treasury.gov/news/press-releases/sm0410> accessed 25 February 2019.

1.3 Extraterritorial enforcement and collective action

This book introduces a collective action perspective as a new account of foreign anti-bribery laws and their extraterritorial enforcement. Analyzing and evaluating extraterritoriality from the perspective of collective action complements the ongoing discussion about the desirability extraterritoriality, in general, and in the specific context of international bribery. Furthermore, politicians, prosecutors, practitioners, researchers, and students in building up their strategies, compliance programs and theories should not rely on a dogmatic analysis of anti-bribery laws and should not blindly follow simplistic data about anti-bribery enforcement tends. The collective action perspective allows these interested in foreign anti-bribery law to understand how enforcement functions in practice, including complex interactions between national enforcement authorities and firms, and how these interactions evolve with the changing enforcement landscape.

The key premise of the perspective is that extraterritoriality can offset failures of some states to regulate international bribery as well as can incentivize new states to step forward with their own anti-bribery enforcement. This gives extraterritoriality a price because it can be an alternative to regulatory failures and markets in which global problems such as corruption and bribery are legal or illegal but in practice not sanctioned. Although extraterritoriality is, and should be, subject to criticism, we should not neglect that extraterritoriality could be effective in initiating collective action to fight societal problems such as international bribery.

The collective action perspective is based on an assumption that states are more effective in addressing global societal problems if they cooperate and coordinate their action in the provision of public goods. In our case, such public good is the enforcement of foreign anti-bribery laws. The problem with the provision of public goods is that those members of the international community of states that invest in enforcement cannot exclude other states from free-riding on the beneficial effects of enforcement (see Olson, 1971). Hence, the collective action problem: if each member of the community prefers to free-ride, then the public good will simply not be provided (see Heather and Peiffer, 2015).[19] In other words, the provision of foreign anti-bribery enforcement is a public good because placing as many corporations as possible under strict regulatory scrutiny facilitates, assumedly, the achievement of the aim of international anti-corruption policy (see Section 2.3.3).[20]

19 Heather and Peiffer (2015) discuss how collective action problems undermine the effectiveness of institutions meant to fight corruption.

20 In this context, the objective of international anti-corruption policy – open and competitive markets – helps to define public goods under the methodology of collective action. In this sense, the objective of open and competitive markets is the justification for resolving the collective action problem.

In the remainder of the book, we will see that the link between extraterritoriality and the provision of the enforcement as a public good is more complicated. Given the steady uptick in countries jumping on the foreign anti-bribery enforcement bandwagon, the provision of public good also requires cooperation and coordination of national enforcement authorities (see Section 2.4). Hence, with the increasing number of states that enforce anti-bribery laws, the real collective action problem lies in multilateral enforcement (for more detail, see Chapter 2). The collective action perspective will reveal how legal institutions and governance mechanisms accompanying multijurisdictional enforcement make a difference between more and less effective solutions to collective action problems (Chapter 7).

1.4 The outline and focus

The main aim of this book is to show how extraterritoriality functions and evaluate to what extent extraterritoriality solves collective action problems associated with foreign anti-bribery enforcement. Chapter 2 introduces a collective action framework as discussed by economic governance scholars, which provides a key methodological innovation and as such a contribution to assessing the effectiveness of legal institutions. The chapter explains what is a collective action problem, why, and in what way, the regulation of international bribery can be viewed as a collective action problem. Moreover, the chapter also discusses the parameters that determine how collective action problems can be resolved.

Chapters 3 and 4 focus on international anti-bribery legislation. Chapter 3 introduces the history of international anti-bribery legislation and explains the key characteristics that distinguish it from domestic anti-corruption legislation. The chapter also explains the evolution of international anti-bribery legislation and analyzes key principles and provisions of the OECD Convention. This book primarily focuses on the OECD Convention because no other international treaty has had a bigger impact on the functioning of foreign anti-bribery extraterritorial enforcement. The book will refer to principles, norms, rules and decision-making procedures related to foreign anti-bribery enforcement as the "OECD anti-bribery enforcement regime."

Chapter 4 analyzes foreign anti-bribery legislation, primarily the OECD Convention and the national laws of the US, and where necessary of other enforcement actors, such as the UK and Germany. This is done from the perspective of collective action, focusing on legal norms determining the provision of enforcement, legal mechanisms that incentivize cooperation and coordination between national enforcement authorities, and legal ambiguities that may cause cooperation and coordination problems.

Chapters 5 and 6 adopt a qualitative approach in order to shed light on what happens beyond the formal legal framework. Numbers and other statistical data are important and can indicate patterns and help to compare enforcement trends, however, their validity is limited because of the complex institutional dimension of foreign anti-bribery enforcement. Chapter 5 explains how foreign anti-bribery cases are structured, provides an overview of the enforcement activity in the US, the UK, and Germany, and an in-depth case study of foreign anti-bribery enforcement practice in three "classic" enforcement schemes, including *Siemens, Bonny Island, and BAE Systems*.

Chapter 6 builds on the in-depth case study in order to identify common patterns of enforcement. The chapter examines 40 largest foreign anti-bribery enforcement actions concluded between from January 2008 to December 2018. The chapter discusses the following questions: How territorial jurisdiction is established? How, and why, do national enforcement authorities use different charges, including the conspiracy charges, to prosecute foreign bribery? And how the concept of corporate liability is interpreted by enforcement authorities when prosecuting MNCs for bribing? What is more, the chapter explains when, how, and why national enforcement authorities cooperate with each other and coordinate their enforcement actions.

Chapters 7 through 9 evaluate extraterritoriality and provide policy recommendations. The value of the collective action framework is materialized in Chapter 7 that explains how, when, and to what extent, extraterritoriality is effective in solving collective action problems.[21] Chapter 7 applies the collective action framework (presented in Chapter 2) and explains in what way and to what extent, extraterritoriality is effective in solving enforcement difficulties of the OECD anti-bribery enforcement regime.

Chapter 8 provides policy and legal reforms proposals. The chapter is relatively narrow as it provides suggestions specific to the OECD anti-bribery enforcement regime so that states and the OECD may consider how extraterritoriality contributes to solving collective action problems, and adopt a policy to foster collective action.

Chapter 9 analyzes alternative solutions to collective action problems, both in the area of anti-bribery and in other fields. Chapter 9 offers explanations why and when an enforcement system supervised by an international tribunal such as the International Criminal Court (ICC), the World Trade Organization (WTO) model, and more de-centralized solutions could work, and why, and when, they could not work. Furthermore, this chapter also discusses the impact of private actors on collective action and indicates how private and public actors can, and should, cooperate to further mitigate collective action problems. As the book presents the link between extraterritoriality and collective action as a general conceptual challenge, final conclusions are relevant not only in anti-bribery law but also in other fields of law.

The final chapter summarizes the book and sets a research agenda for the future.

21 The notion of regime effectiveness is commonly understood as "the extent to which regimes contribute to solving or mitigating the problems that motivate those people who create the regimes" (Young, 2011: 19854) referring to (Young, 1999: 109).

References

Coffee, J. C. (2014) 'Extraterritorial Financial Regulation: Why E.T. Can't Come Home' 99 Cornell Law Review 1259.

Colangelo, A. J. (2014) 'What Is Extraterritorial Jurisdiction' (2014) 99 Cornell Law Review 1303.

Cuervo-Cazurra, A. (2006) 'Who Cares about Corruption?' 37 Journal of International Business Studies 807.

Danielsen, D. (2005) 'How Corporations Govern: Taking Corporate Power Seriously in Transnational Regulation and Governance' 46 Harvard International Law Journal 411.

Heather, M. and Peiffer, C. (2015) Corruption and Collective Action. U4 Anti-Corruption Resource Center, Research Paper 32 <http://publications.dlprog.org/CorruptionandCollectiveAction.pdf> accessed 25 February 2019.

Hock, B. and Gomtsian, S. (2018) 'Private Order Building: The State in the Role of the Civil Society and the Case of FIFA' 17 The International Sports Law Journal 186.

Kennedy, D. (1999) 'The International Anti-Corruption Campaign' 14 Connecticut Journal of International Law 455.

Keohane R. O. (2005) 'Global Governance and Democratic Accountability' In R. Wilkinson (Ed.) *Global Governance Reader* (pp. 121–139). London: Routledge.

Koehler, M. (2010) 'The Facade of FCPA Enforcement' 41 Georgetown Journal of International Law 907.

Leisinger, K. M. (2009), 'The Role of Corporations in Shaping Globalization with a Human Face' In J. Straus (Ed.), *The Role of Law and Ethics in the Globalized Economy* (pp. 1–19). Berlin: Springer.

Méon, P-G. and Khalid S. (2005) 'Does Corruption Grease or Sand the Wheels of Growth?' 122 Public Choice 69.

Nichols, P. M. (2000) 'The Myth of Anti-Bribery Laws as Transnational Intrusion' 33 Cornell International Law Journal 627.

OECD (2011) Convention on Combating Bribery of Foreign Public Officials in International Business Transactions and Related Documents <http://www.oecd.org/daf/anti-bribery/ConvCombatBribery_ENG.pdf> accessed 25 February 2019.

Olson, M. (1971) *The Logic of Collective Action: Public Goods and the Theory of Groups*. Cambridge, MA: Harvard University Press.

Parrish, A. L. (2009) 'Reclaiming International Law from Extraterritoriality' (2009) 93 Minnesota Law Review 815.

Rose-Ackerman, S. (2011) 'Anti-Corruption Policy: Can International Actors Play a Constructive Role?' (2011) 440 Yale Law & Economics Research Paper.

Rose, C. (2015) *International Anti-Corruption Norms: Their Creation and Influence on Domestic Legal Systems*. Oxford: Oxford University Press.

Ryngaert, C. (2015) 'Symposium issue on Extraterritoriality and EU Data Protection' 5 International Data Privacy Law 221.

Sandler, T. (2004) *Global Collective Action*. Cambridge: Cambridge University Press.

Salbu, S. R. (1999) 'Extraterritorial Restriction of Bribery: A Premature Evocation of the Normative Global Village' 24 Yale Journal of International Law 223.

Scott, J. (2014) 'Extraterritoriality and Territorial Extension in EU Law' 62 American Journal of Comparative Law 87.

Shleifer, A. and Vishny, R. W. (1993) 'Corruption' 108 Quarterly Journal of Economics 599.

Spalding, A. B. (2010) 'Unwitting Sanctions: Understanding Anti-Bribery Legislation as Economic Sanctions Against Emerging Markets' 62 Florida Law Review 351.

Teachout, Z. (2016) *Corruption in American: From Benjamin Franklin's Snuff Box to Citizens United*. Cambridge, MA: Harvard University Press.

Westbrook, A. D. (2011) 'Enthusiastic Enforcement, Informal Legislation: The Unruly Expansion of the Foreign Corrupt Practices Act' 45 Georgia Law Review 489.

Young, O. R. (1999) *Governance in World Affairs*. Ithaca, NY: Cornell University Press.

Young, O. R. (2011) 'Effectiveness of International Environmental Regimes: Existing Knowledge, Cutting-Edge Themes, and Research Strategies' 108 Proceedings of the National Academy of Sciences of the United States of America 19853

Zagaris, B. (2015) *International White Collar Crimes: Cases and Materials*. Cambridge: Cambridge University Press.

Zerk, J. A. (2010) 'Extraterritorial Jurisdiction: Lessons for the Business and Human Rights Sphere from Six Regulatory Areas' (Harvard University, John F. Kennedy School of Government <https://www.hks.harvard.edu/sites/default/files/centers/mrcbg/programs/cri/files/workingpaper_59_zerk.pdf> accessed 25 February 2019.

2 International bribery and collective action problems

2.1 Introduction

Many global societal problems persist because states fail to act collectively when addressing them (Sandler, 2004: 46). International bribery is one of these problems. This form of corruption is detrimental to economic growth, the rule of law, political, and economic competition, and government legitimacy, and, thus, the achievement of public goods.[1] Yet, despite its harmfulness, countries have for a long time refrained from fighting it, and from cooperating with each other, even if the international community, as well as their own citizens, would have benefited from reducing international bribery.

The enforcement of foreign anti-bribery laws is a public good in its own right. The enforcement is in-built in multiple international anti-corruption treaties. What makes it a public good is its function to provide deterrent sanctions, recovery of stolen assets, and restitution. Sanctions and related enforcement tools promote anti-bribery compliance by providing constraints to corporations that seek to improve their competitive position by engaging in bribery.[2] Moreover, effective enforcement expresses the states' commitment to promote integrity and ethics in international business transactions. States, however, have struggled to act collectively when providing foreign anti-bribery enforcement.

States' struggle to establish collective action because more than one of them generally needs to contribute to the provision of public goods in situations where opportunism and temptations to free-ride are ever present (Ostrom, 2004). The lack of political will and resources and ineffective governance systems result in some states' free-riding on the enforcement of others. Despite the fact that a number of states have recognized that the mitigation of international bribery requires specific legislation, and adopted such legislation, not many have enforced their legislation (Section 3.2.3.). This collective action

1 See the analysis of the economic effects of corruption and bribery in Section 2.3.3 below.

2 It will be also argued that international anti-corruption policy is based on economic rationales, such as those that markets are more competitive if international bribery is mitigated. For the discussion about the economic effects of corruption and bribery and international anti-corruption policy, see Sections 2.3.3 and 2.3.4 below.

problem prevents placing corporations under more stringer regulatory scrutiny, hence companies might seek to improve their competitive position by engaging in bribery more easily.[3]

The inability to overcome collective action problems stands behind multiple market failures, notably those associated with problems of coordination, enforcement, and the provision of public goods (Ferguson, 2013: 5). Economic governance scholars developed research tools that explain how various collective action problems arise and how to solve them.[4] This chapter introduces these tools and explains first why, and in what way, the regulation of international bribery is a collective action problem.[5] Second, this chapter presents an analytical framework that explains how extraterritorial enforcement, defined broadly as the application and enforcement of national laws to subjects acting beyond the borders of a given country, contributes to the resolution of the indicated collective action problem.

The rest of the chapter is organized as follows. In its first part, the theory of collective action, its purpose, and normative justification are introduced. The second part discusses why enforcement of foreign anti-bribery laws is a collective action problem. It focuses on questions such as: Why are corruption and international bribery harmful? What are the main elements of international bribery schemes? Who regulates international bribery and why international bribery is a regulatory challenge? Last, the chapter presents an analytical framework of the role of extraterritoriality in mitigating or hampering a collective action problem.

2.2 The theory of collective action

Scholars concerned with protecting global commons such as competitive markets, peace, and environment have long been familiar with difficulties to generate and sustain collective action. This section provides an introduction to collective action as discussed in the field of economic governance. This introduction explains the foundations of the analytical framework within which the following chapters present foreign anti-bribery law and its application in practice.

2.2.1 The logic of collective action

Collective group behavior is not natural for rational individuals with common interests. This thought, first presented by Olson (1971), focuses on the question why individuals do not act collectively. Olson (1971: 2) describes a situation where individual motivations and group motivations conflict, and

3 It will be also argued that international anti-corruption policy is based on economic rationales, such as those that markets are more competitive if international bribery is mitigated. For the discussion about the economic effects of corruption and bribery and international anti-corruption policy, see Sections 2.3.3 and 2.3.4 below.

4 See, generally, the discussion in Sections 2.2.1 and 2.2.2 below.

5 For more detail about why the regulation of foreign bribery is a collective action problem, how countries free-ride on the enforcement of foreign bribery laws by other countries, and the role of extraterritoriality in overcoming this problem, see Sections 1.1 above and 2.5 below.

where the achievement of individual goals would have a detrimental effect for the group as a whole. The key issue is that individuals will not act to achieve their common or group interests unless they act in a relatively small group or they are incentivized to act in their common or group interest by coercion. Later on, Hardin (1971) related this thesis to the N-person prisoner's dilemma paradigm that does not focus on "one-shot-interactions" but on the cooperation within larger groups whose members interact repeatedly. These models of group behavior have established a new field of study in economics, political science, and social sciences at large.

The main purpose of collective action is the provision of a public good that is characterized by non-excludability and non-rivalrous consumption of the properties of such public good. The mitigation of international bribery, as discussed in the section below, is a public good.[6] While a public good is costly to produce, all members of a relevant group can freely consume its properties without leaving less for other members – non-rivalrous consumption. For example, if state X decides to invest in measures that make international markets less corrupt, other states might enjoy a non-rivalrous benefit of, for example, more transparent, competitive, and efficient global markets.

Moreover, for state X, it is difficult to exclude other beneficiaries (Cooter and Ulen, 2012: 40–41). The problem is that profit-maximizing actors may struggle to induce others to share the costs of the supply of public goods or create additional public goods by themselves. In other words, all members of a group, as rational actors, may be incentivized to free-ride. For example, while all relevant actors want to benefit from less corrupt business environment, some do not want to contribute to such environment because they already enjoy benefits produced by others. This is because in all standard economic models, the decision of actors whether to free-ride or engage in the provision of public goods depends on their rational calculation. The actors provide public goods only if underlying costs are lower than expected benefits (see Olson, 1971).

Consequently, if all actors rely on the provision of public goods by other actors, the public goods will simply not be provided. While state X may decide to invest into anti-bribery enforcement systems in a first place, it will not provide such public good, or provide less of it, if the supply of such public good turns to be too costly because of the free-rider problem. In the discussed case of foreign anti-bribery enforcement, the fact that the US has started enforcing its foreign anti-bribery laws extraterritorially implies that its returns from such enforcement are high, making such action individually rational.[7] Extraterritoriality, as will be explained in sections below, changes the value of enforcement.

6 See the analysis of the economic effects of corruption and bribery in Section 2.3.3 below.

7 In such scenario, the free-riding by other countries is technically no longer a collective action problem, but a more general problem of opportunism. The problem of opportunism is a broader concept than the problem of collective action because it does not have to lead to the non-production or under-production of public goods. In this work, these terms are used interchangeably.

2.2.2 The use of collective action theory as an analytical framework

Collective action as discussed in the field of economic governance provides a framework that structures societal problems. This framework is useful to examine complicated transnational legal regimes that can hardly be grasped by dogmatic legal analysis. Unlike lawyers, economists explain in what situations actors decide to free-ride and in what situations they act in common interest of a group. The determination of these situations and their appropriate resolutions are based on a number of variables such as the size of a group, material incentives, reciprocity, emotions, trust, and other social relations (Dixit, 2003; Kahan, 2003). In addition, the resolution of collective action problems is determined by a number of contextual variables such as the level of excludability of public goods, the dependence on a public good, the common understanding of problems that a group faces, the presence of leadership, etc. (Ostrom et al., 2002).[8]

While Olson's thesis has arguably not developed in a full-blown theory of collective action, economists and other social scientists have advanced it (see Ostrom, 2000; Keohane, 2005). A number of authors provide empirical observations about how and why groups have historically sustained cooperation. Ostrom (1990: 90; 2002) observes cases of self-organization and from these observations derives a number of design principles that contribute to the sustainability of these institutions. Collective action, for instance, is more likely to sustain if a group has rules that enable participants to identify members and non-members of a group. Some of these principles fundamentally question the Olson's thesis because despite the existence of collective action problems, groups often maintained cooperation even without a centralized authority. Other authors confirm this by multiple empirical studies of collective action, notably studies exemplifying collective behavior in the rubber smallholder economy (Landa, 1981), diamond industry (Bernstein, 1992), and the rise and fall of middle ages merchant guilds (Greif, Milgrom and Weingast, 1994).

Said approaches are not only relevant to private communities, whether informal social networks or more formal associations, but also to nation-states. Like private communities, nation-state builds informal networks, associations, and organizations that are more formal.[9] For example, Todd Sandler studies elements that promote or hinder collective action of nation states to face global challenges such as international terrorism and global warming (Sandler, 2004). Barnett and Duvall (2005) focus on how institutional power may unilaterally determine international rules and solve cooperation and coordination dilemmas. Nation-states are conventionally considered as single agents that need international regimes and international legal norms to enhance cooperation in a relative anarchy of relationships they operate in

8 Ostrom et al. focus on the so-called common-pool resources that are, differently from public goods, rivalrous because they can be overused. Example may be water or coal.

9 For discussion about the role of transgovernmental networks, see Chapter 9.

(see Sandler, 2016). The collective action perspective applied in this book helps establish an order in that anarchy.

The collective action perspective can structure legal analysis because it shows which legal institutions matter, and how, and which institutions matter less. The key focus is on appropriate institutional design that groups and international regimes should adopt in order to resolve free-rider problems and ensure cooperation (North, 1991: 97).[10] The resolution of these problems requires relatively stable group with good set of information about its members, prohibited behavior and consequences of misbehavior. Furthermore, such group must be able to identify unacceptable behavior and sanction non-compliance (Dixit, 2009: 16–17).

These conditions are easier to achieve in smaller groups as opposed to larger groups. In smaller groups, collective action may be based on trust build by repeated interactions of homogenous actors (see Kahan, 2003). For example, a small number of national enforcement authorities can sustain cooperation and provide public goods without external governance and rules that are too specific. In larger groups, however, such external governance is necessary for collective action (see Dixit, 2014). Numerous works discuss how larger groups may struggle to observe and share information about the behavior of each member, to define desirable and undesirable behavior, and to sanction members that free-ride (Hadfield and Weingast 2012; Gibbons and Henderson, 2012; Masten and Prüfer, 2014).

The establishment of external governance is costly and may be undermined by the free-rider problem of its own. It means that for the provision of a public good it is also important whether the group is able to establish a governance mechanism that incentivizes cooperation and coordination. In other words, the members of a group face two choices whether to cooperate or free-ride (Heckathron 1989; Ferguson, 2013). First, each actor has to decide whether to join a given group and participate in activities connected with the production of public goods, for example, by adopting and enforcing foreign anti-bribery law. However, the members must also cooperate at the second level in order to maintain a governance mechanism that enhances cooperation and sanctions free-riding. These two levels of collective action are interdependent. The first-stage problems are problems of market failure. The successful resolution of the first-stage problems, however, requires at least some prior resolution of the second-stage problems because a governance mechanism facilitates collective action at the first stage. By this reason, the creation of effective governance system is considered to be a public good in itself (Heckathorn 1989: 80–81; Ferguson, 2013: 5–6). These findings indicate that extraterritoriality, as will be discussed in Chapter 6, functions differently in small and large regimes.

10 When speaking about an organization, it is generally referred to an authority that can decide how formal institutions are structured and/or implement formal institutions. Institutions are then rules of the game, i.e. formal "constrains that structure political, economic and social interaction."

2.2.3 Normative justification of collective action

Other than a framework that conceptualizes difficulties that states face in social dilemma situations, the collective action perspective provides a normative framework to assess international regimes and their institutions. The ability to overcome the said difficulties is an important indicator of whether states are able to mitigate the problems they are supposed to address and provide public goods. From this perspective, the failure to provide public goods is one of the sources of market failures. In economics, market failures are not socially desirable because they lead to a bad equilibrium (Cooter and Ulen, 2012: 38). In other words, market failures plague the competitive trade of commodities and services, hence, resources are not distributed based on their most valued use. The resolution of collective action problems is necessary in order to move toward the well-functioning markets and economic development (Ferguson, 2013: 4–5, 15). In this context, the fact that international anti-corruption policies are based on economic rationales, such as those that argue that markets are more competitive if international bribery is mitigated, makes collective action framework ideal for the normative assessment of international regimes.

More specifically, the collective action perspective allows to evaluate the effectiveness of institutions, including international law and national laws. The effectiveness of institutions is essential for successful mitigation of major societal problems such as international bribery. According to Douglass North:

> [E]ffective institutions raise the benefits of cooperative solutions or the costs of defection, to use game theoretic terms. In transaction cost terms, institutions reduce transaction and production costs per exchange so that the potential gains from trade are realizable.
>
> (North, 1991: 97–98)

Furthermore, North (1990) also argues that the institutions that are designed to solve collective action problems do not have to be socially optimal in order to lower the transaction costs, and hence promote economic development. For example, one powerful state may orchestrate an international regime that primarily serves the state's own interests rather than collective interests. Nevertheless, such international regime can still reduce transaction costs and promote cooperation that in the long term may result in societally more optimal institutions. These premises will resonate in Chapter 6 that shows how and to what extent extraterritorial enforcement is effective.

The following section introduces international bribery and explains why it is a collective action problem.

2.3 Why the regulation of international bribery is a collective action problem

2.3.1 Defining corruption and bribery

This section focuses on bribery as a form of corruption. Corruption is most frequently understood as "the abuse of public office for private gains" (Farrales, 2005). It is also common to assume a broader view that includes abuses of private power into the definition. Transparency International (TI), for instance, defines corruption as "an abuse of entrusted power for private gain" (TI, 2009: 14). Scholars and experts have converged around these and similar operational definitions when discussing how corruption emerges, persists, and affects social phenomena.

The operational definition of corruption relates to the definition of bribery. Bribery in its various forms, such as political contributions or gift giving, always involves at least two parties that interact. The active party usually offers, promises, or gives something of value to the passive party, namely a public official. The passive party is then expected to do or to refrain from doing something in the exercise of its office. In many cases, corruption and bribery involve monetary and similar *quid pro quo* transactions and are so closely related, as phenomena, that a number of works and legal instruments use them as synonyms (Boersma, 2012: 33). For this reason, the operational understanding of corruption is that which best suits the purposes of this work, that aims to discuss one of its forms: international bribery.

The operational understanding of corruption is only one out of several possible working definitions. In some studies, corruption is defined by a political dilemma that relates to the distribution of power and wealth and is not primarily concerned with a transaction between bribers and bribed parties (Johnston, 2010). Other studies focus on a feedback loop between the causes and effects of corruption. This loop means that corruption is self-constituting because it is determined by an old level of corruption (Arnone and Borlini, 2014: 4–6). As these causes and effects depend on the cultural, legal, and market context, it is not feasible to examine all of the elements and effects of corruption at the same time. Researchers should rely on working definitions that best suit their research objectives.

The goal of this study is not to add to the debates on the nature of corruption, or to measure the effects of corruption and how it is perceived. Rather, the following part introduces the main features of international bribery schemes.

2.3.2 The complexity of international bribery schemes – Hewlett Packard

Bribery is a widespread phenomenon in international business transactions. In the international business context, bribery is an element of economic and business globalization, a process characterized by economic, political, and cultural discourses within society (OECD 2013: 13–52). International business transactions that are infiltrated by bribery are commonly composed of (1) the main parties, i.e. bribers and bribed parties, (2) third parties that are controlled by or act on behalf of the main parties, and (3) transnational means of communication. The bribery scheme involving Hewlett-Packard (HP) Company illustrates very well how international bribery schemes are organized.

HP was in April 2014, a multinational corporation organized under US law with the main office in Palo Alto, California. As a global market player in information technology, HP employed roughly 302,000 employees and operated through its subsidiaries, agents, and other groups and individuals in some 106 countries.[11] Since 1961, HP has been listed on the NYSE.

HP and its wholly owned subsidiaries in Russia, Poland, and Mexico engaged from 2000 to 2007 in three international bribery schemes. The US authorities stood in the center of the investigation and prosecution of the group. Nevertheless, Germany and Poland have also investigated several natural persons.

The core of *HP* scheme is the so-called Russian GPO Deal that attracted the attention of the German Public Prosecutor in Dresden.[12] What is more, at the request of the prosecutor, the Russian authorities raided HP's offices in Moscow on 14 April 2010. From 2001 to 2006, HP allegedly funneled around €8 million to various foreign bank accounts in order to secure a €35 million deal on supply of computer systems with the Russian federal prosecutor's office. The German prosecutors have issued an indictment of four natural persons and requested HP to be an associated party to the case.[13] One the day after the raid, the US authorities opened an investigation as well. The US investigation resulted in the set of settlements agreed in 2014. The relevant legal documents contain detailed information about the organization of the so-called buy-back scheme. Figure 2.1 below illustrates its core elements.

HP Russia saw the Russian deal as the "golden key" to the Russian market. In a first stage, HP Russia concluded teaming contracts with a Swiss and a US intermediary. HP intended to use these intermediaries as shell companies for illicit purposes. The US intermediary would be used if the Russian government decided to finance the project via US government-backed financing. However, as that did not happen, HP Russia tried to use the Swiss intermediary as a principal contractor. The second option did not work either, because

11 Hewlett-Packard, *Annual Report 2014, 17 and 51* <http://h30261.www3.hp.com/~/media/Files/H/HP-IR/documents/reports/2015/hpq-annual-report-2014.pdf> accessed 15 February 2017.

12 The analysis is based on Information, *United States vs. ZAO Hewlett-Packard A.O., No. 14-cr-201* (April 9, 2014), 8–18. Some data are derived from Trace, *Trace Compendium: Hewlett-Packard Company* <https://www.traceinternational.org/TraceCompendium/Detail/175?class=casename_searchresult&type=1> accessed 28 December 2018.

13 Individuals were charged with bribery, breach of trust and tax evasion.

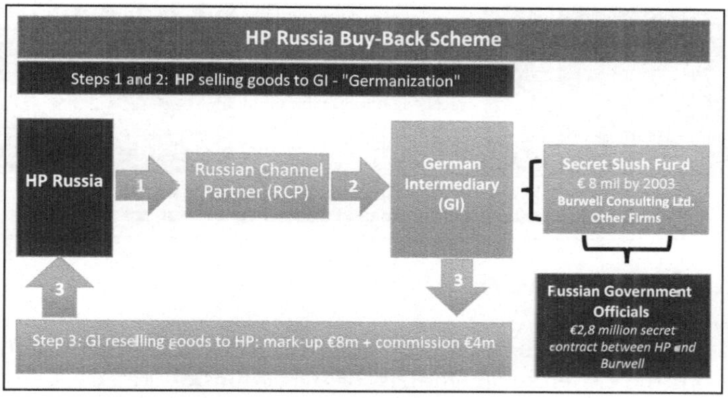

Figure 2.1 HP Russia buy-back scheme.

HP headquarters did not approve the Swiss intermediary. For that reason, HP Russia made the third attempt and switched to a German intermediary with an intention to acquire German government-backed financing. These changes resulted in the termination of the original procurement contract by the Russian side.

In order to secure the deal, endangered after the termination, HP Russia concluded a secret contract with Burwell Consulting Ltd., a shell company associated with a Russian government agency, for approximately €2.8 million. The Russian government then switched to German financing, and the German intermediary became part of the tender. HP's internal compliance mechanisms proved to be too weak to identify the true nature of the project.

To sum up, HP Russia was able to create a slush fund without the knowledge of its headquarters. In a first stage, HP Russia sold goods to a Russian Channel Partner that, at the second stage, resold the goods to the German intermediary – the so-called germanization. The German intermediary at the last stage sold the goods back to HP Russia, enabling HP to acquire German government-backed financing. The buy-back scheme allowed HP Russia to acquire the same goods with a mark-up of €8 million and commission fees of €4 million. In the end, the German intermediary kept only about €200,000, "passing on the rest on third parties – mostly bank accounts in the names of shell companies. These shell companies then laundered most of the money through multiple dimensions of additional shell companies."[14]

The *Russian GPO Deal* is only one of many types of international bribery schemes. These schemes will be examined in depth in Chapters 4 and 5. The discussed example, nevertheless, alludes the complexity of international bribery and may raise some questions about the value and costs of extraterritoriality already at this point, for example, why and how the US authorities

14 Information *United States vs. ZAO Hewlett-Packard A.O., No. 14-cr-201* (April 9, 2014), 16.

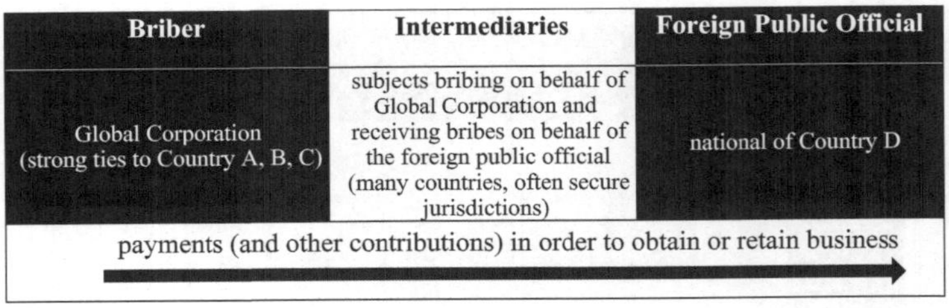

Figure 2.2 The international bribery scheme.

sanctioned Russian corporation for its activities in Russia and Germany? What implications the US enforcement has for the actions of non-US enforcement authorities? Would HP-related corporations be sanctioned at all without US enforcement? This discussed the complexity of schemes such as the *Russian GPO Deal* is generalized in Figure 2.2 below that provides "The international bribery scheme." The scheme represents a starting point for the subsequent analysis and will be used as a reference point in the following chapters.

2.3.3 Foreign anti-bribery enforcement is a public good

To explain why the enforcement of foreign anti-bribery laws is a public good, the section discusses why corruption and international bribery are harmful, how their absence is a public good, and how enforcement as a public good relates to international bribery and collective action.[15]

2.3.3.1 Corruption and international bribery are harmful

Corruption is the source of poverty, the unequal distribution of income, political instability, and other harmful phenomena (see Rose-Ackerman, 1999). Yet, it was not always straightforward to assume that corruption is harmful (see, generally, Pasculli and Ryder, 2019). Corruption was considered to be an efficient phenomenon by some economists, mainly in the context of its function in developing countries. In the past, some scholars have used simple price system models and argued that corruption serves as "grease in the wheels of commerce" (see Huntington, 1968; Mishra, 2005: 15). These models describe bribery and corruption as an efficient part of bargaining processes in corrupt bureaucracies, which allow only the lowest cost firms to win a "bribery auction." Moreover, facilitation payments, and other forms of corruption that companies and individuals may use in order to speed up transactions, were understood as tools that improve dysfunctional administration (Bardhan, 1997: 1322–1323; Mishra, 2005: 15–16).

15 Note that findings related to corruption are also generally applicable to international bribery.

However, later research found that the weak performance of a corrupt government is usually a systemic problem. In the short term, higher corruption rates might improve the government's performance, but in the long term, corruption enhances systemic inefficiencies. For instance, Pranab Bardhan provides that:

> [...] it is usually presumed that a given set of distortions are mitigated or circumvented by the effects of corruption; but quite often these distortions and corruption are caused or at least preserved or aggravated by the same common factors. The distortions are not exogenous to the system and are instead often part of the built-in corrupt practices of a patron client political system.
>
> (Bardhan, 1997: 1322)

In addition, Bardhan's reverse hypothesis, i.e. that corruption sands, rather than greases, the wheels of commerce, was supported by later scholarship (Méon and Khalid, 2005). Therefore, the claim that corruption is efficient is oversimplified.

Nowadays, corruption is generally recognized as a negative economic phenomenon. Be it based on its effects on economic growth, incentives to invest, or value for money, a large amount of research shows that corruption undermines overall productivity and public welfare (Méon and Khalid, 2005). The secrecy of corruption undermines value for money in public expenditures because it shifts government preferences to useless projects (Shleifer and Vishny, 1993). Furthermore, the authors also investigated links between corruption, poverty, and income inequalities (Lambsdorff, 2006: 23–24). It is also agreed that corruption and the allocation of government resources from the poor to the rich are closely related, and that the result undermines distributive justice and leads to undesirable economic effects (Davis and Trebilcock, 2008). Besides the said challenges, the negative economic effects of corruption also directly and indirectly affect the rule of law, government legitimacy, as well as political and economic competition (Mishra, 2005: 24–26). For instance, empirical evidence shows that corruption affects government legitimacy and creates a culture of distrust. Such a perception moves the society toward even more institutional instability and inefficiency (Melgar, Rossi and Smith, 2010). This indicates that the mitigation of corruption and international bribery is beneficial for society at large.

2.3.3.2 The absence of international bribery as a public good

Corruption has increasingly been viewed as the problem of collective action (Heather and Peiffer, 2015). The limitation of negative effects of corruption provides the group's benefits associated with positive social outcomes such as good governance, health, economic development. These positive outcomes make the limitation of corruption, and international bribery, a public good. Moreover, the collective action perspective indicates that the absence of corruption is a public good in itself because it promotes trust and cooperation among citizens, in international business transactions, and within other social relationships (Eigen and Eigen-Zucchi, 2003: 576–603; Heather and Peiffer, 2015: 3–4). The collective action perspective goes beyond the search for concrete linkages between a cost–benefit calculation of rational players who seek a private benefit, and negative effects associated with corrupt actions. The focus on trust and cooperation is an important complement to more instrumental understanding of corruption and bribery that view them primarily as a principal–agent problem.

The fact that the absence of international bribery is a public good is reflected in numerous anti-corruption instruments such as international treaties, national laws, and in documents of non-state actors. These instruments typically enumerate a number of concepts which justify the mitigation of international bribery, including the promotion of efficient international markets, economic growth, poverty alleviation, and the legitimacy of institutions (Rose-Ackerman, 2011: 8–12). These policy rationales are important because the reduction of corruption and international bribery is not an end in itself, but rather an element how to improve the well-being of people.

In international business transactions, the anti-corruption public good is provided by international anti-corruption actors. Rose-Ackerman (2011: 3–6) suggests that these actors can be divided into four main categories: (1) lending organizations such as the World Bank (see Manacorda and Grasso, 2018), (2) international non-profit organizations such as TI, (3) the International Chambers of Commerce and other business associations,[16] and (4) civil[17] and criminal law enforcement agencies.

Each of these categories of international actors has a different role and available tools to tackle international bribery. First, the enforcement of hard law by state agencies as well as the global self-regulation of businesses, have, arguably played a key role in mitigating international bribery. No matter how advantageous law enforcement through private market relations might be as compared to state enforcement, businesses have not been able to govern international bribery effectively, whether through formal or informal business associations, without incentives provided by state enforcement (see Section 9.6.). Second, other players such as lending associations and aid agencies have relatively narrow competence. They can enforce their own anti-bribery

16 International Chamber of Commerce <http://www.iccwbo.org/about-icc/> accessed 25 February 2019.

17 International arbitration is a typical example of a civil law enforcement agency. In practice, however, international arbitration as a framework to fight transnational corruption is uncertain, inter alia because arbitration tribunals such as the International Centre for Settlement of Investment Disputes (ICSID), usually deny jurisdiction or the accessibility of a claim in cases where corruption is present. See, for example, The Republic of Croatia v. MOL Hungarian Oil and Gas Plc, PCA Case 2014–15. An exception is *World Duty Free Co. vs. Republic of Kenya*, ICSID Case No. Arb/00/007 (2006).

standards as far as it concerns projects supported by them, and together with non-profit organizations provide support in the form of advice, monitoring reports, and education (see Simone and Zagaris, 2014).

The mitigation of international bribery schemes, such as the *HP* scheme discussed above, requires formal law that is effectively enforced. This work focuses predominantly on extraterritoriality of foreign anti-bribery laws, a feature of state enforcement. This feature has been the key to the provision of state enforcement and the most important incentive for corporations to refrain from bribing.

2.3.3.3 Foreign anti-bribery enforcement as a public good

Enforcement as the key tool to mitigate corruption and international bribery is in-built in multiple international anti-corruption treaties that nation-states ratified. From the perspective of international anti-corruption policy, foreign anti-bribery enforcement is a public good because it makes markets more open and competitive. This is based on the premise that corrupt public officials and their business counterparts can not only exclude other competitors but also negatively influence the content of contracts and distort public choices (Rose-Ackerman, 2011). For example, the OECD Convention is part of the OECD's mission to promote the economic and social well-being of people by helping governments "to restore confidence in markets and the institutions and companies that make them function" (OECD, 2011: 9). Similarly, also the FCPA was adopted in order to "enhance the integrity and functionality of the global market" (Nichols, 2016: 208). In light of these instruments, foreign anti-bribery enforcement should make markets more competitive, thereby creating more economic prosperity. Behind a broad definition of policy rationales of international anti-corruption instruments is the objective of foreign anti-bribery enforcement that is relatively narrow in its focus.

This objective is not without controversy. Besides open and competitive markets, foreign anti-bribery legislation and its enforcement also carry important political, cultural, and economic consequences, both in the home countries of the MNCs and in foreign markets. David Kennedy highlights how, despite a general agreement that international corruption and bribery are detrimental, initiatives fighting international corruption were ideological projects since the outset, these projects tend to "stigmatize some economic policies and some legal regimes at the expense of other precisely without analyzing their distributional or social consequences in any specific detail" (Kennedy, 1999: 465).[18] It is, for instance, evidenced by some studies that foreign anti-bribery enforcement has negatively influenced the inflow of foreign

18 In addition, other scholars consider anti-corruption policies as a way to put the blame on developing countries, rather than on these that supply corruption (Fouladvand, 2019: 295).

direct investment in developing countries (Cuervo-Cazzura, 2006). These principal clashes are the origin of opportunism and temptations to free-ride.

This criticism of foreign anti-bribery enforcement does not negate the fact that enforcement is a public good because removing corruption and international bribery from international business transactions can make these international markets more competitive. Enforcement assumedly decreases bribery because it provides constraints to corporations that seek to improve their competitive position by engaging in bribery. The establishment of open and competitive markets as well as other rationales of international anti-corruption policies, including poverty alleviation and economic growth, are globally shared values notwithstanding potentially diverging interests of state, business, and other actors underlying these rationales (Rose-Ackerman, 2011: 78–79). In other words, the provision of enforcement as a public good is legitimate, despite the fact that such enforcement may be opportunistic in some instances.

After all, the basis for the provision of foreign anti-bribery enforcement as a public good has developed in practice. Many states under the auspices of international organizations such as the United Nations (UN),[19] the Council of Europe (CoE),[20] the EU,[21] the Organization of American States (OAS),[22] and the OECD, have ratified international anti-corruption treaties.[23] In general, these treaties provide a minimal anti-corruption standard that signatory states implement and enforce at the national level, without a direct supervision of a centralized authority. As the enforcement remains in hands of independent states, national protectionism, institutional problems, and the lack of economic capacity to enforce foreign anti-bribery laws are factors that make free-riding a real threat. This brings us back to a more general discussion about the states' struggle to establish collective action. The next section explains why the enforcement of foreign anti-bribery laws is a collective action problem.

2.3.4 *Why the enforcement of foreign anti-bribery laws is a collective action problem*

The complexity of international bribery schemes makes national states struggle to provide enforcement collectively. While international bribery is harmful and the enforcement of foreign anti-bribery laws is a public good, the provision of enforcement includes a number of political and institutional

19 UNCAC.

20 Council of Europe Criminal Law Convention on Corruption, Strasbourg, 27 January 1999, in force 1 July 2002, Eur. T.S. No. 173.

21 Convention Drawn up on the Basis of Article K. 3 (2) (c) of the Treaty on European Union, on the Fight against Corruption Involving Officials of the European Communities or Officials of Member States of the European Union (OJ C 195, 25 June 1997).

22 Inter-American Convention against Corruption, 29 March 1996, in force 3 March 1997, 35 ILM 724.

23 See the analysis of the OECD Convention in Chapter 3 below.

problems that prevent the establishment of collective action. This collective action problem prevents placing corporations under stringer regulatory scrutiny, hence companies might seek to improve their competitive position by engaging in bribery more easily. This is undesirable because less MNCs under strict regulatory scrutiny means also less public goods under the perspective of collective action.

This section conceptualizes political and institutional problems that nation-states and their enforcement authorities face by introducing the "credibility problem" and the "clarity problem"; concepts at the research frontier in institutional economics (Gibbons and Henderson, 2012: 1351).

2.3.4.1 Introducing the credibility and clarity problems

The credibility and clarity problems are conceptualizations of difficulties that prevent the establishment of collective action. The credibility problem reflects a situation in which states are not able to persuade each other to keep their promises and refrain from free-riding (Gibbons and Henderson, 2012: 1351). The credibility problem limits the provision of public goods, in our case foreign anti-bribery enforcement. Foreign anti-bribery enforcement, as will be discussed in Chapter 6, is undermined by several types of credibility problems such as the lack of will to enforcement foreign anti-bribery laws, low institutional capacity to sanction corporations that bribe, the lack of cooperation and coordination of national enforcement authorities, and enforcement conflicts. These problems are associated with a lack of trust and with negative perceptions that state authorities might have about the future actions of one another. In effect, credibility problems prevent the creation of alliances, weaken cooperation inside existing alliances, or even lead to their demise (see Bachman and Zaheer, 2006).

The clarity problem is associated with administrative-managerial problems within an alliance that aim to produce public goods. If an alliance does not have a mechanism in place in order to clarify the terms of the original promise – issues that cannot be agreed upon in advance – then, they are likely to have clarity problems (see Bachman and Zaheer, 2006; Gibbons and Henderson, 2012).[24] These problems are tricky because an alliance cannot recognize, and solve, clarity problems in advance, even if the alliance generally knows how to provide public goods and is motivated to provide it (Gibbons and Henderson, 2012: 1351–1352).

The case of the car manufacturer Toyota, famous for its effective production system, illustrates the logic of clarity problems. The success of its production system was primarily owed to making all its work a series of ongoing experiments.

24 The clarity problem undermines the constituent agreements of the alliance and, consequently, increases the credibility problem. The lack of cooperation between members of an alliance to maintain an effective governance system that provides clarity is also a credibility problem. The terms "credibility problem" and "clarity problem" are used throughout this work in line with definitions provided in Gibbons and Henderson (2012).

These experiments coupled "the explicit specification of how work is going to be done *before it is performed*" with "testing work *as it is being done*. The end result is that gaps between what is expected and what actually occurs become immediately evident" (Spear, 2004). Although the production system has been studied and followed by other firms, many were not able to replicate Toyota's practices successfully. These firms failed mainly because they focused on tools and tactics instead of operating principles (Spear and Bowen, 1999; Gibbons and Henderson, 2012: 1355–1358).

The public sector faces different clarity problems as compared to the private sector but the essence is the same. International relations, considerations of public interest, and other issues make the operations of states, and their alliances, different from those of firms and their employees. Furthermore, the dynamic interplay of individuals within firms are not comparable to state interactions. Even so, the central challenge is the same for both firms and states: How can states achieve more clarity by testing enforcement "as it is being done" and integrating their findings into explicit agreements about how enforcement "is going to be done before it is performed"?

2.3.4.2 Two orders of a collective action problem: a public good and a classifying mechanism

Difficulties that prevent the establishment of collective action can be so strong that a public good may simply not be provided. A relatively better outcome from the perspective of collective action are scenarios in which credibility problems are alleviated by hegemonic states that provide public goods unilaterally.[25] Naturally, such hegemons do not act from purely altruistic reasons, their benefits must offset their costs (see Snidal, 1985). Nevertheless, it is relatively common for powerful countries to adopt and enforce new legal norms and in so doing to produce externalities associated with a collective consumption of public goods, for example, less corruption in the global economy. They do so despite the existence of free-rider problems, for example, if other countries do not pay enforcement expenses. This was the case in the area of international bribery, which was not regulated until 1977, and until the late 2000s, foreign anti-bribery laws were enforced scarcely. This move from a non-existence of an international anti-bribery regime to the establishment of the OECD anti-bribery enforcement regime is well documented by academics (Windsor and Getz, 1999: 425).

An alliance of states that produces public goods, in our case placing collectively corporations under stringer regulatory scrutiny is, arguably, superior to a hegemonic enforcement (Falvey and Lloyd 1999: 15–16). Anne-Marie Slaughter and David Zaring argue that if multiple authorities enforce a standard that was initially established by unilateral enforcement, the existing

25 Note that institutions that are designed to solve collective action problems do not have to be socially optimal in order to lower transaction costs, and hence promote economic welfare.

regime could reach a new, and better, equilibrium, should they cooperate with each other, rather than use enforcement predominantly as a foreign policy tool (Slaughter and Zaring, 1997). Similarly, the economic literature provides that "each country would benefit from cooperative multilateral actions taken by other countries, acting in their combined interests" (Falvey and Lloyd, 1999: 16).

The mere existence of a formal alliance, however, should not necessarily imply a cooperative outcome that, from the perspective of the provision of public goods, is always better than a non-cooperative outcome. For example, there is an evidence that different types of formal cooperation based on international agreements can, in fact, deliver outcomes that are close to non-cooperation (see Perrings, 2014: 164). In other words, while a multilateral enforcement regime has generally better potential to provide enforcement as a public good than a hegemonic state, the actual outcome will depend on contextual conditions such as the size of a group, and how these fit into the institutional design of a regime.

The success of a multilateral regime largely depends on its ability to adapt its institutional design to new conditions. In this context, after the solution of initial collective action problem, in our case, the lack of enforcement of foreign anti-bribery laws, second-order collective action problems will appear. The key issue in dealing with these problems is an institutional mechanism that classifies individual behavior of group members as wrongful or not. This is crucial in areas that are not directly agreed upon but are necessary in order to move toward the fulfillment of the original agreement (Hadfield and Weingast 2012: 471). Chapter 6 will discussed that these problems include questions such as when, how, and which corporations should be sanctioned for bribery, how sanctions should be divided between multiple enforcement authorities, and how to coordinate overlapping enforcement efforts. If a regime does not have an institution administrating such clarity problems, the lack of knowledge will undermine the understanding of the original agreements of the regime and consequently increase credibility problems (see Ferguson, 2013: 43 et seq.).

The classifying institution is crucial for decentralized enforcement regimes, such as the one the OECD anti-bribery enforcement regime. An alternative to the decentralized model of enforcement is a centralized authority such as an international court established either by an international treaty[26] or by an authority of an international organization.[27] For example, the International Criminal Court (ICC) may exercise very broad jurisdiction, even quasi-universal jurisdiction according to some scholars, over crimes such as genocide. The Office of Prosecutors, as an independent organ of the ICC, is complementary to national enforcement and prosecute cases only if national

26 For example, the International Criminal Court (ICC).

27 For example, the International Court of Justice of the UN or the Dispute Settlement Body of the World Trade Organization (hereinafter WTO).

enforcement authorities are not willing to do so.[28] While such centralized authorities may face a number of challenges such as the lack of state cooperation, including when it comes to the enforcement of the tribunal's orders or the lack of a fair trial, they are in many respects successful in producing impartial and fair decisions, which include the settlement of disputes between states (see Cogan, 2002). However, there is no judicial body with universal or at least limited cross-border jurisdiction over international bribery schemes. Therefore, classifying institution will prove crucial for the regime's effectiveness (see Chapter 8).

Rather, the OECD anti-bribery enforcement regime relies on national extraterritorial enforcement. State compliance in this area is incentivized by a variety of soft instruments such as the open method for coordination, self-assessments, peer reviews, and the publication of reports with recommendations. These processes of multilateral surveillance are coordinated by international organizations that either lack the authority to decide upon a dispute between states or to enforce compliance with the standard (Schäfer, 2006). Large responsibilities to mitigate clarity problems remain in the hands of nation-states. The following section explains the last element in our framework, the way how extraterritoriality relates to the discussed collective action problem.

2.4 How extraterritoriality relates to the collective action problem

Extraterritoriality, defined broadly as the application and enforcement of national laws to subjects acting beyond the borders of a given country, has been a game-changer that to a certain extent facilitated the resolution of collective action problems related to foreign anti-bribery enforcement. First and foremost, extraterritoriality shall be recognized as a technical instrument that limits possibilities for MNCs to use their networks and flexibility in order to hide their illicit activities, by for instance using foreign intermediaries and by operating in so-called secure jurisdictions or tax havens (see Reed and Fontana, 2011). In this way, extraterritorial enforcement, as compared to enforcement limited by national borders, improves the provision of public goods by placing relatively more corporations under stringer regulatory scrutiny. This technico-legal function of extraterritoriality is embedded in several international treaties such as the OECD Convention that require states to implement legislation that provides for a broad application of national anti-bribery laws to subjects acting beyond the borders of their countries.

Moreover, extraterritoriality has also a politico-economic function. When collective action is concerned, extraterritoriality is a politico-economic instrument of national enforcement authorities. Following sections explain the relationship between the politico-economic function of extraterritoriality and collective action in more detail.

28 International Criminal Court, '*How the Court Works*' <https://www.icc-cpi.int/about/how-the-court-works/Pages/default.aspx#legalProcess> accessed 26 February 2019.

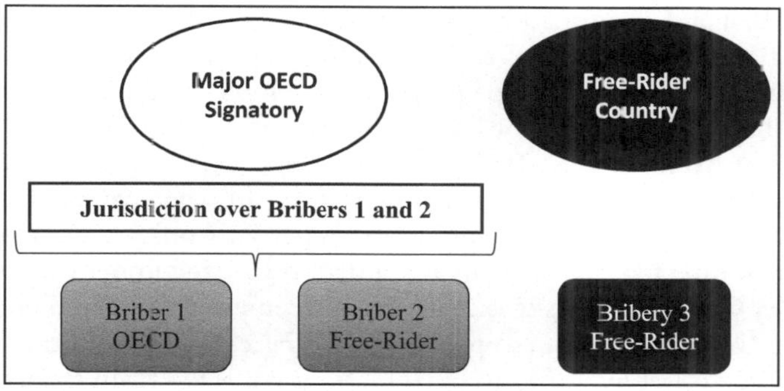

Figure 2.3 Extraterritoriality alleviates the lack of enforcement.

2.4.1 Extraterritoriality and the provision of enforcement as a public good

Extraterritoriality improves collective action because it alleviates the lack of enforcement of foreign anti-bribery laws. Even if some states free-ride by not engaging in enforcement, extraterritoriality may offset their inactivity by providing additional public goods. For example, if even one major state uses extraterritoriality to govern international bribery in overseas markets where both corporations headquartered in that major state and foreign corporations compete, markets will be, assumedly, more open and competitive. This link between extraterritoriality and collective action is illustrated in Figure 2.3 below.

Figure 2.3 above illustrates a hypothetical situation in which three firms that compete on the same market – "Bribers" – engage in an international bribery scheme. Briber 1 is organized under the laws of a "Major OECD Signatory," a country that actively enforces its foreign anti-bribery laws. Briber 2 and Briber 3 are firms organized under the laws of a "Free-Rider Country" that does not actively enforce its anti-bribery laws (if it has any). Without extraterritoriality, we could consider Briber 1 to have a competitive disadvantage as compared to Briber 2 and Briber 3, because Briber 1 would have to defend itself against potential enforcement action by the Major OECD Signatory, while Briber 2 and Briber 3 would not be under such danger. Briber 1 could therefore have significant problems when seeking to invest in emerging markets.

Without extraterritorial jurisdictions, some bribers can easily escape liability for their bribing because countries that should sanction them are not active in foreign anti-bribery enforcement. Under such scenario, the Major OECD Signatory could be incentivized to lower its regulatory standards in order to increase the competitiveness of Briber 1 (see Stephan, 2012).[29] This would mean that enforcement as a public good would simply not be provided.

29 This phenomenon in the literature is referred to as a "race to the bottom" and is in principle undesirable.

Nevertheless, as Figure 2.3 illustrates, thanks to extraterritoriality, the situation of Briber 1 is, arguably, not as disadvantageous as it might seem. It is true that because the Major OECD Signatory has jurisdictional limits, some firms such as Briber 3 still escape prosecution. However, because of the transnational character of the Major OECD Signatory's anti-bribery enforcement, certain firms from the Free-Rider Country, such as Briber 2, can be reached by the Major OECD Signatory's jurisdiction. In this way, we see that the lack of enforcement of the Free-Rider Country is partially offset by extraterritorial enforcement directed toward Briber 2, a firm organized under the laws of the Free-Rider Country.[30] It is true that the enforcement costs would be borne by the Major OECD country, as opposed to the Free-Rider Country, but these costs could be offset by, for example, sanctions collected from Briber 2.

While the use of extraterritoriality may be technically and economically demanding, especially for countries with legal principles that do not favor extraterritoriality and small economies, extraterritorial enforcement is used in practice. We will see in Chapters 5 and 6 that the US enforcement authorities have regularly claimed jurisdiction in order to investigate and eventually punish German, French, Dutch, and Swiss firms for their operations outside the US. Moreover, this hegemonic extraterritorial enforcement has incentivized several other states to become more active in their legislative and enforcement responses to international bribery. The implications of this move to a more multilateral response to international bribery are discussed in the following section.

2.4.2 Extraterritoriality and multilateral enforcement

Giant strides have been made to research when unilateral extraterritorial enforcement may emerge and, possibly, initiate a multilateral enforcement action. It has been the case in the area of international bribery in which the provision of enforcement has developed from a unilateral action to the OECD anti-bribery enforcement regime as a more active international network of states.

This move was not immediately apparent because the mere existence of a formal alliance, the OECD anti-bribery enforcement regime, did not lead to a cooperative outcome. In 2004, scholars still argued that "the U.S. pressure succeeded only in getting other countries to sign the Convention, not in changing the underlying game being played by other countries" (Tarullo, 2004: 667). The underlying game change only since the US started actively enforcing their foreign anti-bribery laws, which was around 2007.[31] At that time, extraterritoriality helped a "unilateral" enforcement regime to evolve into a multilateral enforcement regime. Kaczmarek and Newman (2011: 747)

30 For the discussion on why the credibility problem is alleviated, see Chapter 6.
31 See the discussion in Chapter 3.

found empirical evidence that countries that experienced US extraterritorial application of anti-bribery laws were "twenty times more likely to enforce their national rules." They also claim that such enforcement has "far-reaching spillover effects, unintentionally altering national decision-making in other countries" (Kaczmarek and Newman 2011: 747). In this multilateral enforcement regime, extraterritoriality operates differently than in a unilateral regime.

In a multilateral regime, extraterritoriality introduces new collective action problems, mainly these related to cooperation and coordination of enforcement. This is common because extraterritorial regimes are considered to be only a limited device for an effective multilateral approach to global problems. While the politico-economic function of extraterritoriality has positive spillover effects when a regime is unilateral, it is rarely resulting in a sustainable and collaborative response to global problems (Parrish, 2012). Extraterritorial enforcement is usually accompanied by loose multilateral arrangements that can hardly ensure cooperation within larger groups of states and coordinate the pursuit of individual interests.

One example of how demanding extraterritorial enforcement is when operating as part of a multilateral enforcement regime is when more than one enforcement authority can prosecute a firm for its bribes. Figure 2.4 shows a hypothetical situation in which four firms that compete on the same market – "Bribers" – engage in an international bribery scheme. Briber 1 is organized under the laws of "OECD Signatory 1," a country that actively enforces its foreign anti-bribery laws. Similarly, Briber 2 is organized under the laws of an active enforcer – "OECD Signatory 2." Briber 3 and Briber 4 are firms organized under the laws of a "Free-Rider Country" that does not actively enforce its anti-bribery laws (if it has any). Both OECD countries can reach, thanks to their wide jurisdictional reach, each other's corporations (and Briber 3).[32]

The jurisdictional overlap illustrated in Figure 2.4, although central to our investigation of collective action, is only one clarity problem introduced by extraterritoriality. Additionally, a number of substantive and procedural legal issues that may prevent effective cooperation between countries relate to this central jurisdictional problem. A solution to this problem is of a great relevance because cooperation and coordination between states can leverage the enforcement reach of the OECD regime, making enforcement less costly and more effective. These jurisdictional conflicts can take a form of large

32 Furthermore, not only may foreign anti-bribery enforcement of two or more countries overlap, but extraterritorial enforcement always overlaps with a domicile jurisdiction of foreign public officials that are bribed by the MNCs. For example, if a corporation headquartered in London would bribe Nigerian public officials, it is possible that the US and the UK authorities may claim their wide jurisdiction, but it is also possible that Nigerian authorities will step in because bribing officials is illegal also under Nigerian domestic anti-corruption laws.

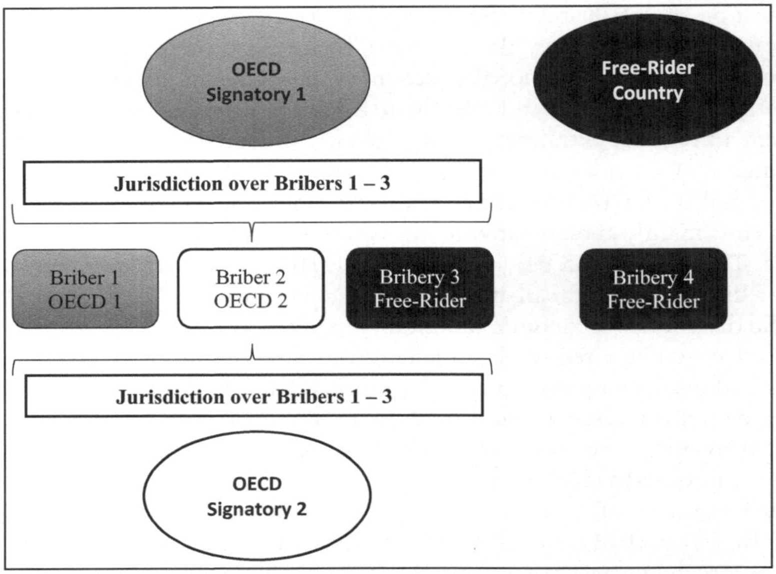

Figure 2.4 Extraterritoriality implies clarity problems.

enforcement conflicts with serious negative implications that either limit overall enforcement activity, or lead to major economic, political, as well as legal clashes (see Chapter 8; Spahn, 2012: 43; Turk, 2013: 325).

2.5 Conclusion

The national enforcement of foreign anti-bribery bribery legislation is a collective action problem because the provision of enforcement is a public good that states often fail to provide. The bribing of foreign public official is harmful because of its negative economic effects on the host country and because of its potential to distort fair and equal competition between foreign firms seeking to do business in the host country. Foreign anti-bribery laws that were specifically adopted to mitigate international bribery schemes are the key legal instrument for the mitigation of international bribery. However, multiple national enforcement authorities operate without a central authority and the enforcement is national. This implies a number of institutional and politico-economic problems that prevent the provision of enforcement as a public good. The ability of a regime to solve these problems provides a normative framework to assess international regimes and their institutions (see Chapter 7).

The framework of collective action is also useful to navigate legal complicated transnational legal regimes. This external perspective can show which legal institutions matter, and how, and which institutions matter less. From this perspective, the key focus should be on extraterritorial legislation that allows states to place corporations, both domestic and foreign, that bribe in foreign markets under strict regulatory scrutiny. In this way, extraterritoriality can alleviate some difficulties associated with the provision of public goods. Furthermore, the framework also shows that a classifying mechanism that ensures the cooperation and coordination of enforcement is crucial for the resolution of second-order collective action problems.

The question that follows is, what legislation is aligned to collective action, how the legislation functions, and what implications, from the perspective of the provision of public goods, such functioning may have for its application in concrete cases? These questions are addressed in Chapters 3 and 4.

References

Arnone, M. and Borlini, L. S. (2014) *Corruption: Economic Analysis and Evolution of the International Law and Institutions*. Cheltenham: Edward Elgar.

Bachmann, R. and Zaheer, A. (2006) *Handbook of Trust Research*. Chteltenham: Edward Elgar.

Bardhan, P. (1997) 'Corruption and Development: A Review of Issues' 35 Journal of Economic Literature 1320.

Barnett, M. and Duvall, R. (2005) 'Power in International Politics' (2005) 59 International Organization 39.

Bernstein, L. (1992) 'Opting Out of the Legal System: Extralegal Contractual Relations in the Diamond Industry' 21 Journal of Legal Studies 115.

Boersma, M. (2012) *Corruption: A Violation of Human Rights and a Crime under International Law?* Cambridge: Intersentia.

Cogan, J. K. (2002) 'International Criminal Courts and Fair Trials: Dificulties and Prospects' 27 Yale Journal of International Law 111.

Cooter, R. D. and Ulen, T. S. (2012) *Law & Economics*. Boston, MA: Addison-Wesley.

Cuervo-Cazurra, A. (2006) 'Who Cares about Corruption?' 37 Journal of International Business Studies 807.

Davis, K. E. and Trebilcock, M. J. (2008) 'The Relationship between Law and Development: Optimists versus Skeptics' 56 American Journal of Comparative Law 895.

Dixit, A. K. (2003) 'Trade Expansion and Contract Enforcement' 111 The Journal of Political Economy 1293.

Dixit, A. K. (2009) 'Governance Institutions and Economic Activity' 99 American Economic Review 5.

Dixit, A. K. (2014) *Lawlessness and Economics: Alternative Modes of Governance*. Princeton, NJ: Princeton University Press.

Eigen, P. and Eigen-Zucchi, Ch. (2003) 'Corruption and Global Public Goods' In I. Kaul (Ed.) *Providing Global Public Goods* (pp. 576–597). New York: Oxford University Press.

Falvey, R. E. and Lloyd, P. J. (1999) 'An Economic Analysis of Extraterritoriality' University of Melbourne Research Paper 675 <https://www.nottingham.ac.uk/gep/documents/papers/1999/99-03.pdf> accessed 26 February 2019.

Farrales, M. J. (2005) 'What Is Corruption? A History of Corruption Studies and the Great Definitions Debate' <http://papers.ssrn.com/sol3/papers.cfm?abstract_id=1739962> accessed 26 February 2019.

Ferguson, W. D. (2013) *Collective Action and Exchange: A Game-Theoretic Approach to Contemporary Political Economy*. Stanford, CA: Stanford University Press.

Fouladvand, S. (2019) 'Corruption and Human Trafficking' In L. Pasculli and N. Ryder (Eds.) *Corruption in the Global Era: Causes, Sources and Forms of Manifestation* (pp. 289–305). Abingdon: Routledge.

Gibbons, R. and Henderson, R. (2012) 'Relational Contracts and Organizational Capabilities' 23 Organization Science 1350.

Greif, A., Milgrom, P. and B. R Weingast (1994) 'Coordination, Commitment, and Enforcement: The Case of the Merchant Guild' 102 Journal of Political Economy 745.

Hadfield, G. K. and Weingast, B. R. (2012) 'What Is Law? A Coordination Model of the Characteristics of Legal Order' 4 Journal of Legal Analysis 471.

Hardin, R. (1971) 'Collective Action as an Agreeable N-Prisoners' Dilemma' 16 Behavioral Science 472.

Heather, M. and Peiffer, C. (2015) 'Corruption and Collective Action. U4 Anti-Corruption Resource Center' Research Paper 32 <http://publications.dlprog.org/CorruptionandCollectiveAction.pdf> accessed 25 February 2019.

Heckathorn, D. D. (1989) 'Collective Action and the Second-Order Free-Rider Problem' 1 Rationality and Society 78.

Huntington, S. P. (1968) *Political Order in Changing Societies*. New Haven, CT: Yale University Press.

Johnston, M. (2010) *Syndromes of Corruption: Wealth, Power, and Democracy*. Cambridge: Cambridge University Press.

Kaczmarek, S. C. and Newman, A. L. (2011) 'The Long Arm of the Law: Extraterritoriality and the National Implementation of Foreign Bribery Legislation' 65 International Organization 745.

Kahan, D. M. (2003) 'The Logic of Reciprocity: Trust, Collective Action, and Law' 102 Michigan Law Review 71.

Kennedy, D. (1999) 'The International Anti-Corruption Campaign' 14 Connecticut Journal of International Law 455.

Keohane, R. O. (2005) *After Hegemony: Cooperation and Discord in the World Political Economy*. Princeton, NJ: Princeton University Press.

Lambsdorff, J. G. (2006) 'Causes and Consequences of Corruption: What Do We Know from a Cross-Section of Countries' In S. Rose-Ackerman (Ed.) *International Handbook on the Economics of Corruption* (pp. 3–51). Chteltenham: Edward Elgar.

Landa, J. (1981) 'A Theory of the Ethnically Homogeneous Middleman Group: An Institutional Alternative to Contract Law' 10 Journal of Legal Studies 349.

Manacorda, S. and Grasso, C. (2018) *Fighting Fraud and Corruption at the World Bank: A Critical Analysis of the Sanctions System*. Cham: Springer.

Masten, S. E. and Prüfer, J. (2014) 'On the Evolution of Collective Enforcement Institutions: Communities and Courts' 43 Journal of Legal Studies 359.

Melgar, N., Rossi, M. and Smith, T. W. (2010) 'The Perception of Corruption' 22 International Journal of Public Opinion Research 120.

Méon, P-G. and Khalid S. (2005) 'Does Corruption Grease or Sand the Wheels of Growth?' 122 Public Choice 69.

Mishra, A. (2005) *The Economics of Corruption*. Delhi: Oxford University Press.

Nichols, P. M. (2016) 'The Neomercantilist Fallacy and the Contextual Reality of the Foreign Corrupt Practices Act' 53 Harvard Journal on Legislation 203.

North, D. C. (1990) *Institutions, Institutional Change and Economic Performance*. Cambridge, MA: Cambridge University Press.

North, D. C. (1991) 'Institutions' 5 Journal of Economic Perspectives Journal of Economic Perspectives 97.

OECD (2011) *The OECD at 50 and Beyond*. OECD <http://www.oecd.org/about/47747755.pdf> accessed 26 February 2019.

OECD (2013) 'Interconnected Economies: Benefiting from Global Value Chains' OECD.

Olson, M. (1971) *The Logic of Collective Action: Public Goods and the Theory of Groups*. Cambridge, MA: Harvard University Press.

Ostrom, E. (1990) *Governing the Commons: The Evolution of Institutions for Collective Action*. Cambridge: Cambridge University Press.

Ostrom, E. (2000) 'Collective Action and the Evolution of Social Norms'14 Journal of Economic Perspectives 137.

Ostrom, E. et al. (2002) *The Drama of the Commons*. Washingron DC: National Academy Press.

Ostrom, E. (2004) 'Collective Action and Property Rights for Sustainable Development, Understanding Collective Action' In R. S. Meinzen-Dick and M. Di Gregorio. *Collective Action and Property Rights for Sustainable Development* (Brief 2). Washington DC: International Food Policy Research Institute.

Parrish, A. L. (2012) 'Domestic Responses to Transnational Crime: The Limits of National Law' 23 Criminal Law Forum 275.

Pasculli, L. and Ryder, N. (2019) 'Corruption and Globalisation' In L. Pasculli and N. Ryder (Eds.) *Corruption in the Global Era: Causes, Sources and Forms of Manifestation* (pp. 3–23). Abongdon: Routledge.

Perrings, C. (2014) *Our Uncommon Heritage, Biodiversity Change, Ecosystem Services, and Human Well-Being*. Cambridge: Cambridge University Press.

Reed, Q. and Fontana, A. 'Corruption and Illicit Financial Flows: The Limits and Possibilities of Current Approaches' U4 Anti-Corruption Research Center < http://www.u4.no/assets/publications/3935-corruption-and-illicit-financial-flows.pdf> accessed 26 February 2019.

Rose-Ackerman, S. (1999) *Corruption and Government: Causes, Consequences, and Reform*. Cambridge: Cambridge University Press.

Rose-Ackerman, S. (2011) 'Anti-Corruption Policy: Can International Actors Play a Constructive Role?' (2011) 440 Yale Law & Economics Research Paper.

Sandler, T. (2004) *Global Collective Action*. Cambridge: Cambridge University Press.

Sandler, T. (2016) 'Strategic Aspects of Difficult Global Challenges' 7 Global Policy 33.

Schäfer, A. (2006) 'A New Form of Governance? Comparing the Open Method of Co-ordination to Multilateral Surveillance by the IMF and the OECD' 13 Journal of European Public Policy 70.

Shleifer, A. and Vishny, R. W. (1993) 'Corruption' 108 Quarterly Journal of Economics 599.

Simone de, F. and Zagaris, B. (2014) 'Impact of Foreign Bribery Legislation on Developing Countries and the Role of Donor Agencies' U4 Anti-Corruption Research Center <http://www.u4.no/publications/impact-of-foreign-bribery-legislation-on-developing-countries-and-the-role-of-donor-agencies/downloadasset/3610> accessed 26 February 2019.

Slaughter, A-M. and Zaring, D. (1997) 'Extraterritoriality in a Globalized World' <https://papers.ssrn.com/sol3/papers.cfm?abstract_id=39380> accessed 26 February 2019.

Snidal, D. (1985) 'The Limits of Hegemonic Stability Theory' 39 International Organization 579.

Spahn, E. K. (2012) 'Multijurisdictional Bribery Law Enforcement: The OECD Anti-Bribery Convention' 53 Virginia Journal of International Law 1.
Spear, S. (2004) 'Learning to Lead at Toyota' 82 Harvard Business Review 78.
Spear, S. and Bowen, K. H. (1999) 'Decoding the DNA of the Toyota Production System' 77 Harvard Business Review 96.
Stephan, P. B. (2012) 'Regulatory Competition and Anticorruption Law' 53 Virginia Journal of International Law 53.
Tarullo, D. K. (2004) 'The Limits of Institutional Design: Implementing the OECD Anti-Bribery Convention' 44 Virginia Journal of International Law 665.
TI (2009) *The Anti-Corruption Plain Language Guide* <http://www.transparency.org/whatwedo/publication/the_anti_corruption_plain_language_guide> accessed 26 February 2019.
Turk, M. C. (2013) 'A Political Economy Approach to Reforming the Foreign Corrupt Practices Act' 33 Northwestern Journal of International Law & Business 325.
Windsor, D. and Getz, K. A. (1999) 'Regional Market Integration and the Development of Global Norms for Enterprise Conduct: The Case of International Bribery' 38 Business & Society 415.

3 The evolution of foreign anti-bribery legislation

3.1 Introduction

This chapter introduces the history of foreign anti-bribery law and its evolution with a special focus on key features that distinguish foreign bribery from domestic anti-corruption legislation.[1] This chapter then introduces the OECD Convention, and not only because it is the most advanced international convention prohibiting foreign bribery, but also because the extraterritorial enforcement of US foreign anti-bribery laws, that sets a precedent for how the extraterritoriality of foreign anti-bribery legislation functions, is part of this framework. Furthermore, this chapter will introduce the implementation of the OECD Convention to national laws of the US, the UK, and Germany.

This chapter provides all information needed to understand the minimum foreign anti-bribery legal standards and the implementation and monitoring processes within the OECD regime. This is important because international legal institutions indicate how, when, and by whom enforcement shall be provided. Moreover, they also show how enforcement shall be provided within a group of multiple national enforcement authorities and how these authorities should cooperate with each other. In the centrum of the discussion will be the principle of functional equivalence that is supposed to alleviate the heterogeneity of national approaches to foreign anti-bribery enforcement. This will lay a foundation for answering the bigger question: What level of heterogeneity of measures is acceptable for achieving collective action within an alliance devoid of a central authority?

Chapter 3, as well as Chapter 4, adopts a rather formalistic approach, meaning that they look at an international regime as one in which there is some kind of international institution, meaning it is visible, distinct regime from the national regimes. An international regime, such as the OECD anti-bribery regime, consists of "principles, norms, rules and decision-making procedures around which actor expectations converge" (Krasner, 1985: 4).

1 Foreign bribery is a narrower concept than "international bribery." This is because foreign bribery relates specifically to the regulation of bribery of foreign government officials in international business transactions.

3.2 The regulation of foreign bribery in historical context

This part sets the evolution of foreign anti-bribery law in a historical context. The analysis is limited to the extent that it is necessary to understand the regulatory context of the contemporary OECD anti-bribery enforcement regime and its dynamics.

3.2.1 Early legislative activities in the US

Until the adoption of the FCPA in 1977, there had been no domestic or international legal instrument that regulated international bribery.[2] This stood in sharp contrast to the fact that there were, for a long time, solid sets of norms criminalizing domestic bribery, both in the US and in many other countries (Noonan, 1984). The 1970s, in particular, brought an increasing amount of domestic anti-corruption laws to the US. Most importantly, the US introduced new legislation that sanctioned the misbehaviors of federally appointed officials, senators, and representatives. This legislation provided rules on the reporting of campaign contributions and obligations connected with the making and keeping of books, records, and accounts over corporations' transactions and their assets (Rossbacher and Young, 1997: 510). However, domestic laws did not cover acts of foreign bribery in their complexity.

Foreign bribery may have been considered unethical by some countries, but the prosecution of such activities was mostly indirect. Thus, firms had, for instance, a legal obligation to disclose some bribery payments to foreign government officials under securities law or they were prohibited from certifying bribes as expenses deductible from income for tax purposes (Noonan, 1984: 677–680). However, foreign bribes themselves were not prohibited. This proved to be insufficient for mitigating foreign bribery. Consider, for instance, disclosure obligations under US securities law that, in practice, resulted in a disclosure of a very narrow scope of foreign payments. The SEC representatives argued that this was because the principle of "materiality" required to disclose only payments that were material to investors in appraising their investments. It means that the mere fact that businesses made a payment abroad did not necessarily have to be disclosed to the SEC.[3]

Therefore, indirect anti-bribery measures and other proposals on how to regulate foreign bribery through indirect means, for example within the scope of anti-trust law (Goodman, 2013) proved to be insufficient for the effective sanctioning of this activity (Noonan, 1984: 677–680; see, generally, Pines, 1994).

2 Note that at the time when the FCPA was adopted, Swedish law was amended in order to regulate foreign bribery (Bogdan, 1979).

3 The Activities of American Multinational Corporations Abroad: Hearings before the Sub-commission on International Economic Policy of the House Committee on International Relations, 94th Cong. 2 (1975), at 69 (statement of Philip Loomis, Comm'r, SEC) in (Koehler, 2012: supra note 69).

However, an exogenous shock changed the US approach to foreign bribery. After a series of political scandals that undermined both US relations with foreign countries and public trust in US political and business leaders, the demand for the extension of domestic anti-bribery legislation to overseas activities increased. The culmination of anti-corruption legislative initiative came with the Lockheed bribery scandals and Watergate scandal (see, for example, Rossbacher and Young, 1997: 510). The former, the Lockheed bribery scandals, relates to how the Lockheed Corporation bribed multiple public officials between the 1950s and the 1970s in order to secure contracts for the supply of military aircraft (Spalding, 2010: 357–360). The latter, the Watergate scandal, concerns a major political scandal related to the Nixon administration, that also included a series of investigations over the financing of US political campaigns.

The Watergate-related investigations revealed the existence of secret political slush funds that were used not only for domestic political contributions but also to bribe foreign government officials. Consequently, the SEC started researching the extent of these practices and promised immunity to US corporations that disclosed foreign bribery payments. The results were striking. Over 450 corporations that participated in the program disclosed bribery payments to foreign public officials exceeding $400 million. These findings motivated the unanimous adoption of the FCPA (Spalding, 2010).

The FCPA makes it an offense to provide[4] anything of value to a foreign official for the purposes of securing any improper advantage in order to assist the actor in obtaining or retaining business.[5] At the same time, the law requires companies that are listed in the US to keep accurate books and records and to create sufficient internal compliance mechanisms.[6] In contrast to American regulation of domestic bribery, the FCPA is special because it concentrates on bribe givers and does not address foreign public officials who are accepting the bribes. It means that the FCPA exclusively affects the supply side of the bribery transaction. Furthermore, the FCPA is a relatively narrow statute because it only addresses public bribery in the context of international business, and only covers foreign bribes that are provided to "foreign public officials."

Finally, it is important to highlight how the FCPA is special because of its jurisdictional provisions that allow prosecutors to reach a wide range of domestic and foreign subjects. During discussions on the enactment of new foreign anti-bribery legislation in the 1970s, there were divergent views on the wide reach of the FCPA. For example, the view of the Department of State was that it would be counterproductive to impose US anti-bribery standards in countries with different histories and cultures. Extraterritorial application of US law, according to the Department of State, was:

4 It includes an offer, payment, promise to pay, or authorization of the payment.

5 15 U.S.C. §§78dd-1(a), 78dd-2(a), 78dd-3(a). Jurisdiction-related issues are discussed in Section 4.7 below.

6 15 U.S.C. §78m.

> [...] viewed by other governments as a sign of U.S. arrogance or even as interference in their internal affairs. U.S. penal laws are normally based on territorial jurisdiction and, with rare exceptions, we believe that is sound policy.[7]

Nevertheless, thereafter, the jurisdictional reach of the FCPA has been only extending. In order to effectively regulate the overseas conduct of US-based corporations and US citizens, the US introduced the principle of nationality. Later on, in the context of the negotiations over the adoption of the OECD Convention, the 1998 amendments to the FCPA introduced provisions allowing enforcement authorities to charge even foreign firms.[8]

3.2.2 Toward the OECD Convention

The legislative process preceding the adoption of the FCPA included extensive discussion about the main rationales of the FCPA. In signing the FCPA, President Carter summarized, in part:

> [B]ribery is ethically repugnant and competitively unnecessary. Corrupt practices between corporations and public officials overseas undermine the integrity and stability of governments and harm our relations with other countries [...].
>
> (Rossbacher and Young, 1997: 519)

In line with the President Trump's words provided in the introductory paragraph of this work, the critique of the FCPA was that it places American firms at a competitive disadvantage to their foreign competitors. Already since the 1970s, some politicians and businesses worried that foreign firms did not have to comply with similar legislation, and hence, faced less compliance costs. Many argue that at the time of the adoption, the FCPA addressed a moral problem, rather than an economic problem, and was a reaction to a domestic ethical crisis (Dalton, 2006; Runnels and Burton, 2012).

The FCPA, however, not only concerns domestic policy but also has large foreign policy and economic rationales. In the last decade, a number of authors have argued that the FCPA has more of an economic rationale, as it originally aimed to advance the foreign policy goals of the US (Spalding, 2010: 384–390). Nichols (2016: 208), for instance, argues that Congress intended for "the Act to enhance the integrity and functionality of the global market." These interpretations indicate that one reason why the US

7 The Activities of American Multinational Corporations Abroad: Hearings before the Subcomm. on Int'l Econ. Policy of the H. Comm. on Int'l Relations, 94th Cong. 2 (1975), at 23–24 (statement of Mark B Feldman, Deputy Legal Advisor, U.S. Dep't of State) in (Koehler, 2012: supra note 14).

8 The International Anti-Bribery and Fair Competition Act 1998.

authorities made a great effort to persuade other countries to adopt similar foreign anti-bribery legislation was to promote a level playing field at the international level (Tarullo, 2004: 674–675). According to George and Lacey (2000: 563), the main expectation of the US was that an international treaty "had potential to solve many troublesome competition issues because all of the major competitor countries would thereafter be working within the same framework of constraints." The FCPA and the subsequent regulation at the international level are clearly linked to the concept of collective action as the politico-economic rationale – open and competitive markets – stood behind both negotiations and initial adoption of the OECD Convention.

The US leadership in the process of internationalization of the fight against international bribery should be also viewed from a wider politico-economic perspective. The internationalization followed the end of the West-East bipolarity after the fall of the Soviet Union, and the consequent globalization of business opportunities (Wolf and Schmidt-Pfister, 2010: 13–16). Within this new politico-economic context, anti-bribery initiatives of that time were influenced by three additional factors (Tarullo, 2004: 675–677). First, the newly elected Clinton administration directed US politics toward development initiatives that were included as a priority for US national interests. Second, increasing efforts by NGOs, research centers and other relevant initiatives boosted the general awareness on the negative effects of international bribery.[9] Finally, important US-based multinationals changed their approach and called for the imposition of similar foreign anti-bribery laws to their competitors (Rose, 2015: 1).

These developments led to the amendment of the FCPA in 1988.[10] The amendment imposed an obligation on the US Administration to negotiate an international agreement on foreign bribery (Pieth, Low and Cullen, 2007: 7–17). The decision was made to settle the discussion within the OECD that was requested to initiate work on an instrument of international law that would combat bribery of foreign public officials. These discussions were connected with the work of the newly established Ad Hoc Group on Illicit Payments, a predecessor of the Working Group on Bribery (WGB).[11] At that time, the move from unilateral US initiative to a more collective legislative response to foreign bribery has started.

9 Transparency International was set up in the early 1990s, see Transparency International, 'Our History' <http://www.transparency.org/whoweare/history> accessed 27 February 2019.

10 Omnibus Trade and Competitiveness Act 1988, 19 U.S.C. §2901 et seq.

11 The OECD first addressed foreign bribery via the Ad Hoc Group on Illicit Payments in 1989. The OECD Working Group on Bribery in International Business Transactions was established in 1994. The WGB is responsible for monitoring the implementation and enforcement and publishes country-monitoring reports. See OECD, 'OECD Working Group on Bribery in International Business Transactions' <http://www.oecd.org/investment/anti-bribery/anti-briberyconvention/oecdworkinggrouponbriberyininternationalbusinesstransactions.htm> accessed 27 February 2019.

The process progressed rapidly after the adoption of the Recommendation of 1994.[12] This document already introduced peer review passages covering follow-up and monitoring processes. Consequently, the decision was made to facilitate the criminalization of "the bribery of foreign public officials in an effective and coordinated manner" (Arner, 2007: 186). Soon after, the Revised Recommendation of 1997 (the 1997 Recommendation)[13] provided concrete substantive-legal foreign anti-bribery standards (Pieth et al., 2007: 14). Finally, just seven months after the adoption of the 1997 Recommendation, the OECD Convention was signed in December 1997. Some members of the WGB admitted that the adoption of the 1997 Recommendation was foreseeable, but not many expected that transnational bribery would be regulated via an international convention.[14]

The OECD Convention is the key legally binding instrument that commits the world's leading exporting countries to make it a crime to bribe foreign public officials in international business transactions.[15] Article 1, that specifies the substantive elements constituting the offense of bribery of foreign public officials, sets the core of the OECD Convention. However, the OECD Convention is not just limited to the definition of the offense of bribery. Article 2 provides that each party shall establish the liability of legal persons in accordance with the national legal principles of each Party. Article 3 then sets a minimal standard on sanctioning.[16] Furthermore, the OECD Convention contains specific substantive requirements on money laundering (Article 7), accounting standards (Article 8), Mutual Legal Assistance (MLA) (Article 9), and extradition (Article 10). Importantly, the OECD Convention also provides procedural rules related to jurisdiction (Article 4), enforcement (Article 5), and a program of systematic monitoring and follow-up (Article 12).

The OECD Convention is supplemented by two Recommendations: the 2009 Recommendation for Further Combating Bribery of Foreign Public Officials (the 2009 Recommendation),[17] that directly succeeds the 1997

12 Recommendation of the Council on Bribery in International Business Transactions, OECD (May 27, 1994).

13 Revised Recommendation of the Council on Combating Bribery in International Business Transactions, OECD (May 23, 1997).

14 See Mark Pieth's speech during the roundtable on the impact of the OECD Anti-Bribery. Mark Pieth, *'Roundtable on the Impact of the OECD Anti-Bribery Convention 15 Years On'* (speech delivered on 11 December 2013) <http://www.oecd.org/corruption/roundtable-oecd-anti-bribery-convention-15-years.htm> accessed 27 February 2019.

15 See OECD, *Third Annual High-Level Anti-Corruption Conference for G20 Governments and Business* (2013) <https://www.oecd.org/daf/anti-bribery/g20-anticorruption-2013.htm> accessed 27 February 2019.

16 Article 3 of the OECD Convention provides that if the criminal responsibility of legal persons is not applicable in the given national system, a given Party shall not be required to establish such a criminal responsibility but rather functionally equivalent non-criminal sanctions. See Article 3(2). Paragraph 20 of the Commentaries (OECD, 2011).

17 Recommendation of the Council for Further Combating Bribery of Foreign Public Officials in International Business Transactions, OECD (26 November 2009). The Recommendation is available in (OECD, 2011: 20–27).

Recommendation, and the 2009 Recommendation on the Non-Tax Deductibility of Bribes.[18] It is important to note that the Recommendations still represent the most important politically binding documents that address international bribery. In particular, the 2009 Recommendation further strengthens the legal framework for fighting bribery through its provisions on facilitation payments, whistleblowing, and communication between public authorities. Finally, the OECD Convention should be interpreted in conjunction with its Official Commentaries (OECD, 2011) that should be understood as *Travaux Préparatoires* to the OECD Convention (Pieth et al., 2007: 26).

3.2.3 Beyond the OECD Convention

The signing of the OECD Convention did not lead to an immediate increase in foreign anti-bribery enforcement. Another set of external shocks was needed to initiate more collective action. Most importantly, the 9/11 terrorist attacks and the Enron scandal, incentivized countries to increase foreign anti-bribery enforcement. After 9/11, the US adopted strict counterterrorism legislation, and the US and other State Parties to the OECD Convention started cooperating more closely on matters related to transnational crime.[19] In addition, a wave of corporate scandals where a number of major corporations engaged in accounting fraud and stock manipulation, initiated the adoption of stringent financial reporting obligations in the US in 2002 (Ashcroft and Ratcliffe, 2012: 30–33).[20] More focus on monitoring of books and records and anti-bribery compliance further strengthened the effectiveness of foreign anti-bribery enforcement (see Chapter 7).

Following these exogenous shocks, most nation-states have outlawed foreign bribery. What is more, since then, the US has conducted all major anti-bribery enforcement actions; in the majority of them, the US relied on the assistance of other State Parties to the OECD Convention (see Chapter 6). The first joint enforcement action resulting into penalties as high as hundreds of millions of dollars was *Siemens* in 2008 (discussed in Chapter 5). *Siemens* should be considered as evidence of a movement from the initial collective action problem to a multilateral enforcement regime. Moreover, it must be also noted, that these processes have generated new anti-bribery instruments such as various monitoring efforts, compliance consultancies, and private anti-bribery standards (see Chapter 9).

It is true that the OECD Convention currently operates in conjunction with a much broader system because states ratified a number of other international anti-corruption treaties. The Inter-American Convention against

18 Recommendation of the Council on Tax Measures for Further Combating Bribery of Foreign Public Officials in International Business Transactions, OECD (25 May 2009). The Recommendation is available in (OECD, 2011: 33–34).

19 Uniting and Strengthening America by Providing Appropriate Tools Required to Intercept and Obstruct Terrorism (US Patriot Act) Act of 2001.

20 The Sarbanes-Oxley Act 2002.

Corruption entered into force in 1997, approximately two years before the OECD Convention.[21] Similarly, the UN,[22] the CoE,[23] and the African Union[24] function alongside the OECD regime. Most importantly, the signature of the UNCAC in December 2003, with currently 140 signatories and 186 parties,[25] was considered as a major milestone in the fight against corruption; not only because of the large number of signatories but also because of its comprehensiveness. For example, differently from the OECD Convention, the UNCAC includes the provisions related to private sector corruption (Article 12), asset recovery (Chapter 5 of the UNCAC), and international cooperation (Articles 37–39 and Chapter IV of the UNCAC). The key problem with the UNCAC is that "the language of its provisions diminishes its potential to contribute to international anti-corruption efforts by penetrating domestic legal systems" (Rose, 2015: 97) and because of so many non-mandatory, vague, and qualified provisions the UNCAC "ultimately represents a relatively ineffective anti-corruption instrument" (Rose, 2015: 98). Therefore, the OECD Convention played a much more important role in the resolution of the initial collective action problem than any other anti-corruption treaty.

Last, the OECD Convention operates in conjunction with a much broader substantive and procedural context. For example, some instruments that are outside the scope of the OECD Convention, or are regulated only vaguely, such as financial reporting, anti-money laundering, and MLA, are relevant from the perspective of collective action. While these issues are alluded, their role in foreign anti-bribery enforcement cannot be well understood without a thorough analysis of foreign anti-bribery enforcement actions. For example, whether and how alternative statutes are applied to the acts of foreign bribery and how MLA is used. These instruments are identified by a case study in Chapter 5, and set into a broader enforcement context in Chapter 6.

3.3 The OECD Convention and functional equivalence

The establishment of collective action, and assumedly open and competitive markets, requires states to adopt effective legislation. The OECD Convention contributes to this end by setting a minimal substantive and procedural standard for such legislation. Legal norms, however, do not have to be completely unified if they have a function that is equivalent to the standard. This

21 Inter-American Convention against Corruption, 29 March 1996, in force 3 March 1997, 35 ILM 724.

22 See UNCAC.

23 Council of Europe Criminal Law Convention on Corruption, Strasbourg, 27 January 1999, in force 1 July 2002, Eur. T.S. No. 173.

24 African Union Convention on Preventing and Combating Corruption, Maputo, 11 July 2003, *in force* 5 August 2006, 43(1) ILM 5.

25 As of 26 June 2018.

so-called principle of functional equivalence is central to the OECD Convention. This part begins with the introduction of functional equivalence and investigates its role in the OECD regime.

The principle of functional equivalence is important for mitigating the credibility and clarity problems that undermine the provision of enforcement as a public good. The principle might be viewed from two interrelated perspectives. First, the question is, what does functional equivalence mean as the general principle of the OECD Convention? And second who, and with what legal effects, decides whether the standards are implemented in a functionally equivalent way? It will be argued that the principle should not be understood as a tool that fills legal gaps. Rather, functional equivalence is an analytical technique used by the WGB in order to evaluate whether the implementation of the OECD Convention into national legal systems is sufficient. Hence, while the principle builds an abstract framework for the implementation of existing minimum standards, it cannot overcome the lack of agreement between signatories.[26]

3.3.1 Functional equivalence as a general principle of the OECD Convention

3.3.1.1 Substance of the principle

The short interval between the adoption of the 1997 Recommendation and the OECD Convention made it a challenge to find a mechanism that would ensure the effective and coordinated implementation of the OECD Convention into national legal systems. Unification and harmonization were not considered appropriate because they are not sensitive to significant differences that existed between national legal orders of the signatory countries (Weiler, 2005: 25–84). The OECD anti-bribery enforcement regime required more flexibility in order to deal with, for example, differences in understanding of the concept of the criminal liability of legal persons. The functional equivalence approach based on the assumption that legal rules can achieve very similar results through different means provides such flexibility (Zweigert, 1972: 466–467).

The term "functional equivalence" is explicitly used in Paragraph 2 of the Official Commentaries. It provides that:

> [T]his Convention seeks to assure a functional equivalence among the measures taken by the Parties to sanction bribery of foreign public officials, without requiring uniformity or changes in fundamental principles of a Party's legal system.
>
> (OECD, 2011)

26 This should not be primarily understood as the critique of the OECD mechanisms. This limitation relates to a more general weakness of the functional comparative method.

Nevertheless, the concept is broader. It should be understood as a general principle that is implicit for the OECD Convention as a whole.[27] The legal basis for that can be seen in the Preamble to the OECD Convention that provides:

> [T]he parties [...] Recognising that achieving equivalence among the measures to be taken by the Parties is an essential object and purpose of the Convention, which requires that the Convention be ratified without derogations affecting this equivalence [...].
>
> (OECD, 2011: 6)

The principle is further materialized throughout the OECD Convention. One example is Article 1, that defines the offense of bribery of foreign public officials, and Paragraph 3 of the Commentaries, that specifies that:

> [...] a statute which defined the offence in terms of payments "to induce a breach of the official's duty" could meet the standard provided that it was understood that every public official had a duty to exercise judgement or discretion impartially and this was an "autonomous" definition not requiring proof of the law of the particular official's country.
>
> (OECD, 2011)

Such standard shall be met by functionally equivalent means, if they do not impose additional conditions that would limit a conviction of a person for the offense of foreign bribery.

Moreover, the principle of functional equivalence is applied by the WGB during its monitoring of the implementation. In light of the principle, the WGB may ask the OECD Convention signatories for clarification or recommend corrective measures. For instance, as the definition of "foreign public official" in German law differs significantly from the wording of the OECD Convention, German authorities were asked to clarify whether the definition is broad enough, meaning that no element of proof beyond those contemplated in Article 1 of the OECD Convention is required.[28] As seen in this example, while the OECD Convention does not require its signatories to utilize its precise terms in defining the offense of bribery, its monitoring mechanisms insist on the interpretation of national provisions to be equivalent to the OECD Convention's standard.

27 International Bar Association, 'Comments of the International Bar Association on the Consultation Paper of the Working Group on Bribery of the OECD' <http://www.ibanet.org/Document/Default.aspx?DocumentUid=E7942B1C-B242–4306-B762–78B03648BE14> accessed 27 February 2019.

28 See OECD (2011) Phase 3 Report on Implementing the OECD Anti-Bribery Convention in Germany, 5–6. For more information about the notion of the foreign public official see Section 4.5 below.

Functional equivalence, however, does not prevent the Parties from being stricter at a certain point – there is no maximum standard. For instance, the given legislator can criminalize an attempt to bribe despite the fact that in the context of domestic bribery, the attempt does not establish criminal liability, or is criminalized less strictly. The Parties can also criminalize negligent violations of the OECD-based anti-bribery laws despite the fact that the standard established by the OECD Convention requires intent (see Article 1(2) of the OECD Convention).[29]

3.3.1.2 Operationalization of the principle – monitoring process

The principle of functional equivalence is operationalized via a monitoring mechanism that provides the basis for effective and coordinated implementation of the OECD Convention in all its signatory states. This is similar to EU directives that should be also implemented with regards to their results. The main difference is that if a state fails to implement an EU directive, the European Commission may take legal action against the state via the Court of Justice of the EU.[30] The OECD does not have a superior body with a mandate to interpret the OECD Convention authoritatively. The monitoring has political and educational, rather than legal, character, and allows the OECD Convention signatories to control, evaluate, and learn from each other. The OECD monitoring mechanism is much softer than the approach developed by the EU.[31]

The "guardian" of the OECD Convention is the WGB, a monitoring body made up of State Parties to the OECD Convention.[32] The WGB relies on Article 12 of the OECD Convention, that sets a program on systematic monitoring and evaluation. The signatory states are obliged to co-operate in carrying out the program and promote the full implementation of the OECD Convention (Article 12 of the OECD Convention). The monitoring process focuses on each Party's implementation and is reviewed by representatives of other Parties. In addition, the role of the Secretariat is crucial because it ensures monitoring processes are fair, equal, and consistently applied.

The monitoring consists of four main evaluative phases. After an assessment of whether implemented national legal texts meet the standards of the OECD Convention and related documents (Phase 1), there follows an examination of national enforcement structures and an assessment of their practical

29 For more discussion about complicity and conspiracy, see Section 4.4.2 below.

30 See Article 258 of Consolidated Version of the Treaty on the Functioning of the European Union [2012] OJ C326/47.

31 Section 14 of the 2009 Recommendation delegates monitoring obligations to the WGB (OECD, 2011).

32 OECD, 'OECD Working Group on Bribery in International Business Transactions' <http://www.oecd.org/investment/anti-bribery/anti-briberyconvention/oecdworkinggrouponbriberyininternationalbusinesstransactions.htm> accessed 27 February 2019.

application (Phase 2). In December 2009, the WGB adopted a more dynamic process based on circular peer review. This so-called Phase 3 circle aims to:

1 monitor progress on weaknesses identified in Phase 2;
2 catch up with possible changes in national legislation; and
3 assess enforcement and other cross-cutting issues such as any previously identified weaknesses and any issues arising from changes in national legislation.[33]

Phase 4 started in 2016 and will last until 2024. Phase 4 pays special attention to unique situation and challenges of each country under evaluation.[34]

All of the Phases are based on "vertical," country-by-country, examinations where two countries are appointed to lead the given examination. The leading examiners choose experts who assist in the preparation of the preliminary report.[35] Consequently, these processes lead to Recommendations, an explicit Summary Record, and a Press Statement that might be supported by additional follow-up measures to increase the effectiveness of the monitoring (Pieth, Low and Bonucci, 2014: 153).

3.3.2 Functional equivalence as a methodological tool

The principle of functional equivalence is not just a general principle of the OECD Convention, but also a methodological tool that is used to assess the effectiveness of the implementation and application of the OECD Convention. A more theoretical basis of this concept lies in the work of comparative lawyers that refer to a "common problem" as the basis of any comparative analysis. As Konrad Zweigert noted:

> [D]ifferent legal systems find equal or at least astonishingly similar solutions – often down to the details – for similar problems, in spite of all differences in historical development, systematical and theoretical concepts and style of practice.
>
> (Zweigert, 1972: 469)

In this context, functional equivalence operates as an analytical tool.

This analytical tool is criticized because of its static character. The use of functional equivalence is based on a presumption that law has a function of solving universal problems (Michaels, 2006: 356–359). According to this view, a researcher should search for and presume evidence of similarity. The pitfall is that the lack of clarity whether and to what extent all problems are the same when societal values differ (Adams and Griffith, 2012: 279–301). For example,

33 OECD, *Phase 3 Country Monitoring of the OECD Anti-Bribery Convention* <http://www.oecd.org/investment/anti-bribery/anti-briberyconvention/phase3countrymonitoringoftheoecdanti-briberyconvention.htm> accessed 22 September 2018.

34 OECD, *Phase 4 Country Monitoring of the OECD Anti-Bribery Convention* <http://www.oecd.org/corruption/oecd-anti-bribery-convention-phase-4.htm> accessed 22 September 2018.

35 Ibid.

one country might be very active in prosecuting individuals, yet inactive in prosecuting corporations. On the other hand, another country might prosecute corporations but not individuals. Are both approaches functionally equivalent? Which country is more compliant with the OECD Convention? In this context, Luhmann (1970: 38) argues that: "although the method of functional equivalence can be abstractly developed as an analytical technique, it is not aimed to be applied in emptiness" (translated in Deth, 2013: 3). In other words, a functional technique needs some substance that indicates what the real problem is.

But should the WGB answer this type of normative questions? Technically, it is possible because the limitations of classical comparative functional schemes have been faced with more dynamic- and context-oriented approaches. Modern comparatists are capable of explaining the nature of institutions and the relationship between legal orders (Larouche, 2013: 258–267). We see elements of this approach in the new Phase 4 that takes into account unique situation and challenges of each country.

However, building a broad descriptive framework is, to a certain extent, always limited by the risk of normative bias (Adams and Griffith, 2012: 279–301). Some countries sometimes referred to these normative biases during the OECD evaluation rounds (Pieth et al., 2014: 154). This leaves the OECD monitoring and evaluation system with a trade-off between a static and a dynamic application of the principle of functional equivalence. The former is limited by clarity problems and may result in only limited validity of the recommendations because of the lack of context. The latter may be criticized as too authoritative and biased.

3.3.3 Minimum standard approach and collective action

Functional equivalence as a general legal principle of the OECD Convention although created to tackle heterogeneity allows for heterogeneity because of institutional reasons and normative constraints. The question is: In what way, and to what extent, is this minimum standard approach conducive to collective action?

The principle of functional equivalence seems more effective when it is used to evaluate whether implemented national legal texts meet relatively concrete textual standards, and when more broad concepts are interpreted in the OECD Convention or the Commentaries. For example, as will be discussed in the following chapter, the heterogeneity is in some cases, such as the definition of the briber and the bribe, relatively narrow and does not cause major clarity problems. In these situations, the principle of functional equivalence may allow national enforcement authorities to operate within the scope of their national legal principles and legal traditions. This flexibility is coordinated by constant evaluation, examinations of enforcement trends, and the work on typologies or cross-country studies. In this context, the OECD mechanism has overcome some of the methodological pitfalls identified by the comparative scholars and is designed to prevent clarity problems that may arise.

However, in areas that lack authoritative interpretation, such as the principles of national enforcement and international cooperation and coordination, heterogeneity is wide. In these cases, it difficult to determine what functionally equivalent solutions are. While the standard of equivalence can be derived from the OECD Convention itself, the Official Commentaries that might further exemplify the OECD Convention's standards, and informally from the WGB through its evaluation processes, the OECD regime does not offer binding "creative" interpretation. By this reason, the regime is not constructed to fully offset the lack of agreement between the OECD Convention signatory countries. In the end, it is up the signatory countries to agree upon what is functionally equivalent because the OECD system does not exclude or eliminate such heterogeneity.[36]

The following section introduces national foreign anti-bribery laws of the US, the UK, and Germany.

3.4 Excursion to national foreign anti-bribery laws

This section gives a brief overview of US, UK, and German anti-bribery laws. Accession to the OECD Convention binds signatory states to ratify and implement its provisions into their national laws in a functionally equivalent manner. The signatories must amend their national legislation in order to comply with "foreign" anti-bribery standards. The implementation not only entails formal transposition of the relevant provisions but also their application in practice. The main questions are: What general features do US law, UK law, and German law have? In what way do they implement the OECD Convention? And how much scope of heterogeneity is there in the implementation of the relevant provisions?

The excursion to national legal systems serves as a necessary basis for the analysis of relevant provisions of the OECD Convention and their implementation into the national laws of its signatory states. US law has been selected as the main jurisdiction, but the analysis also provides comparative notes to UK law and German law. These jurisdictions are relevant, among other reasons, because they are the three largest economies out of seven most active enforcers of the OECD Convention (together with Israel, Italy, Norway, and Switzerland) accounting for 21.2% of world exports (TI, 2018).

3.4.1 US law

The US signed the OECD Convention on 17 December 1997 and implemented it into its legislation by the enactment of the International Anti-Bribery and Fair Competition Act of 1998 that amended the FCPA. The FCPA represents a specific legal instrument against foreign bribery. It contains both the anti-bribery provisions[37] and the accounting provisions.[38] Hence, not only

36 The problem is that if the WGB engages in more creative evaluations, it may be criticized because of the potential of normative bias.

37 15 U.S.C. §§78dd-1, 2, and 3.

38 15 U.S.C. §§78m(b)(2)(A), 78m(b)(2)(B),78m(b)(5).

does the FCPA make it illegal to bribe foreign public officials, but it also requires issuers to "make and keep books, records, and accounts, which, in reasonable detail, accurately and fairly reflect the transactions and dispositions of the assets...,"[39] as well as devise and maintain a sufficient system of internal accounting controls.[40] The enforcement of the statute is centralized. The DOJ is responsible for criminal enforcement and shares the responsibility with the SEC when it comes to civil matters. The SEC has the jurisdiction over listed companies – issuers (DOJ and SEC, 2012: 2).

The US legal system recognizes criminal liability for both natural and legal persons. US law sanctions the offense of bribery of foreign public officials via a combination of criminal and civil sanctions. For example, for each violation of the anti-bribery provisions, criminal penalties can reach up to $2 million for corporations and up to $100,000 and five years' imprisonment for natural persons; for books and records, penalties can reach up to $25 million for corporations and up to $5 million and 20 years' imprisonment for natural persons. However, the fines can be increased above the maximum level once the given company gains profits under a bribery scheme that exceeds such a maximum.[41]

3.4.2 German law

Germany signed the OECD Convention on 17 December 1997 and implemented it into its legislation via an enactment of a transposition act – Gesetz zur Bekämpfung Internationaler Bestechung (IntBestG).[42] The German approach is not based on a special code. The IntBestG is an auxiliary act that operates in combination with other statutes that deal with liability for bribing domestic public officials. In November 2015, the offense of foreign bribery was incorporated into the German Criminal Code – Strafgesetzbuch (StGB) by introducing a new §335a StGB.[43] In this context, the function of the IntBestG and the StGB is to ensure the equal treatment of both domestic and foreign bribery. Unlike the US, the German enforcement model is decentralized. Multiple public prosecuting authorities that operate within 16 regions – Länder – are responsible for the enforcement.

German law sanctions the offense of bribery of foreign public officials via a combination of criminal and administrative sanctions. The criminal liability

39 15 U.S.C. §78m(b)(2)(A).

40 15 U.S.C. §78m(b)(2)(B).

41 Criminal penalties may be increased to as much as twice the benefit sought by the violation, see The Alternative Fines Act, 18 U.S.C. §3571(d). See also US Sentencing Guidelines §1A1.1 (2011) that provides a detailed methodology how to determine sanctions.

42 Gesetz zu dem Übereinkommen vom 17. Dezember 1997 über die Bestechung ausländischer Amtsträger im internationalen Geschäftsverkehr, the Act entered into force on 15 February 1999 (hereinafter IntBestG).

43 Strafgesetzbuch in der Fassung der Bekanntmachung vom 13. November 1998 (BGBl. I S. 3322), das zuletzt durch Artikel 1 des Gesetzes vom 1. März 2017 (BGBl. I S. 386) geändert worden ist (hereinafter StGB). Gesetz zur Bekämpfung der Korruption vom 20. November 2015 (BGBl. I S. 2025).

of natural persons under German law is based on §§334–338 of the StGB. The available duration of imprisonment depends on the type of offense and its severity. For example, the basic sanction for the offense of bribery of a public official under §334(1) StGB ranges from three to five years' imprisonment, or fine up to €10.8 million. The offense of serious bribery under §335 ranges from one to ten years' imprisonment. The key procedural principles can be found in the German Code of Criminal Procedure – Strafprozeßordnung (StPO).[44]

Unlike natural persons, legal persons are only subject to provisions of administrative law, due to German law not recognizing criminal liability for legal persons. Administrative sanctions for legal persons are based on the Administrative Offences Act – Gesetz über Ordnungswidrigkeiten (OWiG).[45] After 30 June 2013, the German legislature has increased maximum administrative penalties up to €10 million. However, the fine can be increased above the maximum level once a given company gains profits under a bribery scheme that exceeds such a maximum.[46] Moreover, the sanctions might increase in the future. In 2018, the German Government announced a possible increase in maximum punitive fine to 10% of the company's turnover.[47] It must also be added that German law does not provide any specific "civil sanctions" for foreign bribery. Nevertheless, general provisions on damages and compensation of the German Civil Code – Bürgerliches Gesetzbuch (BGB) – are applicable to bribery of foreign public officials.[48]

3.4.3 UK law

The UK signed the OECD Convention on 14 December 1998 and implemented it into its legislation via an amendment of its old anti-corruption statutes, most importantly of which are the Prevention of Corruption Act 1906 and the Public Bodies Corrupt Practices Act 1889, as well as the common law offense of bribery.[49] The UK approach was harshly criticized by the WGB for its ineffectiveness and the lack of compliance with the OECD

44 Strafprozeßordnung in der Fassung der Bekanntmachung vom 7. April 1987 (BGBl. I S. 1074, 1319), die zuletzt durch Artikel 2 des Gesetzes vom 1. März 2017 (BGBl. I S. 386) geändert worden ist (hereinafter StPO).

45 See §30 and §130 OWiG.

46 See Gibson Dunn, *Tenfold Increase of Corporate Fines for Compliance Violations in Germany* (9 July 2013) <https://www.gibsondunn.com/tenfold-increase-of-corporate-fines-for-compliance-violations-in-germany/> accessed 27 February 2019.

47 OECD (2018) Phase 4 Report on Implementing the OECD Anti-Bribery Convention in Germany, 69.

48 See §§823(2) and 826 BGB.

49 The Prevention of Corruption Act 1906 (c. 34). The Public Bodies Corrupt Practices Act 1889 (c.69). See also OECD (2010) United Kingdom Phase 1 Ter: Report on the Application of the Convention on Combating Bribery of Foreign Public Officials in International Business Transactions and the 2009 Revisited Recommendation on Combating Bribery in International Business Transactions.

Convention's standards.[50] For this reason, in April 2010, the UK enacted a new comprehensive anti-bribery statute – the Bribery Act 2010 (the Bribery Act). The Bribery Act is considered to be the strictest legislation on foreign bribery in the world. It covers not only active and passive bribery on a public level but also private-to-private bribery. Furthermore, the Bribery Act provides for wide jurisdiction by, for instance, introducing a corporate offense for the failure to prevent bribery (Section 7).

The UK legal system recognizes criminal liability for both natural and legal persons. The Bribery Act enables a judge to punish an individual with a sentence of up to ten years and impose an unlimited fine (Section 11(1)). Legal persons are punishable by an unlimited fine (Section 11(2) and (3)). In addition, a criminal conviction might lead to confiscation orders, civil recovery orders, serious crime prevention orders, and debarment.[51] The leading enforcement authority in the UK is the Serious Fraud Office (SFO). The competence of the SFO, however, to some extent overlaps with other enforcement authorities including the Crown Prosecution Service, National Crime Agency International Corruption Unit, and Financial Conduct Authority. It must be noted that the Crown Office and Procurator Fiscal Service is in charge of the prosecution of foreign bribery in Scotland.

3.5 Conclusion

The adoption of the FCPA should be recognized as a new and unique step that overcame limitation of domestic (internal) regulation on bribery and corruption. The FCPA allowed the US enforcement authorities to prosecute bribery occurring at the international level. The US sent a strong signal to the international community, that bribery in international business transactions is unacceptable. As a consequence, the OECD anti-bribery enforcement regime evolved from markets where foreign bribery was not regulated at all (before 1977), through one where only the US formally prohibited foreign bribery (1977–1998), to today's situation in which 44 countries have adopted the OECD Convention, and most of the other countries adopted other anti-corruption treaties such as the UNCAC.

The OECD Convention is the most advanced international legal instrument that sets the basis of how extraterritorial enforcement should provide public goods and how collective action problems should be resolved. The leading principle of the OECD Convention is functional equivalence. Although created to alleviate the heterogeneity of national approaches to

50 See, generally, OECD, 'United Kingdom: Review of Implementation of the Convention and 1997 Recommendation' (1999).

51 See, generally, Barry Vitou and Richard Kovalevsky, *Part 1 – When It Goes Wrong: Penalties for Bribery* (thebriberyact.com, 2012) <http://thebriberyact.com/2012/05/14/part-1-%E2%80%93-when-it-goes-wrong-penalties-for-bribery/> accessed 27 February 2019.

foreign anti-bribery enforcement, the principle allows for heterogeneity because of institutional reasons and normative constraints.

The elimination of heterogeneity could solve some credibility and clarity problems that undermine collective action. The principle of functional equivalence can help with the elimination of heterogeneity in situations when national laws are required to meet relatively concrete textual standards of the OECD Convention, and when more broad concepts are interpreted in the OECD Convention or the Commentaries. In areas that lack authoritative interpretation, however, for example, questions of appropriate jurisdiction, it is difficult to determine what functionally equivalent solutions are. This may limit collective action.

The following chapter will analyze the extent of this heterogeneity with a special focus on the provision of the OECD Convention that is relevant from the perspective of collective action.

References

Adams, M. and Griffiths, J. (2012) 'Against "Comparative Method": Explaining Similarities and Differences' In M. Adams and J. Bomhof (Eds.) *Practice and Theory in Comparative Law* (pp. 279–301). Cambridge: Cambridge University Press.

Arner, D. W. (2007) *Financial Stability, Economic Growth, and the Role of Law*. Cambridge: Cambridge University Press.

Ashcroft, J. and Ratcliffe, J. (2012) 'The Recent and Unusual Evolution of an Expanding FCPA' 26 Notre Dame Journal of Law, Ethics & Public Policy 25.

Bogdan, M (1979) 'International Trade and the New Swedish Provisions on Corruption' 27 American Journal of Comparative Law 665.

Dalton, M. M. (2006) 'Efficiency v. Morality: The Codification of Cultural Norms in the Foreign Corrupt Practices Act' 2 The NYU Journal of Law and Business 583.

Deth Van, J. W. (2013) *Comparative Politics: The Problem of Equivalence*. Colchester: ECPR Press.

DOJ and SEC (2012) 'A Resource Guide to the U.S. Foreign Corrupt Practices Act' (2012) 10 < https://www.justice.gov/sites/default/files/criminal-fraud/legacy/2015/01/16/guide.pdf> accessed 27 February 2019.

George, B. C. and Lacey, K. A. (2000) 'A Coalition of Industrialized Nations, Developing Nations, Multilateral Development Banks, and Non-Governmental Organizations: A Pivotal Complement to Current Anti-Corruption Initiatives' 33 Cornell International Law Journal 547.

Goodman, J. (2013) *The Anti-Corruption and Antitrust Connection*. The Antitrust Source. <http://www.americanbar.org/content/dam/aba/publishing/antitrust_source/apr13_goodman.authcheckdam.pdf> accessed 27 February 2019.

Koehler, M. (2012) 'The Story of the Foreign Corrupt Practices Act' 73 Ohio State Law Journal 929.

Krasner, S. D. (1985) *Structural Conflict: The Third World against Global Liberalism*. Berkeley: University of California Press.

Larouche, P. (2013) 'Legal Emulation between Regulatory Competition and Comparative Law' In P. Larouche and P. Cserne (Eds.) *National Legal Systems and Globalization: New Role, Continuing Relevance* (pp. 247–287). The Hague: T.M.C. Asser Press.

Luhmann, N. (1970) *Soziologische Aufklärung*. Opladen: Westdeutscher Verlag.
Michaels, R. (2006) 'The Functional Method of Comparative Law' In M. Reimann and R. Zimmermann (Eds.) *Oxford Handbook of Comparative Law* (pp. 339–382). Oxford: Oxford University Press.
Nichols, P. M. (2016) 'The Neomercantilist Fallacy and the Contextual Reality of the Foreign Corrupt Practices Act' 53 Harvard Journal on Legislation 203.
Noonan, J. T. (1984) *Bribes*. New York: Macmillan.
OECD (2011) Convention on Combating Bribery of Foreign Public Officials in International Business Transactions and Related Documents (2011) <http://www.oecd.org/daf/anti-bribery/ConvCombatBribery_ENG.pdf> accessed 25 February 2019.
Pieth, M., Low, L. A. and Bonucci, N. (Eds.) (2014) *The OECD Convention on Bribery: A Commentary*. Cambridge: Cambridge University Press.
Pieth, M., Low, L. A. and Cullen, P. J. (Eds.) (2007) *The OECD Convention on Bribery: A Commentary*. Cambridge: Cambridge University Press.
Pines, D. (1994) 'Amending the Foreign Corrupt Practices Act to Include a Private Right of Action' 82 California Law Review 185.
Rose, C. (2015) *International Anti-Corruption Norms: Their Creation and Influence on Domestic Legal Systems*. Oxford: Oxford University Press.
Rossbacher, T. W. and Young, H. H. (1997) 'The Foreign Corrupt Practices Act within the American Response to Domestic Corruption' 15 Dickinson Journal of International Law 509.
Runnels, A. M. and Burton, M. B. (2012) 'The Foreign Corrupt Practices Act and New Governance: Incentivizing Ethical Foreign Direct Investment in China and Other Emerging Economies' 34 Cardozo Law Review 295.
Spalding A. B. (2010) 'Unwitting Sanctions: Understanding Anti-Bribery Legislation as Economic Sanctions Against Emerging Markets' 62 Florida Law Review 351.
Tarullo, D. K. (2004) 'The Limits of Institutional Design: Implementing the OECD Anti-Bribery Convention' 44 Virginia Journal of International Law 665.
TI (2018) *Exporting Corruption: Progress Report 2018: Assessing Enforcement of the OECD Convention on Combating Foreign Bribery, available at* <https://www.transparency.org/whatwedo/publication/exporting_corruption_2018> accessed 27 February October 2019.
Weiler, J. (2005) 'Mutual Recognition, Functional Equivalence and Harmonization in the Evolution of the European Common Market and the WTO' In F. Padoa-Schioppa (Eds.) *The Principles of Mutual Recognition in the European Integration Process* (pp. 25–84). Basingstoke: Palgrave Macmillan.
Wolf, D. and Schmidt-Pfister, S. (Eds) (2010), *International Anti-Corruption Regimes in Europe: Between Corruption, Integration, and Culture*. Baden-Baden: Nomos.
Zweigert, K. (1972) 'Methodological Problems in Comparative Law.' 7 Israel Law Review 465.

4 The OECD Anti-Bribery Convention and national foreign anti-bribery laws

4.1 Introduction

This chapter analyzes foreign anti-bribery legislation, primarily the OECD Convention and the national laws of the US, and where necessary of other enforcement actors, such as the UK and Germany. This will be done from the perspective of collective action, focusing on legal norms determining the provision of enforcement, legal mechanisms that incentivize cooperation and coordination between national enforcement authorities, and legal ambiguities that may cause cooperation and coordination problems. It will be argued that the substantive standard introduced by the OECD Convention sets a good basis for prosecuting many MNCs for bribing. However, the key problem is how to deal with certain clarity challenges, such as which authority should enforce foreign anti-bribery laws and how enforcement authorities should cooperate and coordinate with each other.

First, when it comes to the provision of enforcement, the legal analysis will focus upon how, and to what extent, foreign anti-bribery laws are applicable to subjects operating in the global market. In order to do so, both the procedural and substantive elements determining the jurisdiction of national enforcement authorities must be identified. From the procedural perspective, the key issue is how jurisdiction is established over operations of foreign and domestic subjects that act outside an enforcing state's territory. Moreover, the scope of application has a deep substantive dimension, as the establishment of jurisdiction depends on many substantive concepts such as the notions of the briber, the bribed party, and the control over subsidiaries, agents, and other intermediaries that act on behalf of the headquarters (indirect bribery).

Second, collective action relates to the question of how legal rules address cooperation and coordination within the OECD anti-bribery enforcement regime. In this context, international cooperation and assistance is important because it lowers enforcement resources and makes it easier to gather evidence and information that is relevant for prosecutors. Furthermore, collective action also depends on coordination mechanisms that clarify ambiguities about the terms of a states' agreement to provide foreign anti-bribery enforcement. The coordination mechanisms are important because they, for example, prevent enforcement conflicts, including conflicts in which large countries enforce foreign anti-bribery laws without coordinating each other's actions. The relevant questions are: Which institutions, if any, does the OECD regime offer to face clarity threats? How does foreign anti-bribery legislation deal with situations where several enforcers claim that they have jurisdiction over the given bribery case? And how is the non-action of enforcement authorities dealt with?

The collective action perspective shows costs associated with the alleviation of heterogeneity of national measures. While the elimination of the heterogeneity could be the solution to some clarity problem, it could undermine the effectiveness of norms that help to provide enforcement. The problem is that an appropriate institutional design to eliminate the heterogeneity depends on the level of collective action that exists within a regime. For example, if the OECD regime is in the stage that lacks the enforcement of foreign anti-bribery legislation, a high level of heterogeneity may be acceptable. In such situation, any foreign anti-bribery enforcement would result in placing relatively more corporations under strict regulatory scrutiny. Yet, heterogeneity could turn to be increasingly undesirable if the provision of enforcement is relatively high. In this scenario, more rigorous governance framework is needed in order to resolve second-order collective action problems, for example, the lack of coordination of enforcement (see Sections 7.2.1 and 8.2).

The investigation in this chapter adopts a more formalistic approach that will be further expanded by an in-depth case study in Chapters 5 and 6. Some provisions of the OECD Convention that are relevant from the perspective of collective action are relatively precise and their implementation into national laws will be discussed in more detail. Other relevant provisions are vague and possibly outside the scope of the OECD Convention. These provisions will be discussed in less detail by exemplifying the key elements of the analyzed national legal systems because their relevance from the perspective of collective action depends on how they are used in enforcement practice

4.2 The offense of bribery of foreign public officials

The signatories to the OECD Convention are obliged to criminalize bribery of foreign public officials. The core of the OECD Convention is the definition of the offense of foreign bribery. The definition in Article 1 includes the most important substantive elements of the offense. The signatories shall ensure that any person in the conduct of international business is prohibited from:

- intentionally
- offering, promising, or giving whether directly or through intermediaries
- any undue pecuniary or other advantage
- to a foreign public official, for that official or for a third party

- in order that the official act or refrain from acting in relation to the performance of official duties
- in order to obtain or retain business, or any other improper advantage.[1]

The analysis that follows below focuses on four elements that are crucial for the provision of enforcement as a public good: (1) the briber (i.e. any person); (2) the liability for acts of third persons (indirect bribery); (3) the bribed party (i.e. foreign public official); and (4) the bribe (i.e. any undue advantage).

4.3 The briber: "any person"

Foreign anti-bribery law shall generally apply to "any person." The OECD signatories should ensure the generality of application of the offense of foreign bribery to all bribers. It means that no special category of potential bribers shall be exempted from the application of the law. In other words, the law should not provide any immunity to existing entities whether natural or legal.[2]

This fundamental obligation of the OECD Convention does not cause heterogeneity in implementation. The FCPA provides a broad definition of the briber and it does not exempt any natural or legal person. The FCPA applies to "issuers," "domestic concerns," and "any persons other than issuer or domestic concern."[3] The UK system contains the word "a person" that entails "a body of persons corporate or unincorporated."[4] In addition, Germany does not provide any special treatment to natural persons.

Some issues may arise in jurisdictions that do not attribute criminal liability to legal persons. Consider Germany that in §334(1) StGB, similarly to the US and the UK, uses the word "anyone" in international business practice.[5] The provision, however, applies only to natural persons. The absence of corporate criminal liability does not, per se, constitute non-compliance with the OECD Convention because the most important is to establish the liability of legal persons in general. Article 2 of the OECD Convention provides that in case a legal system of a Party does not recognize criminal responsibility for legal persons, such Party shall ensure that legal persons shall be subject to non-criminal sanctions.[6] Under German law, the requirement of Article 2 is operationalized by §30 and §130 OWiG. These provisions of German administrative law provide that any legal person might be held liable for offenses committed by relevant natural persons.[7]

1 Article 1 of the OECD Convention.
2 For instance, the immunity of the Head of State might be an exception (Pieth et al., 2007: 98).
3 15 U.S.C. §§78dd-1, 2, and 3. For further discussion about these notions see Section 4.7.3.
4 The notion of 'a person' under the Bribery Act is defined in the Interpretation Act 1978 (c. 30), Section 5 and Schedule I.
5 See §2 of the IntBestG.
6 Article 3(2) of the OECD Convention (see Section 4.8.3).
7 See §30 OWiG See summary in OECD (2013) Germany: Follow-up to the Phase 3 Report & Recommendations, 8. For the analysis of §30 and §130 OWiG see Section 4.4.1 (German Law).

Jurisdictions that recognize corporate criminal liability and these that do not recognize such liability will tend to have different enforcement priorities and policy objectives. For instance, German enforcement authorities may tend to focus more than the US authorities on the prosecution of natural persons rather than corporations. Without specifying in more detail how equivalent these two diverse approaches to corporate liability are, collective action can be undermined because of clarity problems.

The liability for the acts of third persons, or indirect bribery – is another crucial requirement of the OECD Convention that concerns liability for acts of both natural and legal persons. This concept is discussed in the following section.

4.4 Indirect bribery: intermediaries and complicity

Corporations that do business globally face a number of institutional and cultural challenges specific to foreign markets in which they operate. To deal with these challenges in an efficient way, they hire or establish local representatives in foreign markets. Foreign intermediaries, subsidiaries, and similar entities, however, frequently engage, whether that be by themselves or under orders of their principals, in bribery of foreign public officials (OECD, 2009: 5–6). Without effective legislation, the principals could bribe freely by instructing foreign intermediaries to bribe on their behalf. The ability of national enforcement authorities to sanction this form of bribery is crucial for the provision of enforcement and collective action.

The OECD Convention aims to limit situations in which intermediaries are used to protect principals from incurring legal responsibility for bribery that the principals in fact organized or benefited from. The key question is whether the OECD Convention and national foreign anti-bribery laws ensure that enforcement authorities have legal means to hold these principals accountable for indirect bribery and impose penalties. The following section introduces the most important legal concepts that relate to the issue of indirect bribery.

4.4.1 Liability for the acts of intermediaries

Generally, a corporation can be held criminally liable for acts of third persons if it fulfills certain subjective and objective elements. The subjective element is connected with the subjective responsibility of an offender.[8] In principle, the concept of subjective responsibility entails two, to a certain extent, overlapping elements: "intent" and "knowledge." The general rule is that the offender acts knowingly if he is aware of the fact that he himself or through another person is committing an offense. At the same time, the offender should have a certain degree of intent to commit a crime, ranging

8 This concept is important for both direct and indirect bribery.

from negligence, through eventual intent – *dolus eventualis*, to direct intent – *dolus directus*. The OECD Convention requires *dolus eventualis* or possibly a stricter form, like negligence for example (Pieth, Low and Bonucci, 2014: 640–645). Such an intent also includes a situation in which the offender intentionally overlooks criminal conduct. In some jurisdictions, this is called "willful blindness," referring to when a corporation is suspicious of a criminal activity but deliberately do not act to mitigate such criminal activity.

The objective element relates to the relevant acts of a company that constitute legal responsibility, including certain acts undertaken by employees, subsidiaries, and other persons. In other words, the key question is whether the relevant acts that caused the violations of foreign anti-bribery laws are, at least in part, attributable to a corporation. There are three main types of relationships that may establish the liability of a corporation for the acts of third persons:

a The first type is the responsibility of the principal for the bribes of its agents. This is frequently connected with activities of independent bodies such as foreign consultancies or distributors who act on behalf of the firms that hired them. As stated above, these types of situations are addressed by Article 1 of the OECD Convention that explicitly refers to the criminalization of indirect bribery through intermediaries.[9]
b The second type is the responsibility of a parent corporation for its subsidiary that enjoys a sufficient level of independence, meaning that the subsidiary is not fully controlled by the parent corporation. These independent subsidiaries are not mentioned in the OECD Convention explicitly. Nevertheless, the 2009 Recommendation indicates that: "a legal person cannot avoid responsibility by using intermediaries, including related legal persons, to offer, promise or give a bribe to a foreign public official on its behalf."[10] It implies that national laws should implement the OECD Convention in such a way as to treat independent subsidiaries as de facto intermediaries (Pieth et al., 2014: 159–165).
c The third type is the liability of a parent corporation for bribes of subsidiaries that are controlled by the parent. In many jurisdictions, the legal responsibility of the parent depends on the degree of control and influence it has over its subsidiaries (see Hill, 2003; Pieth et al., 2014: 150–151). For example, case studies in Chapters 5 and 6 will show that in a number of US enforcement actions, if a firm (daughter) is wholly owned and managed by another firm (parent), the parent is considered

9 Article 1 provides that the bribing can be conducted "directly or through intermediaries". Paragraph 6 of the Commentaries makes also clear that "the conduct described in paragraph 1 is an offence whether the offer or promise is made or the pecuniary or other advantage is given on that person's own behalf or on behalf of any other natural person or legal entity" OECD (2011).

10 Annex I., C) of the Recommendation 2009. OECD (2011).

to have control and the actions of the daughter are imputed to its parent (see Section 6.4.2). As these daughter companies are only branches operating under the instructions of their parent, the parent is fully responsible for their acts.

The key problem with the liability for the acts of third persons is that the OECD Convention does not specify the conditions for when subsidiaries and intermediaries are independent from their principals. This may result in a heterogeneity in implementation that is problematic from the clarity point of view, as well as it could limit the enforcement reach of the OECD regime. The following part discusses how the issue is approached by US law, as well as German law and UK law.

4.4.1.1 US law

US law is explicit about how a corporation can be held liable for the acts of its intermediaries and subsidiaries. The FCPA provides that liability for the cases of indirect bribery can be triggered if a company corruptly authorized, directed, or controlled others to bribe. It means that corporations and natural persons shall not corruptly offer, pay, promise, or authorize anything of value to "any person, while knowing that all or a portion of such money or thing of value will be offered, given, or promised, directly or indirectly, to any foreign official [...]."[11] The clause dealing with indirect bribery operates with two key concepts: "corruptly" and "knowingly."

The first concept "corruptly" is not defined by the FCPA. The US Resource Guide to the US Foreign Corrupt Practices Act (DOJ and SEC, 2012: 14) explains that "corruptly" "means an intent or desire to wrongfully influence the recipient." Liability of the briber is neither determined by achieving its purpose, nor by the fact that a foreign official actually receives, accepts or solicits the bribe (DOJ and SEC, 2012: 14). The second term "knowingly" is defined by the FCPA and relates to a conduct, a circumstance, or a result if[12]:

- i such person is aware that such person is engaging in such conduct, that such circumstance exists, or that such result is substantially certain to occur; or
- ii such person has a firm belief that such circumstance exists or that such result is substantially certain to occur.

"Knowingly" also includes the situation of "willful blindness," meaning when a person intentionally avoid the knowledge of a conduct (DOJ and SEC, 2012: 22 and 27).

11 15 U.S.C. §§78dd-1(a), 2(a), and 3(a).
12 15 U.S.C. §§78dd-1(f)(2)(A); §78dd-2(h)(3)(A); §78dd-3(f)(3)(A).

The clause dealing with indirect bribery allows the US enforcement authorities to establish the liability of corporations for acts of third entities in two main ways.[13] First, the FCPA can punish a company for indirect bribery if that company sufficiently participates in the bribing activity, for example, if the company authorizes the misconduct of the entities.[14] Second, the DOJ and the SEC provide that another way to trigger corporate liability for violations of the FCPA is based on "traditional agency principles"; mainly agency control. The DOJ and the SEC have significant discretion in interpreting agency principles. As will be seen in chapters below, they evaluate the parent's control not only on the basis of general criteria, such as their ownership but also on the bases of the specific context of a transaction (DOJ and SEC, 2012: 27).

It must be noted that the FCPA's accounting provisions are yet another way to make corporations accountable for the acts of third persons. In the context of criminal liability, a person shall not "knowingly circumvent or knowingly fail to implement a system of internal accounting controls or knowingly falsify any book, record, or account…"[15] In the context of the liability of issuers, the FCPA establishes strict civil liability, meaning that no knowledge of an issuer about a violation is required. Therefore, the accounting provisions might provide for even broader jurisdiction than the anti-bribery provisions.

4.4.1.2 German law

In many civil law jurisdictions such as Germany, indirect bribery is not regulated explicitly but based on general principles of law. The key difference with US law, that may be problematic from the perspective of collective action, is that the liability of legal persons is always to some extent derived from the liability of natural persons – corporations under German law do not have an autonomous will. In this context, §25 StGB provides that "Any person who commits the offense himself or through another shall be liable as a principal." As German law does not recognize criminal liability for legal persons, this provision of the criminal code should be read together with §30 and §130 OWiG, that establish administrative liability.

First, under §30(1) OWiG a legal person may be held liable for the criminal or administrative offenses of natural persons that are responsible for the management of the legal person.[16] The natural person responsible for the management is a person acting "as an entity authorized to represent a legal person

13 This is relevant for the parent–subsidiary relationship, the principal–agent relationship, and the successor–predecessor relationship.

14 See *United States vs. Biomet Inc, No. 12-cr-80* (26 March 2012); *Securities and Exchange Commission v. Biomet Inc, No. 1:12-cv-00454* (26 March 2012).

15 15 U.S.C. §78m (b)(5).

16 Note that Germany under §15 StGB conditions the liability of the offense of foreign bribery to intentional acts.

or as a member of such an entity," chairmen of an executive committee or an agent. These persons must commit an offense "as a result of which duties incumbent on the legal person" [...] "have been violated or the legal person" [...] "has been enriched." It must be noted that under §30(4) OWiG, German law provides a possibility to prosecute legal persons even if a proceeding against a natural person has not commenced or is discontinued.

Second, under §130 OWiG, German law covers failures of managers and other employees to sufficiently supervise the business. Thus, the legal person might be also sanctioned for the illegal actions of its subordinate employees if they resulted from the breach of a supervision duty at the managerial level.[17] The OECD Phase 3 report further elaborates on the use of §130 OWiG[18]:

> [...] the corporation is not made liable for the breach per se but for a natural person's intentional or negligent failure to carry out his/her supervisory duties – this failure having led to the breach. In this case, the criminal liability of an individual at a lower level may have triggered the administrative liability of lack of supervision, itself triggering the liability of the company.

The interpretation of these concepts, and mainly the committing of an offense through another person under §25 StGB, is a matter of case law and doctrine. Nevertheless, the OECD reports repeatedly state that the German approach, at least as black-letter law, complies with the requirements of the OECD Convention standard on indirect bribery.[19]

Yet, the German approach is principally different from the US approach. Such heterogeneity is transferred to the enforcement of foreign anti-bribery laws. The German enforcement authorities focus more than the US authorities on the prosecution of natural persons (Section 5.3.2). This fact reflects a deeper clarity problem in defining common policy objective of the OECD anti-bribery enforcement regime. Second, the German approach, arguably, limits the enforcement reach of the German authorities and results in a low corporate enforcement rate.[20]

4.4.1.3 UK law

Under UK law, the liability for acts of third persons is built on different principles than US law and German law. Generally, as stated in Sections 3(3)–(5) and 4 of the Bribery Act, a person should perform his function and activity in good

17 See summary in OECD, Germany: Follow-Up (n 7) 8.

18 OECD (2011) Phase 3 Report on Implementing the OECD Anti-Bribery Convention in Germany 24.

19 OECD, Germany: Phase 3 (n 18) 27.

20 OECD (2018) Phase 4 Report on Implementing the OECD Anti-Bribery Convention in Germany, 66–67.

faith, impartially, and should comply with the expectation of trust. Section 5 provides that these conditions of improper performance should be tested by "what a reasonable person in the United Kingdom would expect [...]."

More specifically, the liability for acts of third persons under UK law is based on the so-called identification doctrine, a doctrine that has been constantly criticized by the WGB.[21] This doctrine provides that a corporation shall be held liable for the illegal acts of third persons if these persons are "directing the mind and will" of the corporation. This concept, however, covers a narrow scope of subjects, concentrating only on members of the board of directors, a managing director, and other superior officers.[22] Therefore, the bribing by lower employees of a company is outside the scope of this concept.

In order to overcome the limitations of UK legislation, the Bribery Act introduced new offenses rather than re-interpreting existing ones. Most importantly, Sections 7–9 of the Bribery Act establish the offense of the "failure of commercial organization to prevent bribery" of the so-called associate person. In this context, Section 8(1) provides that an associated person "is a person who performs services for or on behalf of" a company. The person may be an employee, an agent or a subsidiary (Section 8(3)). Under Section 7, the company is liable for the failure to prevent bribery of such a person. It must be noted that the failure to prevent bribery is a key novelty in the UK foreign anti-bribery system with potentially broad extraterritorial application. This novelty gives UK enforcement authorities potentially strong tools to provide more enforcement as a public good.

However, the WGB is still not convinced about the suitability of this solution, because the concept of associated person might be too narrow.[23] Section 8(1) requires prosecutors to prove that an associated person performs services for or on behalf of a defendant. Such proof must be provided "disregarding any bribe under consideration."[24] In other words, the mere bribing by associated persons on behalf of the defendant is not a sufficient link. This, however, means that, for instance, a shell company "who performs no service other than to pay a bribe would not be an associated person."[25] In this context, the UK authorities argue that: "The fact that an organization benefits indirectly from a bribe is very unlikely, in itself, to amount to proof of the specific intention required by the offence" (Bribery Act Guidance: para 42).

21 OECD (2012) Phase 3 Report on Implementing the OECD Anti-Bribery Convention in the United Kingdom, 14–18.

22 The theory establishes liability of a corporation based on proving a culpable act of each one individual who acts within a company. The proof of such liability, arguably, is very challenging.

23 See generally OECD (2017) Phase 4 Report on Implementing the OECD Anti-Bribery Convention in the United Kingdom, 77.

24 This does not stand for employees who are presumed to perform services. See Section 8(5) of the Bribery Act.

25 OECD, United Kingdom: Phase 3 (n 21) 17.

4.4.2 Complicity and conspiracy

The application of complicity and conspiracy principles is the second possibility how the liability for the acts of third persons can be established. Article 1(2) of the OECD Convention provides that:

> [E]ach Party shall take any measures necessary to establish that complicity in, including incitement, aiding and abetting, or authorisation of an act of bribery of a foreign public official shall be a criminal offence. Attempt and conspiracy to bribe a foreign public official shall be criminal offences to the same extent as attempt and conspiracy to bribe a public official of that Party.

This provision indicates that the complicit conduct and the conspiracy are treated differently.[26]

Regarding complicity, the OECD Convention provides that, under said convention, those who are intentionally helping, initiating, or authorizing a crime shall be criminally liable for participating in the crime. Article 1(2) of the Convention needs to be interpreted in line with Commentary 11 providing that if the offenses under Article 1(2) do not lead to further action, and the complicity is not itself punishable under domestic law, "then the Party would not be required to make it punishable with respect to bribery of a foreign public official." In all of the analyzed national legal systems, complicit conduct is dependent on the commitment of the main offense.[27] Therefore, the usage of complicity is limited in foreign anti-bribery law, and complicit conduct such as aiding and abetting depends on the commitment of the main offense.

Regarding conspiracy, a concept focusing on an agreement of several parties to bribe, the OECD Convention has a modest aim of placing the conspiracy to commit domestic bribery at the same level as the conspiracy to commit foreign bribery. As the OECD Convention does not provide any further guidance regarding conspiracy, it is up to the signatories to decide upon how they regulate this area. In some countries, such as the US, conspiracy is an

26 The same standard stands for an attempt, however, the offense of foreign bribery is a conduct crime, completed once an act, not necessarily an effect of the act, takes place. Thus, this is hard to find an example of attempted bribery.

27 See 18 U.S.C. §2; §§26 and 27 StGB, see the analysis in OECD (1999) Germany: Review of Implementation of the Convention and 1997 Recommendation, 4. Regarding the UK: "The U.K. authorities state that, under the common law, it is an offence to aid, abet, counsel or procure an offence, including any offences under the Bribery Act. The Accessories and Abettors Act 1861 further provides that any person who does so can be proceeded against as if he/she were the principal offender." OECD (2010) United Kingdom Phase 1 Ter: Report on the Application of the Convention on Combating Bribery of Foreign Public Officials in International Business Transactions and the 2009 Revisited Recommendation on Combating Bribery in International Business Transactions, 7.

independent offense, and in other countries such as Germany and the UK, conspiracy is not an independent offense which implies the heterogeneity of approached. The following section shortly introduces differences in how the selected jurisdictions deal with the concept of conspiracy because the application of conspiracy charges is very important for the provision of enforcement and collective action (Section 6.6).

4.4.2.1 US law

In the US, the federal conspiracy law provides that:

> [I]f two or more persons conspire either to commit any offense against the United States, or to defraud the United States, or any agency thereof in any manner or for any purpose, and one or more of such persons do any act to effect the object of the conspiracy, each shall be fined under this title or imprisoned not more than five years, or both. [...][28]

The essential elements of conspiracy under US law are (1) an agreement to commit an offense; (2) between at least two persons that knowingly participate in the conspiracy; and (3) an overt act in furtherance of conspiracy that is not necessarily the crime or its element (Doyle, 2016: 2).

It will become apparent during the analyses of anti-bribery foreign anti-bribery enforcement actions in Chapter 6 that conspiracy charges allow the US enforcement authorities to extend their jurisdiction to a wide net of persons involved in foreign bribery schemes (Section 6.6.2). One reason for this is that the US Supreme Court interprets the jurisdiction of conspiracy offenses widely. This is also reflected in the Resource Guide (DOJ and SEC, 2012: 34) that provides that:

> [A] foreign company or individual may be held liable for aiding and abetting an FCPA violation or for conspiring to violate the FCPA, even if the foreign company or individual did not take any act in furtherance of the corrupt payment while in the territory of the United States. In conspiracy cases, the United States generally has jurisdiction over all the conspirators where at least one conspirator is an issuer, domestic concern, or commits a reasonably foreseeable overt act within the United States.[29]

Moreover, the use of complicity and conspiracy charges has yet another important dimension: it can stretch the statute of limitations.[30] In the US, the

28 18 U.S.C. §371 (Conspiracy to commit offense to defraud United States).

29 The Resource Guide refers to *United States vs. Winter, 509 F.2d 975, 982 (5th Cir. 1975)* and *United States vs. MacAllister, 160 F.3d 1304, 1307 (11th Cir. 1998).*

30 The OECD Convention provides in Article 6 that there should be "an adequate period of time for the investigation and prosecution...."

enforcement authorities must start a proceeding within a certain time after the offense has been committed. Such period is generally five years, but can, under certain circumstances, be prolonged by another three years.[31] In this context, the statute of limitations operates differently in relation to conspiracy charges. Specifically, the limitation period starts running with the last act that was undertaken in furtherance of the conspiracy (see, generally, Doyle, 2016: 10 and 17). For example, if two persons conspire to violate the FCPA, one bribe a foreign public official in order to obtain a public procurement contract in 2013, and the other bribe the same official in order to retain the same public procurement contract in 2015, the statute of limitations period would be counted since 2015 for both persons (Section 6.6.2).

4.4.2.2 German law and UK law

Under German law and UK law, conspiracy charges are less relevant for establishing corporate liability for the acts of third persons than under US law. In the UK, "the agreement" to commit an offense is the essential condition to be met for something to be considered conspiracy, as also provided for under the Criminal Law Act 1977.[32] Under Section 1(1) of the Act, the agreement shall be carried out in accordance with the intentions of the conspiring parties, which is an extra condition compared to the US approach. Hence, it is more difficult to convict a person, because enforcement authorities have to prove the knowledge and intent of persons regarding their entering into the agreement, the purpose of the agreement, and the relevant circumstances that should lead to the fulfillment of the purpose of the agreement (Ferguson, 2015: Chapter 3, 42–43).

The civil law approach to conspiracy is significantly different from common law systems. In Germany, "conspiracy is a mode of attempted participation that merges into the crime once it is attempted or committed" (Okoth, 2014: 74–75). However, such conspiracy only applies to very serious crimes that are punishable by a minimum sentence of one year's imprisonment. Therefore, since the offense of bribery is not considered a very serious crime, the conspiracy provisions do not apply to it.[33] Rather, in Germany, §129 StGB establishes an independent crime of "forming a criminal organization," an independent crime that penalizes acts that contribute to the existence and rise of the criminal organization, for instance, by recruiting new members.[34]

31 18 U.S.C. §§ 3282, 3290 and 3292. See also OECD (2010) Phase 3 Report on Implementing the OECD Anti-Bribery Convention in the United States, 16.

32 Criminal Law Act 1977 Chapter 45. In Scotland conspiracy is the matter of common law, see OECD, United Kingdom Phase 1 Ter (n 27) 8.

33 §30 (2) and §12(1) StGB. See also OECD, Germany: Review (27) 5.

34 For more about the use of alternative charges in Germany and the regulation of organized crime, see Section 6.3.3.

4.4.3 Concluding remarks

While the OECD Convention provides a strong basis for mitigating collective action problems related to the lack of enforcement, it also allows for significant heterogeneity of measures. First, US law provides a wide array of possibilities how to sanction indirect bribery. The main are the provisions related to the liability of corporations for the actions of other persons – being it the liability determined by a parent–subsidiary, a principal–agent, and a successor–predecessor relationship – and the liability based on conspiracy charges. Second, German law is more limited because the liability of legal person is under German law derived from the liability of natural persons. Furthermore, persons cannot be charged for conspiracy to bribe, because bribery is not considered a "very serious offense." Last, the UK law thanks to the Bribery Act has significantly extended opportunities to prosecute indirect bribery. Yet, the application of conspiracy charges on foreign bribery cases is under UK law limited.

The examination of the implementation of the OECD Convention into German law and UK law raises some concerns whether these jurisdictions can provide enforcement as a public good sufficiently, and whether they will be able to cooperate and coordinate their actions with the US and other enforcement authorities. Chapters 5 and 6 will test how the concepts related to the problem of indirect bribery are interpreted and applied in practice and whether the US enforcement can mitigate the potential lack of enforcement in other countries. These chapters will also explain the scope of clarity problems caused by the heterogeneity.

4.5 The bribed party: "foreign public official"

At the heart of the OECD Convention stands the notion of foreign public official. The notion has raised a lot of discussion, mainly among businesses, because it is constructed broadly, and might cause ambiguities (Koehler, 2010).[35] Most importantly, the legal division between "private" and "public" is understood differently in various cultures. Hence, the interpretation of notions such as the status of a public body or the manifestation of the dominant influence of a state, both of which are relevant for determining whether an official is a public official, might vary. In this context, it would be problematic and probably ineffective to accept a definition based on the legal system of the country of the bribed party. Therefore, the OECD Convention establishes its own standard by an autonomous definition that is further specified by official Commentaries.[36]

35 Koehler (2010: 964–971) argues that the concept of foreign public officials is in an urgent need of judicial scrutiny.

36 See Paragraphs 12–18 of the Commentaries. OECD (2011) Convention on Combating Bribery of Foreign Public Officials in International Business Transactions and Related Documents (2011) <http://www.oecd.org/daf/anti-bribery/ConvCombatBribery_ENG.pdf> accessed 25 February 2019.

The OECD Convention defines a foreign public official as:[37]

a Any person holding a legislative, administrative, or judicial office of a foreign country; and any official or agent of a public international organization.
b Any person exercising a public function for a foreign country, including for a public agency or public enterprise; or for an international organization.

The first part of the definition reflects a formal (institutional) perspective that is derived from a well-known separation of powers model. Under this model, the state power is divided into three branches: a legislative, an executive, and a judiciary. From this perspective, a foreign public official is a person who, whether appointed or elected, is a member of a governmental institution of a foreign country.[38] The OECD Convention further specifies the notion of foreign country that includes all levels and subdivisions of government, from national to local.[39] This is not limited to a traditional definition of the state, but also covers any organized foreign area or entity such as an autonomous territory or a separate customs territory.[40] Furthermore, the institutional definition covers any official or agent of a public international organization that, according to official Commentary 17, includes any international organization formed by states, governments, or other public international organizations, whatever the form of organization and scope of competence (see Pieth, Low and Cullen, 2007: 77–79).

The second part of the definition reflects the functional principle of the OECD Convention, that is, under Article 1(4)(a), operationalized by the term "public function." It means that a foreign public official does not have to formally belong to one of the three governmental branches, because the critical issue is the nature of a given activity. Hence, the term covers persons who perform any activity in the public interest delegated to them by a foreign country.[41] This is, for instance, the performance of a task delegated by a foreign country in connection with public procurement.[42]

37 Article 1(4)a) provides that foreign public official means "any person holding a legislative, administrative or judicial office of a foreign country, whether appointed or elected; any person exercising a public function for a foreign country, including for a public agency or public enterprise; and any official or agent of a public international."
38 Article 1(4)a) of the OECD Convention.
39 Article 1(4)b) of the OECD Convention.
40 Paragraph 18 of the Commentaries. OECD Convention and Related Documents (n 36).
41 Paragraph 13 of the Commentaries. OECD Convention and Related Documents (n 36).
42 Paragraph 12 of the Commentaries. OECD Convention and Related Documents (n 36). A foreign public official is any person who assists in a tendering procedure. It might be, for instance, ITs, architects, financial and other experts who provide comments on tenders.

The functional part of the definition is further clarified by the Commentaries that define elements of public function. The public function can be carried out by a public agency, a public enterprise and, in special circumstances, can also be informally carried out by the de facto performance of an influential person who does not have legal authorization to officially carry out public functions. These notions are defined by the OECD Convention as follows:

a A public agency is an entity that is constituted under public law in order to fulfill specific tasks in the public interest.[43]
b A public enterprise is any enterprise regardless of its legal form, over which a government, or governments, directly or indirectly, exercise a dominant influence.[44] The key point here is the term "dominant influence." This notion is defined by the Commentaries via a demonstrative enumeration. The dominant influence might be constituted, for instance, when the government holds a majority of shares in the enterprise or can appoint a majority of the members of the enterprise's administrative body, managerial body, or superior board.[45] Officials of these enterprises are by principle considered to perform a public function. This is however not the case when the enterprise operates in the relevant market based on a normal competition, meaning free of any subsidies or other privileges.[46]
c The term foreign public official also includes a special category of persons who exercise a public authority without any legal title. This, however, happens just in special circumstances, and if it is recognized by national legal principles of the Parties.[47]

It is important to note that acts of foreign public officials are only relevant when such an official "act[s] or refrain[s] from acting in relation to the performance of official duties." It "includes any use of the public official's position, whether or not within the official's authorized competence."[48] For example, an act of a government official who informally influences another official to "award a contract to that company" shall be considered as the use of that first official's position.[49]

While differences in implementation may exist, the OECD Convention and its official Commentaries provide a concrete definition of the term foreign public official. By this reason, the OECD monitoring mechanism can correct undesirable differences between countries. Nevertheless, the sensitivity of the

43 Paragraph 13 of the Commentaries. OECD Convention and Related Documents (n 36).
44 Paragraph 14 of the Commentaries. OECD Convention and Related Documents (n 36).
45 Paragraph 14 of the Commentaries. OECD Convention and Related Documents (n 36).
46 Paragraph 15 of the Commentaries. OECD Convention and Related Documents (n 36).
47 Paragraph 16 of the Commentaries. OECD Convention and Related Documents (n 36).
48 Article 1(4)c) of the OECD Convention.
49 Paragraph 19 of the Commentaries. OECD Convention and Related Documents (n 36).

issue for businesses, cultural differences in understanding the differences between "public" and "private" function, and existing differences in national approaches, justify a closer analysis of national approaches. What will now be discussed, is how on the one hand, US law and UK law follow the approach of the OECD Convention by adopting the two-sided (formal–functional) definition of the foreign public official. Whilst, on the other hand, the German approach has a more autonomous structure because it is derived from the national definition of a domestic official.

4.5.1 US law

The FCPA provides a very broad definition of foreign public official. It covers any officer or employee of a foreign government or any department, agency, or instrumentality thereof, or of a public international organization. From a functional perspective, it also applies to "any person acting in an official capacity." It means "for or on behalf of any such government or department, agency, or instrumentality [...] or public international organization."[50] The FCPA explicitly provides that the definition of a foreign public official also concerns "any foreign political party or official thereof, or to any candidate for foreign political office [...]"[51]

Despite the fact that the FCPA provides a broad definition of a foreign public official, it does not cover private, commercial bribery. It will be discussed below that these limitations are overcome by an expansive interpretation of the term (Section 6.3.1 – other alternative statutes). For example, procurement managers of Chinese state-owned entities[52] or doctors in public hospitals were considered to be foreign public officials under the FCPA.[53] Furthermore, what will also be discussed is how the US authorities use other acts, separately or together with the FCPA, in order to cover corporations, and their employees, that bribed quasi-public officials.[54]

4.5.2 UK law

Currently, the most expansive legal approach regarding the definition of a foreign public official is represented in the UK Bribery Act that, not only criminalizes bribery of public officials but also private, commercial bribery.[55] This stands in sharp contrast to the old UK legislation that, prior to the

50 15 U.S.C. §§78dd-1(f)(1), 78dd-2(h)(2), 78dd-3(f)(2).

51 15 U.S.C. §§78dd-1(a)(3), 78dd-2(a)(3), 78dd-3(a)(3).

52 See, for example, *United States vs. Control Components, No. 09-cr-162* (22 July 2009).

53 See, for example, *United States vs. Johnson & Johnson (Depuy), No. 11-cr-99* (8 April 2011).

54 In the light of alternative statutes and alternative charges that can be applied to foreign bribery, division between public and private officials has become less relevant (Section 6.3.1).

55 See Section 3(2)(b) of the Bribery Act. See also Bribery Act Guidance para 18.

adoption of the Bribery Act, was subject to harsh critique.[56] At present, new UK laws use very similar wording to the OECD Convention. Section 6(5) of the Bribery Act provides that a foreign public official is an individual who "holds a legislative, administrative or judicial position of any kind, whether appointed or elected, of a country or territory outside the United Kingdom (or any subdivision of such a country or territory)." The institutional definition exists parallel to the functional and includes a person who exercises a public function for, or on behalf of, a foreign government, any public agency or public enterprise. The foreign public official is, under the Bribery Act, also an official or agent of a public international organization.[57] Sections 1–5 (the general offenses) of the Bribery Act are broader because they cover bribery that is not limited to a public official.

4.5.3 German law

The German definition of a foreign public official is different from the approach of the OECD Convention. The definition and related terms are based on §§334–338 of the StGB, that regulate these issues in the domestic context.[58] §335a StGB transfers these provisions also to foreign public officials, including judges and other public official of a foreign state; judges at international courts, public official and other member of the staff of international organizations, European public officials, and foreign soldiers.[59] German law also provides specific provisions dealing with members of a legislative body of a foreign state and parliamentary assembly of an international organization.[60]

Furthermore, §335a also contains a functional definition of a foreign public official. This definition widens the scope of the notion to a person entrusted to exercise a public function for a foreign State. German law does not explicitly mention that a foreign public official is also an official entrusted to exercise a public function for a public enterprise.[61] Because of this, doubts arose as to whether the definition of the term "public function" fully implemented Article 1 of the OECD Convention. These doubts also relate to some earlier foreign bribery investigations in which the notion of the foreign public official was interpreted too narrowly to establish criminal liability.[62] Moreover, the offense of foreign bribery has often been prosecuted through

56 See generally OECD (1999) United Kingdom: Review of Implementation of the Convention and 1997 Recommendation' (1999).
57 Section 6(6) of the Bribery Act.
58 § 11(1) ad 2 and following of the StGB.
59 §2(1) of the IntBestG.
60 The reason is that Members of Parliament were not considered as public officials before the enactment of IntBestG. OECD, Germany: Review (27) 3.
61 Note that this was the case before the introduction of §335a in 2015, see §2(1) of the IntBestG.
62 See the judgment of The Federal Supreme Court (Bundesgerichtshof), Judgement of 29 August 2008 (2 StR 587/07).

other provisions of German law.[63] Nevertheless, in the light of the case law of the German enforcement authorities, the WGB considers the German definition as compliant with Article 1 of the OECD Convention.[64]

4.5.4 Concluding remarks

The OECD Convention and its official Commentaries provide a concrete definition of the notion of the foreign public official. By this reason, the OECD monitoring mechanism can correct undesirable differences between countries, and should not constitute undesirable heterogeneity in implementation. The functional principle, in most of the cases, makes the term foreign public official broad because it includes not only officials that formally belong to one of the three governmental branches, but also those who perform a public function. The broad definition is well implemented in the US and the UK, both going beyond the standard of the OECD Convention. Germany has a different approach because the definition of foreign public official is derived from the national definition of a domestic official. Yet, this approach is functionally equivalent and should not have any significant negative effect from the perspective of collective action.

4.6 The bribe: "any undue advantage"

After researching legal aspects related to the main actors that engage in foreign bribery, it is necessary to analyze the object of their interaction – the bribe. The following analysis will include two problems. The first problem is how the OECD Convention defines the bribe. The second, is when a bribe is undue, which also includes the question of statutory exceptions and defenses. As will be seen, while these exceptions and defenses could potentially lead to negative heterogeneity between the OECD Convention signatories, they apply only to very specific situations and are not likely to undermine collective action.

4.6.1 The bribe

The OECD Convention defines the bribe broadly as "any undue pecuniary or other advantage."[65] The scope of the offense covers bribes that are offered, promised, or given to a foreign public official or to a third party. State should not be considered as a third-party beneficiary (Pieth et al., 2007: 98). The form of the bribe might be material or immaterial. It may include a bank transfer or a cash payment, but also any other identifiable monetary

63 For example, through §266(1) of StGB dealing with breach of trust. Note that German law also prohibits active and passive private commercial bribery under §299.

64 OECD, Germany: Follow-Up (n 7) 6 and 30. OECD, Germany: Phase 4 (n 20) 29–30.

65 Article 1(1) of the OECD Convection.

contribution, such as the establishment of new business contacts, access to a golf club, or awarding a degree *honoris causa* (see other examples in DOJ and SEC 2012: 14–17).

The legal standard of "the bribe" is concrete and conceptually similar to the notion of the briber. The FCPA uses a broad definition that prohibits "payment of any money [...]" or "[...] anything of value."[66] Similarly, the Bribery Act also uses the wording "any financial or other advantage."[67] Germany uses the term "benefit" (*Vorteil*) that, as indicated by a judicial interpretation, covers all material and immaterial benefits.[68]

A more complicated issue is what distinguishes undue (criminal) advantage and due advantage. This is discussed in the following section.

4.6.2 Undue advantage

Reasonable payments and other contributions to public officials may be legitimate and lawful. Before buying certain products and services, for example, a public buyer may want to examine them or discuss them with sellers. If guests, public officials, are invited to visit the premises of a business, it might be expected to show some level of hospitability. Another example of a reasonable payment is a registration fee and a notary fee mandated by written regulations. This section discusses local law exceptions and other statutory defenses that clarify a line between legitimate and undue expenses.

4.6.2.1 Local law exception

The OECD Convention provides some guidance regarding what "due advantage" is. Commentary 8 provides that the advantage is due if it "was permitted or required by the written law or regulation of the foreign public official's country, including case law." This means that payments allowed by the written law are due, but payments that are merely a common practice arising from a local custom or payments that are tolerated by public authorities shall not be exempted. It must be also noted that the value of the advantage is irrelevant.[69]

Both the FCPA and the Bribery Act provide for a statutory defense when an advantage provided to a foreign public official is permitted under the written law of the official's country. The FCPA provides that the defense might be raised if a bribe "was lawful under the written laws and regulations of the foreign official's [...] country."[70] The burden of proof is on the person raising the defense. Similarly, the Bribery Act provides that a person can be

66 15 U.S.C. §78dd-1(a).
67 Section 6(3)(a) of the Bribery Act.
68 OECD, Germany: Review (27) 2.
69 Paragraph 7 of the Commentaries. OECD Convention and Related Documents (n 36).
70 15 U.S.C. §§78dd-1(c)(1), §§78dd-2(c)(1), 78dd-3(c)(1).

considered to be bribing only if a foreign public official is neither permitted nor required by the written law applicable to the official, to be influenced in the official's capacity by bribery.[71] *A contrario* a person cannot be considered a briber if such an official is, by written law, permitted or required to be influenced by the bribe. The Bribery Act focuses on the legality of the influence and not on the advantage provided to the official.[72]

German law does not recognize any formal local law exception because a lawful performance by a foreign public official cannot, in any case, constitute an offense of bribery (Pieth et al., 2014: 136). It is also unlawful to bribe in order to influence a foreign public official's discretion.[73] In addition, German law does not recognize any *de minimis* rules or other special defenses.[74]

4.6.2.2 Other statutory defenses

Apart from the local law exception that is directly addressed by the Commentaries, the FCPA and the Bribery Act include three specific defenses. First, the FCPA recognizes the so-called reasonable and bona fide expenditures defense. This affirmative defense covers, for instance, expenses directly related to the promotion of a companies' products or travel expenses associated with training.[75] The DOJ and SEC (2012: 24) provide many examples of these expenditures and clarify conditions under which these expenditures are considered lawful.

The Bribery Act does not recognize a similar defense. However, the UK authorities claim that hospitality, promotion, and other business expenditures will not be prosecuted if they are reasonable and proportionate to the nature of the given business activities (Bribery Act Guidance: paras 26–32). Second, the Bribery Act, in contrast to the FCPA, also recognizes an exception for national security activities.[76] Third, the Bribery Act also provides the so-called adequate procedures defense, related to internal corporate compliance mechanisms.[77]

4.6.2.3 Small facilitation payments

The issue of small facilitation payments is not explicitly mentioned in the OECD Convention, but the Commentaries and the 2009 Recommendation

71 Section 6(3)(b) of the Bribery Act.

72 This approach could lead to a narrow application of UK foreign anti-bribery law. OECD, United Kingdom: Phase 3 (n 21) 14.

73 OECD, Germany: Phase 4 (n 20) 28.

74 See OECD, Germany: Review (27) 2.

75 15 U.S.C. §78dd-1(c), 15 U.S.C. §§78dd-2(c)(2), 78dd-3(c)(2).

76 Section 13 of the Bribery Act. See the analysis in Fine (2011: 20). A defense is, for example, if a conduct that may be charged with bribery offense was necessary for the proper exercise of an intelligence service.

77 Section 7(2) of the Bribery Act. See the analysis in Fine (2011: 21).

provide some guidance. The Commentaries recognize the negative effects of small facilitation payments. At the same time, the Commentaries provide that their criminalization is impractical and ineffective. The facilitation payments should, rather, be fought by programs of good governance.[78] In addition, the 2009 Recommendation specifies that signatories should: (a) periodically review their policies and approach on small facilitation payments; (b) encourage companies to face this phenomenon via adequate internal company controls, ethics, and compliance programs; and (c) ensure that these payments are accounted for in the books and records of companies.[79]

The treatment of small facilitation payments differs in jurisdictions this book is concerned with. The FCPA provides an exception, stating that provisions of the FCPA do not apply to "any facilitating or expediting payment" aiming to facilitate "a routine governmental action."[80] On the other hand, the Bribery Act provides "zero-tolerance" (Bribery Act Guidance: paras 44–47). The UK enforcement authorities, however, can use prosecutorial discretion and possibly not prosecute facilitation payments (Bribery Act Guidance: paras 49–51). German law also does not recognize any exception for small facilitation payments. Such exception was considered to exist de facto, because the German approach limits the offense of bribery "to official acts in violation of official duties [...] to the exclusion of lawful acts."[81] This issue has been clarified during Phase 4 monitoring, payments to public officials that aim to influence their discretion are unlawful.[82]

4.6.3 Concluding remarks

The OECD Convention and its official Commentaries provide a concrete definition of the notion of bribe: "any undue pecuniary or other advantage."[83] This definition does not constitute any concerns regarding collective action, because the OECD monitoring mechanism can correct undesirable differences between countries. Regarding the core of the definition, "pecuniary or other advantage," US law, UK law, and German law subsume all material and immaterial benefits provided to foreign public officials under the notion of bribery. Furthermore, the OECD Commentaries specify that an advantage is "due" only if it is permitted or required by the written law of the official's country. In this context, all analyzed jurisdictions follow this

78 Paragraph 9 of the Commentaries. OECD Convention and Related Documents (n 36).

79 Section VI of the 2009 Recommendation. OECD Convention and Related Documents (n 36). According to Section VII of the 2009 Recommendation, Member states are recommended to raise awareness of their public officials on their domestic bribery and solicitation laws with a view to stop the solicitation and acceptance of small facilitation payments.

80 15 U.S.C. §78dd-1(b), 15 U.S.C. §§78dd-2(b), 78dd-3(b).

81 OECD, Germany: Phase 3 (n 18) 21.

82 OECD, Germany: Phase 4 (n 20) 28 and 32.

83 Article 1(1) of the OECD Convection.

requirement. Hence, the notion of bribe should not constitute a heterogeneity in implementation that would limit the enforcement reach of national enforcement authorities and that would cause clarity problems.

Some problems may be related to the fact that both US and UK law provide several statutory exceptions. Furthermore, national legal systems differ in regulating small facilitation payments because the US allows the payments facilitating routine governmental actions but the UK and Germany do not allow facilitation payments. While these exceptions might limit enforcement, they apply only to very specific situations and target low-scale contributions to foreign public officials.

After the analysis of the most important elements of the offense of bribery of foreign public officials, i.e. the briber, indirect bribery, the bribed party, and the bribe, the analysis will focus the issue of jurisdiction.

4.7 Jurisdiction

Global bribery schemes can hardly be eliminated by legislation that is strictly limited by state borders, because MNCs could then be hiding in secure jurisdictions or be shielded from liability by their intermediaries (Sections 4.4.1 and 6.4). That is the reason why effective jurisdictional provisions are the key issue for the provision of enforcement as a public good and for establishing collective action. A wide interpretation of jurisdiction might capture many MNCs who operate and/or are established outside the territories of OECD Convention signatory states. A narrow interpretation, on the other hand, would block both the investigation and sanctioning of some MNCs. The approach advocated by the OECD Convention is that national enforcement authorities should be equipped with a wide jurisdictional ambit.

Theories of international law include three main categories of jurisdiction: to prescribe, to adjudicate, and to enforce (see, generally, Ireland-Piper, 2013: 69–72; Zerk, 2010). These established concepts developed by classical, territoriality-based, approaches, are challenged by new forms of transnational law-making, including foreign anti-bribery law (see, generally, Berman, 2005, 2007; Ryngaert, 2008). The analysis in this section focuses on what Paul Berman calls "legal jurisdiction," i.e. a set of provisions determining (1) that national laws apply and (2) that a given state can decide a case (Berman, 2005: 530–534). In this context, the OECD Convention is based on two jurisdictional principles: territoriality and nationality. The analysis below discusses the two principles in more detail and discusses how jurisdictional conditions that the OECD Convention prescribes are implemented in the selected national legal systems.

4.7.1 Territorial jurisdiction

The principle of territoriality is the leading standard of the OECD Convention. The OECD Convention requires its signatories to interpret territorial basis for jurisdiction broadly. Article 4(1) provides that "each Party shall [...] establish its jurisdiction [...] when the offence is committed in whole or in part in its territory." The word "committed" under Article 4(1) might be interpreted in a way that an act (1) itself (subjective territoriality) or (2) its effects (objective territoriality) occurred within the territory of a given state. The latter, objective territoriality, known as the effects doctrine, might be especially asserted over a wide range of foreign activities. Moreover, Paragraph 25 of the Commentaries provides that "the territorial basis for jurisdiction should be interpreted broadly so that an extensive physical connection to the bribery act is not required."[84]

The OECD Convention, however, does not provide any clear limitation. National enforcement authorities can use broad jurisdictional claims based on acts or effects of acts that have just a minimal link to a territory of a given country (Zerk, 2010: 18–19). That such standard may be implemented in a way that any means of transnational commerce such as the use of emails, telephone, or banking system shall be sufficient for the establishment of territorial jurisdiction, are discussed in Chapters 5 and 6.

4.7.2 The principle of nationality

An alternative to the principle of territoriality is the principle of nationality that requires an assertion of jurisdiction against a state's own nationals who committed a crime abroad (active nationality). Article 4(2) of the OECD Convention provides that:

> [E]ach Party which has jurisdiction to prosecute its nationals for offences committed abroad shall take such measures as may be necessary to establish its jurisdiction to do so in respect of the bribery of a foreign public official, according to the same principles.

This means that, for instance, if a signatory state does not apply the principle of nationality to other offenses, it is not required to do so in the context of foreign bribery either. This requirement has become obsolete because all OECD countries have recognized the nationality principle over at least some "foreign offenses." Therefore, the principle of nationality is de facto mandatory for all signatory countries (Pieth et al., 2017: 11–12 and 281).

The second part of Article 4(2): "[...] establish jurisdiction [...] according the same principles" reflects the fact that historically, the nationality principle was viewed as a narrow concept (Inazumi, 2005: 24).[85] It was limited by additional requirements such as dual criminality, a complaint by the victim,

84 Paragraph 25 of the Commentaries. OECD Convention and Related Documents (n 36).

85 Harvard Research in International Law, 'Draft Convention on Jurisdiction with Respect to Crime' (1935), 519 in Inazumi (2005: 24).

or the availability of the suspect (Pieth et al., 2017: 283–285). In this context, Commentary 26 gives a sign that such limitations shall not go too far. It provides that, if national laws would limit the imposition of the nationality principle by the requirement of dual criminality, such a requirement "should be deemed to be met, if the act is unlawful where it occurred, even if under a different criminal statute [...]." For instance, it shall be sufficient for the application of the nationality principle if the country of a foreign public official would criminalize only domestic bribery (Pieth et al., 2017: 11–12 and 283–284).

The right to assert jurisdiction on the basis of nationality is undisputed (see Cryer, 2007: 47–49). Nevertheless, the globalization of economy makes the use of this principle broader – with uncertain limits. Most importantly, there is no single test in place to determine the nationality of MNCs. Thus, the signatories may take into account the place of incorporation, the corporation's seat, the place where the most business is done, or the "nationality" of the corporation's controlling entity. This gives the OECD Convention signatories the discretion either to claim jurisdiction against a wide range of MNCs or to stay silent. The following section discusses the implementation of the OECD Convention's standard in the selected jurisdictions.

4.7.3 National approaches

4.7.3.1 US law

The FCPA recognizes both territorial jurisdiction and the principle of nationality. Generally, the FCPA asserts territorial jurisdiction over both nationals and foreigners who act within the territory of the US. The FCPA also contains "the alternative jurisdiction" based on the principle of nationality.[86]

The US authorities claim that territorial jurisdiction will be interpreted and applied broadly to three main categories of actors: issuers, domestic concerns, and any other persons and entities bribing or furthering a bribery scheme while in the territory of the US.[87] The following text introduces the key characteristics of the three categories.

1 An "issuer" is a company that has a class of securities registered under Section 12 of the Securities & Exchange Act.[88] Thus, foreign companies organized outside the US can also qualify as issuers. Furthermore, US territorial jurisdiction can also be extended to associated persons, meaning "any officer, director, employee, or agent of such issuer or any stockholder thereof acting on behalf of such issuer."[89]

86 15 U.S.C. §§78dd-1(g), §§78dd-2(i).
87 15 U.S.C. §78dd-1(a), 15 U.S.C. §§78dd-2(a), 78dd-3(a).
88 15 U.S.C. §78dd-1.
89 15 U.S.C. §78dd-1(a).

2 A "domestic concern" is any citizen, national or resident of the US and any corporation or other legal entity which has its principal place of business in the US or which is organized under US law.[90] Similarly as with the issuers, the associated persons are also under the territorial jurisdiction of the US.[91]
3 "Any persons other than an issuer or a domestic concern" is any person other than a national who engages in any acts in the territory of the US. The term "any person" includes both physical persons and business entities.

The underlying rule connected with the assertion of territorial jurisdiction is that companies should have relevant territorial nexus with the US. Some confusion may arise because the FCPA does not formally treat all categories in the same way.[92] The territorial jurisdiction for issuers and domestic concerns is triggered if there is interstate commerce nexus, meaning if they "make use of the mails or any means or instrumentality of interstate commerce corruptly [...]."[93] The FCPA provides that the term interstate commerce means:

> [...] trade, commerce, transportation, or communication among the several States, or between any foreign country and any State or between any State and any place or ship outside thereof, and such **term includes the intrastate** [emphasis added] use of – (A) a telephone or other interstate means of communication, or (B) any other interstate instrumentality.[94]

In case that an issuer or domestic concern does not meet this requirement, territorial jurisdiction cannot be established.

In order to fill potential jurisdictional gaps, an amendment of the FCPA in 1998 established an alternative jurisdiction based on the nationality principle. The amendment provides, in essence, that the interstate commerce requirement is not applicable when US issuers and domestic concerns act corruptly outside the US.[95] Therefore, if these bribers are not captured by territorial jurisdiction, they shall be prosecuted based on the alternative jurisdiction.

Foreign issuers and other foreign entities cannot be subjected to the alternative jurisdiction because they are not US persons. This means that enforcement authorities must find nexus with the US territory if they want to prosecute foreign entities. As discussed above, the nexus for foreign issuers is the interstate (intrastate) commerce criterion. Foreign entities under §78dd-3

90 15 U.S.C. §78dd-2(h).
91 15 U.S.C. §78d-2(a).
92 For the analysis of the reason, see the discussion in OECD, 'United States: Review of Implementation of the Convention and 1997 Recommendation' (1999) 14.
93 15 U.S.C. §78dd-1(a) and §78dd-2(a).
94 15 U.S.C. §78dd-2(h)(5); §78dd-3f)(5).
95 15 U.S.C. §§78dd-1(g); §§78dd-2(i).

Entity	Territorial Jurisdiction	The Principle of Nationality
Domestic Concerns US Issuers	Interstate commerce nexus	If there is no interstate commerce nexus, then **alternative jurisdiction (the nationality principle)**
Foreign Issuers	Interstate commerce nexus	If there is no interstate commerce nexus, then **no jurisdiction**
Any Foreign Person	Any act in furtherance of bribery while in the territory of the US	If there is no territorial nexus, then **no jurisdiction**

Figure 4.1 Jurisdiction under the anti-bribery provisions of the FCPA.

can be prosecuted if they commit relevant acts "while in the territory of the US." For the sake of clarity, the relevant subjects and conditions under which they can be prosecuted by the US enforcement authorities are illustrated in Figure 4.1.

4.7.3.2 UK law

The Bribery Act, like the FCPA, recognizes the nationality and territoriality principles. Generally, the Bribery Act asserts territorial jurisdiction over any act under Sections 1, 2, and 6, if such act takes place in England, Wales, Scotland, or Northern Ireland and forms any part of the offense there.[96] In case no such act takes place in the UK, the UK authorities can rely on the nationality principle under two conditions:

a the act would form part of a bribery offense if done or made in the UK;
b the briber has a close connection with the UK,[97] i.e. a person is a British citizen or one of the eight other categories of persons as provided in Section 12(4).[98]

96 Section 12(1) of the Bribery Act. For the establishment of territorial jurisdiction, such an act does not have to be an essential part of the underlying conduct. See OECD, United Kingdom Phase 1 Ter (n 27) 16.
97 Section 12(2) and (3) of the Bribery Act.
98 These are British overseas (1) territories citizens, (2) nationals, and (3) citizens; (4) a person who under the British Nationality Act 1981 was a British subject, (5) a British protected person within the meaning of that Act, (6) individuals ordinarily resident in UK, (7) a body incorporated under the law of any part of the UK, and (8) a Scottish partnership.

Section 7 of the Bribery Act that creates an offense for the failure of commercial organizations to prevent bribery, provides for wider jurisdictional provisions than Sections 1, 2, and 6. Under Section 7, the UK authorities may use two bases for jurisdiction: (a) nationality and (b) territoriality if a company carries on a business in the UK. It must be noted that jurisdiction should be asserted no matter "whether the acts or omissions which form part of the offence take place in the United Kingdom or elsewhere."[99] Section 7 applies to any domestic or foreign company that, whilst carrying out business in the territory of the UK, fails to prevent bribery by its associated persons. It means that a foreign company can be investigated and punished under Section 7 for the bribes of its business partners. The Bribery Act is applicable even if such business partners bribe outside the territory of the UK and have no direct effect in UK territory.[100]

Hence, the jurisdictional reach of the Bribery Act is, in theory, broader than the one under the FCPA. The main problem with the UK approach is that the Bribery Act does not apply to some illegal activities that take part in the Crown Dependencies or Overseas Territories. This is constantly criticized by the WGB that claims that the UK considers some of these places offshore financial centers. Typically, these offshore centers are often used for various types of economic crimes such as tax evasion, money laundering, and foreign bribery.[101] According to the WGB, corporations that do not carry out business in the territory of the UK, but only in its Crown Dependencies or Overseas Territories, might be subjected to lower anti-bribery standards. For example, such corporations are not subjected and cannot be held liable when they fail to prevent bribery by their associated persons.[102] For many years, the UK is being recommended to extend the jurisdiction of the Bribery Act to legal persons incorporated in its Crown Dependencies or Overseas Territories.[103]

4.7.3.3 German law

Similar to the FCPA and the Bribery Act, German law also recognizes the principles of territoriality and nationality. §3 StGB provides that German criminal law applies if an act is committed in German territory.[104] It must be noted that in Germany, bribery is a conduct crime. This means that the crime is completed once an act, not necessarily the effect of the act, takes place. §9(1) StGB provides that:

99 Section 12(5) of the Bribery Act. See also Section 12(6).
100 See Section 7 and Section 12(5) and (6) of the Bribery Act.
101 OECD, United Kingdom: Phase 3 (n 21) 6.
102 OECD, United Kingdom Phase 1 Ter (n 27) 20.
103 See OECD, United Kingdom: Phase 4 (n 23) 25–28.
104 §3 StGB: "*Das deutsche Strafrecht gilt für Taten, die im Inland begangen werden.*"

> [...] an act is committed at every place the perpetrator acted [...] should have acted, or at which the result, which is an element of the offense, occurs or should occur according to the understanding of the perpetrator.[105]

§9(1) indicates that the establishment of sufficient territorial nexus is largely based on conduct taking place in Germany, rather than on a mere threat of negative effects that such conduct could have in Germany. This makes the establishment of jurisdiction based on the principle of territoriality narrower than in the US and the UK.

Germany also recognizes the nationality principle regarding acts of German citizens committed abroad. §5(15) StGB extends jurisdiction to all offenses involving foreign public officials, pursuant to §§331–337 StGB. However, the principle of nationality seems to be narrower than in the case of the Bribery Act and the FCPA. What may be limiting is that, under German law, the corporate sanction is an incidental consequence of a criminal offense committed by the natural person. While it does not mean that a criminal conviction of an individual is needed to establish the administrative liability of a corporation, corporate liability is always to some extent derived from liability for a natural person.[106] It may be a reason why in practice, the German enforcement authorities use alternative offenses to prosecute foreign bribery. §5(15) StGB, however, likely does not apply to these alternative offenses. This fact could limit German foreign anti-bribery enforcement.[107]

4.7.4 Concluding remarks

The OECD Convention requires that the territorial basis for jurisdiction is to be interpreted broadly and that the principle of nationality is de facto mandatory for all signatories. The analysis shows that the selected national systems comply with these requirements to a great extent, and even common law jurisdictions such as the US and the UK, that used to be absolutely territorial, have recognized the principle of nationality.[108] The analysis revealed that the US and the UK adopted broad jurisdictional frameworks. These legal systems may capture a wide range of foreign subjects who bribe outside of the territories of these jurisdictions. This supports collective action because more bribers can be reached. Nevertheless, some problems persist. The Bribery Act still applies to the UK Crown Dependencies and the Overseas Territories with limitations. For this purpose, Article 4(4) of the OECD Convention

105 German Law Archive (Translation) http://germanlawarchive.iuscomp.org/ accessed 1 May 2019.

106 OECD, Germany: Phase 4 (n 20) 60–61.

107 OECD, Germany: Phase 4 (n 20) 50.

108 Prior to the 1998 amendment of the FCPA, the US approach was based on territorial jurisdiction. The UK changed the approach several years later, see generally OECD (2003) United Kingdom Phase I Bis: Review of Implementation of the Convention 9–10.

provides that the Parties should review the effectiveness of their jurisdictional basis and take remedial steps if they find them ineffective.[109]

Overall, US law, and also UK law and Germany law, rely on jurisdictional provisions that can cover a wide array of actions. While this fact supports the provision of enforcement as a public good, the questions are which corporations are not covered by foreign anti-bribery laws and whether the US enforcement, or other foreign anti-bribery enforcement, can mitigate the potential lack of enforcement in other countries. Furthermore, wide jurisdiction may cause internal challenges within the OECD regime, because of the lack of credibility and clarity at the enforcement stage. For example, without the cooperation and coordination of national enforcement authorities, enforcement conflicts may arise. The part below focuses on legal aspects of law enforcement, including investigation, prosecution, and sanctioning, and the most important cooperation and coordination mechanisms.

4.8 Enforcement

Collective action depends largely on law enforcement, including the independence, the professionalism, and the discretion of investigators and prosecutors. In this work, the term enforcement is mainly used in the context of state enforcement, including investigation, prosecution, and the sanctioning of offenders for bribing foreign public officials. The problem is that enforcement mechanisms that are relevant from the perspective of collective action are either vague or outside the scope of the OECD Convention. The OECD Convention, in line with the principle of functional equivalence, recognizes that prosecutorial discretion should be based on national rules and principles applicable to the investigation and prosecution.[110] Hence, how signatory states ensure the independence and professionalism of their investigations and prosecutions are, generally, left up to them.

Because of this wide heterogeneity, the relevance of national mechanisms depends on their use in practice. That is the reason why this section focuses only on the most important of them by exemplifying the key elements of the US system. If appropriate, comparative notes are provided to UK law and German law. This part starts by introducing the core standards related to law enforcement as provided by Article 5 of the OECD Convention. The focus is on the four issues that are the most important from the perspective of collective action:

1 The independence and professionalism of enforcement.
2 The structure and core principles of national enforcement systems.

109 Article 4(4) provides that "Each Party shall review whether its current basis for jurisdiction is effective in the fight against the bribery of foreign public officials and, if it is not, shall take remedial steps."

110 See Paragraph 27 of the Commentaries and Article 5 of the OECD Convention. OECD Convention and Related Documents (n 36).

3 The availability of effective, proportionate, and dissuasive penalties.
4 The types of proceedings and resolutions that can be used.

4.8.1 The independence and professionalism of enforcement

One problem with anti-bribery enforcement is that national enforcement authorities, mainly investigators and prosecutors, might lack prosecutorial independence. Despite the fact that the degree of formal independence from the executive branch is a matter of political choice, once it is defined, it should not be influenced by political or other improper motives (Monti, 2016: 184). Such an influence could lead to selective enforcement, protectionism, and ultimately, more corruption and bribery in international business transactions. Therefore, independence requires the non-intervention of politics into the investigation and prosecution of foreign bribery cases, and a transparent relationship between politics and enforcement authorities.

In order to protect the main objectives of the OECD Convention, its Article 5 introduces a minimal standard for the independence and professionalism of investigation and prosecution.[111] First, the OECD Convention specifies that such political pressure should not influence independent enforcement by considerations of national economic interest, the potential effect upon relationship with other states, or the identity of persons involved.[112] Hence, prosecutors should exercise their discretion based on professional motives and political authorities should not intervene by instructing investigators and prosecutors. Second, this threat should be prevented by building citizens' trust by issuing policy guidelines and clarifying relations between political representatives and prosecution. Last, the requirement of independence and professionalism is also connected with adequate resources dedicated to enforcement (Pieth et al., 2007: 312–313).[113]

4.8.1.1 US anti-bribery enforcement system

The US is a federal republic that consists of 50 states where both the federal government and the states prosecute criminal offenses. As the FCPA is US federal law, the investigation and prosecution of the offense of foreign bribery is the responsibility of the executive branch of government. The enforcement system is centralized and all federal prosecutors are part of a single government body – the DOJ. At the apex of the DOJ stands the US Attorney General that is appointed by the US President and is part of the President's

111 The OECD Convention does not explicitly address the independence of judges. However, judges and other authorities should apply sanctions that are effective, proportionate and dissuasive. See Article 3(1).

112 See Article 5 of the OECD Convention.

113 See Paragraph 27 of the Commentaries. OECD Convention and Related Documents (n 36).

cabinet. The US Senate confirms the appointment.[114] Nearly all of the functions of other officers, agencies, and employees of the DOJ are vested with the US Attorney General.

The centralized system of US prosecution is formally part of the executive branch. Thus, the DOJ does not formally have much independence. Factually, however, the DOJ exercises a high level of independence. The OECD reports, for example, provide that:

> [F]CPA prosecution decisions are based on the merits of the case, not political or economic considerations. Political bodies and non-criminal government bodies have no influence on the investigation and prosecution of cases involving bribery of foreign public officials.[115]

Furthermore, the US enforcement system has been increasingly specialized. The Criminal Division of the DOJ has jurisdiction over criminal matters that fall under the FCPA, and therefore authorizes the investigation and prosecution of all criminal cases. The Fraud Section of the Criminal Division and its FCPA Unit are then in charge of the investigation and prosecution. The main enforcement partner of the FCPA Unit is the Federal Bureau of Investigation (FBI) that established three specialized international corruption squads in 2015. These squads focus on the investigation of foreign bribery. The DOJ and its FCPA unit work in close cooperation with the SEC that is responsible for civil enforcement related to issuers. The SEC also has a specialized FCPA Unit.[116]

4.8.1.2 UK and German anti-bribery enforcement systems

Unlike the US, the UK enforcement model is less centralized. The SFO has been the leading enforcement authority in the UK for investigating and prosecuting foreign bribery in England, Wales, and Northern Ireland (Section 5.3.3). The main focus of the SFO is to tackle bribery, corruption, and fraud both in the UK and overseas. It must be noted that the Crown Office & Procurator Fiscal is in charge of the prosecution of foreign bribery in Scotland.[117] What is more, as will be discussed below, the Financial Conduct Authority (FCA), a specialized enforcement agency for financial insti-

114 28 U.S. Code §503. See Organization of American States, 'Guide to Criminal Prosecution in the United States' (*Information Exchange Network,* 2007) <https://www.oas.org/juridico/mla/en/usa/en_usa-int-desc-guide.html> accessed 29 April 2019.

115 OECD, United States Review (n 92) 16.

116 Securities and Exchange Commission (2010) *SEC Names New Specialized Unit Chiefs and Head of New Office of Market Intelligence* <https://www.sec.gov/news/press/2010/2010-5.htm> accessed 1 May 2019.

117 Crown Office & Procurator Fiscal Service <http://www.copfs.gov.uk/> accessed 1 May 2019.

tutions, has also conducted a number of important foreign bribery-related enforcement actions.[118] Last, some foreign bribery cases are prosecuted by the Crown Prosecution Service that handles foreign bribery cases through its Specialist Fraud Division as well as an International Team. The Crown Prosecution Service works together with the National Crime Agency International Corruption Unit that carries out foreign bribery investigations. While the mandate of the Unit overlaps with the mandate of the SFO, both should enforce the Bribery Act, the Unit specifically focuses on bribery and corruption affecting priority countries, money laundering, and politically exposed persons.[119] Therefore, the UK enforcement model has been to some extent decentralized and it is currently not clear how relevant enforcement authorities will coexist in the future.

Unlike the US, and to a great extent the UK, the German enforcement model represents a decentralized system without a central anti-corruption authority. Each of the 16 regions in Germany that are responsible for the enforcement may have different structure. According to Lord (2011: 151), such decentralized system "minimises the risk of one-sided and partial procedures and political influences." Moreover, such a system can be viewed as a cooperative network. The key role in this system has *Bundeskriminalamt* (Federal Criminal Police Office) that has a mandate from the German Constitution to coordinate the actions of state and federal authorities in criminal matters. Moreover, *Bundeskriminalamt* is also the leading agency in terms of international exchange of information and cooperation.[120]

Yet another key difference between Germany and the US and the UK are the principles related to the discretion of prosecutors. These principles, opportunity and legality, are discussed in the following part that mainly focuses on the example of US system, based on the principle of opportunity, because it is the key driver of the foreign anti-bribery enforcement. A short comparative note is provided to outline the German approach that in criminal matters relies on the principle of legality.

118 The corporations authorized under the Financial Services and Markets Act 2000 "have a regulatory obligation to put in place and maintain policies and processes to prevent bribery and corruption and to conduct their business with integrity." Financial Conduct Authority (2016) *Anti-Bribery and Corruption* <http://www.fca.org.uk/about/what/enforcing/anti-bribery-and-corruption> accessed 29 July 2016. The FCA does not enforce the Bribery Act. The predecessor of the FCA was the Financial Service Authority (FSA).

119 OECD, United Kingdom: Phase 4 (n 23) 29–30. For more discussion about the differences between the International Corruption Unit and the SFO, see Clare, L. and Elvin, R. (2016) *Fighting Corruption and Fraud – The UK International Corruption Unit (ICU) and Serious Fraud Office*. The National Law Review <http://www.natlawreview.com/article/fighting-corruption-and-fraud-uk-international-corruption-unit-icu-and-serious-fraud> accessed 29 April 2019.

120 Bundeskriminalamt, 'The BKA' <https://www.bka.de/EN/Home/home_node.html> accessed 2 May 2019.

4.8.2 The principles of opportunity and legality

The high level of discretion to prosecute cases is a key feature of the US enforcement system. According to the principle of opportunity, the leading principle not only in the US but also in the UK, prosecutors are not obliged to prosecute every potential offense that they know about (Lord, 2016: 95–102). For example, they can decide whether, when, against whom, and on what basis to open or withdraw a criminal proceeding. Furthermore, they have enforcement policies that prioritize specific types of anti-bribery schemes and they negotiate prosecution agreements.[121] The problems associated with such level of discretion, including its potential abuse, the lack of transparency, and a lack of legal certainty, may undermine collective action.

In order to minimize the potential abuse of this discretion, and to increase the transparency and predictability of prosecution, the US authorities promote "the reasoned exercise of prosecutorial authority."[122] In this line, they have published a number of guidelines and memoranda. The core principles and policies of the prosecution can be found in the US Attorneys' Manual that serves as the internal guide for US federal authorities. The most general principles regarding the decision-making process of the prosecutors are contained in the Principles of Federal Prosecution and the Principles of Federal Prosecution of Business Organizations.[123] The US prosecutors consider nine main factors such as the nature and seriousness of the offense, wrongdoing within corporation, and remedial actions, when exercising their discretion.[124] The nine factors also apply in the area of foreign anti-bribery enforcement. While these documents and policies are in themselves the guarantee of the reasoned exercise of the discretion, they are also subject to external audit control as provided by the US Government Accountability Office (GAO).[125] The GAO, for example, in one of its audit reports analyzed how the principles of federal prosecution influenced the decision-making of prosecutors when choosing the type of criminal resolution.

Moreover, the DOJ publishes specific foreign bribery-related memoranda that contain enforcement policies and compliance guidance. Furthermore, the DOJ established the Foreign Corrupt Practices Act Opinion Procedure that enables "issuers and domestic concerns to obtain an opinion of the Attorney General as to whether certain specified, prospective, but not hypothetical,

121 See U.S. Attorneys' Manual, 9–27.000 – Principles of Federal Prosecution.

122 See U.S. Attorneys' Manual, 9–27.110 – Purpose.

123 See U.S. Attorneys' Manual, 9–27.110 – Purpose; U.S. Attorneys' Manual, 9–28.000 – Principles of Federal Prosecution of Business Organizations.

124 United States Government Accountability Office (2009) *Corporate Crime: DOJ Has Taken Steps to Better Track Its Use of Deferred and Non-Prosecution Agreements, but Should Evaluate Effectiveness* 10 <http://www.gao.gov/assets/300/299781.pdf> accessed 19 April 2019.

125 United States Government Accountability Office, *About GAO* <http://www.gao.gov/about/index.html> accessed 30 April 2019.

conduct conforms to the Department's present enforcement policy."[126] Last, the DOJ and the SEC issued non-binding guidelines, the Resource Guide (DOJ and SEC, 2012), clarifying key legal aspects of the FCPA.

The above-discussed enforcement policies not only represent the stick that incentivizes corporations and individuals to comply with the FCPA, but also the carrot. For example, the Weismann memo, published in April 2016, provides that the principal goal of the DOJ is to promote corporate accountability by:

> [...] motivating companies to voluntarily self-disclose FCPA-related misconduct, fully cooperate with the Fraud Section, and, where appropriate, remediate flaws in their controls and compliance programs.[127]

Hence, the discretion of the US enforcement authorities can be exercised in favor of corporations whose self-reporting, good cooperation with the US authorities, and high quality of compliance programs may even be rewarded by prosecutors. For example, prosecutors may choose to offer lower penalties or even decide not to prosecute.

Unlike in the US, the German system is partially based on the principle of legality and partially on the principle of opportunity. The principle of legality that applies to criminal offenses committed by natural persons is considered by the German constitution (*Grundgesetz*) as the guarantee of the rule of law. The principle is closely related to another leading principle: the principle of equality of all persons before the law (Gleichheitsgrundsatz) (Lord, 2016: 97–100). In this context, according to §152(2) StPO, "the public prosecution office shall be obliged to take action in relation to all prosecutable "criminal offenses, provided there are sufficient factual indications."[128] This means that German enforcement authorities have less discretion than the US enforcement authorities do.[129]

These principles have also implications for the prosecution of corporations that, contrary to the prosecution of natural persons, is led by the principle of opportunity. Yet, the liability of legal persons is always to some extent derived from the liability of natural persons. This superiority of the prosecution of natural persons undermines the use of corporate liability because, as found during

126 Sec 80.1 of the Foreign Corrupt Practices Act Opinion Procedure Regulation, 28 C.F.R. part 80 as of July 1, 1999.

127 Department of Justice (2016) *The Fraud Section's Foreign Corrupt Practices Act Enforcement Plan and Guidance* 2 <https://www.justice.gov/criminal-fraud/file/838416/download> accessed 19 April 2019.

128 German Law Archive (Translation) http://germanlawarchive.iuscomp.org/ accessed 2 May 2019.

129 Note that the principle of legality implies a certain level of discretion for deciding whether to prosecute all foreign bribery cases. For example, German prosecutors do not have to prosecute minor offenses, can use the statute of limitations in order to "miss the deadline," and employ other strategies in order to prioritize between cases (Lord, 2016: 98–99).

Phase 4 on-site visits, "consideration to initiating proceedings against legal persons is taken at a later stage of the proceedings against the natural persons."[130]

The supremacy of the prosecution of natural persons may be the reason why unlike in the US, German authorities do not systematically provide enforcement guidelines that would define their enforcement policy. The mandatory prosecution of all natural persons does not require such enforcement policy because it could weaken the principle of equality of all persons before the law and the principle of legality. The enforcement policy is, however, desirable when it comes to corporate liability.

German enforcement authorities, unlike in the case of natural persons, have a wide prosecutorial discretion to initiate and discontinue proceedings against legal persons. This prosecutorial discretion, to be exercised reasonably, requires certain degree of transparency and external control. Moreover, the discretion needs to be coordinated because the German system is based on a decentralized enforcement system of 16 independent enforcement authorities which implies the need to deal with heterogeneity of approaches between those enforcement authorities. The lack of control of the prosecutorial discretion in Germany is a problem that undermines collective action.

4.8.3 Sanctions

The effectiveness of an anti-bribery regime, from the perspective collective action, can be guaranteed only if the legislator ensures that foreign bribery is sufficiently sanctioned. The OECD Convention, in its Article 3(1), provides that the offense of foreign bribery should be "punishable by effective, proportionate and dissuasive criminal penalties."[131] The most common tools to sanction this type of conduct are monetary penalties and the imprisonment of natural persons. It was discussed above that all of the selected jurisdictions sanction the offense of foreign bribery by many years of imprisonment for natural persons and financial fines for both legal and natural persons (Section 3.4).

Furthermore, there are alternative sanctions. Article 3(3) of the OECD Convention requires states to adopt measures that ensure the seizure or confiscation of the bribes and the gains made from bribing. We will see below in the study of enforcement schemes that the SEC heavily relies on the disgorgement of ill-gotten gains, an ancillary equitable remedy.[132] Furthermore, the US enforcement authorities can impose compliance-related obligations such as the appointment of an independent corporate monitor who assesses a company's obligations to improve its internal compliance program and system of internal controls (DOJ and SEC, 2012: 71–72). Last, a foreign bribery conviction may result in the more serious consequence of a company be-

130 OECD, Germany: Phase 4 (n 20) 68.

131 Article 3(1) of the OECD Convention.

132 According to some scholars, disgorgement is in fact used as "a remedy at law, or even a punitive remedy" (Ryan, 2013: 2).

ing suspended (debarment) from contracting with public authorities or face ineligibility to receive export licenses (Acorn, 2016). Such a threat might incentivize companies to engage in negotiations with enforcement authorities in order to mitigate or even avoid such collateral consequences.

The key issue from the perspective of collective action is whether and how national enforcement authorities sanction foreign bribery in practice. This will be discussed in more detail in Chapters 5 and 6. The following subsection introduces the key types of negotiated resolutions that the US authorities rely upon when enforcing the FCPA.

4.8.4 Resolutions of foreign bribery cases

The OECD Convention does not oblige national states to implement any specific procedure to resolve foreign bribery cases. While in some cases, a wrongdoer can face a trial and the case is decided by a court, the use of out-of-court settlements is dominant in the area of foreign anti-bribery enforcement. Written negotiated agreements have been frequently used by prosecutors because they lead to fast and effective resolution of foreign bribery cases. In exchange for the cooperation, corporations might receive lower penalties and avoid a criminal conviction. On the other hand, settlements imply clarity problems associated with the lack of regulatory oversight and transparency (Corruption Watch, 2016: 2–4; Oduor, 2014). The following section introduces the main aspects of negotiated settlements.

4.8.4.1 The US settlement procedures

The use of negotiated agreements, rather than adjudication, in order to resolve allegations of foreign bribery, is a typical in the US. These negotiations may result in a written agreement that usually contains a statement of facts, the calculation of penalties, and agreed upon obligations regarding internal compliance. The DOJ and the SEC rely on the following three main types of out-of-court resolutions.

1 **Guilty plea**: The guilty plea is an agreement between a wrongdoer and the US enforcement authority that has to be reviewed by a judge. According to Rule 11 of the Federal Rules of Criminal Procedure, before a court accepts a plea of guilt, it needs to determine that the facts constitute an offense and that the plea is voluntary. The parties may recommend to the court the amount and type of sanctions that should be awarded. The guilty plea has the same legal effects as the conviction for a crime (DOJ and SEC, 2012: 74; Oduor et al., 2014: 34). Guilty pleas are published on the websites of the DOJ and the SEC.[133]

133 DOJ, <https://www.justice.gov/criminal-fraud/related-enforcement-actions>; SEC <https://www.sec.gov/spotlight/fcpa/fcpa-cases.shtml> accessed 8 May 2019

2 **Deferred prosecution agreement** (DPA): A DPA is, similarly to the guilty plea, an agreement between an accused person and the US enforcement authority that is filed with a court. Unlike, a guilty plea, when a DPA is reached, the US authorities agree to postpone a prosecution of an accused person for a certain period. If the agreement is fulfilled, the authorities dismiss the charges (DOJ and SEC, 2012: 74; Oduor et al., 2014: 34). Hence, DPAs do not constitute the conviction for a crime. DPAs are published on the websites of the DOJ and the SEC.

3 **Non-prosecution agreement** (NPA): An NPA is, from the perspective of a person, the softest resolution, because the US authorities agree not to file charges. NPAs are published on the websites of the DOJ and the SEC. However, they contain less information than guilty pleas and DPAs (DOJ and SEC, 2012: 74; Oduor et al., 2014: 34).

It must be noted that the SEC not only relies on DPAs and NPAs but can also file a civil injunctive action in which it "seeks a court order compelling a person to obey the law in the future," and may initiate various administrative proceedings (DOJ and SEC, 2012: 76). In addition, the DOJ can also fill civil complaints in order to seek forfeiture.

4.8.4.2 Settlement procedures in Germany and the UK

UK law and German law also recognize the possibility of settlements. Unlike the US, however, the role of the judge is much more important.

In the UK, a DPA is an agreement between a prosecutor and a corporation only. It is not possible for a natural person to conclude such an agreement. The UK introduced the settlement mechanism – DPAs – in Schedule 17 of the Crime and Courts Act 2013 (the 2013 Act), that came into force on 24 February 2014. Similarly to the US, in the UK, a legal person "can avoid prosecution for certain economic or financial offenses by entering into an agreement on negotiated terms with a prosecutor…"[134] A DPA is used in the prosecutor's discretion, that can, but does not have to, invite a corporation to negotiate. Prosecutors should follow the Deferred Prosecution Agreement Code of Practice when negotiating DPAs, applying to the court for the approval, and overseeing DPAs.[135]

Unlike US law, UK law has established more stringent conditions for being awarded a DPA. This is mainly because the court is more involved in the process, and under Sections 7 and 8 of Schedule 17, must approve or decline an agreement. This is done in two stages. In a preliminary, private hearing,

134 Para 1 of *Serious Fraud Office and Standard Bank PLC, Approved Judgement of the Crown Court at Southwark* (30 November 2015) <https://www.judiciary.gov.uk/wp-content/uploads/2015/11/sfo-v-standard-bank_Final_1.pdf> accessed 3 May 2019.

135 Deferred Prosecution Agreements <https://www.sfo.gov.uk/publications/guidance-policy-and-protocols/deferred-prosecution-agreements/> accessed 3 May 2019.

the court assesses whether an agreement is likely to be in the interest of justice, and whether the proposed terms of the DPA are fair, reasonable, and proportionate.[136] The court should state reasons for or against the declinations. If the court approves the terms of the agreement, the prosecutor may enter into the agreement with a legal person. Once it is done, the court must still approve or decline the agreement in the final, public hearing.[137] Therefore, in the UK the role of a court in relation to DPAs is more important than in the US.

Negotiating agreements is also possible in Germany. This possibility is, however, available only to natural persons. Legal persons can enter into purely administrative resolution with the prosecution. Starting with natural persons, §153a StPO establishes an exception from the legality principle by allowing a prosecution office to provisionally dispense or terminate proceedings. §153a StPO can be applied only with the consent of an accused natural person and a court, and when it is in the public interest. Furthermore, German law also offers under §257c StPO the possibility to enter into negotiated sentencing agreement with the court.[138] Such agreement can be reached only if the defendant confesses the crime and if the judge proposes such agreement.[139] The court is not bound by such an agreement if it is not appropriate because "legal or factually significant circumstances have been overlooked or have arisen."[140]

Regarding legal persons, German law does not formally provide any possibility to negotiate and resolve foreign bribery cases prior to a trial. Nevertheless, this possibility in a limited form exists because legal persons can enter into a purely administrative resolution with the prosecution based on the violation of supervisory duties by senior management under §130 OWiG. For example, the German enforcement authorities can use a forfeiture order against corporations, considering corporations as third parties, without holding them liable under §30 OWiG.[141] Under this procedure, as discussed in Phase 4 monitoring report, the amount of the confiscatory component of the regulatory fine is to a large extent influenced by estimates provided by a corporation to a prosecutor.[142] The problem is that the use of forfeiture orders is not equivalent to deferred prosecution agreements and other mechanisms in which corporate liability is at stake.[143] This may undermine the provision of enforcement as a public good and lead to clarity problems.

136 Section 7 of the 2013 Act.
137 Section 8 of the 2013 Act. See also (Corruption Watch, 2016: 19–24).
138 Note that under §257c StPO, legal persons can also enter into this type of agreement with the court.
139 §257c (1) and (3) StPO.
140 §257c(4) StPO.
141 §29a OWiG.
142 OECD, Germany: Phase 4 (n 20) 64.
143 OECD, Germany: Phase 4 (n 20) 65–66.

4.8.5 Concluding remarks

From the perspective of collective action, national enforcement authorities should be independent, professional, and have a certain degree of discretion. The OECD Convention leaves it up to signatory states how they ensure the independence and professionalism of their investigations and prosecution. In the main, Article 5 of the OECD Convention stresses that political influence such as the considerations of national economic interest should not interfere with prosecution and investigation. This requirement overlaps with more general international legal obligations established by, for instance, the CoE and the UN.[144] These standards, similarly as the OECD Convention, provide that prosecutorial discretion should be based on national rules and principles applicable to the investigation and prosecution.[145]

The discussed national enforcement models show significant heterogeneity. While the enforcement models of the US and the UK are based exclusively on the principle of opportunity, the prosecution of natural persons in Germany is based on the principle of legality. The discussed national legal systems also differ in a way how they use negotiated agreements. While, the US enforcement authorities are generally not limited by courts when using negotiated agreements, under UK and German law, the role of the courts in supervising these negotiations is much more important.

The principle of opportunity allows for national enforcement authorities prioritize between cases and use the most effective enforcement strategy when prosecuting them. At the same time, however, too much discretion may be detrimental to collective action because of its unpredictability. For example, national enforcement authorities could refuse enforcement in order to save enforcement resources or protect national economic interests. Such uncertainty may also undermine collective action because national enforcement authorities may be prevented from cooperating with each other and coordinating their enforcement actions. The cooperation and coordination mechanisms that the OECD Convention and that some national laws have established are discussed in the following section.

4.9 Cooperation and coordination

Next to a wide jurisdictional ambit of foreign bribery laws, collective action requires cooperation and coordination between national enforcement

144 See, for instance, Council of Europe, Recommendation Rec(2000)19 of the Committee of Ministers to Member States on the Role of Public Prosecution in the Criminal Justice System. Para 11(f) of the recommendation provides that "instructions not to prosecute in a specific case should, in principle, be prohibited. Should that not be the case, such instructions must remain exceptional [...]." See also Guidelines on the Role of Prosecutors, Eighth United Nations Congress on the Prevention of Crime and the Treatment of Offenders, U.N. Doc. A/CONF.144/28/Rev.1 at 189 (1990).

145 See Paragraph 13 of the Commentaries and Article 5 of the OECD Convention. OECD Convention and Related Documents (n 36).

authorities. Cooperation and coordination increase the effectiveness of investigations and prosecution, because they make it easier for enforcement authorities to obtain information and evidence from countries that have better access to them. Furthermore, MLA and similar mechanisms save enforcement resources (OECD, 2012: 3–4). Despite these positive aspects, however, countries may refrain from cooperating because of credibility and clarity problems. For example, sharing evidence is associated with economic costs that some states may not be willing to pay. Moreover, the wide jurisdiction over foreign bribery cases and the use of out-of-court settlements raise the question of which national enforcement authority should be in charge of the enforcement of a case, and whether a case was or was not already resolved by another signatory state.

The importance of cooperation and coordination is recognized in the Preamble of the OECD Convention. The Preamble provides that "all countries share a responsibility to combat bribery in international business," and the responsibility requires the "prompt criminalisation of such bribery in an effective and co-ordinated manner."[146] The following text analyzes the three most important legislative and regulatory mechanisms of cooperation and coordination. These are:

1 Assistance mechanisms for cooperation such as MLA.
2 Mechanisms of coordination of jurisdictional conflicts that arise before and after a resolution of a foreign bribery case.
3 Direct cooperation mechanisms such as joint investigation.

4.9.1 Assistance mechanisms for cooperation

Collective action largely depends on cooperative assistance between countries. Such assistance may be challenging to obtain because of legal barriers, the lack of resources, a lack of professionalism, and political tensions. According to the OECD, in December 2015, 70% of officials that were responsible for anti-bribery enforcement reported that their work was negatively affected because of challenges related to obtaining information and evidence from other countries.[147] This so-called MLA is the key legal, formal, mechanism for strengthening such assistance.

Article 9(1) of the OECD Convention obliges the signatories to provide MLA to another signatory for the purpose of both criminal and non-criminal proceedings. In general, such assistance should be effective and prompt, and the requested party should, without delay, inform the requesting party about

146 See the Preamble of the OECD Convention. OECD Convention and Related Documents (n 36).

147 OECD, *International Cooperation in Combating Foreign Bribery* (2016) <https://www.oecd.org/daf/anti-bribery/Anti-Bribery-Ministerial-International-Cooperation-Discussion-Paper.pdf> accessed 3 May 2019.

the status and the outcome of the request, and about all additional issues that are needed to fulfill the request.[148] Furthermore, the OECD Convention refers to other MLA instruments that can be used for the purposes of anti-bribery enforcement. First, the Preamble refers to the work of organizations such as the UN, the EU, and the CoE that have developed a number of cooperation and coordination mechanisms alongside the OECD framework. Second, Article 9(1) of the OECD Convention provides a general reference to other existing treaties. Last, Section XIII(iv) of the 2009 Recommendation encourages the signatories to "make full use of existing agreements and arrangements for mutual international legal assistance and where necessary, enter into new agreements or arrangements for this purpose." The OECD Convention does not aspire to provide a bribery-specific MLA standard.

The OECD Convention signatories are part of a much larger legal framework consisting of various multilateral, regional, or bilateral MLA agreements. These include international anti-corruption treaties, such as the UNCAC, that in its Article 46 provides a number of rules dealing with MLA, general multilateral MLA treaties, such as the European Convention on Mutual Assistance in Criminal Matters[149] and bilateral agreements.[150] These legal instruments provide for a number of tools and mechanisms that not only include MLA, but other more traditional tools and mechanisms, such as extradition, information sharing, the detention and transfer of prisoners, and arrest warrants.

The freezing and confiscation of assets, and bank secrecy, as well as the exchange of tax information, are, or could be, relevant for the OECD anti-bribery enforcement regime. For example, transnational regulation of tax matters relies on a number of consistency tools including a global standard on automatic exchange of key indicators such as profits, taxes paid, and assets of MNCs. These alternative legal frameworks, no matter how they differ in substantive and objective scope, can be used in other fields and are endorsed by international anti-bribery legislation (Section 9.5).

4.9.2 Jurisdictional conflicts and their coordination

Cooperation and coordination are not only about seeking assistance from other countries, but also about parallel investigations and resolutions. Either because of the lack of credibility or because of the lack of clarity between national enforcement authorities, foreign anti-bribery enforcement of several

148 In addition, Article 9(2) of the OECD Convention deals with "dual criminality" and Article 9(3) states that bank secrecy shall be no reason for a refusal of MLA.

149 See Article 21 of the European Convention on Mutual Assistance in Criminal Matters, Strasbourg, 20 April 1959, *in force* 12 June 1962, ETS No. 030.

150 The central authority in the US responsible for gathering international evidence in criminal matters is the Office of International Affairs. The Office, together with the Department of State, negotiates treaties and bilateral agreements.

enforcement authorities may overlap. Without coordination, such parallel enforcement may have a number of undesirable effects on collective action, and thereby on ensuring open and competitive markets. For example, punishing one corporation multiple times for the same acts is not effective from the perspective of the provision of public goods, because of wasted enforcement resources that could be spent to bring additional cases. Alternatively, the lack of coordination may also result in clarity problems associated with the non-resolution of a bribery case because all of the enforcement authorities that may potentially be involved could see themselves as not having the appropriate jurisdiction.

The OECD Convention offers a coordination mechanism based on a consultation procedure between relevant Parties that aims to mitigate coordination problems. Article 4(3) provides that:

> [W]hen more than one Party has jurisdiction over an alleged offence described in this Convention, the Parties involved shall, at the request of one of them, consult with a view to determining the most appropriate jurisdiction for prosecution.

Because of its open character, Article 4(3) of the OECD Convention raises some controversy. The question is whether the provision should be read more broadly or more narrowly. Those who read the article broadly argue that the OECD Convention itself is the source of the protection against overlapping enforcement. Those who read it more narrowly argue that the signatories have only an obligation to consult and not to decline prosecution if another signatory already decided the case (Ferguson, 2015: Chapter 6, 74; Van Alstine, 2012: 1349–1350). The latter argument is supported by the fact that Article 4(3) does not specify what the most appropriate jurisdiction is and how a jurisdictional conflict between the signatories should be resolved procedurally.

In other words, the OECD Convention provides no substantive criteria and no procedural mechanism of the consultation referred to in Article 4(3). Moreover, the consultation mechanism does not provide for any legal consequences for cases where the signatories do not reach an agreement about the most appropriate jurisdiction. Because of its open character, therefore, Article 4(3) represents an invitation to use the doctrine of international comity rather than directly protecting enforcement overlaps (International Bar Association, 2009: 229–230). The doctrine of international comity is discussed in the following section.

4.9.3 International comity

The doctrine of international comity does not have a single definition. In essence, it means that states, in the assertion of their sovereign power, should take into account legislative, executive, and judicial acts, as well as the interests of other countries. We can recognize between the positive comity and the negative comity. The former reflects a request of one country to another country to consider the one's country interests when enforcing legislation and to take remedial actions if deemed appropriate. The latter is based on the notification of one country to other countries that its enforcement proceedings may have an effect on their interests (OECD, 1999).

However, it does not mean that international comity is only a matter of good will. In *Hilton vs. Guyot*, the US Supreme Court provided that "'Comity', in the legal sense, is neither a matter of absolute obligation, on the one hand, nor of mere courtesy and good will, upon the other."[151] The doctrine of international comity is often institutionalized on a bilateral basis. For example, the EU/US cooperation agreements in the field of competition law have proven successful in increasing cooperation and coordination between competition enforcement authorities in transnational cases (see, generally, Guzman, 2011). Unlike the use of comity in competition laws, no such specific agreements, have been concluded regarding foreign anti-bribery enforcement. Nevertheless, the US and other countries such as the UK have concluded guidelines for handling criminal cases affecting both countries.[152] More recently, the DOJ issued a policy of coordination of corporate resolution penalties.[153] These policies also influence other forms of cooperation and coordination such as the application of the principle *ne bis in idem* and issues related to direct cooperation and coordination.

The discussed jurisdictions recognize the possibility to consult each other with a view of determining the most appropriate jurisdiction for prosecution. For example, the OECD reports indicate how in practice, the US provides regular consultations.[154] Germany refers to the European Convention on Mutual Assistance in Criminal Matters,[155] diplomatic consultations, and an extradition request.[156] In the UK, the SFO provides that its approach is to:

> [h]ave a frank and open discussion with the overseas agency/ies regarding the ambit of the respective investigations and seek to agree to co-operate. This includes updating on progress of the respective investigations, and

151 See *Hilton vs. Guyot, 159 U.S. 113, (1895)* 163–164.

152 UK (2007) Attorney General's Domestic Guidance for Handling Criminal Cases Affecting both England, Wales, or Northern Ireland and the United States of America' <https://www.publications.parliament.uk/pa/ld200607/ldlwa/70125ws1.pdf> accessed 3 May 2019. See also Crown Prosecution Service (2013) Director's Guidance on the Handling of Cases where the Jurisdiction to Prosecute is Shared with Prosecuting Authorities Overseas <http://www.cps.gov.uk/publications/directors_guidance/director_s_guidance_on_concurrent_jurisdiction.html> accessed 3 May–October 2019.

153 United States Department of Justice (2018) 'Policy on Coordination of Corporate Resolution Penalties' <https://www.justice.gov/opa/speech/file/1061186/download> accessed 3 May 2019.

154 OECD, United States Review (n 92) 14.

155 See Article 21 of the European Convention on Mutual Assistance in Criminal Matters.

156 OECD, Germany: Review (27) 10.

> discussing lines of enquiry and intelligence sharing. [...] there should be a preliminary presumption that a prosecution should take place in the jurisdiction where the majority of the criminality occurred or where the majority of the loss was sustained. When reaching a decision, prosecutors should balance carefully and fairly all the factors both for and against commencing a prosecution in each jurisdiction where it is possible to do so.[157]

Moreover, all of the discussed jurisdictions also ratified the UNCAC, that provides some additional guidance and incentivizes bilateral agreements regarding coordination.[158] Therefore, the doctrine of international comity plays an important role in the area of foreign anti-bribery enforcement.

4.9.4 Ne bis in idem

The doctrine of international comity is not the only possible solution to coordination problems. Both civil and common law systems rely on mechanisms that help them prevent possible enforcement conflicts. Civil law recognizes the old Roman law principle called *ne bis in idem*, that is, in a way, similar to the double jeopardy clause in common law jurisdictions. These two concepts may be of some use in preventing the discussed credibility and clarity problems. Whether potential conflict is identified before the prosecution of a MNC, at the time of the conclusion of a foreign bribery case, or after the conclusion, *ne bis in idem* and similar principles could provide more clarity in what jurisdiction is appropriate in the given foreign bribery case (but see Section 8.4.5.2). In result, more clarity could also prevent credibility problems such as enforcement opportunism (Sections 6.7.3, 7.4.3 and 8.4).

In the area of foreign anti-bribery enforcement, discussed states do not provide any obligatory modes of *ne bis in idem* and double jeopardy. It means that the coordination of enforcement remains an issue of international comity as a default rule. The DOJ, in its recent policy on the coordination of corporate resolution penalties, indicates that it should endeavor, as appropriate, "to coordinate with and consider the amount of fines, penalties, and/or forfeiture paid to other federal, state, local, or foreign enforcement authorities that are seeking to resolve a case with a company for the same misconduct."[159] This means that the US deals with the issue of overlapping jurisdiction on a case-by-case basis, while taking into account many variables, such as reciprocity. The US claims that this is necessary because of credibility problems, mainly that in many cases their counterparties do not cooperate even if the US provides them with evidence of foreign bribery.[160]

157 OECD, United Kingdom: Phase 4 (n 23) 47.
158 See Article 48(1)(e) of the UNCAC.
159 Policy on Coordination of Corporate Resolution Penalties (n 153).
160 OECD, Phase 3 Report on the United States (31) 22–23.

In Germany, the OECD reports indicate that German authorities are open to cooperation with other enforcers but are otherwise silent about the issue of overlapping jurisdictions. Furthermore, the problem with the *ne bis in idem* principle is that it prevents the subsequent prosecution and conviction of the same case only in criminal matters, and only once a court reaches a final decision.[161] Hence, German authorities may not be able to apply the principle to cases resolved by out-of-court agreements. Regarding the UK, the UK authorities argue that a person may not be convicted twice for the same offense based on facts that are substantially similar.[162]

From a more general perspective, *ne bis in idem* and double jeopardy usually only apply to domestic cases (Oduor et al., 2014: 58–59). US law does not recognize any general standard preventing jurisdictional overlap at the international level. Moreover, the US Supreme Court uses the so-called dual sovereignty doctrine that limits the effective use of the double jeopardy defense when more than one sovereign is prosecuting the case. Colangelo (2009: 773) in his extensive analysis of the double jeopardy defense comments:

> [b]y labelling successively prosecuting entities separate sovereigns, the Court permits multiple prosecutions and ends all further discussion under the Constitution's Double Jeopardy Clause.

Furthermore, the effectiveness of the discussed principles is limited also in other fields, even within much more homogenous systems than the OECD anti-bribery enforcement regime such as EU competition law.[163] Therefore, *ne bis in idem* and double jeopardy do not have high potential to be effective in facing the discussed cooperation and coordination problems. In all, as in the case of international comity, the case study of this work, that is in the following two chapters, will confirm whether *ne bis in idem* and double jeopardy play some role in coordinating foreign anti-bribery enforcement.

4.9.5 Direct cooperation and joint investigation teams

In order to avoid overlapping investigations and resolutions, signatories may, in some cases, cooperate and coordinate their parallel investigation directly, without what are often lengthy MLA requests. Furthermore, more informal and direct communication between national enforcement authorities may help hold MNCs accountable for bribing more effectively. This is also recognized by Section XIII(i) of the 2009 Recommendation that recommends that the signatories:

161 OECD, United Kingdom: Phase 4 (n 23) 48.

162 OECD, United Kingdom: Phase 3 (n 21) 31.

163 Even in the EU system, the *ne bis in idem* principle causes very complex legal questions, see Michele Simonato (2016) *Ne Bis In Idem in the EU: Two Important Questions for the CJEU*. European Law Blog <http://europeanlawblog.eu/?p=3071> accessed 3 May 2019. More generally see OECD (2014).

> [c]onsult and otherwise co-operate with competent authorities in other countries, and, as appropriate, international and regional law enforcement networks involving Member and non-Member countries, in investigations and other legal proceedings concerning specific cases of such bribery, through such means as the sharing of information spontaneously or upon request [...]

The quality of direct cooperation refers to in Section XIII(i) of the Recommendation is to a great extent based on trust and good relationships between national enforcement authorities. In specific cases, direct cooperation can be strengthened by agreeing on ad hoc memoranda of understanding. More generally, direct cooperation is also facilitated by various international networks and organizations in the area of transnational economic crime.

Elements of more direct cooperation and coordination have been formalized in a number of enforcement policies. For example, the UK and the US formalized on a bilateral Guidance for handling criminal cases affecting the UK and the US.[164] The Guidance specifies in its para 13 the consultation procedure between the US and the UK prosecutors:

> [D]iscussions between UK and US prosecutors should take place with the aim of developing a case strategy on issues arising from concurrent jurisdiction. The information shared between the UK and the US should include the facts of the case, key evidence, representations on jurisdictional issues, and, as appropriate, any other consideration which will enable the prosecutors to develop a case strategy and resolve issues arising from concurrent jurisdiction.[165]

Furthermore, national enforcement authorities do not have to cooperate and coordinate their actions only while maintaining their own separate investigations, but they can also establish a joint investigation team (JIT) (OECD, 2012: 47–55). In essence, the JIT is a team established by an agreement for a fixed period, with a specific purpose to investigate a specific case.[166] Currently, the only formal international legal mechanism for establishing JITs is the 2000 EU Convention on Mutual Legal Assistance (2000 MLA Convention).[167] Under the 2000 MLA Convention, the establishment and operation

164 UK, Attorney General's Domestic Guidance (n 152).

165 UK, Attorney General's Domestic Guidance (n 152) para 13.

166 Article 13 of the Council Act of 29 May 2000 establishing in accordance with Article 34 of the Treaty on European Union the Convention on Mutual Assistance in Criminal Matters between the Member States of the European Union (OJ C 197, 12 July 2000) (hereinafter 2000 MLA Convention).

167 Note that in order to speed up the implementation of JITs, the EU Member States agreed on the Council Framework Decision 2002/465/JHA on joint investigation teams [2002] OJ L 162.

of the JITs amongst the EU Member States can be supported by the EU agencies Europol and Eurojust.[168] Furthermore, the notion of JIT is defined in a number of international legal instruments such as the UNCAC (Article 49) and the UN Convention against Transnational Organized Crime.[169] These instruments recommend concluding framework agreements and ad hoc agreements to establish JITs. Therefore, the EU JIT project remains the only formal mechanism, and Germany and the UK have implemented relevant legislation on JITs into their national legal orders.[170] JITs are also an important concept in the US, with the US having concluded bilateral, multilateral, and ad hoc agreements (Ferguson, 2015: Chapter 6: 16).[171]

4.9.6 Concluding remarks

The key problem that limits collective action is that the OECD Convention signatories do not sufficiently cooperate, nor coordinate their actions, when enforcing their national laws. When it comes to the provision of enforcement, obtaining information and evidence from other countries is crucial. The OECD Convention obliges its signatories to provide MLA, and encourages them to use a broad range of other legal instruments that exist outside the OECD legal framework. This fact provides for a wide heterogeneity, and many alternative mechanisms may be relevant. These mechanisms were discussed only briefly because their relevance for foreign anti-bribery enforcement depends on whether they are applied by national enforcement authorities when investigating and prosecuting concrete cases.

Furthermore, a lack of cooperation and coordination may lead to undesirable forms of jurisdictional conflicts. The OECD Convention anticipates these challenges, however, it merely provides a limited solution: an obligation to consult each other in order to establish who has the appropriate jurisdiction over a foreign bribery case. This represents an invitation to use the doctrine of international comity. Alternative mechanisms for cooperation and coordination such as the *ne bis in idem* and double jeopardy defense, presumably, cannot be effectively used in international cases. Rather, more informal and direct mechanism such as JITs have the potential to make enforcement more effective (Sections 6.7.2 and 8.2).

168 Council of the European Union, Joint Investigation Teams Manual (2011) 13–14 <https://www.europol.europa.eu/sites/default/files/documents/st15790-re01.en11.pdf> accessed 3 May 2019.

169 UN Convention against Transnational Organized Crime, 15 November 2000.

170 See references to national legislation in Joint Investigation Teams Manual (168) 19 and 22. Regarding German law see Gesetz über die internationale Rechtshilfe in Strafsachen vom 27. June 1994 (BGBI. I S. 1537). See generally Schomburg et al. (2012). Regarding UK law see Police Reform Act 2002 (c. 30), Sections 103 and 104 and Crime (International Cooperation) Act 2003 (c. 32), Section 16. See also OECD (2012) 51.

171 Regarding the cooperation with the EU, see the Agreement on Mutual Legal Assistance between the European Union and the United States of America, [2003] OJ L 181.

4.10 Conclusion

This chapter sets a framework for the qualitative study of foreign anti-bribery enforcement actions by analyzing foreign anti-bribery legislation. This was done from the perspective of collective action. While the analysis of US law, UK law, and German law shows that the implementation of the OECD Convention provides a good potential to hold MNCs liable for foreign bribery, the heterogeneity of approaches may limit this potential.

When it comes to the provision of enforcement, the OECD Convention introduces several substantive standards that have the potential to alleviate collective action problems. These standards allow national states prosecute a wide range of transnational activities of domestic corporations as well as foreign corporations. In this context, the OECD Convention defines certain notions, including the notions such as the "offense of foreign bribery," "briber," "bribed party," and "bribe," relatively precisely. Hence, the potential of undesirable heterogeneity is low. Other relevant provisions are also defined relatively precisely, however, their functioning largely depends on the execution of prosecutorial discretion and on other mechanisms that are outside the scope of the OECD Convention. The most important are the following:

1 The OECD Convention requires that the territorial basis for jurisdiction is to be interpreted broadly and that the nationality principle is de facto mandatory for all signatories.
2 Corporations can be held liable for actions of other persons such as intermediaries and subsidiaries (indirect bribery).
3 Indirect bribery can also be sanctioned via conspiracy charges; hence, for example, if a corporation headquartered in Japan conspires with a corporation based in the US, the US authorities may, in theory, extend their jurisdiction to cover also the Japanese co-conspirator.

Last, some relevant provisions, including the standard for MLA and the standard for the performance of enforcement discretion, are either vague or completely outside the scope of the OECD Convention.

Because of the heterogeneity, some enforcement authorities may face legal limitations to hold MNCs liable for foreign bribery. Furthermore, there may be different views about who and how should be prosecuted. For example, US law allows the enforcement authorities to charge corporations independently from the liability of natural persons. In Germany, on the other hand, the liability of legal person is derived from the liability of natural person. Hence, German law creates more incentives than US law to prosecute natural persons rather than corporations. This indicates that the heterogeneity may not only limit the enforcement reach but it also opens the question of how to determine the appropriateness of enforcement.

Furthermore, the heterogeneity may undermine collective action because of clarity problems that may block cooperation and coordination between national enforcement authorities. The lack of cooperation and coordination can, for instance, lead to jurisdictional conflicts associated with either non-prosecution of a given case or multiple prosecutions of the same case. The OECD Convention addressed jurisdictional conflicts through a coordination mechanism based on a consultation procedure. However, it provides no substantive criteria and no procedural mechanism that would govern such a consultation and define its desirable outcome. It was discussed that a number of these problems may be eliminated if national enforcement authorities engage in direct cooperation, for example, by establishing JITs.

In all, the OECD Convention is part of a much broader legal framework, factual anti-bribery regime that can only be understood by investigating the enforcement of the law in concrete cases. In this context, the interpretation of certain concepts that influence (1) the assertion of jurisdiction, such as the notion of territorial nexus and indirect bribery and (2) the cooperation and coordination of enforcement is absolutely key issue because it determines the functioning of extraterritoriality and its relation to collective action. Hence, the case analysis in Chapters 5 and 6 further extends the findings of this chapter and identifies what elements of this factual regime are dominant and how they function in practice.

References

Acorn, E. (2016) *The Power of Procurement in the Fight against Foreign Bribery*. 2016 OECD Integrity Forum.

Berman, P.S. (2005) 'From International Law to Law and Globalization' 43 Columbia Journal of Transnational Law 485.

Berman, P.S. (2007) 'Global Legal Pluralism' 80 Southern California Law Review 1155.

Colangelo, A. J. (2009) 'Double Jeopardy and Multiple Sovereigns: A Jurisdictional Theory' 86 Washington University Law Quarterly 769.

Corruption Watch (2016) 'Out of Court, Out of Mind: Do Deferred Prosecution Agreements and Corporate Settlements Fail to Deter Overseas Corruption' <http://www.cw-uk.org/wp-content/uploads/2016/03/Corruption-Watch-Out-of-Court-Out-of-Mind.pdf> accessed 19 January 2019.

Cryer, R. (2007) *An Introduction to International Criminal Law and Procedure*. Cambridge: Cambridge University Press.

DOJ and SEC (2012) 'A Resource Guide to the U.S. Foreign Corrupt Practices Act' (2012) 10 <https://www.justice.gov/sites/default/files/criminal-fraud/legacy/2015/01/16/guide.pdf> accessed 27 February 2019.

Doyle, Ch. (2016) 'Federal Conspiracy Law: A Brief Overview' Congressional Research Service, 2 <https://www.fas.org/sgp/crs/misc/R41223.pdf> accessed 31 December 2018.

Ferguson, G. (2015) *Global Corruption: Law, Theory and Practice*. Creative Commons License <http://icclr.law.ubc.ca/global-corruption-law-theory-and-practice> accessed 23 April 2019.

Fine, M. (2011) 'Coordinating UK Bribery Act & FCPA Compliance'. LNT's Ethics & Compliance.

Guzman, A. T. (2011) *Cooperation, Comity, and Competition Policy*. New York: Oxford University Press.

Hill, J. (2003) 'Corporate Criminal Liability in Australia: An Evolving Corporate Governance Technique?' Journal of Business Law 1.

Inazumi, M. (2005) *Universal Jurisdiction in Modern International Law: Expansion of National Jurisdiction for Prosecuting Serious Crimes under International Law*. Antwerpen: Intersentia.

International Bar Association (2009) Report of the Task Force on Extraterritorial Jurisdiction. IBA Legal Practice Division Task Force on Extraterritorial Jurisdiction.

Ireland-Piper, D. (2013) 'Prosecutions of Extraterritorial Criminal Conduct and the Abuse of Rights Doctrine' 9 Utrecht Law Review 68.

Koehler, M. (2010) 'The Facade of FCPA Enforcement' 41 Georgetown Journal of International Law 907.

Lord, N. (2011) 'Regulating Transnational Corporate Bribery in the UK and Germany' (Cardiff University PhD Thesis 2011) <https://orca.cf.ac.uk/26844/1/Nicholas%20Lord_PhD%20Thesis_May%202012%20-%20NEW.pdf> accessed 2 May 2019.

Lord, N. (2016) *Regulating Corporate Bribery in International Business: Anti-corruption in the UK and Germany*. London: Routledge.

Ministry of Justice (2011) *The Bribery Act 2010 Guidance* <https://www.justice.gov.uk/downloads/legislation/bribery-act-2010-guidance.pdf> accessed 27 December 2018.

Monti, G. (2016) 'Independence, Interdependence and Legitimacy: The EU Commission, National Competition Authorities, and the European Competition Network' In D. Ritleng (Ed.) *Independence and Legitimacy in the Institutional System of the European Union* (pp. 180–205). Oxford: Oxford University Press.

Oduor, J. et al. (2014) 'Left Out of the Bargain: Settlements in Foreign Bribery Cases and Implications for Asset Recovery' Stolen Asset Recovery Initiative <http://star.worldbank.org/star/sites/star/files/9781464800863.pdf> accessed 7 January 2019.

OECD (1999) CLN Report on Positive Comity <https://www.oecd.org/daf/competition/prosecutionandlawenforcement/2752161.pdf> accessed 3 May 2019.

OECD (2009) 'Typologies on the Role of Intermediaries in International Business Transactions' OECD.

OECD (2011) Convention on Combating Bribery of Foreign Public Officials in International Business Transactions and Related Documents <http://www.oecd.org/daf/anti-bribery/ConvCombatBribery_ENG.pdf> accessed 25 February 2019.

OECD (2012) Typology on Mutual Legal Assistance in Foreign Bribery Cases <http://www.oecd.org/daf/anti-bribery/TypologyMLA2012.pdf> accessed 3 May 2019.

OECD (2014) Challenges of International Co-operation in Competition Law Enforcement <https://www.oecd.org/daf/competition/Challenges-Competition-Internat-Coop-2014.pdf> accessed 3 May 2019.

Okoth, J. R. A. (2014) *The Crime of Conspiracy in International Criminal Law*. The Hague: Asser Press.

Pieth, M., Low, L. A. and Cullen, P. J. (Eds.) (2007) *The OECD Convention on Bribery: A Commentary*. Cambridge: Cambridge University Press.

Pieth, M., Low, L. A. and Bonucci, N. (Eds.) (2014) *The OECD Convention on Bribery: A Commentary*. Cambridge: Cambridge University Press.

Ryngaert, C.(2008) *Jurisdiction in International Law*. Oxford: Oxford University Press.

Ryan, R. N. (2013) 'The Equity Façade of SEC Disgorgement' 4 Harvard Business Law Review Online.

Schomburg, W. et al. (2012) *Internationale Rechtshilfe in Strafsachen = International Cooperation in Criminal Matters*. München: C. H. Beck.

Van Alstine, M. P. (2012) 'Treaty Double Jeopardy: The OECD Anti-Bribery Convention and the FCPA' 73 Ohio State Law Journal 1321.

Zerk, J. A. (2010) 'Extraterritorial Jurisdiction: Lessons for the Business and Human Rights Sphere from Six Regulatory Areas' (Harvard University, John F. Kennedy School of Government <https://www.hks.harvard.edu/sites/default/files/centers/mrcbg/programs/cri/files/workingpaper_59_zerk.pdf> accessed 25 February 2019.

5 Foreign anti-bribery enforcement schemes

5.1 Introduction

Looking at foreign anti-bribery law from a formalist perspective may lead to misconceptions. From this perspective, national enforcement authorities should charge these that bribed predominantly with anti-bribery charges and the bribers should, at least in some occasions, contest the charges in court. Moreover, common sense may indicate that a bribery scheme related to a project in an African country should constitute a separate case, from a scheme, perpetrated several years later in Asia. These shared premises about enforcement against those who engage in acts of giving a bribe to a foreign public official in order to obtain undue advantage are misleading.

However, many foreign bribery cases bundle separate acts at different times in different jurisdictions, include charges based on accountancy law, AML law, competition law, and other alternative laws, and are resolved by out-of-court settlements. This also means that the enforcement of foreign anti-bribery legislation does not rely only on the provisions of the OECD Convention but operates within a broad substantive and procedural context. This chapter investigates how the most relevant legal concepts such as jurisdiction and indirect bribery function within that broader context, and how the discretion of national enforcement authorities is exercised. The collective action perspective will reveal that problems related to foreign anti-bribery enforcement are about complex institutional dimension of the OECD anti-bribery enforcement regime, rather than about the lack of substantive legal provisions.

The rest of this chapter is organized as follows. Section 2 defines key concepts such as "enforcement action," "case," and "enforcement scheme" and discusses the most important studies of foreign bribery cases and their methodology. Section 3 provides an overview of the most important foreign bribery cases and enforcement trends in the US, the UK, and Germany. The last section presents three "classic" case studies: *the Siemens* bribery scheme, *the Bonny Island* bribery scandal, and *the BAE Systems* bribery scheme (BAE). The qualitative study of these foreign anti-bribery enforcement schemes will explain which legal elements of OECD anti-bribery enforcement regime are important in practice, and will navigate the analysis of a broader set of enforcement schemes in Chapter 6.

5.2 Foreign bribery resolution: formal and functional understanding

Foreign bribery schemes are complex. These schemes not only include bribers and bribed parties, but frequently also third parties that are controlled by or act on behalf of the main parties, and are further complicated by transnational communication channels and payment systems. The complexity of foreign bribery places substantial pressure on national enforcement authorities to be creative. Should prosecutors, for instance, present various acts of bribery as a single, continuing, violation of anti-corruption laws or as multiple violations?[1] Moreover, foreign bribery is usually part of many interrelated corporate processes, including accountancy, tax, and security. Which charges should be used? In one case, foreign bribery charges could be appropriate. Yet, accounting, export, and tax fraud charges could be more appropriate in other, very similar case. These examples show that the provision of enforcement as a public good can be provided by several ways that may differ in their substance and procedure.

The extent to what national enforcement authorities are successful in their effort to enforce foreign anti-bribery laws is conventionally expressed in terms of resolution numbers and sanctions awarded to wrongdoers. There is, however, not a single notion of a foreign bribery resolution. Four main notions are used when discussing foreign anti-bribery enforcement: "settlement," "matter," "case," and "enforcement scheme." These notions are defined as follows:

- *Settlement* is used widely as "any procedure short of a full trial" including, for instance, administrative decisions (Oduor et al., 2014: 18).
- *Case* (in a narrow sense) includes "settlement" and the final "decision" of the court.
- *Matter* is a broader notion than the settlement and the case as it refers to a set of settlements/cases related to the same or similar subject matter. These settlements are concluded in one country with one company or companies in a parent–subsidiary or successor–predecessor relationship if they are sanctioned jointly and severally.[2]
- *Enforcement scheme* refers to the combined set of bribery cases related to the same or similar subject matter. For example, an enforcement scheme may include four bribery settlements with four corporations that acted as business partners and coordinately bribed public officials.

1 Another examples of procedural difficulties are negotiated settlements. Negotiated settlements may constitute *res judicata* in one jurisdiction but not in other jurisdictions.

2 For example, a situation in which a parent company settles with the US authorities and two subsidiaries of the parent plead guilty for related conduct is not considered as three cases but as one matter. The US approach, therefore, is more concerned with facts of a single bribery scheme, whereas the OECD approach, with procedural issues.

The notions of settlement, matter, case, and enforcement scheme are used to formalize substantive and procedural complexities of foreign anti-bribery enforcement.

The problem is that while we measure success in terms of resolution numbers, we know little about the discussed procedural complexities and the subject matters that anti-bribery settlements and cases include. Consider, the below discussed *Siemens* case. Siemens AG accepted responsibility for bribes in projects such as the construction of a metro transit system in Venezuela, the construction of metro trains and signaling devices in China, the building and servicing of power plants in Israel, the installation of mobile telephone service in Bangladesh, and the design and installation of a traffic system in Russia.[3] According to the SEC, Siemens AG made 4,283 bribery payments totaling approximately $1.4 billion between 12 March 2001 and September 2007.[4] All of these payments are bundled into one resolution consisting of seven settlements.[5]

5.2.1 Approaches to study foreign bribery cases

Several approaches are used to study foreign bribery cases. The Foreign Bribery Report of the OECD refers to the term "case" as "a single enforcement action or sanction by a law enforcement agency."[6] The US authorities rather use the term "matter" that includes "a set of related cases involving legal persons and individuals and that 'matter' number is the one recorded in the Enforcement Data Table for the purposes of the monitoring" (Oduor et al., 2014: 148).[7] This means that, for example, if a parent corporation settles with the US authorities and two subsidiaries of the parent plead guilty for the related conduct, the three underlying proceedings are not counted as three cases but as one matter. The US approach, therefore, is more concerned with facts of a single bribery scheme whereas the OECD approach is concerned with procedural issues.

3 Paragraphs 38–72 of the Complaint, *Securities and Exchange Commission vs. Siemens Aktiengesellschaft, No. 08-cv-2167* (15 December 2008).

4 Paragraphs 36 of the Complaint, *Securities and Exchange Commission vs. Siemens Aktiengesellschaft, No. 08-cv-2167* (15 December 2008). The DOJ provides slightly different numbers, see Paragraph 87 of the Statement of Offense, *United States vs. Siemens Aktiengesellschaft, No. 08-cr-367* (15 December 2008).

5 Please note that the *Siemens* matter includes seven settlements between the headquarters, its three subsidiaries and the German and the US authorities, one being reached in 2007 and six in 2008. In the US, the headquarters concluded two settlements, one with the DOJ and one with the SEC.

6 OECD (2014) OECD Foreign Bribery Report: An Analysis of the Crime of Bribery of Foreign Public Officials 11 <http://www.oecd.org/corruption/oecd-foreign-bribery-report-9789264226616-en.htm> accessed 28 December 2018.

7 The US definition is closely connected with the so-called core approach, a method used for calculating the FCPA statistics (see Koehler, 2014: 964).

Furthermore, studies of foreign anti-bribery enforcement include cases based on different substantive criteria. In one case, a similar set of facts may qualify as foreign bribery and in another case as, for example, accounting fraud, money laundering, and commercial bribery. Some studies are narrower, such as the Foreign Bribery Report of the OECD, and focus on violations of Article 1 of the OECD Convention. Other reports such as the OECD monitoring reports are more detailed as they include alternative anti-corruption charges.[8] The most inclusive is an annual report provided by Transparency International (TI). The report includes foreign bribery cases that were sanctioned by wide range of laws, including bribery, money laundering, tax evasion, fraud and violations of accounting, and disclosure requirements.[9] According to this study, for example, the conviction of a corporation of money laundering counts as a foreign bribery case if the money came from the corporation's involvement in foreign bribery.

Consequently, the total number of foreign anti-bribery and related enforcement actions differs. Nevertheless, existing studies indicate that national enforcement authorities have concluded several hundreds of foreign anti-bribery enforcement actions:

1 *OECD Data:* OECD Foreign Bribery report indicates that between 15 February 1999 and 1 June 2014, 427 enforcement actions – 263 individuals and 164 corporations "have been investigated, prosecuted and reached a final law enforcement outcome for the specific crime of bribery of foreign public officials in international business transactions."[10] Other OECD report indicates that at least 253 entities have been sanctioned in criminal, administrative and civil proceedings for foreign bribery between 1999 and the end of 2016. 235 entities have been sanctioned for alternative offenses related to foreign bribery.[11]
2 *TI Exporting Corruption Reports:* For the period 2014–2017, 208 enforcement actions were concluded with sanctions, of which 101 led to substantial sanctions.[12] As noted above, TI included also alternative offenses related to foreign bribery. The TI's count involves some level of discretion as cases involving multiple defendants and charges "are counted as

8 OECD, *Country monitoring of the OECD Anti-Bribery Convention* <http://www.oecd.org/corruption/countrymonitoringoftheoecdanti-briberyconvention.htm> accessed 12 October 2018. See also OECD, 2016 *Data on Enforcement of the Anti-Bribery Convention,* available at <http://www.oecd.org/daf/anti-bribery/Anti-Bribery-Convention-Enforcement-Data-2016.pdf> accessed 14 October 2018.

9 Transparency International, *Exporting Corruption: Progress Report 2018: Assessing Enforcement of the OECD Convention on Combating Foreign Bribery*, available at <https://www.transparency.org/whatwedo/publication/exporting_corruption_2018> accessed 14 October 2018.

10 OECD (2014) OECD Foreign Bribery Report: An Analysis of the Crime of Bribery of Foreign Public Officials 11 <http://www.oecd.org/corruption/oecd-foreign-bribery-report-9789264226616-en.htm> accessed 28 December 2018.

11 OECD, 2016 *Data on Enforcement of the Anti-Bribery Convention* (n 8).

12 Transparency International, *Exporting Corruption: Progress Report 2018* (n 9)118.

one if they are commenced as a single proceeding. If in the course of proceeding cases against different defendants are separated, they may be counted as separate concluded cases."[13]

To conclude, statistical data on foreign anti-bribery enforcement are important because they indicate enforcement patterns and help compare enforcement trends. Yet, given the procedural and substantive complexity of foreign anti-bribery enforcement, we need to interpret enforcement numbers with caution. Qualitative approaches, including the functional understanding of foreign bribery cases, are needed to understand whether, how, and why the provision of enforcement is provided. Before case studies of foreign anti-bribery enforcement are presented, the following section provides an overview of the most important foreign bribery cases and enforcement trends in the US, the UK, and Germany.

5.3 Enforcement in the US, the UK, and Germany

The US, the UK, and Germany are, together with Israel, Italy, Norway, and Switzerland, the only countries that belong to the category of "active enforcers" of the OECD Convention according to the TI analysis.[14] With more than 21% of world exports, the three jurisdictions have high potential to provide enforcement as a public good. This is particularly important if we consider that the vast majority of other countries do not actively enforce their own foreign anti-bribery laws. The following part introduces some basic facts regarding the level of enforcement in the selected jurisdictions. This book provides a comprehensive picture of enforcement as of 1 January 2019. It must be noted that the situation is constantly changing, with new cases and techniques of enforcement coming in. The reader can follow up-to-date databases such as the TRACE Compendium[15] and enforcement reports of legal firms such as the Sherman & Sterling's bi-annual FCPA Digest[16] study forthcoming cases and enforcement trends.

5.3.1 The United States

The US is the leader in the enforcement of foreign anti-bribery laws. Robust enforcement is, however, relatively recent practice as the US has concluded biggest bribery resolutions only after 2007. While between from 2002 to 2006,

13 Transparency International, *Exporting Corruption: Progress Report 2018* (n 9) 118.
14 The US, the UK, and Germany account for 21.2% of world exports. Transparency International, *Exporting Corruption: Progress Report 2018* (n 9) 4.
15 The Trace Compendium <https://www.traceinternational.org/compendium> accessed 11 March 2019.
16 See, for example, FCPA Digest 2019 <https://www.shearman.com/perspectives/2019/01/shearman-fcpa-digest-2019-and-recent-trends-and-patterns-in-fcpa> accessed 11 March 2019.

the DOJ and the SEC conducted in average three enforcement actions against corporations per year, it increased to an average 14.25 enforcement actions between from 2007 to 2014. The US authorities imposed financial penalties, meaning fines, disgorgement, and pre-judgment interest, amounting to $87 million in 2006, $1.8 billion in 2010, and $1.57 billion in 2014.[17]

In recent years, the enforcement trend has changed in a way that the US enforcement was supplemented by the enforcement of other enforcement authorities, mainly from the UK, Brazil, Germany, and the Netherlands. Between from 2016 to 2018, the US authorities lead a number of global anti-bribery enforcement actions that resulted in the award of very high sanctions, in 2017 for instance: *Rolls-Royce* ($800 million globally), *Telia Company* ($966 million globally), *Keppel Offshore & Marine Ltd.* ($422 million globally), SBM Offshore ($238 million in the US). The US authorities imposed financial penalties amounting $2.4 billion in 2016, $958 million in 2017, and $2.2 billion in 2018.[18] The US enforcement schemes represent the vast majority of enforcement actions and cases discussed in this work.

5.3.2 Germany

The German foreign anti-bribery enforcement against corporations occurs at a much lower rate than in the US. The TI data indicate that between from January 2014 to December 2017, the German authorities concluded six major cases compared to 66 major cases concluded by the US authorities. Germany scores the second in the TI rankings because it concluded 43 minor cases compared to 32 minor cases in the US.[19] Furthermore, Germany scores high mainly because of enforcement against natural persons. According to the OECD monitoring reports, between from January 2005 to December 2010, 69 individuals were sanctioned in Germany,[20] Since Phase 3 evaluation and as of December 2017, 259 additional individuals were sanctioned.[21]

German enforcement authorities, however, enforce foreign anti-bribery law against corporations less frequently than against individuals. The Phase 3 report indicates that between 2007 and 2010, six legal persons were awarded an administrative sanction after a court decision,[22] Since Phase 3 evaluation and as of February 2018, 13 additional legal persons were held liable for

17 Shearman & Sterling (2015) FCPA Digest: Cases and Review Releases Relating to Bribes to Foreign Officials under the Foreign Corrupt Practices Act of 1977, iv–vi <http://www.shearman.com/~/media/Files/NewsInsights/Publications/2015/01/Recent-Trends-and-Patterns-FCPA-Digest-FCPA-LT-010515.pdf> accessed 22 December 2018.

18 Stanford Law School, *Foreign Corrupt Practices Act Clearing House* <http://fcpa.stanford.edu/statistics-analytics.html?tab=2> accessed 18 December 2018.

19 Transparency International, *Exporting Corruption: Progress Report 2018* (n 9) 10–11.

20 OECD (2011) Phase 3 Report on Implementing the OECD Anti-Bribery Convention in Germany, 9.

21 OECD (2018) Phase 4 Report on Implementing the OECD Anti-Bribery Convention in Germany, 13.

22 OECD, Germany: Phase 3 (n 20) 22–23.

foreign bribery.[23] This study has not identified any other major case as of December 2018. Therefore, between from 2007 to 2018, Germany concluded 19 corporate enforcement actions in total.

Out of the 19 corporate enforcement actions, nine include substantial penalties. These nine actions relate, in fact, to six enforcement schemes:

1 Three cases relate to the *Siemens* enforcement scheme.[24]
2 German prosecutors sanctioned two units of MAN AG, the Truck unit,[25] and the Turbo engines unit.[26] In 2009, MAN AG has paid €250 million in fines and investigation costs.[27]
3 In 2011, The Munich I Public Prosecutor's Office imposed a fine against Ferrostaal AG in the amount of nearly EUR 140 million.[28]
4 In 2011, Linde AG allegedly agreed to pay to the state of Bavaria €35 million to resolve corruption allegations.[29]
5 In 2014, Rheinmetall Defence Electronics settled with the Bremen prosecutor office and agreed to pay a EUR 37 million fine.[30]
6 In February 2018, Airbus Space and Defence GmbH settled with the Munich I Prosecutor Office and agreed to pay a EUR 81.25 million fine.[31]

Unfortunately, many German enforcement actions cannot be analyzed in detail because the German authorities rarely publicize detailed information about concluded foreign bribery cases, for what Germany faces criticism by the OECD.[32]

23 OECD, Germany: Phase 4 (n 21) 13.
24 The scheme is analyzed in Section 5.5 below.
25 Stolen Asset Recovery Initiative, *MAN/Trucks Unit* <http://star.worldbank.org/corruption-cases/node/20102> accessed 5 February 2017, referring to the *Decision of Munich I Public Prosecution office of 10 December 2009 against the Trucks unit of MAN*. The decision based on §§130 and 30 OWiG; awarded fine was €75.3 million.
26 Stolen Asset Recovery Initiative, *MAN/Turbo Engines Unit* <http://star.worldbank.org/corruption-cases/node/20103> accessed 5 February 2017, referring to the *Decision of a Munich I Regional Court of 10 December 2009 against the Turbo engines Unit of MAN*. The decision based on §§334 and 222 StGB; awarded fine was €75.3 million.
27 Letzien, C. (2014) *MAN AG Discloses $344 Million in Penalties and Costs for Bribe Scandal*. The FCPA Blog <http://www.fcpablog.com/blog/2014/4/10/man-ag-discloses-344-million-in-penalties-and-costs-for-brib.html#sthash.SRsMJcdb.dpuf> accessed 18 December 2018.
28 OECD, Germany: Phase 4 (n 21) 132. Ferrostaal AG is a former subsidiary of MAN SE.
29 Trace, *Trace Compendium: LINDE* <https://www.traceinternational.org/TraceCompendium/Detail/492?class=casename_searchresult&type=1> accessed 18 December 2018. Palazzolo, J. (2011) *Linde To Pay 35 Million Euros To Settle Corruption Allegations*. The Wall Street Journal <http://blogs.wsj.com/corruption-currents/2011/06/08/linde-to-pay-35-million-euros-to-settle-corruption-allegations/> accessed 18 December 2018.
30 OECD, Germany: Phase 4 (n 21) 134. *Case Bremen 2013/1 (Rheinmetall Defence Electronics)*. Note that some cases do not include a corporate liability. Notably, in *Case Bremen 2013/2 (Atlas Elektronik GmbH)* only a forfeiture of EUR 48 million was imposed.
31 OECD, Germany: Phase 4 (n 21) 135.
32 OECD, Germany: Phase 3 (n 20) 25–26. OECD, Germany: Phase 4 (n 21) 11.

5.3.3 The United Kingdom

The UK is the third most active enforcer of foreign anti-bribery laws. The TI data indicate that between from January 2014 to December 2017, the UK concluded nine major cases and two minor cases.[33] According to the OECD monitoring reports, from 2009 to January 2017, the UK enforcement authorities convicted 13 individuals and 8 legal persons. Between from February 2017 and December 2018, the UK enforcement authorities convicted nine natural persons in still ongoing *F.H. Bertling* matter related to shipping contracts in Angola.[34]

Before the UK authorities started enforcing the Bribery Act more actively, the SFO concluded several corporate enforcement actions under the old UK anti-corruption laws. Regarding criminal enforcement, the first case under the UK's identification doctrine was concluded in *Mabey & Johnson* where the corporation bribed officials in Jamaica, Ghana, and Iraq, and as a result received £6.6 million criminal sanction.[35] The bribes were discovered during a civil proceeding initiated by *Mabey & Johnson* against the former employees of its agent. In *BAE*, bribes related to defense and security systems in Saudi Arabia, Central and Eastern Europe, and Africa, the SFO faced government pressure to stop the investigation because of national economic interests.[36] Last, the UK cooperated with the US in *Innospec*, bribery of Iraqi and Indonesian officials at refineries in order to secure the supply of chemicals, settling for £8.3 million.[37] Besides *Mabey & Johnson*, *Innospec*, and *BAE*, there has not been any remarkable criminal enforcement until November 2015.

The application of the Bribery Act is a very recent trend. The SFO applied the Bribery Act for the first time in December 2014, charging Gary L. West and Stuard J. Stone in relation to the *Sustainable AgroEnergy* fraud scheme.[38] When it comes to legal persons, no enforcement action under the Bribery Act had been successfully completed until November 2015, when the SFO

33 Transparency International, *Exporting Corruption: Progress Report 2018* (n 9) 10–11.

34 Note that there are also other corruption cases such *as Skansen Interiors*, the first conviction for failure to prevent – domestic – bribery, and *Tesco Stores*, related to accounting practice. These are, however, not cases of international bribery.

35 Serious Fraud Office, *Mabey & Johnson Ltd Sentencing* (25 September 2009) in Trace, *Trace Compendium: Mabey & Johnson* <http://star.worldbank.org/corruption-cases/sites/corruption-cases/files/documents/arw/Mabey_Johnson_UK_SFO_Press_Release_Sentencing_Sep_25_2009.pdf> accessed 5 February 2017.

36 *Regina vs. Bae Systems Plc (Note for Opening, 22 November 2010).*

37 *Regina vs. Innospec Limited, [2010] EW Misc 7(EWCC)* (26 March 2010). Serious Fraud Office, *Innospec Ltd* (Case Information) <https://www.sfo.gov.uk/cases/innospec-ltd/> accessed 24 December 2018. See the criticism of the settlement by Lord Justice Thomas Judiciary of England and Wales, *In the Crown Court at Southwark Regina v Innospec Limited Sentencing remarks of Lord Justice Thomas* (26 March 2010).

38 Serious Fraud Office, *City Directors Convicted in £23m Green Biofuel Trial* (Press Release 5 December 2014) <https://www.sfo.gov.uk/2014/12/05/city-directors-convicted-23m-green-biofuel-trial/> accessed 24 December 2018.

settled with ICBC Standard Bank for $33 million. The ICBC enforcement action, related to a bribery to carrying out a private placement on behalf of the Government of Tanzania, highlights the importance of DPAs in the UK enforcement system. The *ICBC* was not only the first application of Section 7 of the Bribery Act, charging the bank for failure to prevent foreign bribery, but also the first UK DPA.[39] DPA was also used in XYZ, a company not yet named, has agreed to pay £6.5 million and in *Rolls-Royce*. The *Rolls-Royce*, British engineering giant, has been the biggest enforcement scheme in the history of the UK foreign anti-bribery enforcement. *Rolls-Royce* indicates how the use of DPA allowed the US, the UK, and Brazilian enforcement authorities to negotiate and split global settlement. The part of this global bribery scheme that was covered by the SFO resulted in a fine of £497 million. The US enforcement element yielded $170 million, and Brazilians $25.6 million.

Despite the recent increase in DPAs, a small number of criminal corporate prosecutions conducted by the SFO has been to a certain extent complemented by civil recovery orders, and enforcement actions of other UK bodies, most importantly the FCA a fiscal institution, and the Crown Office & Procurator Fiscal Service, a criminal prosecutor in Scotland.[40] First, the biggest civil recoveries were concluded in *Macmillan*,[41] approximately £11.26 million, and *MW Kellog*,[42] approximately £7 million. The latter is discussed as part of the *Bonny Island* in-depth study.[43] Second, the FCA is also significant because it concluded four enforcement actions related to foreign bribery against financial institutions. Most importantly, in September 2009, the FCA charged Aon Limited with £5.25 million when the company also settled with the DOJ and the SEC for $16.2 million.[44] Later on, in July 2011, the FCA

39 *Serious Fraud Office and Standard Bank PLC, Approved Judgement of the Crown Court at Southwark* (30 November 2015) <https://www.judiciary.gov.uk/wp-content/uploads/2015/11/sfo-v-standard-bank_Final_1.pdf> accessed 23 December 2018.

40 See, for instance, *Crown Office & Procurator Fiscal Service vs. International Tubular Services* (17 December 2014).

41 Serious Fraud Office, *Action on Macmillan Publishers Limited* (Press Release 22 July 2011) http://www.ethic-intelligence.com/wp-content/uploads/macmillan_sfo_press_release.pdf accessed 5 February 2017.

42 Serious Fraud Office, *MW Kellogg Ltd to Pay £7 million in SFO High Court Action* (16 February 2011) <https://www.sfo.gov.uk/press-room/press-releasearchive/press-releases-2011/mw-kellogg-ltd-to-pay-7-million-in-sfo-high-court-action.aspx> accessed 1 February 2015.

43 See Section 5.6.4 below.

44 Financial Conduct Authority, *FSA Final Notice 2009: Aon Limited*, (6 January 2009) <https://www.fca.org.uk/publication/final-notices/aon.pdf> accessed 23 December 2018. For the US settlements see *Securities and Exchange Commission vs. Aon Corporation, No. 11-cv-2256* (20 December 2011). Department of Justice, *Aon Corporation Agrees to Pay a $1.76 Million Criminal Penalty to Resolve Violations of the Foreign Corrupt Practices Act* (20 December 2011) <https://www.justice.gov/opa/pr/aon-corporation-agrees-pay-176-million-criminal-penalty-resolve-violations-foreign-corrupt> accessed 23 December 2018.

charged also Willis Limited with £6,895 million that has been the largest fine related to foreign bribery imposed by the FCA or the FSA to date.[45]

The analysis of the UK enforcement approach, similar to the German approach, is limited because the UK authorities are not praised for their transparency. The OECD in the Phase 3 report provides that "the full facts of several of these cases are not available. Consequently, it is unclear whether the sanctions imposed in these cases were effective, proportionate and dissuasive as required by the Convention."[46] It must be noted, however, that the Phase 3 follow-up report and Phase 4 report refer to an improvement in the UK approach that can be, for example, seen in SFO's DPAs with *Standard Bank* and *Rolls-Royce*.[47]

5.3.4 Concluding remarks

The level of anti-bribery enforcement is uneven in the selected jurisdictions, both as to the amount and transparency thereof. On the one hand, the US authorities regularly impose sanctions as high as hundreds of million dollars and publish settlements. On the other hand, Germany and the UK lag behind. While Germany occasionally enforces huge cases, such as *Siemens*, *MAN*, *Ferrostaal*, and *Airbus Space*, they are rarely public. The UK differs from Germany because it concluded larger amount of corporate cases and published more information about them. However, the UK enforcement actions are, with the exception of Rolls-Royce, much smaller than the US, and usually linked to the US enforcement.

5.4 Qualitative study – analytical framework

The enforcement of foreign anti-bribery legislation does not rely only on the provisions of the OECD Convention but operates within a broad substantive and procedural context. This section illustrates how the most relevant legal concepts function within that broader context. The analysis of three major foreign anti-bribery enforcement actions will show how enforcement authorities exercise their discretion, including which legal procedures, substantive charges, and cooperation mechanism they use. Before discussing the enforcement actions, the following part presents the analytical framework of key legal aspects that are addressed by the qualitative study.

45 Financial Conduct Authority, *FSA Final Notice: Willis Limited* (21 July 2011) <https://www.fca.org.uk/publication/final-notices/willis_ltd.pdf> accessed 23 December 2018. The FCA imposed higher fines related to money laundering, for example, Barclays Bank was sanctioned £72 million. Financial Conduct Authority, *FSA Final Notice: Barclays Bank plc* (25 November 2015) <https://www.fca.org.uk/publication/final-notices/barclays-bank-nov-2015.pdf> accessed 23 December 2018.

46 OECD, Germany: Phase 3 (n 20) 8.

47 OECD (2017) Phase 4 Report on Implementing the OECD Anti-Bribery Convention in the United Kingdom, 59–60.

The collective action perspective indicates that problems related to foreign anti-bribery enforcement are about complex institutional dimension of the OECD anti-bribery enforcement regime, rather than about the lack of substantive legal provisions. The main legal aspects of this dimension are (1) the offense of bribery (2) jurisdiction, including the problem of indirect bribery, and (3) cooperation and coordination.

5.4.1 Offense of bribery

When studying foreign anti-bribery schemes from the perspective of collective action, one needs to focus on the use of substantive laws covering international bribery. The schemes will illustrate how enforcement authorities charge MNCs. The discussion will pay attention to the nature of legal provisions applied by enforcement authorities, the character of legal persons who were charged, and consider other legal and factual information contextualizing enforcement schemes. For example, in *Siemens*, it will be seen that a thicket of procedural and substantive laws may cover foreign bribery, and that one enforcement scheme can be divided into multiple interrelated settlements covering a set of thousands of individual bribes.

5.4.2 Jurisdiction

Collective action is to a large extent dependent on the ability of enforcement authorities to stretch their jurisdiction and sanction foreign corporations in foreign markets. The enforcement schemes illustrate how enforcement authorities establish their jurisdiction. This depends on how the principles of territoriality and nationality are interpreted, including what territorial nexus establishes sufficient connection with the US territory. Furthermore, the question of jurisdiction is closely connected with the interpretation of concepts related to corporate liability such as corporate control, including ownership and factual control, and the liability for acts of intermediaries. Last, the application of conspiracy charges plays a key role in asserting jurisdiction. For example, *Bonny Island* illustrates how the US authorities use conspiracy charges in order to sanctions foreign corporations that act completely outside the territory of the US.

5.4.3 Cooperation and coordination

Cooperation and coordination between national enforcement authorities can be supported by a number of formal legal tools as well as by informal interactions between enforcement authorities. The analysis will focus on three types of information:

a Whether enforcement authorities cooperate before the final resolution of a case, for example, by using MLA;

b Whether and how they coordinate their enforcement before, at the time, and after the final resolution of an enforcement action by using, for example, the doctrine of international comity and applying the principle of *ne bis in idem*.

c Whether and how they engage in more direct forms of cooperation such as by establishing JITs.

5.4.4 Types of foreign bribery schemes

The complexity of foreign anti-bribery enforcement is also reflected in a way how foreign bribery enforcement schemes are structured. The discussion below introduces three types of foreign anti-bribery enforcement schemes.

1 *Endemic bribery*: First, prosecutors focus on situations encompassing thousands of payments in substantively unrelated projects. In fact, these schemes sanction the continuation of an endemic bribery scheme that is attributable to one company. This type of scheme will be illustrated on *Siemens*, one of the biggest enforcement schemes in the history of foreign anti-bribery enforcement. *Siemens* is understood by scholars and practitioners as the one that has changed the global approach toward foreign bribery. It also provides a great deal of material for studying how the US and German foreign bribery laws function, and how these and other authorities cooperate and coordinate when conducting global settlements.

2 *We will catch them all*: Second, authorities in some cases include multiple companies into one enforcement scheme. This means that they sanction together multiple firms that conspire to bribe in concrete projects. This type of scheme will be illustrated on the *Bonny Island* scheme that, similarly to the *Siemens* scheme, has gained notoriety in the field of anti-corruption. In *Bonny Island*, acts of foreign bribery are relatively concrete. What is important is that the scheme shows how extraterritoriality operates when it comes to complicated systems of corporate veils that were involved in the bribery process. *Bonny Island* includes multiple settlements agreed between enforcement authorities and a number of companies that conspired with each other or aided and abated the commission of foreign bribery.

3 *International bribery and alternative laws*: Third, when we refer to a substantive complexity of international bribery, what we mean is that foreign anti-bribery enforcement is in many cases based on alternative laws, such as export laws. There are many reasons why to use alternative laws, it may be simply a matter of perspective, some cases can be more about failures of compliance system rather than about bribery. In other cases, alternative laws can stretch the jurisdictional reach of enforcement authorities and offset other weaknesses of foreign anti-bribery laws. This substantive fragmentation will be illustrated on the *BAE* scheme. In *BAE*, these were the US export laws that helped to make up for potential

limitations of the US jurisdiction. What is more, *BAE* is the most significant scheme that involved UK authorities. *BAE* illustrates how the UK foreign anti-bribery approach proved highly ineffective in capturing huge enforcement schemes. The failure of UK criminal justice system to investigate and prosecute the BAE scheme in full incentivized a legislative change and the adoption of the Bribery Act.

These typologies illustrate that foreign anti-bribery enforcement is based on a broad menu of legislative tools whose application is largely a matter of enforcement strategy adopted by the enforcement authorities.

5.5 Endemic bribery: *Siemens*

5.5.1 The core of the enforcement scheme

Siemens Aktiengesellschaft (Siemens AG) was, at the end of 2008, a multinational corporation organized under German law with main offices in Berlin and Munich.[48] As a global market player in telecommunications, electronics, electrical engineering, transportation, and medicine, the Siemens Group employed roughly 405,000 employees and operated through its subsidiaries, agents, and other groups and individuals in some 190 countries.[49] Since 12 March 2001, Siemens has been listed on the NYSE.[50]

5.5.2 Offense of bribery

The Siemens Group was subject to various corruption scandals in multiple jurisdictions. Already in 2006, the Italian authorities sanctioned Siemens AG for bribing the Italian energy utility corporation Enel.[51] The German prosecutor in Darmstadt consequently opened a criminal investigation against several Siemens employees to complement the Italian enforcement. The German authorities at that time did not sanction the company.[52]

The core of *Siemens* enforcement scheme lays in the US and German cases that cover business projects in many countries. For instance, the official documents provide that Siemens AG accepted responsibility for bribes in projects such as the construction of a metro transit system in Venezuela, the construction of metro trains and signaling devices in China, the building and

48 In different context, *Siemens* was analyzed in Hock (2017: 329–336).

49 Siemens, *Annual Report 2009,* 36–37 <http://www.siemens.com/investor/pool/en/investor_relations/e09_00_gb2009.pdf> accessed 21 December 2018.

50 Paragraph 2 of the Statement of Offense, *United States vs. Siemens* (n 4).

51 Stolen Asset Recovery Initiative, *Siemens AG (Italy Settlement)* (2013).

52 The OECD points out that in *Enel*, individuals were charged with an offense other than foreign bribery because a German court did not consider Enel's representatives as foreign public officials. OECD, Germany: Phase 3 (n 20) 13.

servicing of power plants in Israel, the installation of mobile telephone service in Bangladesh, and the design and installation of a traffic system in Russia. Siemens AG also participated, via its French, Turkish, and other subsidiaries in the Oil-For-Food Program bribery scheme in Iraq.[53]

The German and the US enforcement authorities used a number of charges in order to sanction the Siemens Group. In a first stage, Germany and the US sanctioned Siemens AG for paying bribes. The SEC concluded that between 12 March 2001 and September 2007, Siemens AG made 4283 bribery payments totaling approximately $1.4 billion.[54] Foreign public officials received bribes through a variety of mechanisms such as direct payments to business consultants, payments to intermediaries, and slush funds controlled by non-Siemens trustees. Siemens even established special cash desks in their offices that served its employees to withdraw cash for the purpose of bribery.[55]

In the second stage, Siemens AG was sanctioned for violating German law and US law because it systematically circumvented internal controls and falsified books and records. Siemens AG was falsifying its books and records already before the criminalization of foreign bribery by the OECD Convention because some of its bribes could have been prosecuted based on domestic anti-corruption laws. During the German and US investigations, it became clear that "[f]rom the 1990s through 2007, Siemens engaged in a systematic and widespread effort to make and to hide hundreds of millions of dollars in bribe payments across the globe."[56] Siemens, for example, used off-books accounts, false invoices and consulting agreements.[57]

The main line of the US and German cases consists of seven settlements between the company and the German and the US authorities, one being reached in 2007 and six in 2008 (the main case). The following overview shows these settlements in more detail.

1 4 October 2007: Germany, Munich Public Prosecution Office vs. Siemens AG. The Munich district court ordered Siemens AG to pay €201 million ($285 million) for bribes of Siemens' Telecommunications Unit in Russia, Nigeria, and Libya. €200 million included unlawfully obtained economic advantages; €1 million was an additional administrative fine.[58]

53 Paragraphs 38–72 of the Complaint, *SEC vs. Siemens* (n 3).

54 Paragraph 36 of the Complaint, *SEC vs. Siemens* (n 3). The DOJ provides slightly different numbers, see Paragraph 87 of the Statement of Offense, *United States vs. Siemens* (n 4).

55 Paragraph 87 of the Statement of Offense, *United States vs. Siemens* (n 4).

56 United States Department of Justice, *Transcript of Press Conference Announcing Siemens AG and Three Subsidiaries Plead Guilty to Foreign Corrupt Practices Act Violations* (15 December 2008) <https://www.justice.gov/archive/opa/pr/2008/December/08-opa-1112.html> accessed 21 December 2018.

57 Ibid.

58 Siemens, *Annual Report 2007*, 162 <http://www.siemens.com/investor/pool/en/investor_relations/financial_publications/annual_reports/2007/e07_00_gb2007.pdf> accessed 21 December 2018.

2 15 December 2008: Siemens AG vs. Germany, Munich Public Prosecution Office. This settlement was part of the main case that Germany coordinated with the US authorities (see ad 3–5 below). The Munich district court ordered Siemens to pay €394.75 million ($529 million) – unlawfully obtained economic advantage, and €250,000 – an administrative penalty.
3 15 December 2008: United States vs. Siemens AG, DOJ. On the same day as the German authorities, the DOJ settled with Siemens for $448.5 million, a criminal fine. Furthermore, sanctions also included implementation of a rigorous compliance system and a four-year review by an independent compliance monitor.[59]
4 15 December 2008: United States vs. Siemens S. A. (Argentina)/United States v. Siemens Bangladesh Limited/United States vs. Siemens S. A. (Venezuela). In three separate proceedings, the DOJ settled with three wholly owned Siemens' subsidiaries. For each of them, the DOJ imposed a $500,000 criminal fine.[60]
5 15 December 2008: United States vs. Siemens AG, SEC. The SEC in a civil proceeding also settled with Siemens AG, which agreed to pay $350 million in a disgorgement of wrongful profits.

The Siemens case shows that the German and the US settlements cover a broad range of illicit conduct including substantively unrelated business projects. *Table 5.1* shows an overview of charges that were used in *Siemens*. The German enforcement authorities concluded two enforcement actions. In the 2007 enforcement against Siemens' Telecommunications Unit, the German court held Siemens AG liable as part of the criminal proceedings, pursuant to §30 OWiG in conjunction with §334 StGB (offering bribe) and §266(1) StGB (breach of trust), held against its former employees. This enforcement action relates to crimes of specific individuals.[61] However, one year later, the German authorities imposed regulatory fines independently from a prosecution of natural persons and focused on the systemic character of the Siemens bribing. They based their claim on the application of §30(1) OWiG and an exception under §30(4).[62] Moreover, they applied §30 OWiG in conjunction with §130 OWiG, which allowed them to cover the breach of a supervision duty, based on acts of lower-ranked employees that were allowed to bribe because of insufficient supervision by managers and other relevant employees.[63]

59 For calculation of the fine and its justification, see Department's Sentencing Memorandum, *United States vs. Siemens Aktiengesellschaft/Argentina/Bangladesh/Venezuela, No. 08-cr-367* (15 December 2008) 12–25.
60 Ibid 10–11.
61 Note that in Germany, corporate liability is to a large extent tied with the liability of natural persons.
62 See the discussion in Section 4.4.1 (German law).
63 The settlement is available online, see *Staatsanwaltschaft München vs. Siemens Aktiengesellschaft (Bußgeldbescheid)* (3 December 2008) <https://www.siemens.com/press/pool/de/events/2008-12-PK/MucStaats.pdf> accessed 21 December 2018.

Table 5.1 Charges in Siemensa

Abbreviations *C = Conspiracy*	*Settlement US*			
Relevant Provisions	***Anti-Bribery*** *§ 78dd-1,2 or 3*		***(1): Books and Records*** *§§78m(b)(2)(A)* ***(2): Internal Controls*** *78m(b)(2)(B)* ***(3): Knowingly*** *78m(b)5*	
	DOJ	*SEC*	*DOJ*	*SEC*
Siemens AG		**78dd1**	**(1)(2)(3)**	**(1)(2)(3)**
Siemens Argentina			**C- (1)(3)**	
Siemens Bangladesh	**C - 78dd3**		**C- (1)(3)**	
Siemens Venezuela	**C - 78dd3**		**C- (1)(3)**	
	Settlement Germany			
Relevant Provisions	**Criminal Proceeding Against Individual** 30 OWiG + STgB		**Independent** 30 (4) OWiG + 130 OWiG	
Siemens AG (2007)	30 OWiG + 334/266(1) STgB			
Siemens AG (2008)			30 (1)(4) OWiG + 130 OWiG	

a Branislav Hock "Transnational Bribery: When Is Extraterritoriality Appropriate?" (2017) 11 Charleston Law Review 305, 335.

The US enforcement includes criminal settlements with the DOJ and a civil settlement with the SEC. The DOJ settled with Siemens AG based on a violation of the FCPA (1) internal controls and (2) books and records provisions under 15 U.S.C. §§78m(b)(2)(A), 78m(b)(2)(B),78m(b)(5), and 78ff(a). While the DOJ took into account many individual acts when determining a criminal fine, the settlement punished a systemic failure of company. The SEC acted similarly as the DOJ but charged Siemens AG not only with the books and records, and internal provisions but also with the anti-bribery provisions under 15 U.S.C. §§78dd-1. The DOJ did not charge Siemens AG with a violation of the anti-bribery provisions, despite the language of the settlement giving the impression that the DOJ collected sufficient evidence to do so.

Furthermore, the settlements with the Siemens headquarters are complemented by relatively minor charges against Siemens foreign subsidiaries.[64] These subsidiaries were bribing foreign public officials on behalf of their headquarters and caused that Siemens AG recorded these bribes as legitimate expenses in its books and records. By that reason, the DOJ charged the subsidiaries with the conspiracy to violate the FCPA books and records provisions under 15 U.S.C. §§78m(b)(2)(A), §§78m(b)(5) (see Sections 4.4.2 and 6.6).[65] In addition, Siemens Bangladesh and Siemens Venezuela were charged with conspiracy to violate the anti-bribery provisions under 15 U.S.C. §§78dd-3.

Last, after the US and German resolutions, many other jurisdictions investigated and sanctioned Siemens. The World Bank, Nigeria and Greece concluded the most significant enforcement actions.[66] First, the World Bank settled in July 2009 with Siemens in relation to its co-financed project in Russia. The consequences for Siemens were significant as it agreed to refrain from bidding on World Bank projects for two years, to dedicate $100 million to combat corruption, and the World Bank debarred Siemens's Russian subsidiary for four years.[67] Second, in November 2010, Siemens settled in Nigeria based on the Nigerian domestic anti-corruption law. The settlement is confidential but secondary sources provide that the sanction of $46 million was paid to the Nigerian government.[68] Third, in April 2012, the Greek parliament adopted an ad hoc legislation that allowed Greece to settle with Siemens AG for approximately €270 million ($355.7 million). Due to a gen-

64 All three subsidiaries were charged $500,000.

65 See §78m(b)(5) provides that "No person shall knowingly circumvent or knowingly fail to implement a system of internal accounting controls or knowingly falsify any book, record, or account" […].

66 For the overview of the scheme see Trace, *Trace Compendium: Siemens AG* <http://www.traceinternational.org/TraceCompendium/Detail/124?class=casename_searchresult&type=1> accessed 21 December 2018.

67 World Bank (2009) *Siemens to Pay $100m to Fight Corruption as Part of World Bank Group Settlement* < https://star.worldbank.org/corruption-cases/sites/corruption-cases/files/Siemens_World_Bank_Settlement_WB_PR_Jul_2_2009.pdf> accessed 6 May 2019.

68 Trace, *Trace Compendium: Halliburton/KBR* <http://www.traceinternational.org/TraceCompendium/Detail/15?type=1> accessed 23 December 2018.

eral character of the settlement and a special immunity granted to Siemens AG for all bribes until the day of the settlement, it is not clear what particular projects the settlement covered (Oduor et al., 2014: 134).

5.5.3 Jurisdiction

The US settlements with Siemens show three relevant aspects of the US enforcement: (1) how jurisdiction over foreign issuers is assessed, (2) what constitutes territorial nexus with the US, and (3) how jurisdiction is asserted over foreign subsidiaries of foreign issuers.

1 Every issuer can be charged with the record-keeping and internal controls provisions

   Although it may be true that Siemens AG is a German-based corporation, Siemens AG was as of 12 March 2001, listed on the NYSE. Thus, it qualified as an "issuer" under 15 U.S.C. §78dd-l(a). In this context, the US authorities do not need to identify the interstate commerce nexus in order to establish their territorial jurisdiction. By virtue of this status, Siemens AG was obliged to comply with the books and records, and internal controls provisions of the FCPA. For the assertion of jurisdiction, it is not relevant whether or not these that bribe foreign government officials are in fact in the territory of the US.[69] A more detailed discussion about how issuers can be charged with these provisions is provided in Chapter 6 below.[70]

2 Interstate commerce nexus – broad definition

   The SEC adopted a different approach than the DOJ because it charged Siemens AG, besides breaches of internal controls, and books and records provisions, with the violation of the anti-bribery provisions. As Siemens AG is a foreign issuer, the nationality principle does not apply, and the SEC had to identify relevant connection with the US territory – the interstate commerce nexus.[71] In the case at hand, the SEC provided an extensive list of situations that qualified as the use of interstate commerce. Accordingly, the SEC claims territorial jurisdictions if an issuer is:

   a Involving US-based subsidiaries and their employees in the bribery schemes;
   b Financing projects by the World Bank or the US Export–Import Bank;
   c Making illegal payments through US banks;

69 Statement of Offense, *United States vs. Siemens* (n 4) 1–2.

70 Regarding the books and records, and internal control provisions, see Section 6.4.3.

71 See Figure 4.1: Jurisdiction under the anti-bribery provisions of the FCPA (Section 4.7.3). Note that books and records, and internal control charges do not require the interstate commerce nexus.

d Using US-based companies as intermediaries, business consultants, and holders of slush funds;
e Conducting meetings in the US in furtherance of a bribery scheme; and
f Transmitting mail, electronic mail, and facsimile messages into and out of the US.[72]

3 Charging foreign subsidiaries of a foreign issuer

The DOJ also asserted territorial jurisdiction over the Argentinian, Venezuelan, and Bangladeshi subsidiaries that qualified as persons "other than an issuer or a domestic concern."[73] The jurisdiction can be considered as extraterritorial because the subsidiaries were not charged directly under §78dd-3 but under conspiracy charges. It means that the liability of the subsidiaries was derived from acts of their co-conspirators, through which they allegedly acted. Furthermore, the DOJ states that the original offense was committed by related individuals, agents, and consulting firms known or unknown while at least one acted within the US territory.[74] Furthermore, it must be noted that also the violations of the books and records, and internal controls provisions were based on conspiracy charges. It illustrates that the US authorities can sanction a foreign subsidiary of a foreign issuer even if the subsidiary could not be sanctioned independently. This may be in cases when the subsidiary's agents act while in the territory of the US, for example by channeling illegal payments through US banks.

The relationship between a parent company and its foreign subsidiaries was also an issue in Germany, but German authorities did not prosecute the Siemens foreign subsidiaries; rather, they sanctioned Siemens AG. Germany had jurisdiction because Siemens AG was a corporation headquartered in Germany and organized under German law. This status required Siemens AG to comply with German foreign anti-bribery laws since February 1999 when they entered into force. In addition, *Siemens* shows that the application of §30(4) OWiG is relatively flexible because the identity of a natural person violating German anti-bribery laws was not needed to sanction Siemens AG.

5.5.4 Cooperation and coordination

Siemens is the first truly global enforcement scheme that includes effective cooperation and coordination of foreign anti-bribery enforcement between multiple national enforcement authorities. The emergence of these global cooperative schemes, as will be discussed in the next chapter, is becoming

72 Statement of Offense, *United States vs. Siemens* (n 4) 32–33.
73 15 U.S.C. §78dd-3.
74 See for instance Statement of Offense, *United States vs. Siemens S.A. (Argentina), No. 08-cr-368*, 9, 11–13; Statement of Offense, *United States vs. Siemens S.A. (Venezuela), No. 08-cr-370*, 5–6, 9.

an enforcement pattern. From the perspective of collective action, *Siemens* illustrates three levels of cooperation and coordination between the US authorities and the German authorities:

a Cooperation before the final resolution of a case by using MLA.

The DOJ in its press release refers to Article 9 of the OECD Convention and states: "The Department and the SEC closely collaborated with the Munich Public Prosecutor's Office in bringing these cases."[75] Most importantly, the US authorities and the German authorities shared information and evidence by applying MLA provisions of the OECD Convention.[76] Moreover, also the SEC acknowledges assistance of the Prosecutor General in Munich, and the UK Financial Services Authority and the Hong Kong Securities and Futures Commission.[77]

b Coordination at all stages of investigation and prosecution.

All relevant enforcement authorities highlighted that the Siemens case was coordinated throughout the entire process of investigation and resolution. For example, the 2008 German settlement states that an administrative fine $250,000 is sufficient because it expected high criminal fines to be imposed by the US authorities. The German district court made also clear that the disgorgement and the administrative fine in the 2008 settlement did not overlap with the previous German settlement in 2007.[78] Furthermore, the SEC confirmed the coordination between the US and Germany by stating that the disgorgement of wrongful profits did not "include profits factored into Munich's fine."[79]

c More direct form of cooperation – parallel investigation.

The coordination through all stages of investigation and prosecution was possible because of a more direct means of cooperation. Even if the US authorities mainly refer to the use of MLA, the authorities cooperated more informally. Acting Assistant Attorney General Friedrich, for example, stated that "we have worked from the beginning in close cooperation with German law enforcement. Indeed, this case began with the execution of searches by German authorities in November of 2006."[80]

75 United States Department of Justice, *Siemens AG and Three Subsidiaries Plead Guilty to Foreign Corrupt Practices Act Violations and Agree to Pay $450 Million in Combined Criminal Fines* (Press Release 15 December 2008) <https://www.justice.gov/archive/opa/pr/2008/December/08-crm-1105.html> accessed 21 December 2018.

76 United States Department of Justice, *Siemens AG and Three Subsidiaries Plead Guilty to Foreign Corrupt Practices Act Violations and Agree to Pay $450 Million in Combined Criminal Fines* (Press Release 15 December 2008) <https://www.justice.gov/archive/opa/pr/2008/December/08-crm-1105.html> accessed 21 December 2018.

77 Securities and Exchange Commission, *SEC Charges Siemens AG for Engaging in Worldwide Bribery* (Press Release 15 December 2008) <https://www.sec.gov/news/press/2008/2008-294.htm> accessed 21 December 2018.

78 *Staatsanwaltschaft München vs. Siemens (Bußgeldbescheid)* (n 63).

79 Securities and Exchange Commission, *SEC Charges Siemens* (n 78).

80 United States Department of Justice, *Transcript of Press Conference* (n 56).

Furthermore, the DOJ and the SEC "closely collaborated with the Munich Public Prosecutor's Office in bringing these cases."[81] The German and the US authorities even announced their resolutions at the same day. Furthermore, in the DOJ press release, the DOJ refers to a combined fine and disgorgement of profit, and indicate that half of the total $1.6 billion includes payments to the US authorities.[82]

However, *Siemens* is not just an example of good cooperation and coordination but also of subsequent resolutions that overlap with the original enforcement. For example, the Greek and Nigerian authorities granted wide immunities to the company (in the Nigerian case also to individuals) in exchange of high monetary fines (Oduor et al., 2014: 134).

Furthermore, also the World Bank settled with Siemens. These enforcement actions, at least to a certain extent, overlap with the main case. For instance, the SEC included into its settlement the Moscow Third Ring Project that was also settled by the World Bank.[83] Furthermore, the Nigerian settlement dealt with the same projects as the US authorities did.[84] The question is for further investigation is whether and to what extent such subsequent enforcement actions might undermine collective action.

One more important aspect must be mentioned. When looking at *Siemens* more closely, we see interactions between more than just domestic and foreign bribery legislation. Siemens's bribing was also subjected to various civil lawsuits, investment arbitrations such as the one under the Convention on the Settlement of Investment Disputes (ICSID),[85] and the application of money laundering provisions. For instance, in November 2013 the Swiss authorities settled a case with Siemens AG because it created and used illegal funds in Swiss banks. The Swiss authorities issued several fines and ordered Siemens to forfeit about $65,000,000.[86]

5.5.5 Concluding remarks

Siemens was the first enforcement action that prosecuted endemic bribery. This was mainly possible because of MLA provided by a number of countries, and because of direct cooperation between the US and the German prosecutors.

81 United States Department of Justice, *Transcript of Press Conference* (n 56).

82 United States Department of Justice, *Siemens AG and Three Subsidiaries* (n 76).

83 Complaint, *SEC vs. Siemens* (n 3) 25–26.

84 Complaint, *SEC vs. Siemens* (n 3) 7, 20–21. The Statement of Offense, *United States vs. Siemens* (n 4) 9.

85 *Convention on the Settlement of Investment Disputes between States and Nationals of Other States*, signed on 18 March 1965, entered into force on 14 October 1966 under the aegis of the World Bank. See *Siemens A.G. vs. The Argentine Republic, No. ARB/02/8* (ICSID).

86 Trace, *Trace Compendium: Siemens AG* (n 67). Forfeiture means "the incurring a liability to pay a definite sum of money as the consequence of violating the provisions of some statute, or refusal to comply with some requirement of law." Black's Law Dictionary Free Online <http://thelawdictionary.org/forfeiture//> accessed 21 December 2018.

The German and the US enforcement authorities divided the case into seven interrelated settlements covering a set of thousands of individual bribes conducted by Siemens's agents, subsidiaries and other person acting on its behalf. In doing so, they evaluated and generalized multiplicity of bribery acts in order to present a relatively homogenous case covering all bribery-related acts in a given period. This is the example of how global settlements are usually structured. It is worth noting that the US enforcement authorities applied not only the anti-bribery charges but also the books and records, and internal controls charges. This helped them to stretch their jurisdiction, and hold the parent corporation liable for bribing by its subsidiaries on a lesser evidentiary burden than if they would have used the anti-bribery charges only.

5.6 We will catch them all: *Bonny Island*

5.6.1 The core of the enforcement scheme

In the core of the *Bonny Island* bribery scandal is the TSKJ joint venture.[87] The entity was established in 1991 to bid for contracts in the project focused on designing and building liquefied natural gas production plants in Nigeria.[88] TSKJ consisted of four members:

a Kellogg Brown & Root, LLC (KBR LLC), a wholly owned US subsidiary of the Halliburton Company – a US "issuer" (Halliburton). After January 2009, a wholly owned subsidiary of Kellogg Brown & Root Inc., a US issuer (KBR Inc.);
b Technip SA (Technip), a company organized under French law and from August 2001 until November 2007 a foreign "issuer";
c Snamprogetti Netherlands B.V. (Snamprogetti), a company organized under Dutch law, a wholly owned subsidiary of ENI S.p.A. (ENI), a company organized under Italian law and a foreign issuer. ENI sold Snamprogetti to Saipem S.p.A. (Saipem) in 2006. ENI owns 43% of Saipem, a controlling share;
d JGC Corporation (JGC), a company headquartered in Tokyo, Japan.

TSKJ operated in Nigeria through several subsidiaries and agents that from 1995 to 2004 acted on behalf of TSKJ. These companies were:

a LNG Service, a company based in Madeira, Portugal (LNG Madeira). TSKJ established LNG Madeira in order to conclude contracts with their agents based in Gibraltar and Tokyo;

87 In different context, *Bonny Island* was analyzed in Hock (2017: 336–343).
88 Plea Agreement – Statement of Facts, *United States vs. Kellogg Brown & Root LLC, No. 9-cr-71* (11 February 2009) 2–3. TSKJ are the initials of the following business partners: Technip, Snamprogetti, Kellogg Brown & Root, and JGC.

- b M.W. Kellogg Limited (MWKL), a UK subsidiary of KBR and JGC that they used in order to channel funds to the LNG Madeira;
- c Tri-Star Investments Ltd. (Tri-Star Gibraltar), a consulting corporation based in Gibraltar, an agent of TSKJ;
- d Marubeni Corporation (Marubeni), a company headquartered in Tokyo, Japan,[89] the agent of TSKJ.

Nigeria LNG, a company established by the Nigerian government that had the right to award contracts related to the Bonny Island Project, was another key actor in the scheme. The biggest shareholder of Nigeria LNG was the Nigerian government-owned corporation Nigerian National Petroleum Corporation (NNPC). NNPC owned 49% of Nigeria LNG.[90]

TSKJ took part in the Bonny Island project from 1995 to 2004. During that time, Nigeria LNG awarded TSKJ four contracts worth more than $6 billion in order to design and build natural gas plants. The TSKJ members participated in the project equally.[91] TSKJ bribed officials and employees of Nigeria LNG, NNPC, and other Nigerian government officials in order to win the contracts. It hired two agents, Tri-Star Gibraltar and Marubeni, and used them for bribing. Tri-Star paid over $130 million to higher ranked officials, Marubeni paid over $50 million to lower ranked officials. The money allocated for bribing was sent from LNG Madeira's account in Amsterdam to Swiss, Monaco, and Japanese banks controlled by the agents. Bank transfers to Switzerland and Monaco were sent via correspondent accounts in New York. This fact played an important role in asserting jurisdiction over the members of the joint venture.[92] The structure of the Bonny Island bribery scheme is demonstrated in Figure 5.1 below.

5.6.2 Offense of bribery

The first legal action was taken by the French authorities who opened an investigation against a former high official of Technip in 2003. The official informed the French authorities about other bribery schemes including *Bonny Island*. Consequently, the French opened an investigation of *Bonny Island* that triggered attention of the US, Swiss, and Nigerian authorities.[93]

The US resolution started with the investigation against Albert "Jack" Stanley, KBR formed chief executive officer (CEO) and was followed by many other prosecutions. From between 2008 to 2012, the US enforcement

89 For summary, see ibid 3–6.

90 Ibid 6–7.

91 Ibid 3.

92 Ibid 7–11 and 13.

93 Cassin, R. L. (2009) *KBR: Nigerians Tell Their Own Story*. The FCPA Blog <http://www.fcpablog.com/blog/2009/3/30/kbr-nigerians-tell-their-own-story.html> accessed 22 December 2018.

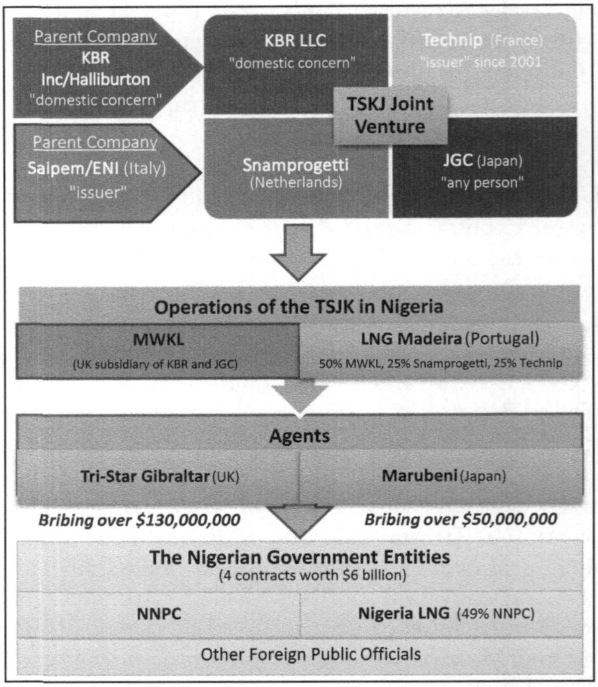

Figure 5.1 Bonny Island scheme.

authorities charge all members of TSKJ, Marubeni as their agent, and several individuals with violations of the FCPA. The enforcement scheme consists of five related cases divided into eight criminal and civil settlements with the DOJ and the SEC. All of these cases deal with the same subject matter. The following overview discusses them in more detail.

a *KBR LLC, KBR Inc., and Halliburton* – $579 million

On 11 February 2009, the DOJ and the SEC in their coordinated enforcement action sanctioned KBR LLC and its parent companies Halliburton and KBR Inc. While KBR LLC pleaded guilty and settled criminal charges with the DOJ for $402 million, Halliburton paid most of the fine – $382 million. The reason for that is an indemnification agreement between Halliburton and KBR entered into during their separation in 2009.[94] Furthermore, the SEC settled with Halliburton and KBR Inc. for a civil penalty of $177 million; Halliburton paid the civil sanction.[95]

94 Shearman & Sterling, 2015 (n 17) 100.

95 Securities and Exchange Commission, *Litigation Release No. 20897A* (Press Release 11 February 2009) <https://www.sec.gov/litigation/litreleases/2009/lr20897.htm> accessed 22 December 2018.

The indemnification agreement did not protect KBR from all consequences; KBR, for instance, agreed with the US authorities to be subject to supervision by an independent monitor for three years.[96]

b *Technip* – $338 million

On 28 June 2010, the second member of TSKJ settled with the DOJ and the SEC. Technip entered into a DPA with the DOJ to pay $240 million.[97] Furthermore, the SEC settled with Technip for a civil sanction of $98 million, and disgorged gains obtained because of bribing.[98]

c *Snamprogetti* (ENI) – $365 million

On 7 July 2010, the third member of TSKJ settled with the DOJ and the SEC. Snamprogetti entered into a DPA with the DOJ to pay $240 million.[99] Furthermore, the SEC entered into a civil settlement with ENI and Snamprogetti, and the corporations agreed jointly and severally to disgorge $98 million of gains obtained because of their bribing.[100] ENI paid the fine as it had agreed to indemnify Saipem for potential losses and charges resulting from the TSKJ investigations.[101]

d *JGC* – $218.8 million

On 6 April 2011, the last member of TSKJ settled with the DOJ. JGC entered into a DPA with the DOJ to pay $218.8 million.[102]

e *Marubeni* – $54.6 million

On 17 January 2012, Marubeni, an agent of TSKJ, entered into a DPA with the DOJ to pay $54.6 million.[103]

All of the corporate defendants also agreed to non-monetary sanctions such as retaining independent compliance monitors, independent consultants and agreed to implement better internal compliance and ethics programs.[104] Furthermore, it is noteworthy to mention that the US authorities sentenced several individuals. For instance, the District Court in Houston sentenced Jeffrey Tesler, an agent who was hired by the TSKJ joint venture to organize bribing, to 21 months in jail, Tesler agreed to forfeit $149 million held in Swiss and Israeli accounts to the US Treasury.[105]

96 Shearman & Sterling, 2015 (n 17) 295.

97 *United States vs. Technip S.A., No. 10-cr-439* (28 June 2010).

98 *Securities and Exchange Commission vs. Technip, No. 10-cv-2289* (28 June 2010).

99 Note that also ENI and Saipem were part of the settlement that was concluded on behalf of Snamprogetti. *United States vs. Snamprogetti Netherlands B.V., No. 10-cr-460* (7 July 2010).

100 *Securities and Exchange Commission vs. ENI, S.p.A. and Snamprogetti Netherlands B.V. 4:10-cv-2414* (7 July 2010) (hereinafter *SEC vs. Eni* and *Snamprogetti*).

101 Saipem, *Annual Report 2013*, 122–123 <http://www.saipem.com/en_IT/static/documents/2738BilSaipem13Eng_F.pdf> accessed 22 December 2018.

102 *United States vs. JGC Corporation, No. 11-cr-260* (6 April 2011)

103 *United States vs. Marubeni Corporation, No. 12-cr-22* (17 January 2012).

104 See, for instance, Exhibit 2 of the Plea Agreement, *United States vs. Kellogg Brown & Root LLC, No. 09-cr-71 No. 09-cr-71* (11 February 2009).

105 Judgment, *United States vs. Jeffrey Tesler No. 09-cr-98* (11 March 2011). See also Trace, *Trace Compendium: Halliburton/KBR* (n 69).

The US case was followed by other enforcement actions conducted by the Nigerian, UK, and Italian enforcement authorities. The investigations in these jurisdictions resulted into additional sanctioning of the TSKJ members. First, between from 2010 to 2011, the Nigerian authorities charged, based on their domestic anti-corruption laws, all TSKJ members. The settlements are confidential but secondary sources indicate that the TSKJ members paid approximately $126 million: JGC paid $28.5 million, Snamprogetti, $32.5 million, KBR/Halliburton, $35 million and Technip, $30 million.[106] The Nigerian settlements, similar to *Siemens*, granted wide immunities to corporations and individuals involved in the scheme, including Dick Cheney, former Halliburton CEO, and former US Vice-President.[107]

Second, on 16 February 2011, the SFO took actions before the High Court against MWKL, the UK based subsidiary of KBR and JPG. The SFO reported that MKWL settled for over £7 million for a civil sanction. The SFO also reported that the court ordered the disgorgement of profits that MWKL acquired as the result of the anti-bribery violations of the third parties. MWKL also agreed to improve its internal controls mechanisms. The court, however, applied an AML statute, Part 5 of the Proceeds of Crime Act 2002, instead of foreign anti-bribery laws.[108] The main reason is that under the Act, the authorities can claim a civil recovery without the need for a criminal conviction.[109]

Third, on 11 July 2013, the Court of Milan in Italy ordered Snamprogetti to pay over €24.5 million (over $31.8 million) as the confiscation of illegally obtained gains related to *Bonny Island*. Moreover, the company paid €0.6 million ($0.78 million) as an administrative fine.[110] The company unsuccessfully appealed the decision to the Milan Court of Appeal in February 2015 as well as to the Court of Cassation in February 2016.[111]

Bonny Island covers a single decade-long bribery scheme. In this scheme, several corporations coming from various jurisdictions conspired to reach the same end: bribery foreign government officials in order to obtain and retain lucrative contracts. The US enforcement authorities settled with five of these

106 The Nigerian Attorney General stated that companies and individuals had paid $170.8 million in total. See Stolen Asset Recovery Initiative, *Bonny Island Liquefied Natural Gas Bribe Scheme* (Nigeria Settlement 2013).

107 Trace, *Trace Compendium: Halliburton/KBR* (n 69).

108 The Proceeds of Crime Act 2002 (c.29) Section 240 provides that the main purpose of civil orders is:

> […] enabling the enforcement authority to recover, in civil proceedings before the High Court or Court of Session, property which is, or represents, property obtained through unlawful conduct, (b) enabling cash which is, or represents, property obtained through unlawful conduct, or which is intended to be used in unlawful conduct, to be forfeited in civil proceedings before a magistrates' court or (in Scotland) the sheriff.

109 Serious Fraud Office, *MW Kellogg* (n 42).

110 Saipem, *Annual Report 2013* (n 102) 122.

111 Saipem, *Annual Report 2017*, 164–165 <http://www.saipem.com/en_IT/static/documents/SaipemBil17Ing.pdf accessed 22 December 2018.

corporations. The DOJ and the SEC based their settlements on substantive violations of the FCPA's (1) anti-bribery, (2) books and records, and (3) internal controls provisions, and on conspiring, aiding and abetting to violate these provisions. *Table 5.2* below shows an overview of charges that were used in *Bonny Island*.

Table 5.2 above shows that the DOJ did not apply the record-keeping and internal controls provisions. Rather, the DOJ settled with the members of TSKJ and Marubeni by applying the anti-bribery provisions.[112] KBR and Technip were sanctioned for substantive violations while the others were qualified as accomplices, either by conspiring with (C) or aiding and abetting (A), KBR and Technip in their violations of the law.[113] The SEC, in contrast to the DOJ, enforced not only the anti-bribery provision but also the books and records, and the internal controls provisions. Nevertheless, in line with the SEC personal jurisdiction, the SEC covered only "issuers" and their subsidiaries, i.e. KBR, Technip, and Snamprogetti.

5.6.3 Jurisdiction

The US case shows four relevant aspects of the US enforcement practices: (1) how jurisdiction over domestic concerns and issuers is ascertained, (2) what constitutes territorial nexus with the US, (3) extraterritorial jurisdiction based on complicity charges, and (4) parent–subsidiary liability.

1 *Domestic issuers, domestic concerns, and issuers*

   Bonny Island provides several examples how the US authorities assert territorial jurisdiction over domestic companies and domestic issuers – KBR LLC, KBR Inc., and Halliburton. These examples mainly relate to the use of US currency and the fact that bribery payments were transferred via US correspondent accounts. Even if the US authorities, however, could not prove that there was an interstate commerce nexus, they could rely on the nationality principle because these companies were headquartered in the US, thus without any dispute fell into the categories of "domestic concern" (KBR LLC) or, domestic "issuers" (KBR Inc. and Halliburton).[114] What is also clear is that, as "issuers," Technip, KBR, Halliburton, and ENI could have been charged for their violations of the books and records, and internal controls provisions because these provisions apply to "every issuer" without any additional condition.

2 *Territorial nexus and foreign corporations – a correspondent account*

   The DOJ charged Technip directly with substantive violations of the anti-bribery provisions. In order to impose such charges to a foreign corporation, however, the US authorities must prove the interstate commerce

112 Cf *Siemens* where the DOJ did not use the anti-bribery provisions at all.

113 For instance, C - 78dd-1 means that a given company conspired with an issuer, while C - 78dd-2 stands for the conspiracy with a domestic concern such as KBR LLC.

114 See Figure 4.1: Jurisdiction under the anti-bribery provisions of the FCPA (Section 4.7.3).

Table 5.2 Charges in Bonny Island

Abbreviations *A = Aiding and Abetting* *C = Conspiracy*	**Anti-Bribery** *§ 78dd-1,2 or 3*		**(1): Books and Records** *§§78m(b)(2)(A)* **(2): Internal Controls** *78m(b)(2)(B)* **(3): Knowingly** *78m(b)5*	
	DOJ	*SEC*	*DOJ*	*SEC*
Settlement 1: KBR LLC/KBR Inc/Halliburton				
KBR LLC	78dd2 C - 78dd1	78dd1 most of the fine paid by Halliburton		A - (1) (2) most of the fine paid by Halliburton
KBR Inc				
Halliburton				(1) (2)
Settlement 2: Technip				
Technip	78dd1 C - 78dd1,2	78dd1		(1) (2)
Settlement 3: Snamprogetti *(all fines paid by ENI)*				
Snamprogetti	C - 78dd1,2 A - 78dd2	78dd1		(3)
ENI				(1) (2)
Settlement 4: JGC				
JGC	C - 78dd1,2 A - 78dd2			
Settlement 5: Marubeni				
Marubeni	C - 78dd1,2 A - 78dd2			

a Hock (2017: 342).

nexus. In the settlements with Technip, the US authorities provided several examples of the relevant territorial link between the acts of Technip and the US territory. The DOJ indicates that the key link was the fact that bribery payments were channeled via US correspondent accounts:

> [S]enior executives and employees of Technip and their co-conspirators caused wire transfers totaling approximately $132 million to be sent from Madeira Company 3's bank account in Amsterdam, The Netherlands, to bank accounts in New York, New York, to be further credited to bank accounts in Switzerland and Monaco [...].[115]

The DOJ did not mention any other concrete example what in the case of Technip constituted territorial nexus with the US, stating only that:

> [T]echnip ... willfully used the mails and means and instrumentalities of interstate commerce corruptly in furtherance of the authorization, promise, and payment of bribes to Nigerian government officials pursuant to the scheme. Stanley, other officers, employees, and agents of KBR, and other co-conspirators committed acts in furtherance of the scheme in Houston, Texas, and elsewhere in the United States.[116]

It is not clear whether the phrase used by the DOJ refers to some other territorial link than just the correspondent bank account link. Similarly, the SEC was in its Complaint general, stating that Technip "routinely made use of the U.S. mails, and of U.S. common carriers, and of other instrumentalities of U.S. interstate commerce."[117]

3 *Extraterritoriality – complicit conduct*

Bonny Island illustrates that it is not always necessary to charge foreign corporations with an evidence of their territorial nexus to the US. It is interesting that from all charged corporations, only Technip, a foreign issuer, was charged directly under the anti-bribery provisions. Other foreign corporations, Snamprogetti, JGC, and Marubeni, were charged only with conspiracy to violate the anti-bribery provisions of the FCPA. This indicates that the US authorities might have had difficulties to prove that the conduct of these other foreign corporations took part in the US territory.

In order to overcome possible jurisdictional issues, the DOJ charged Snamprogetti, JPG, and Marubeni exclusively with conspiracy, and aiding and abetting violations of the anti-bribery provisions of the FCPA.[118]

115 Deferred Prosecution Agreement, *United States vs. Technip* (n 98) 10.
116 Ibid 8.
117 Complaint, *SEC vs. Technip* (n 99) 4.
118 These charges make the concerned firms punishable in the same way as principal violators. See 18 U.S.C. §2.

In other words, the conspiracy charges allowed the DOJ to charge foreign corporations that were not domestic issuers, domestic concerns, nor acted within the territory of the US. This leverage of the US jurisdiction to foreign entities that act outside the territory of the US is a powerful enforcement strategy that potentially mitigates the collective action problem and, assumedly, ensures more open and competitive markets.

4 Foreign subsidiaries of a foreign issuer

The US authorities asserted jurisdiction over a foreign subsidiary of a foreign issuer. This is similar to *Siemens*, albeit with a critical difference that the case was also decided by the SEC and not only by the DOJ. The SEC did not charge Snamprogetti with conspiracy but directly with violating §78dd-1 of the FCPA as an agent of its parent – ENI, and with books and records and internal controls violations of the FCPA. Furthermore, the parent company ENI was not charged based on the anti-bribery provisions of the FCPA at all. The legality of the SEC approach may be problematic because, according to the FCPA, the SEC should find a relevant link between an issuer and non-issuer if it wants to charge a non-issuer directly by §78dd-1. This link between the parent (issuer) and the subsidiary (non-issuer) with regard to the bribery scheme, however, is in very loose in *Bonny Island*. The SEC merely stated, "ENI exercised control and supervision of its wholly-owned indirect subsidiary Snamprogetti during the relevant time and on certain of its business decisions, such as Snamprogetti's entry into the joint venture."[119]

The loose interpretation of parent–subsidiary liability, both by the DOJ and the SEC, is critical because it further extends the scope of the US jurisdiction. What will be discussed in the following chapter, is how foreign subsidiaries are charged with the anti-bribery violations instead of their parent corporations, as was seen in *Halliburton/KBR* or *ENI/Snamprogetti*. This is a pattern that strengthens the position of the US authorities when negotiating out-of-court settlements.

5.6.4 Cooperation and coordination

From the collective action perspective, *Bonny Island* illustrates cooperation by using MLA, and some signs of a more direct and informal cooperation between the US and the UK authorities.

a *Cooperation before the final resolution of a case by using MLA*

The DOJ and the SEC refer to cooperation with other foreign enforcement authorities. The DOJ mentioned a significant assistance provided by French, Italian, Swiss, and the UK authorities. The SEC was more

119 Paragraph 12 of the Complaint, *SEC vs. Eni and Snamprogetti* (n 101).

general stating that it acknowledges assistance provided by foreign authorities in Europe, Asia, Africa, and the Americas.[120]

b *Coordination of investigation and prosecution*

Bonny Island is also an example of subsequent resolutions of states that provided MLA to the US authorities. Except Switzerland, that was an important partner regarding the forfeiture of assets stored in Swiss banks, all of the jurisdictions that provided "a significant assistance" also investigated and resolved part of the Bonny Island enforcement scheme. While French authorities reportedly imposed rather symbolic fines on two individuals,[121] in Italy, courts imposed significant civil and administrative sanctions to Saipem (to be paid by ENI/Snamprogetti),[122] in particular, civil sanctions and confiscation of illegally obtained gains. These sanctions might overlap with the US resolution. Last, the SFO shows also signs of a more direct cooperation as it indicated that it worked in partnership with the DOJ, and disgorged profits that MWKL (UK subsidiary of KBR) received in relations to *Bonny Island*.[123]

Bonny Island also illustrates non-cooperative and non-coordinated enforcement. Most importantly, the Nigerian settlements based on the Nigerian domestic anti-bribery laws, similarly to *Siemens*, granted wide immunities to the corporations and individuals. The only difference is that the US settlements with JPG and Marubeni were concluded after the Nigerian settlements with these corporations. It is also important to note that Halliburton also settled a class action with its shareholders. No payment of damages was imposed, only compliance requirements.[124]

5.6.5 Concluding remarks

Bonny Island, with total penalties over $1.8 billion, is one of the largest enforcement schemes in the history of foreign anti-bribery enforcement. *Bonny Island*, differently from *Siemens*, is constructed as large conspiracy aiming to prosecute all major corporations and individuals that participate in the scheme. Despite the high amount of corporate enforcement actions, eight resolved under the FCPA charges, the scheme is homogenous and illegal acts are defined concretely. The main message is that once enforcement authorities find a territorial link with a member of the conspiracy, every related

120 All Bonny Island-related press releases contain similar information regarding the cooperation and coordination, see, for instance, United States Department of Justice, *Kellogg Brown & Root LLC Pleads Guilty to Foreign Bribery Charges and Agrees to Pay $402 Million Criminal Fine* (Press Release 11 February 2009) <http://www.justice.gov/opa/pr/kellogg-brown-root-llc-pleads-guilty-foreign-bribery-charges-and-agrees-pay-402-million> accessed 23 December 2018.

121 Trace, *Trace Compendium: Halliburton/KBR* (n 69).

122 Ibid.

123 Serious Fraud Office, *MW Kellogg* (n 42).

124 Trace, *Trace Compendium: Halliburton/KBR* (n 69).

corporation may be charged as well. Indeed, TSKJ consisted of only one US-based company but in the end, all non-US members and their agent fell under the US jurisdiction.

The scheme also shows an increasing level of cooperation and coordination. Most of the countries that provided a "significant assistance" (France, Italy, and the UK) also resolved relatively minor bribery matters. Bonny Island is the first truly global enforcement action in the region and has been followed by further investigations. Recently, for example, Italian prosecutors filed a case against Royal Dutch Shell and Eni over the $1.3 billion OPL 245 oil deal in Nigeria. The Nigerian government has filled civil lawsuits in London and Milan, requesting the return of $1.1 billion.[125]

5.7 International bribery and alternative laws: BAE

5.7.1 The core of the enforcement scheme

BAE Systems PLC was, in 2010, a multinational corporation organized under UK law with the main office in Farnborough, England. As a global player in defense and security systems and services, BAE employed roughly 98,000 employees and operated through its subsidiaries, agents, and other groups and individuals in five key home markets – US, UK, Saudi Arabia, Australia, and India. Under US and UK government support, BAE focused on export of its products.[126] As of 11 February 1981, BAE was listed on the London Stock Exchange.[127] The predecessor of the company was British Aerospace.

BAE and it's business partners have allegedly bribed foreign public officials in Saudi Arabia, Central and Eastern Europe, and Africa. From 2004 to 2011, BAE was investigated by the UK, US, Austrian, Swiss, and South African authorities. However, only the US and UK enforcement actions resulted in convictions.

5.7.2 Offense of bribery

The first investigation related to the so-called al-Yamamah project, an exchange of arms for oil agreed between the governments of the UK and Saudi Arabia. In more than 20 years of its existence, the project has brought to BAE

125 Financial Times (2018) *Nigeria files $1.1bn legal claim against Shell, Eni over 2011 oil deal* (13 December 2018) <https://www.ft.com/content/9ddb8f0a-ff0d-11e8-ac00-57a2a826423e> accessed 23 December 2018.

126 BAE Systems, *Annual Report 2010* <http://investors.baesystems.com/~/media/Files/B/Bae-Systems-Investor-Relations-V3/PDFs/results-and-reports/reports/2011/ar-2010.pdf> accessed 23 December 2018.

127 London Stock Exchange, *BAE Systems PLC* <http://m.londonstockexchange.com/exchange/mobile/stocks/summary.html?fourWayKey=GB0002634946GBGBXSET1> accessed 23 December 2018.

the revenue of approximately £43 billion. The SFO opened investigation in 2004, however, was pushed by the UK government to drop the investigation in 2006 because of the "need to safeguard national and international security."[128] The discontinuation of the investigation was subject to judicial review. At first, the UK High Court found that the discontinuation was unlawful because of political influence. However, the House of Lords in 2008 held that the discontinuation shall not be subject to judicial review, and was therefore lawful, because of the discretion given to the prosecution.[129] In this context, the WGB prepared a report specially addressing the al-Yamamah project, concluding that the WGB is "disappointed and seriously concerned with the unsatisfactory implementation of the Convention by the UK."[130] In BAE, the UK clearly violated Article 5 of the OECD Convention related to the independence and professionalism of investigation and prosecution.

The SFO also focused on BAE's activities in the Czech Republic, Hungary, Romania, South Africa, and Tanzania. In the end, the UK authorities resolved only a bribery scheme in Tanzania by a settlement in February 2010. BAE admitted a failure to keep adequate accounting records and agreed to pay £30 million, the Crown Court also ordered BAE to pay £225,000 costs of proceedings.[131]

Despite the fact that BAE is a UK company, the core of the BAE enforcement scheme lays in the settlements with the DOJ and the US Department of State (DOS).[132] The DOJ provides that BAE's system of internal controls did not comply with the requirements of the FCPA, thus BAE also did not ensure that its agents and marketing advisors complied with the US anti-bribery standards. After May 2001, BAE made suspicious payments, more than £149 million, through various offshore companies "even though in certain situations there was a high probability that part of the payments would be used in order to ensure that BAE was favoured in the foreign government decisions regarding the sales of defense articles."[133] As the result of these allegations, BAE agreed to pay a $400 million criminal fine, retain an independent compliance monitor, and implement a better compliance program.[134] One year later, BAE settled with the DOS in the related civil enforcement action. BAE agreed to pay $79 million a civil penalty and implement anti-bribery

128 Trace, *Trace Compendium: BAE Systems* <https://www.traceinternational.org/TraceCompendium/Detail/140?class=casename_searchresult&type=1> accessed 23 December 2018.

129 Ibid.

130 OECD (2008) Phase 2bis Report on Implementing the OECD Anti-Bribery Convention in the United Kingdom, 4 and 70.

131 *Regina vs. Bae Systems Plc (Note for Opening, 22 November 2010).*

132 The DOS is responsible for the US foreign policy. See the DOS's website <http://www.state.gov/>.

133 Department of Justice, *BAE Systems PLC Pleads Guilty and Ordered to Pay $400 Million Criminal Fine* (Press Release 1 March 2010) <https://www.justice.gov/opa/pr/bae-systems-plc-pleads-guilty-and-ordered-pay-400-million-criminal-fine> accessed 23 December 2018.

134 Ibid.

compliance measures. Three BAE subsidiaries were debarred from all applications for export licenses in the US.[135]

Neither the UK nor the US authorities sanctioned BAE for violations of foreign anti-bribery laws. The DOJ charged BAE for a conspiracy "to defraud the United States by impairing and impeding its lawful functions"[136] through:

1 making false statements in violation of 18 U.S.C. §1001;
2 violating the Arms Export Control Act, 22 U.S.C. §2751, et seq.[137];
3 violating the International Traffic in Arms Regulation (ITAR), 22 C.F.R. §§120, et seq.[138]

The enforcement was complemented by the civil enforcement action concluded by the DOS that refers to 2591 violations of ITAR.[139]

The UK authorities limited their enforcement only to crimes that BAE committed in Tanzania. According to the UK authorities, BAE "aided and abetted, counselled and procured the commission of the offence contrary to Section 221 (5) of the Companies Act 1985 by the officers of British Aerospace Defence Systems Limited." Thus, British Aerospace as a predecessor of BAE failed to comply with the accounting provisions.[140]

5.7.3 Jurisdiction

BAE illustrates that the use of alternative charges further extends the scope of the US jurisdiction. The key issue is that BAE used US military technology subject to export license requirements. This fact linked international business transactions related to this technology with the US territory and established the US jurisdictional hook. In other words, as one of the conditions of acquiring export licenses in the US was to disclose all commissions paid to advisers and agents that relate to the licensed technology, creating slush funds with the view to sell weapons based on such technology by bribing foreign public officials, constitutes a violation of US export laws. This extension of jurisdiction in *BAE* was very important because the DOJ stressed that BAE's US subsidiary was not involved in the bribery scheme, and BAE is headquartered in the UK.[141] Hence, as territorial jurisdiction related to actual

135 Department of State, *Settlement of Alleged Violations of the AECA and ITAR and Agrees to Civil Penalty of $79 Million* (Press Release 17 May 2011) <https://www.foley.com/files/BAES_StateDeptRelease18may11.pdf> accessed 24 December 2018.

136 Department of Justice, *BAE Systems PLC Pleads Guilty* (n 135).

137 The Arms Export Contol Act 1976.

138 See *United States vs. BAE Systems Plc, No. 10-cr-035* (4 February 2010).

139 Department of State (n 137).

140 *Regina v BAE Systems* (n 133).

141 Department of Justice, *BAE Systems PLC Pleads Guilty* (n 135).

bribing was not proved, it was not possible to apply the FCPA. Therefore, the interplay between export control laws and foreign bribery laws further extends the US anti-bribery standard. Alternative laws in cases such as *BAE* increase the provision of foreign anti-bribery enforcement as a public good.

5.7.4 Cooperation and coordination

BAE is an important illustration of how ineffective enforcement in one country can be partially corrected by enforcement in another country (see Section 2.4.1). Foreign anti-bribery enforcement that is based on alternative laws can be used to improve collective action. Even if some states, such as the UK in *BAE*, free-ride by not engaging in enforcement, extraterritoriality offsets their inactivity by providing additional public goods. The following parts discuss two key elements of cooperation and coordination in *BAE*: MLA and the "offsetting" of the UK ineffective enforcement by the US authorities.

a *Cooperation before the final resolution of a case by using MLA*
Regarding cooperation between various enforcement authorities, the DOJ and SFO expressed mutual appreciation for one another's assistance. No other official or other person were prosecuted elsewhere. Moreover, signs of a more direct cooperation are expressed by the DOJ that appreciated the "ongoing partnership in the fights against overseas corruption" with the SFO.[142] No other jurisdiction was recognized as cooperative.

b *Coordination of investigation and prosecution*
BAE shows the weaknesses of the old UK anti-bribery enforcement system, and mainly that political influence and considerations of national interest can paralyze prosecutors. While the UK prosecutors were ready to charge the *BAE*, they were pressured by the political leadership not to do so. The US authorities partially offset the inability of the UK authorities to effectively enforce their international anti-bribery legislation. As discussed above, the US authorities covered a significant part of the BAE's crimes in Saudi Arabia, the Czech Republic, and Hungary.

Once the UK authorities dropped their investigation in the al-Yamamah matter, the US authorities made a formal diplomatic protest to the UK, and raised the issue at the meeting of the WGB in Paris.[143] Furthermore, in the BAE Sentencing Memorandum, the DOJ stated that:

142 Ibid.
143 Jarrett, T. and Taylor, C. (2010) *Bribery Allegations and BAE Systems*, 3 <researchbriefings.files.parliament.uk/documents/SN05367/SN05367.pdf> accessed 25 February 2017.

> [...] the plea agreement only binds the Department and not any foreign authority. Similarly, the recommended sentence here relates only to the offense charged in the criminal Information to which BAES is pleading guilty, and not to any matters under investigation by any authorities other than the Department, including any foreign authorities.[144]

On the other hand, the UK still covered the foreign bribery scheme in Tanzania. This very limited enforcement result was presented differently from the US, i.e. as a "ground breaking global agreement."[145] Furthermore, the SFO announced that it took into account BAE's settlement with DOJ, and "has determined that no further prosecutions will be brought against BAE Systems in relation to the matters that have been under investigation by the SFO."[146] However, this indirect reference to the international comity serves rather as an excuse of the UK because, for example, the US settlement did not refer to the bribery scheme in South Africa. Hence ceding jurisdiction completely is not justifiable as well as it is not clear why the US should have more appropriate jurisdiction over foreign bribery of the UK-based corporation than the UK.

5.7.5 Concluding remarks

BAE illustrates that foreign anti-bribery enforcement can be based on alternative laws, such as export laws. The US export law charges can further leverage the US jurisdiction over corporations that might otherwise fall outside the territorial scope of the FCPA. In *BAE*, these laws were used by the US enforcement authorities as a response to the UK enforcement passivity. The OECD, the US and other countries, and the civil society harshly criticized the UK authorities for their inactivity, and it became clear that the old UK anti-corruption system is not good enough to cover foreign bribery effectively. The UK was not able to protect the SFO from improper political influence as is required by Article 5 of the OECD Convention. The adoption of the Bribery Act followed shortly after *BAE*.

5.8 Conclusion

The enforcement of OECD-based anti-bribery laws is part of a broad substantive and procedural regime that goes outside the scope of the OECD Convention. In this context, concurrence of substantive laws, broad interpretation

144 Guilty Plea, *United States vs. BAE* (n 140) 2.

145 Serious Fraud Office, BAE Systems plc (Press Release 5 February 2010) <https://www.sfo.gov.uk/press-room/latest-press-releases/press-releases-2010/bae-systems-plc.aspx> last accessed 18 February 2017. Note the *BAE* related SFO press releases were not available on the SFO's web in December 2018.

146 Ibid.

of territorial jurisdiction, the liability for acts of associated persons, the application of conspiracy charges to extend jurisdiction, and cooperation and coordination are the key issues that determine the functioning of extraterritoriality within the factual regime.

The analyzed enforcement schemes illustrate that extraterritorial enforcement is not only determined by jurisdictional criteria derived from general provisions related to jurisdiction. Extraterritoriality also depends on the questions how facts of cases are qualified, and what laws are applied to them. Foreign bribery schemes have several typologies. *Siemens* is an example of an endemic bribery that is not confined to one business project but includes an array of different bribes scattered throughout the world. On the other hand, *Bonny Island* relates to four homogeneous business contracts and is legally constructed as a large conspiracy that covers all major corporations and individuals that participated in the contracts. Yet another type is *BAE* that is constructed as an export law scheme. The concurrence of various substantive laws that factually cover foreign bribery goes beyond export laws and include accountancy, AML, anti-trust, domestic anti-corruption laws, and other laws. This provides further potential how to provide more enforcement as a public good.

Furthermore, the US authorities interpret what constitutes territorial nexus with the US territory broadly. One example of what constitutes such a nexus is the use of a correspondent bank account as a jurisdictional hook. Moreover, US law provides several tools to extend jurisdiction over foreign corporations that never acted in the US. For example, Marubeni, a foreign agent of TSKJ, was charged with the conspiracy to violate the anti-bribery provisions of the FCPA because some of its co-conspirators were found to bribe while being in the territory of the US. Last, another mechanism illustrated in *Siemens* and *Bonny Island* is that the US authorities interpret principal–agent and parent–subsidiarity liability broadly in order to hold corporations liable for acts of third persons.

Last, the studies illustrate a number of legal mechanisms and practices related to cooperation and coordination. First, all of the analyzed schemes include some element of cooperation by the use of MLA. Furthermore, in all enforcement schemes, some of the jurisdictions that provided MLA also complemented the US enforcement by their own enforcement actions. Second, *Siemens* illustrates a more direct and informal cooperation. In *Siemens*, the US and the German enforcement authorities worked together throughout the entire enforcement process, and even announced their resolutions at the same day. Third, such direct and informal cooperation resulted into a more coordinated enforcement. The question is, whether these illustrations are common patterns in the US enforcement, or whether they are less common, and what implications, from the perspective of the collection action, such patterns may have for the effectiveness of enforcement? These questions are addressed in Chapter 6 below.

References

Hock, B. (2017) 'Transnational Bribery: When Is Extraterritoriality Appropriate?' (2017) 11 Charleston Law Review 305.

Koehler, M. (2014) 'A Foreign Corrupt Practices Act Narrative' 22 Michigan State International Law Review 3.

Oduor, J. et al. (2014) 'Left out of the Bargain: Settlements in Foreign Bribery Cases and Implications for Asset Recovery' Stolen Asset Recovery Initiative <http://star.worldbank.org/star/sites/star/files/9781464800863.pdf> accessed 7 January 2019.

6 Patterns of foreign anti-bribery enforcement

6.1 Introduction

This chapter identifies patterns of US foreign anti-bribery enforcement that are relevant from the perspective of collective action. The issues are: How territorial jurisdiction is established? How, and why, do national enforcement authorities use different charges, including the conspiracy charges, to prosecute foreign bribery? And how the concept of corporate liability is interpreted by enforcement authorities when prosecuting MNCs for bribing? What is more, the chapter addresses the question whether, and how, national enforcement authorities cooperate with each other and coordinate their enforcement actions. If they do, is it part of a particular legal practice? If they do not, why?

The patterns pointed out in this chapter have deep implications for collective action. It will be argued that the US enforcement authorities use a number of legal techniques in order to extend their jurisdiction. The application of alternative statutes, the broad interpretation of territorial jurisdiction, piercing the corporate veil, and the use of conspiracy charges, are in practice very effective tools to hold both US corporations and foreign corporations liable for bribing. These enforcement techniques alleviate credibility problems related to the provision of enforcement as a public good. Moreover, they have also incentivized other states to be more active in their legislative and enforcement responses to international bribery: enforcement invites enforcement.

Not only is the provision of enforcement relevant from the perspective of collective action, but also the cooperation and coordination of enforcement. Yet, such cooperation and coordination are undermined by clarity problems. Without more knowledge about what substantive laws apply, what bribery acts are covered, what procedures are used, and who is in charge of enforcement, the effective responses to these problems are difficult, and the provision of public goods limited. It will be argued that more direct and informal cooperation between national enforcement authorities is key to ensure that foreign bribery schemes are prosecuted in their complexity, and negative implications of clarity problems alleviated.

The rest of this chapter is organized as follows. Section 2 discusses how territorial nexus with the US territory is interpreted. The concurrence of substantive laws in the US as well as in Germany and the UK is analyzed in Section 3. Indirect bribery, including parent–subsidiary liability, agency relationship, successor' liability, and conspiracy are discussed in Section 4. Last, Section 5 analyzes the emergence of multijurisdictional settlements and the cooperation and coordination of enforcement.

6.2 Foreign bribery and territorial nexus with the US

The US territorial jurisdiction over issuers and domestic concerns is based on the interstate commerce nexus (Section 4.7.3). In addition, nexus with the US territory is the key concept for establishing jurisdiction over corporations that are foreign non-issuers. In line with the detailed definition provided by the FCPA, the Resource Guide further specifies that the term interstate commerce nexus:

> [...] also includes the intrastate use of any interstate means of communication, or any other interstate instrumentality. Thus, placing a telephone call or sending an e-mail, text message, or fax from, to, or through the United States involves interstate commerce – as does sending a wire transfer from or to a U.S. bank or otherwise using the U.S. banking system, or traveling across state borders or internationally to or from the United States.[1]

In fact, the Resource Guide summarizes the main practices developed by the DOJ and the SEC when enforcing the FCPA.

Some of these practices have appeared to be controversial because only a minimal link with the US territory is arguably sufficient for the US authorities to claim jurisdiction over foreign corporations. The controversy is linked with a large discussion about the constitutional limits of the Congress's power to regulate foreign commerce under the commerce clause and reflects a broader problem regarding the division between federal power and the power of the states.[2] In this context, the FCPA is considered as a "pure foreign-nexus offense," thus is not controversial in its essence. Regulating bribery outside the US is constitutional in principle (Lewi, 2015: 643). Yet, the interstate commerce nexus criterion sets the limit of US jurisdiction because the US shall have power to "regulate commerce 'with foreign Nations,'

1 United States Department of Justice and United States Securities and Exchange Commission, 'A Resource Guide to the U.S. Foreign Corrupt Practices Act' (2012) 11 <https://www.justice.gov/sites/default/files/criminal-fraud/legacy/2015/01/16/guide.pdf> accessed 25 December 2018.

2 Note that the commerce clause includes three elements, the Interstate Commerce Clause, the Indian Commerce Clause, and the Foreign Commerce Clause (Sullivan, 2015: 1957).

not a general, global power to regulate commerce 'among foreign Nations'" (Colangelo, 2010: 954). The following section illustrates how the territorial jurisdiction is interpreted by US prosecutors when charging corporations.

6.2.1 The US territorial jurisdiction in practice

Starting with a less controversial example how the US territorial jurisdiction functions, *HP* illustrates a number of clear territorial links (Section 2.3.2). These links usually relate to the physical presence of relevant individuals in the US. For example, HP Poland organized a trip for a Polish public official in San Francisco in order to obtain business with a Polish agency. They organized various drinks and dinners in Las Vegas and a flight over Grand Canyon. Moreover, representatives of HP Russia organized a business meeting related to the scheme with HP headquarters management in the US.[3]

More controversial are territorial links established by the use of electronic communication and the US bank system. First, the US dollar is a global currency, and the vast majority of business transactions passes through correspondent accounts in the US. The jurisdiction in the *Bonny Island*-related settlements and many other settlements with US authorities is based on the correspondent account criterion.[4] Second, the US authorities regularly refer to the use of electronic communications. For instance, in *Magyar Telekom*, a Hungarian telecommunication company owned by Deutsche Telekom (DT) bribed Macedonian government officials in order to delay legal changes related to the liberalization of the Macedonian telecommunication market. The only concrete jurisdictional criterion mentioned in settlement documents is that electronic communications such as drafts of agreements with the foreign public officials, "were transmitted by Magyar Telekom employees and others through U.S. interstate commerce or stored on computer servers located in the United States."[5] The employees were unaware that they are using servers located in the US. To justify their jurisdiction, the US authorities, similarly to *Magyar Telekom*, used general language in a number of other cases.[6]

It might be possible that, for instance, passing an email via a US server is by itself not a sufficient territorial link to establish jurisdiction. Despite possible jurisdictional limitations of the FCPA, however, corporations do not

3 Guilty Plea, *United States vs. ZAO Hewlett-Packard A.O., No. 14-cr-201* (April 9, 2014) 21–22.

4 For example, *Siemens* and *Total*.

5 Order, *Securities and Exchange Commission vs. Magyar Telekom PLC and Deutsche Telekom A.G., No. 11-cv-9646* (29 December 2011) 8. See similarly also *United States vs. Daimler AG, No. 10-cr-63* (24 March 2010).

6 See Section 6.4.2. for the discussion about anti-bribery charges and consent jurisdiction over subsidiaries.

challenge the US authorities by going to court.[7] This may be explained by a number of reasons such as that the overall bargaining position of the US authorities is better than the one of corporations, or simply because the discussed settlements are not fully transparent about available evidence and the factual and legal background of bribery schemes. Nevertheless, there is a clear link between the US technological capacity and its ability to regulate foreign markets. The technological and business globalization allows the US authorities to apply their jurisdiction over transactions and acts that are extraterritorial. The following part explains that despite some doubts as to the effective application of the interstate commerce nexus criterion, potential legal barriers are not a real concern when enforcing the US foreign anti-bribery laws.

6.2.2 Legal barriers are not a real concern

Before the raise of the US foreign anti-bribery enforcement, the effectiveness of the US approach raised some questions, mainly regarding the jurisdiction over foreign issuers. There were concerns that foreign issuers that cannot be prosecuted under the "alternative jurisdiction" might have been in some cases outside the reach of US law even if they would bribe "while in the US territory" (Section 4.7.3). In 2002, the OECD monitoring report provided two hypothetical examples when the criterion may not be satisfied:

> [...] when an e-mail is not sent until long after a bribe has been paid even where it discusses the now-completed bribe, and in the case when a private mail carrier is used, if it does not cross state lines and does not qualify as an "interstate" facility.[8]

Such scenarios, however, are extremely unlikely to happen in practice, and the interstate commerce nexus covers practically all relevant actions of subjects while they are in the territory of the US. In the light of frequent US enforcement actions against foreign issuers and other foreign corporations, the formally different treatment between US issuers (interstate commerce nexus) and non-US issuers (while in the territory of the US) is not a practical concern. The main reason is that the interstate commerce nexus covers

7 Yet, in cases concerning natural persons, the US courts have been narrowing the scope of US jurisdiction. In *United States vs. Lawrence Hoskins, No. 16-cr-1010*, the court indicated that the government can hold a foreign national liable for the conspiracy to violate the FCPA only if it can evidence that they are an employee or an agent of either an issuer or a domestic concern, or that they acted on American soil. Furthermore, the US courts clarified that in cases against individuals, the territorial jurisdiction shall be based on some "minimal contact" with the US. In *Securities and Exchange Commission vs. Elek Straub, Andras Balogh and Tamas Morvai., No. 11-civ-9645* (S.D.N.Y 2013), the court argued that such minimal contact includes a conduct designed to violate US securities regulations, hence directed toward the US, even if not principally directed there.

8 OECD (2002) United States: Phase 2 Report on the Application of the Convention on Combating Bribery of Foreign Public Officials, 31.

nearly all activities with territorial nexus to the US. This also stands for any foreign corporation acting while in the territory of the US because, arguably, even in that case, for example, the use of US e-mail servers might suffice. In other words, the terms "interstate commerce nexus" and acting "while in the territory of the US" have practically the same substance.

To conclude, the US enforcement authorities interpret grounds of their territorial jurisdiction broadly. This includes both the interstate commerce nexus and how the territorial link is established between the US territory and corporations that are foreign non-issuers. The collective action perspective, however, reveals that the provision of enforcement as a public good is not only a problem of territorial limitations. In some cases, foreign bribery interacts with other economic crimes. This raises the question what substantive laws should be enforced to held corporations liable. The following part explains how and why in some cases US authorities use other statute than the FCPA in order to sanction foreign bribery.

6.3 Foreign bribery and concurrence of substantive laws

This section discusses the use of alternative charges in the US with comparative notes to UK enforcement and German enforcement. Alternative charges are important because the provisions of the OECD Convention overlap with legal provisions regulating other aspects of transnational economic crime. The US often applies the anti-bribery charges of the FCPA, with the alternative charges being supplementary. This usually helps the US enforcement authorities to stretch their jurisdiction and overcome certain limitations of the FCPA, for example, its exclusive application to foreign public officials as opposed to private officials. The UK and Germany use alternative charges either to mitigate limitations of their foreign anti-bribery laws or because it is procedurally efficient. The use of alternative charges by the UK and German authorities raises sometimes concerns of whether they are equivalent to foreign anti-bribery charges.

6.3.1 The US approach

The US enforcement authorities have wide discretion to decide which charges they use to prosecute international corruption. In foreign bribery cases, US authorities use a number of alternative statutes such as the Racketeer Influenced and Corrupt Organization Act (RICO),[9] the Travel Act, and the federal anti-money-laundering statutes, together with or instead of the FCPA. While the US authorities mainly apply the anti-bribery and the accounting provisions of the FCPA in order to prosecute foreign bribery schemes, alternative charges have been used as important supplements to the FCPA charges. In some cases, alternative laws allow the US authorities to

9 Section 901(a) of the Organized Crime Control Act of 1970, Public Law No. 91-452, 18 U.S.C. §§ 1961 – 1968.

sanction foreign bribery by indirect means even if its underlying acts are outside the US jurisdiction.[10] In other cases, the application of RICO and other statutes attenuates the distinction between public and private foreign bribery, and supply and demand side of foreign bribery. *FIFA Gate*, a corruption conspiracy case under investigation by US and Swiss authorities shows it all: The bribes of marketing multinational corporations can be seen as foreign, quasi-public, bribes as well as racketeering, breach of internal controls, books and records provisions, or money laundering.[11]

6.3.1.1 RICO as a special conspiracy: FIFA

In *FIFA Gate*, the US authorities applied RICO and its predicate offenses instead of the FCPA. Fédération Internationale de Football Association (FIFA), an international association registered under Swiss law with its main office in Zurich, was established with the aim to promote the game of football, organize international football tournaments, regulate the game, and promote integrity, ethics and fair play.[12] While FIFA is in principle a non-profit organization, the sports business is in large part based on operations of sport marketing corporations that commercialize the media and marketing rights to various sport events. International bribery of these corporations forms a large part of the *FIFA Gate* enforcement scheme.

The US authorities provide in their original 47-count indictment a detailed description of twelve criminal schemes. Ten out of the twelve schemes, including Confederación Sudamericana de Fútbol (CONMEBOL) Copa América scheme, the Confederation of North, Central American and Caribbean Association Football (CONCACAF) Gold Cup scheme, and the Brazilian Football Confederation (CBF) Sponsorship, are related to international bribery by sport marketing firms.[13] The rest included the 2010 FIFA World Cup Vote and the 2011 FIFA Presidential Election. Furthermore, in December 2015, the US authorities released a 92-count "superseding indictment" that was even bigger than the original indictment.[14] The superseding indictment included bribery schemes related to, for example, FIFA World Cup qualifications and friendly matches, and the bribery of sport marketing firms.[15]

10 See, for example, the use of export laws in *BAE* (Section 5.7.).

11 *United States vs. Webb et al., No. 15-cr-252* (20 May 2015) and *United States vs. Hawit et al., No. 15-cr-252* (25 November 2015).

12 See, generally, *FIFA Statutes: Regulations Governing the Application of the Statutes Standing Orders of the Congress*, April 2015 <http://www.fifa.com/mm/document/affederation/generic/02/58/14/48/2015fifastatutesen_neutral.pdf> accessed 26 December 2018.

13 Copa América is an international championship of South America organized by the South American Football Confederation – CONMEBOL. Gold Cup is a regional championship of North America, Central America, and the Caribbean organized by CONCACAF. CONMBEBOL and CONCACAF are two of the six confederations of FIFA.

14 *United States vs. Hawit et al., No. 15-cr-252* (25 November 2015).

15 United States Department of Justice, *Sixteen Additional FIFA Officials Indicted for Racketeering Conspiracy and Corruption* (Press Release 3 December 2015) <https://www.justice.gov/opa/pr/sixteen-additional-fifa-officials-indicted-racketeering-conspiracy-and-corruption> accessed 26 December 2018.

Bribes and other crimes in *FIFA Gate* were presented by the US enforcement authorities as the 24-year racketeering conspiracy during which the FIFA officials received well over $200 million in bribes and kickbacks. By December 2015, 41 individuals and corporations, including FIFA officials, sports marketing executives, agents operating in the broadcasting business, were charged with the racketeering conspiracy charges under RICO, and many of them pleaded guilty to the same charge.[16] Some of those who pleaded guilty agreed to pay significant sums of money in forfeiture – Darian Warmer (FIFA) $1.1 million, Charles Blazer (FIFA) $1.9 million, and José Hawilla (owner of the Traffic Group) over $151 million, and in total more than $190 million.[17] As of 17 December 2018, 22 individuals pleaded guilty or were convicted. Four corporations pleaded guilty or reached a DPA. Most of the sentencing is scheduled for the first half of 2019.[18]

RICO is a powerful tool that can be applied to big criminal schemes in their complexity by cumulating several offenses under a special type of conspiracy charges. The DOJ specifies in the original indictment that:

> [...] persons employed by and associated with the enterprise, which engaged in, and the activities of which affected, interstate and foreign commerce, did knowingly and intentionally conspire to violate Title 18, United States Code, Section 1962(c), that is, to conduct and participate, directly and indirectly, in the conduct of the affairs of such enterprise through a pattern of racketeering activity, as defined in Title 18, United States Code, Sections 1961(1) and 1961(5).[19]

The pattern of racketeering included:

1 wire fraud in violation of 18 U.S.C. §1343[20];
2 money laundering in violation of 18 U.S.C. §§1956–1957;[21]
3 interstate and foreign travel in aid of racketeering enterprises in violation of 18 U.S.C. §1952 (Travel Act);[22]

16 Ibid
17 Ibid
18 DOJ, *FIFA Prosecution United States v. Napout, et al. and Related Cases* <https://www.justice.gov/usao-edny/file/799016/download> accessed 27 December 2018.
19 Paragraph 265 of the Indictment, *United States vs. Webb* (n 11)
20 Wire fraud 18 U.S.C. §1343:

> [W]hoever, having devised or intending to devise any scheme or artifice to defraud, or for obtaining money or property by means of false or fraudulent pretenses, representations, or promises, transmits or causes to be transmitted by means of wire, radio, or television communication in interstate or foreign commerce, any writings, signs, signals, pictures, or sounds for the purpose of executing such scheme or artifice, shall be fined under this title or imprisoned not more than 20 years, or both.

21 Money Laundering Control Act 1986.
22 The Travel Act 18 U.S.C. §1952 (a):

> [W]hoever travels in interstate or foreign commerce or uses the mail or any facility in interstate or foreign commerce, with intent to - (1) distribute the proceeds of any

4 obstruction of justice in violation of 18 U.S.C. §1512;
5 commercial bribing and commercial bribe receiving in violation of §180.03 and §180.08 of the New York State Penal Law.

RICO has all the advantages of classic conspiracy statutes and adds some extra functions. In the classic conspiracies, for example, corporations and individuals may be held liable for the crimes of each other provided that such crimes are committed in furtherance of the conspiracy (Section 4.4.2). However, RICO offers more because its notion of criminal enterprise, a special kind of conspiracy, gathers together bribe-givers, bribe-takers, and other relevant entities. In *FIFA Gate*, businesses and a private association formed an association serving a legitimate purpose. However, the association was infiltrated by a mafia-like enterprise based on bribery relationships between the businesses and these in charge of FIFA. In effect, these subjects channeled money out of FIFA and corrupted the entire process. Constructing the scheme as a RICO criminal enterprise allows the US authorities to sanction foreign persons that even indirectly participated in the conduct of affairs of the enterprise, for example, by violating some of the predicate offenses of RICO.[23]

Furthermore, RICO allows the US authorities to impose generally harsher penalties than the anti-bribery charges allow. Under RICO, defendants might face imprisonment for up to 20 years, mandatory restitution, or forfeiture.[24] What is also important is that the racketeering charges based on a number of predicate offenses such as money laundering, commercial bribery, or wire fraud, reach long-lasting bribery schemes in their complexity.[25] RICO extends the statute of limitations and allows the prosecution of decade-old criminal schemes (Section 4.4.2). Such a broad reach is, however, not without controversy.

Federal and state courts have been long divided in their interpretation of how far RICO and other US statutes can reach outside the US territory. Lower US courts have adopted several lines of reasoning in RICO cases,

---

unlawful activity; or (2) commit any crime of violence to further any unlawful activity; or (3) otherwise promote, manage, establish, carry on, or facilitate the promotion, management, establishment, or carrying on, of any unlawful activity, and thereafter performs or attempts to perform - (A) an act described in paragraph (1) or (3) shall be fined under this title, imprisoned not more than 5 years, or both; or (B) an act described in paragraph (2) shall be fined under this title, imprisoned for not more than 20 years, or both, and if death results shall be imprisoned for any term of years or for life.

23 Criminal enterprise is a broad concept that may be either structured in a formal matter but maybe also a "group of individuals associated in fact." RICO, 18 U.S.C. §1961(4).

24 United States Department of Justice, *Nine FIFA Officials and Five Corporate Executives Indicted for Racketeering Conspiracy and Corruption* (Press Release 27 May 2015) <https://www.justice.gov/opa/pr/nine-fifa-officials-and-five-corporate-executives-indicted-racketeering-conspiracy-and> accessed 27 December 2018.

25 This cannot be done in a FCPA scheme directly because the FCPA is not a RICO predicate. Nevertheless, the FCPA is a predicate of the Travel Act. Thus, as the Travel Act is a predicate of RICO, FCPA violations may indirectly become predicate acts of RICO once they fell under the Travel Act.

some allows for broad application,[26] others, more restrictive, test whether the nature of the enterprise is domestic.[27] The latest approach, the so-called theory of predicate offenses, is somewhat a middle ground as it is based on an assumption that the US jurisdiction should reach as far as the jurisdiction over the RICO predicate offenses (for further discussion, see Gideon, 2013; Otey, 2015).[28] This approach was also used by the US Supreme Court in *RJR Nabisco Inc. v. European Community* (*Nabisco*) where the EU and its Member States filed a civil complaint in the US against RJR Nabisco, a corporation selling tobacco and food products.[29]

In line with *Morrison*[30]and *Kiobel*,[31] the Supreme Court in *Nabisco* narrowed the extent of US jurisdiction by foreclosing a private right of action for injuries suffered outside the US. Nevertheless, regarding criminal liability, the Supreme Court stated that RICO is "the rare statute that clearly evidences extraterritorial effect despite lacking an express statement."[32] Therefore, in some cases, RICO can be applied extraterritorially if its predicates, such as money laundering, do.

6.3.1.2 Other alternative statutes

The US authorities charged companies and individuals in foreign bribery schemes with a number of RICO predicates and other offenses. For example, in *Nexus Technologies*, a privately held US corporation bribed employees of a Vietnamese state-owned enterprise in order to acquire confidential information related to bids for supply contracts. In this case, the US authorities used the Travel Act together with the FCPA in order to prosecute both the corporation and its employees who bribed quasi-public officials.[33] The defendants tried to challenge that by arguing:

> [M]ere control of an entity by a foreign government no more makes that entity's employees "foreign officials" than control of General Motors

26 *United States vs. Chao Fan Xu, 706 F.3d 965* (9th Cir. 2013).

27 Laundering money through the US banks, for example, does not establish a sufficient link to the US territory once the criminal enterprise was entirely foreign *Cedeno vs. Intech Group, Inc., 733 F.Supp. 2d 471* (S.D.N.Y 2010).

28 *European Community vs. RJR Nabisco Inc et al., No. 11-cv-2475* (2nd Cir. 2014).

29 *RJR Nabisco, Inc. et al. vs. European Community et al., 579 U.S._* (2016).

30 Narrowing the extraterritorial application of US securities laws. *Morrison vs. Nat'l Austl. Bank, 561 U.S. 247* (2010).

31 Narrowing the extraterritorial application of the Alien Tort Claims Act.P908F *Kiobel vs. Royal Dutch Petroleum Co., 569 _* (2013).

32 Opinion of the Court, *RJR Nabisco, INC vs. European Community 579 U.S._*(2016) 12.

33 United States Department of Justice, *Nexus Technologies Inc. and Three Employees Plead Guilty to Paying Bribes to Vietnamese Officials* (Press Release 16 March 2010) <https://www.justice.gov/opa/pr/nexus-technologies-inc-and-three-employees-plead-guilty-paying-bribes-vietnamese-officials> accessed 27 December 2018. *United States vs. Nexus TechnologiesNo. 08-cr-522* (28 October 2009). Similarly, see *United States vs. Control Components, No. 09-cr-162* (22 July 2009).

by the U.S. Department of the Treasury makes all GM employees U.S. officials.[34]

The US authorities responded to Nexus's motion to dismiss the indictment by increasing the charges from 5 to 28, and the company ceased to exist at the end.[35] Therefore, both corporations and individuals should not rely on formalistic arguments related to the public vs. private nature of foreign bribery. In practice, this distinction is not too important, as the application of alternative statutes such as the Travel Act can overcome the fact that the FCPA regulates exclusively the bribery of public officials.

Furthermore, in a number of cases, both individuals and corporations were charged with violating the Money Laundering Control Act 1986.[36] At the side of individuals, as can be seen in *Esquenazi*, money-laundering charges in the FCPA schemes result in longer sentences. In *Esquenazi*, Joel Esquenazi and Carlos Rodriguez, executives of a US corporation, bribed directors of a Haitian state-owned telecommunication company in order to receive a preferential telecommunication rate for their corporation. Rodriguez and Esquenazi were charged with FCPA and money-laundering violations and received sentences of 7 and 15 years in prison respectively. In addition, the US authorities extended their jurisdiction to foreign officials who were bribed.[37] At the side of corporations, the money-laundering charges may activate forfeiture proceedings, and by that increase financial implication of their prosecution. Furthermore, statutes such as the Bank Secrecy Act[38] and Title III of the Patriot Act[39] provide additional deterrence, mainly to financial institutions.

34 Bohn, M. A. (2010) *Are GM Employees Government Officials?* FCPA Blog <http://www.fcpablog.com/blog/2010/4/22/are-gm-employees-government-officials.html> accessed 27 December 2018.

35 The charges included conspiracy to violate the FCPA, nine substantive FCPA violations, nine counts of money laundering, and nine counts of Travel Act violations, see *Nexus Technologies and Three Employees Plead Guilty* (n 33).

36 See *United States vs. Nexus Technologies* (n 33). United States Department of Justice, *Executive Sentenced to 15 Years in Prison for Scheme to Bribe Officials at State-Owned Telecommunications Company in Haiti* (25 October 2011) <https://www.justice.gov/opa/pr/executive-sentenced-15-years-prison-scheme-bribe-officials-state-owned-telecommunications> accessed 27 December 2018.

37 See, for example, United States Department of Justice, *Former Haitian Government Official Sentenced to Nine Years in Prison for Role in Scheme to Launder Bribes* (21 May 2012) <https://www.justice.gov/opa/pr/former-haitian-government-official-sentenced-nine-years-prison-role-scheme-launder-bribes> accessed 27 December 2018.

38 The Financial Recordkeeping and Reporting of Currency and Foreign Transactions Act of 1970 (Bank Secrecy Act).

39 Uniting and Strengthening America by Providing Appropriate Tools Required to Intercept and Obstruct Terrorism (US Patriot Act) Act of 2001.

Other alternative charges in the FCPA schemes relate to, for example, the export law, anti-trust law, and accounting law violations. First, the above-discussed *BAE* illustrates that if businesses bribe foreign officials and US military technology and other US-origin goods subjected to export license requirements are involved, the bribers can be sanctioned based on export laws.[40] Second, in some schemes, bribes in public procurement are not only used to influence the bidding process but can also be used to mask bid-rigging and price-fixing. Hence, the FCPA operates in tandem with the Sherman Act that prohibits anti-competitive activities. In *Bridgestone*, a Japanese corporation that sells chemical and electronic products were charged with conspiring to violate the Sherman Act and the FCPA. The corporations were part of a conspiracy that in furtherance of an international bid-rigging, price-fixing, and market allocation conspiracy, bribed foreign public officials in Latin America.[41] Last, the application of books and records, and internal controls charges is commonly used in foreign anti-bribery enforcement actions. The use of these charges is discussed in depth in Section 6.4 dealing with indirect bribery.

6.3.2 The UK approach

At least, in theory, the UK enforcement authorities do not have incentives to use specific laws against criminal enterprises or to apply alternative statutes in such a magnitude as the US. The Bribery Act provides for a wide extraterritorial jurisdiction, covers both bribe givers and bribe takers, and it is indifferent whether bribe-recipients are private officials or public officials. Yet, the UK authorities still do not have much experience with applying the Bribery Act in practice. The Bribery Act was enforced for the first time in November 2015. Before that, the UK authorities tend to use civil recovery orders more frequently than punitive fines.[42] While civil recovery orders are a solution that overcomes evidentiary problems connected with the old identification doctrine, they are not equivalent to criminal charges.[43]

In practice, the application of alternative charges is still important because the UK enforcement authorities are more limited in the way how they assign their jurisdiction over foreign anti-bribery cases than their US counterparts. Unlike US law, UK law has established more stringent conditions for being

40 See also *United States vs. Weatherford, No. 13-cr-733 and No. 13-cr-734* (26 November 2013). *Securities and Exchange Commission vs. Weatherford International Ltd, No. 13-cv-3500* (26 November 2013).

41 *US vs. Bridgestone Corporation, No. 11-cr-651* (15 September 2011). See also *Petrobras*, Trace, *Trace Compendium: Petroleo Brasileiro SA (Petrobras)* <https://www.traceinternational.org/TraceCompendium/Detail/594?type=1> accessed 14 January 2019.

42 OECD (2012) Phase 3 Report on Implementing the OECD Anti-Bribery Convention in the United Kingdom, 33. See also Harris, K. (2012) *The Territoriality of the Bribery Act.* MLex Magazine 60.

43 For the discussion about the identification doctrine, see Section 4.4.1. (UK law).

awarded a DPA. Furthermore, the UK does not automatically assume jurisdiction over every issuer and do not interpret the agency theory as loosely as the US. This is reflected in the Bribery Act 2010 Guidance:

> [T]he Government would not expect, for example, the mere fact that a company's securities have been admitted to the UK Listing Authority's Official List and therefore admitted to trading on the London Stock Exchange, in itself, to qualify that company as carrying on a business or part of a business in the UK and therefore falling within the definition of a "relevant commercial organisation" for the purposes of section 7. Likewise, having a UK subsidiary will not, in itself, mean that a parent company is carrying on a business in the UK, since a subsidiary may act independently of its parent or other group companies.[44]

These examples indicate that even if in theory the Bribery Act has a wider reach than the FCPA and related US anti-corruption laws, in practice this is not the case.

Regarding the UK approach to transnational economic crime more generally, we do not see a UK alternative to RICO. Only the UK anti-money-laundering regulation, mainly the Proceeds of Crime Act 2002, is to some extent comparable to the US approach. The Act, like RICO, cumulates a number of predicate offenses that may lead to money-laundering charges, but cannot reach so wide because the Act does not focus on an agreement between the members of a criminal enterprise, but rather on criminality related to property. Another possibility under UK law is the application of conspiracy charges. The UK conspiracy charges are again much narrower than RICO because of their inability to cover all offenses of criminal enterprises (Section 4.4.2). It is interesting to note that the US substituted the use of purely conspiracy charges for RICO particularly because they were considered ineffective in reaching criminal networks (Dubber and Hörnle, 2014: 644).

To summarize, the UK enforcement authorities do not use alternative charges to strengthen their enforcement. The wide reach of the Bribery Act finds its limits in the restrained freedom of UK enforcement authorities to conclude DPAs, in a narrower interpretation of what constitutes a relevant conduct in the UK, and how the agency theory is interpreted. This indicates that in some cases, the enforcement authorities might be incentivized to apply alternative charges such as civil recovery orders. Civil recovery orders, however, are not considered as functionally equivalent to criminal charges.

44 United Kingdom, *The Bribery Act 2010 Guidance*, para 36 <https://www.justice.gov.uk/downloads/legislation/bribery-act-2010-guidance.pdf> accessed 27 December 2018.

6.3.3 The German approach

The use of alternative charges is an important part of the German foreign anti-bribery enforcement practice. In the majority of cases, the German enforcement authorities used either the breach of trust charges (§266 StGB), commercial bribery charges (§299 StGB), and forfeiture orders (29a OWiG) instead of the foreign bribery charges (§334 StGB).[45] The use of alternative charges, especially the breach of trust and forfeiture orders, is likely to leave certain criminal acts outside of the scope of prosecution and are not an alternative to holding corporations fully liable for foreign bribery.[46]

One key reason why the German authorities have relied on the alternative provisions is that they generally require a lower level of evidence than foreign bribery charges. For example, the breach of trust does not require a proof that a bribe-taker is a foreign public official. It proved useful in *Siemens* in which the use of breach of trust charges helped to overcome evidentiary problems. Especially, there were doubts whether bribe-takers could qualify as foreign public officials under German law (Section 5.2.2). When it comes to forfeiture orders, these, similarly as the UK civil recovery orders, do not include a punitive element but a mere disgorgement of illicit gains.[47]

Another key element is the fact that German law does not allow the use of parallel charges, which is a common practice in the US. According to §261(9) StGB, a person punished for a predicate offense of money laundering, for example, the offense of foreign bribery, cannot be at the same time punished for money laundering.[48] This makes the German enforcement less effective because it narrows down the choice of German prosecutors how to construct an enforcement scheme. This, for example, also means that Germany cannot prosecute bribe-givers and bribe-takers in a single bribery scheme as easily as the US and the UK.

Regarding the German approach to transnational economic crime in general, we do not see a German alternative to RICO. One reason is that the vagueness of RICO and related US statutes would not pass the constitutional scrutiny of the German Federal Constitutional Court.[49] Furthermore, practitioners and policy-makers also acknowledged that the legal construction of organized crime would create too much controversy (Paoli, 2014: 21–22).

45 OECD (2018) Phase 4 Report on Implementing the OECD Anti-Bribery Convention in Germany, 30–32.

46 Ibid 65–66. OECD (2011) Phase 3 Report on Implementing the OECD Anti-Bribery Convention in Germany, 50.

47 OECD, Germany: Phase 4 (n 45) 65–66.

48 See, generally, Money Laundering Act Gesetz über das Aufpüren von Gewinnen aus schweren Straftaten vom 23 Juni 2017 (BGB1 I S. 1822, last amended 10 July 2018) (Geldwäschegesetz). See the discussion in OECD, Germany: Phase 4 (n 45) 78–79.

49 The question of constitutional conformity regarding RICO was an issue in the US too (see Bauerschmidt, 1990).

Hence, Germany adopted narrower and more precise provisions against organized crime than the US did. To give an example, German law under §129 StGB extends to "forming criminal organization" that penalizes acts that contribute to the existence and rise of the criminal organization, for instance, recruiting new members. Germany also sometimes expands the punishment of underlying crimes that were committed by a member of a gang (Dubber and Hörnle, 2014: 644).[50]

In all, the German authorities are relatively flexible and pragmatic in choosing charges. For example, they use alternative charges because they may be procedurally more efficient. This approach, arguably, is not equivalent to the use of foreign bribery charges. Moreover, the German enforcement authorities cannot use AML charges and foreign bribery charges in parallel. Last, German law does not recognize a concept of criminal enterprise similar to the one provided by RICO.

6.3.4 Concluding remarks

The use of alternative charges may have positive effects on collective action because their application can in some cases increase the jurisdictional reach of US law. For example, by applying export laws, the US enforcement authorities can reach bribing that does not otherwise have sufficient territorial links with the US. Furthermore, the US authorities apply alternative charges in order to make up for limitations of the FCPA, mainly in cases on the edge of private and public bribery, and in cases where they want to prosecute bribe-givers together with bribe-takers.

The use of alternative charges, however, is in some cases not equivalent to the use of the foreign bribery charges. If, for example, foreign bribery would be qualified as a Travel Act violation rather than a FCPA violation, a defendant might face lower sanctions. Similarly, in Germany, the use of the breach of trust charges and forfeiture orders instead of foreign bribery charges helps overcome a number of legal barriers but may lower the standard provided by the OECD Convention. In the UK, civil recovery orders are not equivalent to criminal charges.

Last, it must be also noted that no matter how functionally equivalent the alternative charges may be, they are followed by their own procedural context that may cause coordination challenges. In this way, coordination and cooperation tools and practices accompanying the enforcement of the alternative laws are also relevant for foreign bribery cooperation and coordination. The following text discusses in detail how the US authorities further extend their jurisdiction by establishing the liability of corporations for acts of third entities – indirect bribery.

50 See §335(2) (3) StGB.

6.4 Indirect bribery: parent–subsidiary liability and agency relationship

The vast majority of foreign bribery cases involved payments through marketing agents, consultants, brokers, distributors, and other intermediaries interacting with government officials.[51] This indicates that the provision of foreign anti-bribery enforcement depends largely on the ability of enforcers to hold corporations liable for bribes of their intermediaries and subsidiaries. We see this in the three main areas that are (1) parent–subsidiary liability, (2) mergers and acquisition, and (3) complicit conduct. This section discusses parent–subsidiarity liability and agency relationship.

US law establishes the liability of corporations for acts of third entities if a corporation sufficiently participates in the bribing activity, meaning that the corporation authorizes, directs, or controls the misconduct of the entities. Another way to trigger the corporate liability for violations of the FCPA is based on the agency control. These two approaches are not only applicable to the parent–subsidiary relationship, but also to the principal–agent relationship, and partially also to the successor–predecessors relationship. The following text discusses how these approaches are applied in concrete cases.

6.4.1 Anti-bribery charges and parent companies

The US enforcement practice indicates that a parent company that is not directly involved in the activity at hand may be liable even if it exercises only a limited general control over its subsidiary and the subsidiary's subsidiaries. In *Alcoa*, Alcoa World Alumina and Chemicals (AWAC), a US limited liability company that operates mining and refining facilities, entered into supply agreements with Aluminum Bahrain B.S.C. (Alba), an aluminum manufacturer owned by the Kingdom of Bahrain. AWAC is a majority-owned subsidiary of Alcoa Int., a US aluminum producer. AWAC used a London-based consultant to make payments to the Bahrain royal family in order to retain Alcoa's business with Alba.[52] The SEC provides five main elements that established the agency relationship. The SEC in the first place claims that subsidiaries of the Alcoa's subsidiary AWAC received policy and strategy directions via the Strategic Council chaired by Alcoa Inc. Second, Alcoa Inc. set business and financial goals, coordinated legal, audit, and compliance functions within the Alcoa group. Third, an Australian subsidiary that was involved in bribing transferred personnel to Alcoa Inc. Fourth, Alba was a

51 OECD (2014) OECD Foreign Bribery Report: An Analysis of the Crime of Bribery of Foreign Public Officials, 8–9 <http://www.oecd.org/corruption/oecd-foreign-bribery-report-9789264226616-en.htm> accessed 28 December 2018.

52 Armstrong, D. and Katz, A. (2014) *Billionaire Found in Middle of Bribery Case Avoids U.S. Probe*. Bloomberg <http://www.bloomberg.com/news/articles/2014-08-14/billionaire-found-in-middle-of-bribery-case-avoids-u-s-probe > accessed 28 December 2018.

customer of Alcoa Inc., and the representative of the two corporations met in order to discuss their business relationship. Finally, Alcoa Inc. was aware of the appointment of the London-based consultant.[53]

Alcoa illustrates that knowledge of the parent over acts of its independent subsidiaries is in practice not needed in order to hold the parent company liable for the violations of the FCPA. Rather, *Alcoa* charges are predominantly based on facts demonstrating the degree of general control between the parent and its subsidiaries. However, except for the fact that Alcoa Inc. was aware that the London-based consultant was appointed by AWAC, the SEC does not provide evidence of how the parent and subsidiary interacted in the context of the bribing activity. Moreover, the SEC provides that its investigation "contains no findings that an officer, director or employee of Alcoa knowingly engaged in the bribe scheme."[54]

Alcoa is similar to *Tyco* where a US corporation (Tyco USA), an indirect subsidiary of a Swiss-based manufacturer of water-based suppression system components (Tyco International), bribed the government officials of Saudi Arabia and other countries. Tyco Switzerland allegedly exerted control over Tyco USA because of the dual roles of its employees. In *Tyco*, the SEC considered this criterion as sufficient despite stating that:

> [W]hile there is no indication that any of these individuals knew of the illegal conduct described herein, through the corporate structure used to hold M/A-COM and through the dual roles of these officers, Tyco controlled M/A-COM.[55]

Therefore, the Alcoa group and Tyco International faced the anti-bribery, books and records, and internal controls charges of the FCPA without evidence of their control over the bribing activities of their subsidiaries, and without clear evidence that the specific purpose of the agency relationship was bribery.[56]

Moreover, in other cases, the US authorities provide practically no information about the bases of the parent's control. In *Pride International*, the DOJ charged Pride International, a US-based corporation operating gas-drilling equipment, without mentioning in what way that corporation was involved in a bribery scheme. The DOJ based its decision on the fact that a vendor of

53 Order, *Securities and Exchange Commission vs. Alcoa Inc, No. 3-15673* (9 January 2014) 4.

54 Ibid.

55 Paragraph 25 of the Complaint, *Securities and Exchange Commission vs. Tyco International Ltd, 12-cv-1583* (24 September 2012).

56 See also Williams, G. M. (2014) *The Alcoa FCPA Settlement: Are We Entering Strict Liability Anti-Bribery Regime?* The Harvard Law School Forum on Corporate Governance and Financial Regulation <http://www.wileyrein.com/resources/documents/2014-02-05-the-alcoa-fcpa-settlement-are-we-entering-strict-liability-anti-bribery-regime.pdf > accessed 28 December 2018.

Pride's Venezuelan subsidiary paid bribes "On behalf of PRIDE INTERNATIONAL."[57] In *Magyar Telekom*, three senior executives of the company, one being also a board member, concluded two secret Protocols of Cooperation with government officials. The executives hid these arrangements from the company and the company's parent DT, and "the existence and true purpose of the agreements were unknown to anyone within MAGYAR TELEKOM and DT other than" the executives and "a relatively small number of participants."[58] Furthermore, in *Bio-Rad*, a US-based corporation Bio-Rad Laboratories, providing life science and clinical diagnosis products, was held liable for the operations of its subsidiaries and agents in Russia, Thailand, and Vietnam. The agency relationship was found on the basis that the General Manager and the Controller of the Bio-Rad's Emerging Markets sub-division dealing with its foreign subsidiaries "ignored red flags, which permitted the scheme to continue for years."[59]

The imposition of vicarious liability under the anti-bribery provisions, based on the agency principle, used to be a pattern only in the context of the SEC enforcement. This pattern, however, has also emerged in some cases of the DOJ.[60] From this perspective, the provision of enforcement as a public good is further strengthened because the DOJ can enforce the FCPA against a much broader set of subjects than the SEC can. The DOJ has jurisdiction not only over the issuers and their affiliated persons but can also cover domestic concerns, and any other person that acts while in the territory of the US. Moreover, either because of reputation or because of the threat of being debarred from public contracting, the DOJ criminal anti-bribery charges have potentially more serious implications that the SEC civil charges. This influences the settlement negotiations between the US authorities and corporations and, as is discussed in the following text, in some cases results in the so-called consent jurisdiction.

6.4.2 Anti-bribery charges and consent jurisdiction over subsidiaries

Despite the discussion in the previous section indicates that in many cases, the US enforcement authorities use aggressive strategies to charge parent corporations for acts by their subsidiaries, the play is also reverse. The DOJ, for

57 Paragraph 36 of the Information, *United States vs. Pride International Inc, No. 10-cr-766* (4 November 2010).

58 *United States vs. Magyar Telekom, Plc, No. 11-cr-597* (29 December 2011). See also *United States vs. Deutsche Telekom AG, Non-Prosecution Agreement* (29 December 2011).

59 Paragraph 2 of the Order, *Securities and Exchange Commission vs. Bio-Rad Laboratories Inc, No. 3-16231* (3 November 2014). See also *United States vs. Bio-Rad Laboratories Inc, Non-Prosecution Agreement* (3 November 2014).

60 *United States vs. Magyar Telekom* (n 58). *United States vs. Ralph Lauren Corporation, Non-Prosecution Agreement* (22 April 2013). *Securities and Exchange Commission vs. Ralph Lauren Corporation, Non-Prosecution Agreement* (22 April 2013). Ralph Lauren is the first "double" non-prosecution agreement.

example, charges foreign subsidiaries on the basis of the anti-bribery provisions of the FCPA more often than parent companies.[61] In some cases, however, the DOJ can hardly justify why the parent company is not charged with violating the anti-bribery provisions of the FCPA. For example, DOJ evidence of endemic bribery at Siemens was very strong. Despite this fact, Siemens pleaded guilty only to the books and records, and the internal controls violations but not to the anti-bribery violations. Another example of this practice is the enforcement actions against Daimler AG, the German maker of Mercedes cars, where the company did not plead guilty at all, and agreed only to a DPA referring to the violations of books and records, and internal controls provisions. The language of the DOJ, however, indicates that foreign bribery was endemic and deeply rooted in the entire corporate network:

> [D]AIMLER engaged in a long-standing practice of paying bribes [...] through a variety of mechanisms, including the use of corporate ledger accounts known internally as "third-party accounts" or "TPAs," corporate "cash desks," offshore bank accounts, deceptive pricing arrangements, and third-party intermediaries. [...] Between 1998 and January 2008, DAIMLER made hundreds of improper payments worth tens of millions of dollars to foreign officials in at least 22 countries [...] to assist in securing contracts with government customers for the purchase of DAIMLER vehicles valued at hundreds of millions of dollars.[62]

Siemens and *Daimler* are examples of what is by some commentators called "jurisdiction by consent" (Pieth, Low and Bonucci, 2014: 635–636). The jurisdiction by consent is the result of the legal possibility given to the US authorities to negotiate an out-of-the-court settlement with corporate defendants (Section 4.8.4). In some enforcement schemes, a parent corporation manages to avoid criminal anti-bribery charges and is charged only with the books and records violations. In other cases, parent corporations are able to defer their prosecution over anti-bribery charges.

The record-keeping provisions of the FCPA and a DPA, instead of a guilty plea for the anti-bribery provisions, serve as a reward to the wrongdoers for agreeing to settle with prosecutors in a way that avoids debarment in jurisdictions that would otherwise debar, or consider debarment, based on the

61 *United States vs. Alstom SA et al., No. 14-245 – 248* (22 December 2014). The Hewlett-Packard's subsidiaries – Mexico, Polska, and ZAO (Russia), see, generally, Trace, *Trace Compendium: Hewlett-Packard Company* <https://www.traceinternational.org/TraceCompendium/Detail/175?class=casename_searchresult&type=1> accessed 28 December 2018. *United States vs. Alcoa World Alumina LLC, No. 14-cr-7* (9 January 2014). *United States vs. Weatherford* (n 40); *United States vs. Tyco Valves and Controls Middle East, No. 12-cr-418* (24 September 2012). *United States vs. Magyar Telekom* (n 58). The Siemens' subsidiaries – Argentina/Bangladesh/Venezuela, see Table 5.1 (Section 5.5.2). The Daimler's subsidiaries – China, Russia, and Dailer Export (Germany), see generally *United States vs. Daimler* (n 5).

62 Government's Sentencing Memorandum, *United States vs. Daimler* (n 5) 4.

anti-bribery charges. Instead of parent corporations, these that plead guilty are often their foreign subsidiaries. Because the jurisdiction is agreed between the corporate group and the authorities, the charges may be based on a limited evidence about the territorial nexus of the foreign subsidiaries with the US.[63] In this way, the US authorities can extend jurisdiction over corporations that in fact acted outside the US territory and are legally outside the US jurisdiction.

A similar trend can also be seen in the SEC enforcement actions. In *HP*, *Halliburton/KBR*, *ENI/Snamprogetti*, *Panalpina*, or *Royal Dutch Shell*, the SEC extended its jurisdiction and charged foreign subsidiaries with the anti-bribery charges as agents of their parents.[64] Some of these allegations are likely outside the SEC's jurisdiction because if it wants to charge foreign subsidiaries of issuers, it should show that an issuer directed or controlled its subsidiaries' decision to bribery or that there is an agency control. To give an example, it was discussed above in *Bonny Island* that ENI and its wholly-owned indirect subsidiary Snamprogetti settled with the SEC. Snamprogetti was charged with violating the anti-bribery provisions of the FCPA without any information of how it actually interacted with ENI in the scheme.

6.4.3 FCPA accounting provisions

The FCPA does not only contain the anti-bribery provisions, but also the accounting provisions.[65] The books and records, and internal controls provisions of the FCPA apply only to issuers, and the person that "knowingly circumvent[s] or knowingly fail[s] to implement a system of internal accounting controls or knowingly falsif[ies] any book, record, or account" of issuers.[66] In *Siemens*, *Daimler* and other, more recent, enforcement schemes, the accounting charges have been regularly used by the DOJ instead of the anti-bribery charges.[67] In many cases, as discussed above, this serves as a reward to corporations that cooperate with prosecutors.

63 *United States vs. Alstom SA et al.* (n 61). *United States vs. Magyar Telekom* (n 58). *United States vs. Ralph Lauren Corporation, Non-Prosecution Agreement* (22 April 2013). *Securities and Exchange Commission vs. Ralph Lauren Corporation, Non-Prosecution Agreement* (22 April 2013). *United States vs. SGA Societe Generale Acceptance, N.V., No. 18-cr-274* (5 June 2018).

64 *Securities and Exchange Commission vs. Hewlett-Packard Company, No. 3-15832* (9 April 2014). *Securities and Exchange Commission vs. Panalpina Inc., No. 4:10-cv-4334* (4 November 2010). *Securities and Exchange Commission vs. Royal Dutch Shell Plc, No. 3-cv-1410 (4 November 2010). Securities and Exchange Commission vs. Halliburton Company and Kbr Inc., No. 4:09-cv-399* (11 February 2009). *Securities and Exchange Commission vs. ENI, S.p.A. and Snamprogetti Netherlands B.V. 4:10-cv-2414* (7 July 2010).

65 See 15 U.S.C. §§78m(b)(2)(A), 78m(b)(2)(B),78m(b)(5).

66 15 U.S.C. §78m(b)(5). The DOJ is required to identify that the accounting provisions were violated with intentional acts, see §78m(b)(4) provides that "No criminal liability shall be imposed for failing to comply with the requirements of paragraph (2) of this subsection except as provided in paragraph (5) of this subsection."

67 See, for example, *United States vs. Alstom SA et al.* (n 61). *United States vs. Panasonic Avionics Corporation, No. 18-cr-118* (30 April 2018).

Yet, in other cases, the accounting provision of the FCPA allows the US enforcement authorities to sanction foreign bribery of corporations that could be otherwise difficult to prosecute via the anti-bribery charges. In *SQM*, the Chilean chemicals and mining corporations were charged with the internal controls and books and records violation of the FCPA. The corporation agreed to pay to the SEC and the DOJ $30.5 million because its former CEO allegedly made payments from a fund under his discretion to various foundations tied with Chilean politicians. In total, nearly $15 million in payments were made without evidence that any goods and services were received. These payments were not properly documented, violated Chilean tax laws, and political financing limits.[68]

The key issue in *SQM* is that both the DOJ and the SEC prosecuted the Chilean corporation without any evidence that the CEO acted in the US; for example, even the alleged payments were in the local currency. The only relevant criterion was the status of the corporation as a foreign issuer.[69] This explains why the US authorities were likely not able to use the anti-bribery charges. It is also worth noting that neither the SEC and the DOJ demonstrated evidence that the payments were bribes, and did not use the term "bribe" in relevant documents. Therefore, the SEC and DOJ may prefer to apply the accounting instead of, or together with, the anti-bribery provisions, if the authorities face evidentiary and jurisdictional difficulties, and to sanction a parent corporation if the enforcement authorities lack evidence about actual bribery payments.

Moreover, the accounting provisions are also special because the SEC charge issuers, and affiliated persons, for the actions of third parties that result in the circumvention of the issuers' books and records even if the issuers do not have actual knowledge about the third parties' behavior. For example, in *HP*, the bribery payments of the HP's subsidiaries were "falsely recorded in the subsidiaries' books and records and, ultimately, in HP Co.'s books and records."[70] The HP headquarters were held liable because they should have known that the bribery acts of the subsidiaries might have taken place, and should have had a compliance program effectively preventing the bribery. In addition, in *Archer Daniels Midland Company* (*ADM*), a manufacturer and seller of food and feed ingredients were held liable for books and records, and internal controls violations. The parent was held liable because its indirect 80%-owned foreign subsidiary bribed Ukrainian officials in order to incentivize Ukrainian officials to return more than $100 million that were owned to the company by tax authorities. After ADM's compliance

68 *United States vs. Sociedad Quimica Y Minera De Chile, No. 17-cr-13* (13 January 2017). *Securities and Exchange Commission vs. Sociedad Quimica Y Minera De Chile, No. 3-17774* (13 January 2017).

69 Ibid.

70 Paragraph 1 of the Order, *SEC vs. Hewlett-Packard* (n 64).

program discovered these payments, the parent corporation self-reported to the US authorities, and was charged even if it had no knowledge about these payments.[71]

Issuers are in fact vicariously liable if majority-owned subsidiaries falsify their books and records.[72] What is more, the SEC has arguably adopted even stronger strategy in the context of the internal controls violations. In some cases, as some commentators claim, the SEC charged the parent for insufficient internal control mechanisms without any evidence that would tie the insufficient internal controls with the alleged bribery actions.[73]

6.4.4 Concluding remarks

The US authorities interpret the agency theory loosely which allows them to charge both US and non-US issuers with the anti-bribery charges even if they have no, or very limited, knowledge about the bribes of their subsidiaries and agents. Moreover, in some schemes, the US authorities charge issuers, and their agents, with the books and records, and the internal controls provision without any evidence that would tie the insufficient internal controls and accountancy with the alleged bribery actions and about actual bribery payments. While these techniques undermine the rule of law, they are extremely effective in terms of the provision of enforcement.

These aggressive enforcement techniques are compromised by the possibility to negotiate agreements with the enforcement authorities. In many enforcement schemes, we see that parent corporations are not charged with the anti-bribery charges and the US enforcement authorities defer their prosecution. These parents often "sacrifice" their foreign subsidiaries that are forced to plead guilty with criminal charge despite jurisdictional and evidentiary problems that the US enforcement authorities face. This phenomenon was discussed as consent jurisdiction. These strategic considerations and background negotiations explain why both the DOJ and the SEC are arguably not consistent in applying the anti-bribery and accountancy provisions.

71 *Securities and Exchange Commission vs. Archer-Daniels-Midland Company, No. 13-cv-2279* (20 December 2013). The DOJ concluded a non-prosecution agreement with the corporation. The Ukrainian subsidiary pleaded guilty.

72 For further clarification, see Resource Guide (n 1) 43.

73 Order, *Securities and Exchange Commission vs. Smith & Wesson Holding Corporation, No. 3-15986* (28 July 2014) 3. See commentary in Fox, T. (2015) *Is Strict Liability Coming to FCPA Enforcement?* FCPA Compliance & Ethics <http://fcpacompliancereport.com/2015/03/is-strict-liability-coming-to-fcpa-enforcement> accessed 28 December 2018

6.5 Successor's liability

Merger and acquisition may enhance efficiency through economies of scale, bigger market share, and tax advantages (see, generally, Ilzkovotz and Meiklejohn, 2006). However, the corporate reorganization could also be used to avoid liability for foreign bribery. The FCPA counts with this problem and mitigates such strategies. A number of FCPA enforcement actions show that both the pre- and post-acquisition bribes of acquired entities may be prosecuted.[74] In *Johnson & Johnson*, a US issuer Johnson & Johnson (J&J) that manufactures and sells medical devices, pharmaceuticals, and health-related products decided to acquire DePuy. Already prior to the acquisition by J&J, DePuy and its subsidiaries paid bribes to Polish and Romanian doctors. In exchange, the doctors were prescribing drugs produced by J&J. After the acquisition, J&J decided not to cease the bribery that was happening prior to the acquisition. This was the reason why J&J was charged with the FCPA violations.[75]

However, the jurisdiction under the FCPA has its limits. The FCPA does not apply to situations where the pre-acquisition conduct of foreign entities was not subject to the US jurisdiction at the time of bribing. The US authorities provide that:

> [S]uccessor liability does not, however, create liability where none existed before. For example, if an issuer were to acquire a foreign company that was not previously subject to the FCPA's jurisdiction, the mere acquisition of that foreign company would not retroactively create FCPA liability for the acquiring issuer.[76]

This guidance was endorsed and further clarified by the DOJ Opinion Procedure Release.[77]

The application of the FCPA to merger and acquisition has important jurisdictional implications. In practice, every company under US jurisdiction must pay special attention to pre- and post-acquisition due diligence, and integrate the acquiring entity into its compliance program. By doing this, corporations that would not be otherwise be subjected to the FCPA standard can be policed. In other words, from the perspective of collective action, the successor's liability either changes many "bad" corporations to corporations that are more compliant, or if they do not change, imposes significant barriers on doing business between these corporations and the compliant

74 *United States vs. Johnson & Johnson (Depuy), No. 11-cr-99,* (8 April 2011). See further *Securities and Exchange Commission vs. Johnson & Johnson Corporation, No. 11-cv-686* (8 April 2011). See also *United States vs. Pfizer H.C.P. Corporation, No. 12-cr-169* (7 August 2012).

75 *United States vs. Johnson & Johnson* (n 74).

76 Resource Guide (n 1) 28.

77 DOJ, Opinion Procedure Release, No. 14-02, 7 November 2014 <https://www.justice.gov/sites/default/files/criminal-fraud/legacy/2014/11/14/14-02.pdf> accessed 30 December 2018.

corporations. Therefore, the imposition of the successor's liability further improves the provision of enforcement as a public good. The following section focuses on the enforcement of conspiracy provisions.

6.6 US enforcement and conspiracy charges

The conspiracy principle has developed in the US federal case law into a powerful tool that can hold one person liable for conduct of another person. Conspiracy involves at least two persons: co-conspirators that are related by an agreement to participate in the conspiracy (Section 4.4.2). This type of vicarious liability is constitutionally permissible if committed crimes are reasonably foreseeable among co-conspirators and are committed in furtherance of conspiracy (Doyle, 2016: 2). In foreign anti-bribery law, conspiracy charges are used as an important tool that improves procedural efficiency, stretches the US jurisdiction, and allows the US enforcement authorities to overcome evidentiary and statute of limitations issues.

6.6.1 Procedural efficiency

The key rationale for applying conspiracy charges is procedural efficiency. This is mainly true in long-lasting and complex bribery schemes. *Siemens*, *Bonny Island*, *Daimler*, *Panalpina*, and *Alcatel-Lucent* exemplify that the US authorities apply the conspiracy charges even if the US authorities can apply the conventional anti-bribery and accounting provisions.[78] For example, *Panalpina* involved operations of Panalpina World Transport, that was in 2010 a Swiss corporation and a non-issuer in the US, specialized in forwarding and logistics services, and its subsidiaries (Panalpina). Panalpina provided services to a number of US issuers operating in the oil and gas industry in Nigeria and at least six other countries. Regarding the Nigerian scheme, Panalpina was bribing Nigerian custom officials on behalf of its customers in order to "avoid local customs and import laws and processes by seeking to import goods without sufficient documentation, without being inspected or without paying the required taxes, duties or fees."[79]

78 *United States vs. Siemens Aktiengesellschaft, No. 08-cr-367* (15 December 2008). *United States vs. Marubeni Corporation, No. 12-cr-22* (17 January 2012). *United States vs. JGC Corporation No. 11-cr-260* (6 April 2011). *United States vs. Technip S.A., No. 10-cr-439* (28 June 2010) (note that the DOJ charged Technip also with substantive anti-bribery charges); *United States vs. Snamprogetti Netherlands B.V., No. 10-cr-460* (7 July 2010). *United States vs. Daimler* (n 5). Regarding *Panalpina* see Securities and Exchange Commission, *SEC Charges Seven Oil Services and Freight Forwarding Companies for Widespread Bribery of Customs Officials* (Press Release 4 November 2010) <https://www.sec.gov/news/press/2010/2010-214.htm> accessed 31 December 2018. *United States vs. Alcatel-Lucent France, S.A., et al., No. 10-cr-20906* (27 December 2010).

79 Paragraph 19 of the Information, *United States vs. Panalpina World Transport (Holding) Ltd, No. 10-cr-769* (4 November 2010).

Panalpina included the conspiracy charges against Panalpina, Pride International, Royal Dutch Shell, and other four corporations, and a number of subsidiaries that were all together fined approximately $236.5 million.[80] While the US authorities structured *Panalpina* as a conspiracy, most of the prosecuted corporations were also charged directly with violating the anti-bribery provisions. Nevertheless, announcing the criminal and civil resolutions at the same day and against all co-conspirators is procedurally efficient.[81]

6.6.2 Conspiracy charges stretch US jurisdiction

The conspiracy charges are also used to overcome legislative and evidentiary limitations. In enforcement schemes such as *Total* and *Alstom*, the US authorities applied the conspiracy charges in order to overcome several jurisdictional problems.[82] For one, although bribery acts cannot be prosecuted if they were completed before the general five-year limitation period, the conspiracy charges extend this period (Section 4.4.2). The trick is similar to the one discussed in *FIFA*: Conspiracy is completed only with the last act in the furtherance of the offense (Section 6.3.1). Second, conspiracy charges extend US jurisdiction also to foreign intermediaries that act outside the US territory and cannot be prosecuted under the agency theory. Third, conspiracy charges are a good vehicle for US authorities to bundle unrelated bribery allegations to encourage defendants into settling multiple charges in a single action. The following sections look into these three issues in more detail.

1 *Conspiracy extends the statute of limitations period*

The impact of conspiracy charges on the statutes of limitation period is clearly illustrated in *Total*. Total, a French issuer in the US market that

80 In the year 2010, the charged companies included: Panalpina, Pride International, Tidewater, Transocean, GlobalSantaFe Corp., Noble Corporation, Royal Dutch Shell, and a number of subsidiaries of these companies. Noble Corporation was formally not part of the conspiracy charges, and it agreed on a NPA, see *Seven Oil Services and Freight Forwarding Companies* (n 78). United States Department of Justice, *Oil Services Companies and a Freight Forwarding Company Agree to Resolve Foreign Bribery Investigations and to Pay More Than $156 Million in Criminal Penalties* (Press Release 4 November 2010) <https://www.justice.gov/opa/pr/oil-services-companies-and-freight-forwarding-company-agree-resolve-foreign-bribery> accessed 31 December 2018.

81 In addition, in 2013, Parker Drilling Company was charged. Together with Parker Drilling Company, the Panalpina scheme contains 17 settlements.

82 United States Department of Justice, *French Oil and Gas Company, Total, S.A., Charged in the United States and France in Connection with an International Bribery Scheme* (Press Release 29 May 2013) <https://www.justice.gov/opa/pr/french-oil-and-gas-company-total-sa-charged-united-states-and-france-connection-international> accessed 30 December 2018. United States Department of Justice, *Alstom Pleads Guilty and Agrees to Pay $772 Million Criminal Penalty to Resolve Foreign Bribery Charges* (Press Release 22 December 2014) <https://www.justice.gov/opa/pr/alstom-pleads-guilty-and-agrees-pay-772-million-criminal-penalty-resolve-foreign-bribery> accessed 30 December 2018.

from 1995 to 2004 bribed Iranian officials in order to re-enter the Iranian oil and gas market, settled with the US authorities in 2013. Most of the bribes took part from 1995 to 1997, and the only concrete territorial nexus to the US was a $500,000 transfer through a correspondent bank account in the US in July 1995.[83] This is raising not only statute of limitations problems but also jurisdictional issues. The 1995 transfer represents only a minimal part of the overall scheme because total paid approximately $60 million in bribes.[84] What is more, the DOJ was open about its struggle to overcome evidentiary challenges.[85] Despite these legal issues, these were the conspiracy charges that stood behind a $398 million settlement in 2013. The sanctions were awarded for conduct that happened from 10 to 18 years before the settlement.

2 *Conspiracy charges and foreign intermediaries that act outside the US territory*

The conspiracy charges further extend the US jurisdiction to certain foreign entities that do not act while in the territory of the US. The power of conspiracy charges can be seen in the case of a French rail transport company Alstom S.A. *Alstom* features a long-lasting scheme, where relevant acts took part from 1998 to 2011. During that period, foreign bribery was used endemically in order to obtain power and infrastructure projects all around the world, including projects in Indonesia, Saudi Arabia, Egypt, and the Bahamas.[86] In Saudi Arabia, for example, the Shoaiba project included the construction of power generating units. The value of the first two stages of the project – involving 11 separate power generating units – was approximately $3 billion.[87] At the end, the headquarters were charged only with the books and records and internal controls charges and subsidiaries with the conspiracy to violate the anti-bribery provision of the FCPA. Together with its subsidiaries and agents, Alstom settled with the DOJ in 2014 and agreed to pay a criminal fine of more than $772 million. The SEC did not have jurisdiction because Alstom de-listed from the NYSE in 2004.

Alstom illustrates that the conspiracy charges have a serious impact on foreign intermediaries. These intermediaries do not necessarily have to bribe while in the territory of the US if there is an evidence that they acted as agents of issuers and domestic concerns. In *Alstom*, the DOJ applied the conspiracy charges to three Alstom subsidiaries in order to overcome statute of limitations and jurisdictional problems. For example,

83 Paragraph 24 of the Deferred Prosecution Agreement, *United States vs. Total S.A., No. 13-cr-239* (29 May 2013). Paragraphs 9–10 of the Order, *Securities and Exchange Commission vs. Total S.A., No. 3-15338* (29 May 2013).

84 *French Oil and Gas Company, Total* (82).

85 Paragraph 24 of the Deferred Prosecution Agreement, *United States vs. Total S.A., No. 13-cr-239* (29 May 2013)

86 *Alstom Pleads Guilty* (n 82). *United States vs. Alstom SA et al.* (n 61).

87 Paragraph 58 of the Information, *United States vs. Alstom SA et al.* (n 61).

a Swiss subsidiary allegedly bribed from 2000 to 2011, while being an agent of an issuer (Alstom SA) from 2000 to 2004 only. As the conspiracy lasted until 2011, the DOJ was still on time with its charges in 2014 and was able to prosecute the subsidiary ten years after Alstom delisted. For the period after the subsidiary ceased to be an agent of an issuer, the DOJ does not provide clear evidence whether the subsidiary actually acted while in the territory of the US. This shows the power of conspiracy charges because once a foreign company is not an agent of an issuer or domestic concern, the DOJ needs to find the US territorial nexus to establish criminal liability.

The fact that the conspiracy charges are in some cases more effective in prosecuting foreign intermediaries than, for instance, the broad use of agency theory is clear in cases of foreign agents that are not subsidiaries of US issuers. Even though foreign agents take no action in the US, they can be charged with conspiring with issuers and domestic concern's violations.[88] Marubeni in *Bonny Island* was a foreign agent of the TSKJ joint venture, non-issuer in the US, and its corporate structure was not related to any TSKJ member. The DOJ charged the corporation with conspiracy and aiding and abetting because Marubeni agreed with its co-conspirators to violate the anti-bribery provisions. The bases for the jurisdiction was that at least one of the co-conspirators violated the anti-bribery provisions of the FCPA while in the US territory.[89]

3 *Conspiracy charges encourage corporations to settle multiple charges*

Yet from another perspective, the conspiracy charges are a good vehicle for US authorities to bundle unrelated bribery allegations to encourage defendants into settling multiple charges in a single action (Hock, 2018). In schemes such as *Teva*, the conspiracy charges allowed the US authorities to sanction the corporate group for a collection of substantively unrelated bribery acts that took part at different times in different jurisdictions.

Teva Pharmaceutical Industries, an Israeli-based manufacturer of pharma products, and its Russian subsidiary agreed with the DOJ and the SEC to pay more than $519 million because they allegedly paid bribes to government officials in Russia, Ukraine, and Mexico. These bribes were used to facilitate the approval of Teva's drugs and increase sales of its drugs. The DOJ charged the headquarters and its Russian subsidiary with the conspiracy to violate the anti-bribery provisions of the FCPA.[90] The DPA with the Israeli headquarters includes three substantively unrelated schemes in Russia, Ukraine, and Mexico. For example, the Russian

88 Resource Guide (n 1) 34.

89 Information, *United States vs. Marubeni* (n 78) 12 and 19.

90 United States Department of Justice, *Teva Pharmaceutical Industries Ltd. Agrees to Pay More than* $283 million to Resolve Foreign Corrupt Practices Act Charges (Press Release 22 December 2016) <https://www.justice.gov/opa/pr/teva-pharmaceutical-industries-ltd-agrees-pay-more-283-million-resolve-foreign-corrupt> accessed 31 December 2018.

scheme includes a series of bribes provided from 2006 through at least 2012 in exchange for influencing public procurement related to Copaxone, a pharma product used in the treatment of sclerosis. In Ukraine, Teva's employees, local subsidiary and foreign agents were bribing a government official between 2001 and 2011. For a decade, the official was paid a monthly consultation fee to retain the registration of TEVA products in Ukraine.[91]

Teva illustrates the added value of the conspiracy charges because the bases of the US jurisdiction are weak. In relevant documents, the DOJ refers to two bank transfers, $10,000 and $16,500, sent through intermediary bank account in New York to the official in Ukraine.[92] The Mexican and Russian schemes are solely based on email communication that was, implicitly, taking part through servers in the US. This shows that although settlements with the US enforcement authorities include multiple charges that some corporations would likely defend if brought in isolation, when faced with the alternative prospect of multiple actions, they preferred to buy these settlements.

Differently from *Teva*, the bundling effect in *Alstom* was achieved by combining the conspiracy charges the accounting charges. As these enforcement schemes illustrate, the bases of the settlement are sometimes striking. In *Alstom*, for example, the parent company pleaded guilty to violations of legal provisions in 2014, including conduct that took part in the period from 1998 till 2011, that did not apply to the company since 2004. Charging Alstom A.S. with the accounting provisions of the FCPA ten years after the Alstom's delisting could be considered as unfair. It could also be considered unfair to reach a DPA based on the anti-bribery charges with Teva without clear jurisdictional bases. Yet, corporations still tend to settle.

Corporations tend to settle because besides the functioning of the conspiracy charges, *Alstom* and *Teva* illustrate once again what was discussed as the jurisdiction by consent. Plead guilty with the anti-bribery provisions if only for some of bribery schemes mentioned in these settlements, would have had major consequences for the entire corporate group. Corporations clearly value the possibility to avoid a significant risk of being barred from the US, the EU and countries such as Canada,[93] or endanger their other business operations.[94]

91 *United States vs. Teva Pharmaceutical Industries, No. 16-cr-20968* (22 December 2016).

92 Paragraphs 68 and 70 of the Information, *United States vs. Teva Pharmaceutical Industries, No. 16-cr-20968* (22 December 2016).

93 For the discussion about the possibility of debarment, see, generally, Acorn (2016).

94 For example, the anti-bribery charges in *Alstom* could have undermined the planned acquisition of Alstom by General Electric. See Debevoise & Plimpton (2014) *FCPA Update: Alstom's $772 Million FCPA Settlement: The Wages of Late Cooperation and Other Lessons of the Settlement* <http://www.debevoise.com/~/media/files/insights/publications/2014/12/fcpa_update_dec_2014_final.pdf> accessed 31 December 2018.

6.6.3 Concluding Remarks

Yet another way to sanction indirect bribery is the use of complicit conduct charges. Conspiracy and aiding and abetting are legal tools that pertain more to substantive liability than jurisdiction, hence might be truly extraterritorial. The strategic consideration and the possibility to negotiate agreements with the enforcement authorities, similar to the parent–subsidiary liability, resulted in the aggressive application of these charges and the use of consent jurisdiction agreements. The conspiracy charges are special because they allow the US enforcement authorities to prosecute bribery schemes that could be otherwise outside the statute of limitations period. Moreover, conspiracy charges allow the US enforcement authorities to prosecute some foreign corporations that neither act in the US territory, nor can they be prosecuted based on the agency theory.

6.7 Cooperation and coordination

Cooperation and coordination, when concerned with enforcement, are crucial for achieving collective action. Legal institutions designed to support cooperation and coordination should build trust between enforcement authorities and contribute to the effective provision of enforcement as a public good. In this section, the three most important elements of cooperation and coordination, as they function in the context of foreign anti-bribery enforcement, are discussed. The first element relates to a more formal MLA that takes part before the final resolution of a case. The second relates to the use of a more informal and direct mechanism of MLA, including, for example, parallel investigation and prosecution. As will be seen, these more direct and informal mechanisms are crucial for the third element: coordination of investigation and prosecution (see, generally, Section 4.9.5).

6.7.1 Cooperation before the final resolution of a case by using MLA

The OECD Convention obliges signatories to provide MLA and encourages them to use a broad range of other legal instruments that exist outside the OECD legal framework, including, for example, general multilateral MLA treaties and bilateral agreements. MLA mechanisms such as obtaining information and evidence from other countries, securing the proceeds of crime, detention and transfer of prisoners, and arrest warrants, are based on both formal and informal interactions. These classic mechanisms are crucial for the effectiveness of enforcement because they initiate cooperation that makes investigation and prosecution more effective and efficient (Section 4.9.1).

While in some enforcement schemes, the US received MLA and cooperated with other countries, in other schemes, MLA was not provided. This is not only because of political and legal obstacles but also because of the lack of relevant data: MLA is confidential in the context of criminal investigation (OECD, 2017: 33). Hence, drawing a full picture of cooperation is a challenging task, and the information available is scare (Oduor, 2014: 63).

Foreign anti-bribery enforcement schemes provide some information how national enforcement authorities cooperate in foreign anti-bribery enforcement. A number of non-US authorities such as police, prosecutors, and courts are involved in providing MLA to the US authorities in foreign anti-bribery cases. For example, a number of MLA mechanisms such as freezing of assets depend on the approval of foreign judges. Furthermore, foreign police departments and specialized squads discover, document, and communicate basic facts, collect evidence, and arrest individuals. Foreign prosecutors share intelligence.[95] The US foreign anti-bribery enforcement to a large extent relies on the help of their foreign counterparts.

The US enforcement authorities recognize MLA provided by other states in press releases of their foreign anti-bribery enforcement actions. These press releases refer to various degrees of MLA that may range from a mere "acknowledgment of assistance"[96] through the "appreciation of the significant assistance"[97] and up to "deep appreciation of significant assistance"[98]. Between from 2008 to 2018, MLA provided from foreign authorities to the US authorities is recognized in 18 out of 27 largest FCPA matters that relate to non-US corporations.[99] No appreciation of MLA is mentioned in relatively older enforcement actions against Swiss-based corporations Weatherford, Panalpina, and ABB, as well as in cases of other non-US corporations including Daimler, Avon, SQM, Teva, Credit Suisse, and Petrobras.[100]

Nevertheless, most enforcement actions include MLA. In *FIFA Gate*, both DOJ indictments were preceded, at the request of the US, by raids by the Swiss police. The Swiss police arrested nine FIFA officials in Zurich just several hours before the US authorities announced the indictments. A number of these FIFA officials were later extradited to the US (Section 6.3.1). Moreover, in *HP*, the criminal scheme became public once the Russian authorities, at the request of the German Public Prosecutor in Dresden, raided the HP offices in Moscow (Section 2.3.2). One day after the raid in Moscow, the US authorities opened their own investigation in the matter.

Furthermore, MLA also includes requests to restrain assets related to foreign bribery. In *HP*, the DOJ refers to law enforcement partners in Mexico, the UK, Lithuania, Latvia, Italy, Spain, and Hungary, some of them assisting

95 See anonymized case studies of MLA in OECD (2012: 75–87) 75–87.

96 For example, *Bio-Rad*: the SEC recognized Bank of Lithuania, Financial and Capital Market Commission of Latvia, and British Virgin Islands Financial Services Commission.

97 For example, in *Magyar Telekom*: Switzerland, Germany, Greece, Hungary, and Macedonia were recognized.

98 *HP*: Poland, Germany, Mexico, the UK, Lithuania, Latvia, Italy, Spain and Hungary were recognized. In *Siemens*: "exceptional help provided, in the form of mutual legal assistance…"

99 Figure 7.2: Nationality of MNCs under the US anti-bribery laws (Section 7.3.2.) provides an overview of the 40 largest foreign bribery matters. Matters related to *Bonny Island* are counted separately. *SBM Offshore*, including an overlapping enforcement of the Dutch and US enforcement authorities, is counted as one matter.

100 Note that in *Teva*, Mexican authorities provided assistance but other relevant jurisdictions, namely Israeli, Russian, and Ukrainian authorities are not acknowledged.

with identification of money chains used for the legitimization of stolen assets.[101] In *FIFA Gate*, the US authorities sent a request to restrain assets to 13 countries and forfeited more than $190 million.[102] In a number of other enforcement schemes, the US enforcement resulted in a forfeiture of the proceeds of crime. Consider schemes such as *Bonny Island*, $149 million held in Swiss and Israeli bank accounts.

Last, sharing and obtaining evidence from abroad was easier thanks to the cooperative networks of the SEC. For example, in *Bio-Rad*, the SEC refers to assistance by banks and market regulators such as the Bank of Lithuania, the Financial and Capital Market Commission of Latvia, and the British Virgin Islands Financial Services Commission. For example, three offshore Russian agents were used by a Bio-Rad subsidiary in order to pay bribes. These agents had bank accounts in Latvia and Lithuania; hence, the assistance of relevant authorities in these countries was important for the SEC in order to gather sufficient bank evidence.[103]

6.7.2 The OECD: the emergence of a more direct cooperative network

The OECD anti-bribery enforcement regime is developing into an active, and rather informal, cooperative network of national enforcement authorities. While a formal MLA is common in foreign anti-bribery enforcement schemes, more direct and informal ways of cooperation between national enforcement authorities are relatively new. Between from 2008 to 2015, national enforcement authorities of countries such as Germany, the UK, Switzerland, and the Netherlands occasionally cooperated and coordinated their enforcement with the US enforcement authorities. This trend has increased in recent years, when between from 2016 to 2018, 7 out of 13 major US foreign anti-bribery enforcement actions against non-US corporations involved some form of direct cooperation and coordination.[104] This trend shows that the time has passed when the US was the only enforcer of foreign anti-bribery laws.

Since the late 2000s, foreign anti-bribery enforcement actions are increasingly concluded by several enforcement authorities rather than by enforcement authorities of one country. In this period, we see an activation of several

101 Ibid.

102 *Additional FIFA Officials Indicted* (n 15).

103 Paragraphs 2, 15, 19 of the Order, *SEC vs. Bio-Rad Laboratories* (n 59). Similarly, in *Alcoa*, the SEC recognized the assistance of authorities such as Liechtenstein Financial Market Authority, Norwegian ØKOKRIM, and United Kingdom Financial Control Authority. In *Panasonic*, the assistance was provided by Switzerland, Ontario, United Arab Emirates, Japan, Singapore, Malaysia, Australia, and Pakistan.

104 These include *Telia, SBM Offshore, Rolls-Royce, VimpelCom, Embraer, Odebrecht/Braskem, and Société Générale.*

major enforcement actors such as Germany, Switzerland, France, the UK, and the Netherlands. The following sections explain key patterns of cooperation that have accompanied foreign anti-bribery enforcement.

6.7.2.1 Siemens as the standard of global resolutions

The first example of a truly direct cooperation in foreign anti-bribery enforcement is *Siemens*, a global resolution in which the German and the US authorities maintained separate but parallel and cooperative investigations (Section 5.5). The authorities of both countries announced their resolutions at the same day, divided penalties between each other, and worked closely together throughout the entire process of investigation and prosecution.

Even if the OECD commended Germany for its excellent cooperation with other jurisdictions,[105] from a broader perspective, Germany is not mentioned by the US as a cooperative enforcement partner very frequently. For example, in *Daimler*, more than one year after *Siemens*, Germany is not mentioned even as an assisting country. Rather, *Daimler* is an example of a corrective function of the US enforcement because the SEC stated that, the Daimler's "conduct dates back to a time when such payments were not prohibited by German law, and therefore were tax deductible according to the German Tax Code."[106]

It must be stressed that the *Siemens* matter sets the standard of global foreign anti-bribery resolutions. Yet, in the context of US–German enforcement cooperation, this form of cooperative enforcement is rather an exception.[107]

6.7.2.2 Switzerland and bank transparency

While the majority of countries in a post-*Siemens* enforcement landscape remain rather passive, some countries have become more active in the investigation and prosecution of foreign bribery and international economic

105 OECD (2011) Phase 3 Report on Implementing the OECD Anti-Bribery Convention in Germany, 48.

106 Complaint, *Securities and Exchange Commission vs. Daimler AG, No. 10-cv-473* (22 March 2010) 4.

107 Note that there are some relatively smaller cases such as *ADM*. In *ADM*, the German and US enforcement authorities worked in a close cooperation with each other, and their parallel investigations resulted in settlements with a parent corporation and its Ukrainian subsidiary in the US. They agreed to pay $54 million to the US authorities. In addition, a German subsidiary of ADM, Alfred C. Toepfer International, was charged in Germany. US authorities deducted the German sanction of more than $1.3 million from the US penalty in order to avoid the duplication of fines. Plea agreement at para 16, *United States vs. Alfred C. Toepfer International Ukraine Ltd, No. 13-cr-20062* (20 December 2013). See also Martin Kopp, *Korruption beim Getreidehändler* (Welt, 15 February 2014) <http://www.welt.de/print/die_welt/hamburg/article124871975/Korruption-beim-Getreidehaendler.html> accessed 8 January 2019.

crimes in general. This transition in international bribery law relates to new developments in international tax law such as the adoption of the new standard for the automatic exchange of information in tax matters. These new standards are pressing some of the biggest offshore wealth centers such as Switzerland to abandon strict bank secrecy protection.[108] More transparency about financial flows and ownership then makes the provision of foreign bribery enforcement easier.

The Swiss transition can also be seen in foreign anti-bribery enforcement. In the post-Siemens landscape, the US targeted a number of Swiss corporations. In these high-profile US enforcement actions including *Weatherford International* ($252 million), *Panalpina* ($82 million), and *ABB* ($58.3 million), the Swiss authorities did not assist or cooperate at all.[109] More recently, however, the Swiss have been more actively cooperating with the US. In enforcement schemes such as *Alstom* and *Alcoa*, both resolved in 2014, the US authorities recognized significant cooperation and assistance provided by the Office of the Attorney General of Switzerland. One year later, in *FIFA Gate*, the US authorities already refer to "continuing outstanding assistance" with Switzerland.[110]

This outstanding assistance has been transformed into direct cooperation that between from 2016 to 2018 allowed the US and other enforcement authorities to resolve foreign bribery cases with record sanctions. In *VimpelCom*, Swiss authorities were the first to initiate a foreign anti-bribery investigation into $114 million bribes paid by VimpelCom to an Uzbek government official in order to enter and remain in the Uzbek telecom market.[111] Consequently, VimpelCom, a US issuer and Amsterdam-based corporations, and its Uzbek subsidiary reached a $795 million global settlement with the US and Dutch enforcement authorities. The crucial issue was that Swiss authorities confiscated hundreds of millions dollars in the investigation and, based on the

108 For the discussion about the automatic exchange of tax information in Section 9.5.3.

109 Securities and Exchange Commission, *SEC Charges Weatherford International With FCPA Violations* (Press Release 26 November 2013) <https://www.sec.gov/News/PressRelease/Detail/PressRelease/1370540415694> accessed 10 January 2019. *Oil Services Companies* (n 80). United States Department of Justice, *ABB Ltd and Two Subsidiaries Resolve Foreign Corrupt Practices Act Investigation and Will Pay $19 Million in Criminal Penalties* (Press Release 29 September 2010) <https://www.justice.gov/opa/pr/abb-ltd-and-two-subsidiaries-resolve-foreign-corrupt-practices-act-investigation-and-will-pay> accessed 10 January 2019.

110 *Additional FIFA Officials Indicted* (n 15). However, cooperation is not mentioned in the *Credit Suisse*, a NPA with the Swiss headquarters and its Hong Kong subsidiary, total combined sanction of $76.8 million. *In re Credit Suisse (Hong Kong) Limited* (24 May 2018).

111 Trace, *Trace Compendium: VimpelCom Ltd.* <https://www.traceinternational.org/Trace-Compendium/Detail/625?class=casename_searchresult&type=1> accessed 9 January 2019. DOJ, *VimpelCom Limited and Unitel LLC Enter into Global Foreign Bribery Resolution of more than $795 million* (18 February 2016) <https://www.justice.gov/opa/pr/vimpelcom-limited-and-unitel-llc-enter-global-foreign-bribery-resolution-more-795-million> accessed 28 December 2018.

request by the US, frozen funds with links to Uzbek government officials.[112] Swiss authorities also played a crucial role in later resolutions such as *Odebrecht/Braskem*[113] and *Societe Generale.*[114]

6.7.2.3 UK, France, and the Netherlands getting over lax enforcement

Until at least 2016, major foreign anti-bribery enforcement schemes that involved the UK and French corporations show a mixed record about the UK and French willingness to cooperate with the US.

The UK enforcement authorities, after the *BAE* fiasco and relatively low levels of foreign anti-bribery enforcement, have shown more cooperation and engagement. In a number of foreign anti-bribery enforcement schemes, the US and UK enforcement authorities cooperated throughout the entire process of investigation and prosecution. In *Innospec*, the US authorities acknowledged "the extensive coordination and cooperation with the SFO," and both the SFO and the DOJ refer to the outcome as "the global settlement."[115] The UK, as well as the US authorities, took into account the potential of Innospec's insolvency. To keep the corporation alive, they agreed to charge the company with lower sanctions, and also agreed to split the sanction of $40.2 million between each other – the DOJ ($14.1), the SEC ($11.2), the Department of the Treasury's Office of Foreign Assets Control (OFAC) ($2.2), and the SFO ($12.7).

Due to their more direct cooperation, supported by several new policies that formally support cooperation and coordination, resolutions in several other parallel anti-bribery enforcement schemes were highly coordinated. In *J&J*, the anticipated penalties in the UK were taken into account.[116] In *AON* and *ICBC*, the US authorities agreed to credit sanctions paid to the UK authorities.[117]

112 Trace, *Trace Compendium: VimpelCom Ltd.* <https://www.traceinternational.org/Trace-Compendium/Detail/625?class=casename_searchresult&type=1> accessed 9 January 2019.

113 *United States vs. Odebrecht S.A., No. 16-cr-00643* (21 December 2016).

114 *United States vs. Société Générale S.A., No. 18-cr-00253* (4 June 2018).

115 United States Department of Justice, *Innospec Inc. Pleads Guilty to FCPA Charges and Defrauding the United Nations; Admits to Violating the U.S. Embargo Against Cuba* (18 March 2010) <https://www.justice.gov/opa/pr/innospec-inc-pleads-guilty-fcpa-charges-and-defrauding-united-nations-admits-violating-us> accessed 10 January 2019. Serious Fraud Office, *Innospec Ltd* (Case Information) <https://www.sfo.gov.uk/cases/innospec-ltd/> accessed 24 December 2018.

116 United States Department of Justice, *Johnson & Johnson Agrees to Pay $21.4 Million Criminal Penalty to Resolve Foreign Corrupt Practices Act and Oil for Food Investigations* (8 April 2011) <https://www.justice.gov/opa/pr/johnson-johnson-agrees-pay-214-million-criminal-penalty-resolve-foreign-corrupt-practices-act> accessed 10 January 2019.

117 Department of Justice, *Aon Corporation Agrees to Pay a $1.76 Million Criminal Penalty to Resolve Violations of the Foreign Corrupt Practices Act* (20 December 2011) <https://www.justice.gov/opa/pr/aon-corporation-agrees-pay-176-million-criminal-penalty-resolve-violations-foreign-corrupt> accessed 11 January 2019.

Clearly, and as will be also discussed in *Rolls-Royce* bellow, splitting of global settlements is becoming a trend that evidences the existence of network of cooperative enforcement authorities. In this context, US–UK interactions have led to activation of the UK authorities, as they have started pursing their own enforcement actions based on the Bribery Act, and applying in practice legal instruments such as DPAs, originally used only in the US in foreign anti-bribery enforcement.

France has experienced similar transition as the UK but a little later. The *Total* resolution, for example, was described as an example of direct cooperation between the US and French enforcement authorities. In 2013, the US authorities indicated that *Total* was:

> [...] the first coordinated action by French and U.S. law enforcement in a major foreign bribery case. Our two countries are working more closely today than ever before to combat corporate corruption, and Total, which bought business through bribes, now faces the criminal consequences across two continents.[118]

At the time of the US settlement with Total, the French prosecution announced that they would bring Total to trial and complement the US enforcement.[119] The first instance court, however, acquitted Total and a number of its executives. Nevertheless, the Paris court of appeals finally charged Total with the fine of EUR 750,000 for bribing Iranian public officials.[120] This is rather low fine when compared to the $398 million resolution of the scheme in the US in 2013. The French case was concluded only in February 2016 with much lower sanctions. This reluctance to fully cooperate was also apparent in other enforcement schemes related to France. At the end of 2014, in the *Alstom* resolution, the US authorities did not recognize a French assistance in the matter, even not in a form of a formal MLA, in their original press release.[121]

France has changed only with Sapin II, new foreign anti-bribery legislation that allows for extraterritorial application, DPAs, and sanctioning

118 *French Oil and Gas Company, Total* (82).

119 Reuters, *Total Oil Company to Face Trial Over Claims of Graft Tied to Iran Contracts* (*NY Times*, 25 November 2014) <http://www.nytimes.com/2014/11/26/business/international/total-to-face-trial-over-claims-of-graft-tied-to-iran-contracts.html?_r=0> accessed 11 January 2019.

120 While in the US Total faced penalties of $398 million, the French enforcement was concluded only in February 2016. Trace, *Trace Compendium: Total SA* <https://www.traceinternational.org/TraceCompendium/Detail/141?class=casename_searchresult&type=1> accessed 11 January 2019.

121 *French Oil and Gas Company, Total* (82). Nevertheless, the US authorities in a press release related to the sentencing by a judge, 11 months after the original settlement, recognized a French cooperation. See United States Department of Justice, *Alstom Sentenced to Pay $772 Million Criminal Fine to Resolve Foreign Bribery Charges* (Press Release 13 November 2015) <https://www.justice.gov/opa/pr/alstom-sentenced-pay-772-million-criminal-fine-resolve-foreign-bribery-charges> accessed 11 January 2019.

corporations for failure to implement effective internal compliance mechanisms even without any bribery taking place.[122] In *Societe Generale*, for the first time, France was able to fully coordinate with the US its first global resolution in a foreign bribery case.[123] The French headquarters, a US issuer, concluded a DPA and its subsidiary based in Curacao pleaded guilty for a conspiracy to violate the anti-bribery provisions of the FCPA.[124] The scheme is based on bribes paid in order to obtain investments made by Libyan state-owned financial institutions worth $3.66 billion. In result, the French group agreed to pay more than $585 million for the FCPA part. The US split the penalties with the French authorities, offsetting up to $292.8 million paid to the Parquet National Financier.[125]

It must be noted that besides the UK and France, a significant increase in enforcement and cooperation can be also seen in the Netherlands, being it evidenced by the above discussed *VimpelCom*, or other enforcement actions such as *SBM Offshore* and *Telia*. *SBM Offshore* is the first major enforcement action resolved by the Dutch enforcement authorities. The Dutch Openbaar Ministerie settled with SBM Offshore N.V. (SBM), a Dutch-based corporation and US issuer that focuses on selling systems and services related to oil and gas industry, for a $240 million fine on account of SBM bribes in Equatorial Guinea, Angola, and Brazil.[126] In Brazil, SBM's most important customer is Petróleo Brasileiro S.A. (Petrobras), partially owned by the Brazilian state. According to Dutch authorities, between 2007 and 2011, the company used sales agents that bribed Brazilian foreign public officials via multiple offshore entities.[127]

It must be noted that *SBM Offshore* was resolved after a number of US enforcement actions against Dutch-based corporations, for example, *Snamprogetti* ($240 million), *Royal Dutch Shell* ($48 million), and *KPMG* ($8.2 million), where the Netherlands was not even mentioned as an assisting country.[128] This activation of the Dutch enforcement only confirms the patter that was illustrated in Germany, the UK, Switzerland, and France.

122 LOI n° 2016–1691 du 9 décembre 2016 relative à la transparence, à la lutte contre la corruption et à la modernisation de la vie économique (Sapin II), available at https://www.legifrance.gouv.fr/affichLoiPubliee.do?idDocument=JORFDOLE000032319792&type=general&legislature=14, accessed 11 January 2019.

123 *United States vs. Société Générale S.A., No. 18-cr-00253* (4 June 2018).

124 Note that one part of the scheme also includes manipulations of interest rates.

125 Deferred Prosecution, *United States vs. Société Générale S.A., No. 18-cr-00253* (4 June 2018), 13–14.

126 Openbaar Ministerie, *SBM-offshore schikt voor 240 miljoen* (Press Release 7 July 2015) <https://www.om.nl/onderwerpen/cybercrime/@89993/sbm-offshore-schikt/> accessed 12 January 2019.

127 Ibid.

128 *Snamprogetti* is part of Bonny Island (Section 5.6.). *Dutch Royal Shell* is part of *Panalpina*, see *Seven Oil Services and Freight Forwarding Companies* (n 78). For *KPMG* see Securities and Exchange Commission, *SEC Charges KPMG Violating Auditor Independence Rules* (Press Release 24 January 2014) <https://www.sec.gov/News/PressRelease/Detail/PressRelease/1370540667080#.UuKqm_30Cu4> accessed 12 January 2019.

6.7.3 Coordination of enforcement

Foreign anti-bribery enforcement schemes in which the US and other countries such as Germany, Switzerland, France, the Netherlands, and the UK directly cooperate usually lead to more coordinated resolutions. More cooperation promotes coordination by preventing the duplication of effort and large conflicts among jurisdictions OECD (2012: 48). From around 2016, the dominant means to achieve large foreign anti-bribery resolutions has become multijurisdictional settlements. As will be discussed in the following section, the key implication of multijurisdictional settlements is that they usually involve negotiations between multiple national enforcement authorities and provide a good chance to achieve a more coordinated resolution. Yet, as will be also discussed, not all settlements are multijurisdictional and not all multijurisdictional settlements lead to coordinated enforcement. In some schemes such as settlements related to the Brazilian state-owned corporations Petrobras, collective action is undermined by the lack of coordination and jurisdictional conflicts.

6.7.3.1 Direct cooperation leads to more coordination: multijurisdictional settlements

Between from 2016 to 2018, the US enforcement authorities concluded 15 foreign anti-bribery enforcement actions with sanctions above $30 million. In 7 of these 15 actions, multiple jurisdictions coordinated their enforcement and divided sanctions.[129] The emergence of multijurisdictional settlements indicates that the foreign anti-bribery enforcement landscape has become an enforcement network with shared jurisdiction over international bribery schemes. These multijurisdictional settlements require not only negotiations with corporations and enforcement authorities, but also with enforcement authorities themselves.[130]

Consider Rolls-Royce plc, the UK-based manufacturer and distributor of power systems, that agreed to pay more than $800 million for its bribes in countries such as Thailand, Brazil, Kazakhstan, Azerbaijan, Angola, Iraq, China, India, Indonesia, Malaysia, Nigeria, and Russia between 1989 and 2013. *Rolls-Royce* is a global corporate resolution with authorities in the US, the UK, and Brazil. *Rolls-Royce* includes an agreement between multiple enforcement authorities to split corporate sanctions. The DOJ indicated that "this successful parallel investigation is a tremendous example of the central

129 SBM Offshore is not included. While the US authorities argue that they credited SBM's previous payment to the Dutch authorities and prospective payments to the Brazilian authorities in calculating its fine, this cannot be considered as fully coordinated resolution.

130 Article 4(3) of the OECD Anti-Bribery Convention and other international anti-corruption instruments envisages negotiations between enforcement authorities.

importance of working cooperatively alongside our international partners to achieve a fair and meaningful resolution."[131] This means that the Brazilian authorities covered bribery related to Petrobras, a Brazilian state-owned petroleum corporation, and sanctioned Rolls-Royce with $25.6 million. The UK part resulted in a fine of £497 million related to corrupt schemes in China, Indonesia, Malaysia, Nigeria, Russia, and Thailand. The US enforcement element yielded $170 million for corruption in Thailand, Kazakhstan, Azerbaijan, Angola, and Iraq. The practice of splitting sanctions and taking into account parallel enforcement of multiple authorities heralds a new pattern. *Table 6.1* below provides more detail about enforcement schemes that include multijurisdictional settlements.

Table 6.1 above also provides schemes in which Brazilian and other enforcement authorities have coordinated their enforcement with the US enforcement authorities. As large sums are involved, foreign anti-bribery enforcement includes complex negotiations between a corporate wrongdoer and multiple enforcement authorities, and between enforcement authorities themselves. In this context, Assistant Attorney General Caldwell commented that:

> [...] sometimes the center of gravity in a case is in another country; it makes sense to do the case there. It's probably no secret to say sometimes there's a bit of negotiation involved. But our default position is not, "We get the case, and you can have the table scraps." [...] it's often appropriate for cases to be prosecuted sometimes in both places, sometimes different people in different countries.[132]

The said negotiations between multiple enforcement authorities are by themselves a form of cooperation that makes it more likely that enforcement is coordinated. The result of these negotiations depends on many variables such as the bargaining position of enforcement authorities, political and economic relations between involved countries, but also the rule of law.

131 DOJ, *Rolls-Royce plc Agrees to Pay $170 Million Criminal Penalty to Resolve Foreign Corrupt Practices Act Case* (Press Release, 17 January 2017) <https://www.justice.gov/opa/pr/rolls-royce-plc-agrees-pay-170-million-criminal-penalty-resolve-foreign-corrupt-practices-act> accessed 12 January 2019. United States vs. *Rolls-Royce PLC, No.2:16-cr-00247* (20 December 2016). Regina v Rolls-Royce plc, Rolls-Royce Energy Systems, Inc. Statement of Facts (17 January 2017) available at https://www.sfo.gov.uk/cases/rolls-royce-plc/ accessed 12 January 2019.

132 The citation taken from Debevoise & Plimpton (2014) *Small Country, Big Punch: The Netherlands' Anti-Bribery Prosecution of SBM Offshore.* 6 FCPA Update 5, p. 21 <https://www.debevoise.com/~/media/files/insights/publications/2014/12/fcpa_update_dec_2014_final.pdf> accessed 14 January 2019. The source refers to "Transcript: Leslie Caldwell Q&A at the American Conference Institute's 2014 FCPA Conference," Main Justice: Just Anti-Corruption (19 November 2012).

Table 6.1 Multijurisdictional Settlements and Penalties

<table>
<tr><th>Multijurisdictional Settlements 2016-18</th><th colspan="3">Penalties in multijurisdictional settlements – countries</th><th colspan="2">Total Penalties</th></tr>
<tr><td>VimpelCom</td><td colspan="3">Netherlands (NL) $397.5 million</td><td colspan="2">$795 million</td></tr>
<tr><td>Embraer</td><td colspan="3">Brazil $20 million</td><td colspan="2">$205 million</td></tr>
<tr><td>Odebrecht/ Braskem</td><td colspan="3">Criminal Odebrecht: Brazil $2.08 billion; Swiss $260 million; US $93 million
Criminal Braskem: Brazil $442.8 million; US and Swiss both $94.9 million
Civil Braskem: Brazil $260 million; US $65 million</td><td colspan="2">$3.39 billion</td></tr>
<tr><td>Telia</td><td colspan="3">NL $274 million; Sweden – court proceedings are ongoing; SEC agreed to credit any disgorged profits paid to the Dutch and Swedish up to half of the total</td><td colspan="2">$965 million</td></tr>
<tr><td>Keppel</td><td colspan="3">Brazil $211 million; Singapore $105.5 million</td><td colspan="2">$422 million</td></tr>
<tr><td>Rolls Royce</td><td colspan="3">UK £497 million; Brazil $25.6 million</td><td colspan="2">$800 million</td></tr>
<tr><td>Societe Generale</td><td colspan="3">France $292.8 million</td><td colspan="2">$585 million</td></tr>
<tr><th colspan="6">Non-US Enforcement Authorities – Coordinated Penalties</th></tr>
<tr><td>Brazil
$3198 mil</td><td>Netherlands
$671.5 mil</td><td>UK
£497 mil</td><td>Switzerland
$354.9 mil</td><td>France
$292.8 mil</td><td>Singapore
$105.5 mil</td></tr>
</table>

6.7.3.2 Petrobras and coordination challenges

The increase in multijurisdictional settlements does not necessarily mean that the enforcement is coordinated. After all, the recent increase of foreign anti-bribery enforcement is taking part under enforcement pressure created by the US enforcement authorities. For example, the focus of US enforcement on Swiss, Dutch, Brazilian, and French corporations incentivized national enforcement authorities of these countries to act. Have countries such as Brazil, the Netherlands, and France not cooperated with the US enforcement authorities, sanctions collected from their national corporate champions would likely go only to the US treasury.

Yet, foreign anti-bribery enforcement provides more public goods only if it is coordinated. And this is not always the case. The key issue is that some multijurisdictional settlements stem a systemic coordination problem. While some multijurisdictional settlements seem coordinated, their conclusion is influenced by considerations of political interest. In some cases, this leads to a situation that resembles a trade war between multiple enforcement authorities that impose tariffs on each other's national corporate champions. The most important example of the systemic coordination problems is Petrobras-related enforcement actions such as *SBM Offshore, Odebrecht/Braskem, Petrobras, Rolls-Royce*, and *Keppel*.[133] This scheme is discussed in the following sections.

1 *Coordination problems and suppliers: SBM Offshore*

The core of Petrobras-related enforcement actions is a cartel formed by companies that were suppliers to the Brazilian state-owned corporations Petrobras. The cartel operated in collusion with Petrobras officials, deciding about the buying needs of Petrobras, overcharging bids, and deciding who would win these bids. These bids were rigged in exchange for kickbacks to the Petrobras officials and Brazilian politicians and political parties.[134]

The first major prosecution related to Petrobras is the above-discussed *SBM Offshore*. If analyzed without a broader context, *SBM Offshore* could be presented as a good example of coordination between the Dutch enforcement authorities and the US enforcement authorities. *SBM Offshore* self-disclosed both in the Netherlands and the US and cooperated with both authorities. The investigation focused on foreign bribery in three countries, Brazil, Angola, and Equatorial Guinea.[135] The settlement included a $40 million criminal fine and $200 million in disgorgement.[136] The majority of bribers, $123.7 million of the $200 million, was paid in relations to Petrobras.[137] When the settlement with the Dutch authorities was reached in November 2014, the DOJ informed *SBM Offshore* that it is not prosecuting the company and has closed the case because of the parallel Dutch settlement.[138]

133 Note that in *Odebrecht/Braskem, SBM Offshore, and Rolls-Royce*, Petrobras-related bribery is only one out of several other bribery schemes that these corporations were involved. See Trace, *Trace Compendium: SBM Offshore N.V.* <https://www.traceinternational.org/TraceCompendium/Detail/478?class=casename_searchresult&type=1> accessed 17 January 2019.

134 Paragraphs 16–17 of the Order *SEC vs Petróleo Brasileiro S.A. – Petrobras, No. 3-18843* (27 September 2018). Note that not all charged companies were necessarily part of the cartel, or at least not in all corrupt projects. For example, the DOJ does not mention any participation of Rolls-Royce in a cartel, rather the DOJ describes how and why bribes were paid in order to obtain a concrete business project.

135 *Trace Compendium: SBM Offshore* (133).

136 Openbaar Ministerie, *SBM* (n 126).

137 Ibid.

138 SBM Offshore, *SBM Offshore achieves settlement with Dutch Prosecutor's Office over alleged payments. United States Department of Justice closes out the matter* (2 November 2014) <https://www.sbmoffshore.com/?press-release=sbm-offshore-achieves-settlement-dutch-public-prosecutors-office-alleged-improper-payments-united-states-department-justice-closes-matter> accessed 16 January 2019.

Yet, the DOJ charged *SBM Offshore* in November 2017 again. As in the settlement with the Dutch authorities, the 2017 settlement relates to foreign bribery in Brazil, Angola, and Equatorial Guinea. On top of that, the DOJ also mentions schemes in Kazakhstan and Iraq.[139] Clearly, the initial coordination with the Dutch authorities did not prevent the DOJ to charge company again.

Furthermore, the Brazilian authorities conducted their own enforcement actions. In July 2015, *SBM Offshore* became one of the 32 companies blocked from signing new contracts with Petrobras.[140] Finally in July 2016, *SBM Offshore*, Petrobras – SBM's customer, and Brazilian authorities came to a settlement totaling $342 million. The way of paying the penalty is rather special. A significant part of the penalty, $149.2 million, was directly transferred to Petrobras.[141] The agreement also includes a 95% reduction for works related to two offshore vessels that will be performed from 2016 to 2030 on behalf of Petrobras; the nominal value of the 95% reduction is $179 million.[142] SBM was under significant pressure to accept such terms because *SBM Offshore* had more than $20 billion in contracts with Petrobras at the time of the settlement.[143]

SBM Offshore was the first settlement related to the Petrobras scheme. The following schemes such as *Odebrecht/Braskem*, *Rolls-Royce*, and *Keppel* are already more coordinated. This may be because the US, Brazilian, and other enforcement authorities have developed more trust and experience. But many enforcement schemes related to Petrobras are still open and it is difficult to predict further evolution.

2 *Systemic coordination problems: political enforcement*

Prior to Petrobras-related enforcement actions, Brazil practically did not enforce its anti-bribery laws. In this context, the enforcement of the Brazilian enforcement authorities can be seen as a systemic activation of enforcement. Once the US decided to enforce their foreign anti-bribery laws, the Brazilian authorities did not have other choice but to start

139 *United States vs. SBM Offshore, N.B., No. 17-cr-686* (21 November 2017).

140 A number of these companies were mentioned in documents of Brazilian authorities including for example, Mitsubishi, Rolls Royce, Samsung, and Skanska. Trace, *Trace Compendium: Petroleo Brasileiro SA (Petrobras)* <https://www.traceinternational.org/Trace-Compendium/Detail/594?type=1> accessed 14 January 2019.

141 Ibid.

142 SBM Offshore, *Leniency Agreement Signed between Brazilian Authorities, Petrobras and SBM Offshore* (Press Release 16 July 2016) <http://www.sbmoffshore.com/?press-release=-leniency-agreement-signed-brazilian-authorities-petrobras-sbm-offshore> accessed 17 January 2019.

143 Note that the Dutch Prosecution Office allegedly promised cooperation to Brazilian authorities in prosecuting individuals in foreign countries. The Brazilian government, however, complained on the lack of cooperation of the Dutch authorities in the *Petrobras* matter. Valle, S. and Millard, P. (2014) *SBM Bribery Probe in Brazil Puts Petrobras Work at Risk*. Bloomberg <https://www.bloomberg.com/news/articles/2014-11-13/sbm-bribery-probe-in-brazil-puts-petrobras-work-at-risk> accessed 17 January 2019.

enforcing as well. This allowed them not only to collect more than $3.2 billion from foreign suppliers of Petrobras but also to prevent devastating financial losses related to the US investigation of Petrobras.

These financial losses are associated with the US plans to sanction Petrobras. As Petrobras is a state-owned corporation, it was in the interest of Brazil to cooperate and coordinate with the US enforcement authorities. In fact, the US pushed Brazil to sanction a corporation it owns. In September 2018, Petrobras reached a global settlement with the DOJ, the SEC, and Brazilian authorities and agreed to pay a criminal fine of $853.2 million and $933 million in disgorgement and prejudgment interest. As the Brazilian enforcement authorities cooperated with the US, Brazil received 80%, approximately $682.5 million of the criminal fine. Moreover, Petrobras was allowed to offset the civil penalty of $933 million from a $2.95 billion resolution that it agreed to pay to its investors that filled a class action in the US.[144]

6.7.3.3 *Large enforcement conflicts are rare*

With the increasing enforcement comes a question whether the provision of public goods is undermined by enforcement conflicts and overlapping enforcement. Indeed, we see a number of relatively small enforcement conflicts. For example, in *Siemens*, *Bonny Island*, and *Teva*, the enforcement authorities of countries such as Greece, Nigeria, and Israel took an advantage of the US enforcement and followed up with their own enforcement. In SQM, the US authorities did not seem to be very much concerned by an existing investigation in Chile and awarded their sanctions without much cooperation and coordination with enforcement authorities in Chile.

While these examples certainly undermine the provision of enforcement as a public good, they are relatively small. It is relatively rare to see over-enforcement and open enforcement conflicts such as the one in *SBM Offshore*. As a matter of illustrations, we do not see the US enforcement authorities sanctioning Chinese corporations and Chinese enforcement authorities, as a revenge, sanctioning US business partners, or competitors, of those Chinese corporations. Rather, China does not sanction foreign bribery at all and the US refrain from sanctioning Chinese corporations.

6.8 Conclusion

The main aim of this chapter was to identify patterns of US foreign anti-bribery enforcement that are relevant from the perspective of collective action. What

144 DOJ, *Petroleo Brasileiro S.A. – Petrobras Agrees to Pay More than* $850 million for FCPA Violations (Press Release, 27 September 2018) <https://www.justice.gov/opa/pr/petrleo-brasileiro-sa-petrobras-agrees-pay-more-850-million-fcpa-violations> accessed 17 January 2019.

was discussed is the fact that the US extraterritorial enforcement alleviates the credibility problem associated with the provision of enforcement. The US enforcement, to some extent, offset the inactivity of other states. There are three main reasons why US foreign anti-bribery enforcement can reach foreign entities all around the world. The first is the broad interpretation of what constitutes territorial nexus with the US. This relates not only to the offense of bribery but also to the use of alternative charges that can increase the jurisdictional reach of US law. By applying alternative laws, the US enforcement authorities can, in some cases, impose sanctions on corporations that are neither headquartered in, nor have a sufficient territorial link with, the US.

Second, foreign bribery cases usually involve payments through marketing agents, consultants, brokers, distributors, and other intermediaries interacting with government officials. These intermediaries can be prosecuted thanks to the possibility to negotiate agreements with the enforcement authorities and the broad interpretation of the liability for the acts of third persons. For example, using the consent jurisdiction, proved to be a pattern that ensures wide enforcement reach. It must be noted that the US enforcement has also incentivized private self-regulation. In the field of merger and acquisitions as well as in the due diligence of suppliers, businesses falling under US anti-bribery laws regularly check their business partners' compliance in order to mitigate the risk of being accountable for the partners' activities. Hence, also these partners have to indirectly comply with US laws.

Third, and finally, yet another way to sanction bribery is the use of complicit conduct charges. The conspiracy and aiding and abetting are legal tools that pertain more to substantive liability than jurisdiction, hence might be truly extraterritorial. The conspiracy charges are special because they allowed the US enforcement authorities to prosecute bribery schemes that could be otherwise outside the statute of limitations period, and allowed to prosecute some foreign corporations that neither act in the US territory, nor could they be prosecuted based on the agency theory.

The above-discussed tools have not only alleviated the credibility problem but have also incentivized other states to be more active in their legislative and enforcement responses to international bribery. Most importantly, the US has further alleviated the credibility problem associated with the lack of enforcement by initiating a relatively strong network of countries that cooperate with each other in terms of MLA as well as by using more informal and direct methods of cooperation. The enforcement schemes with a more direct cooperation between the US and other countries such as Germany, Switzerland, the Netherlands, Brazil, France, and the UK illustrate that parallel investigation and close cooperation between enforcement authorities is effective in achieving coordinated enforcement.

Moreover, while a formal MLA is common, more direct and informal ways of cooperation, including parallel investigations and JITs, are less common.

On the one hand, in some enforcement schemes, states were reluctant to cooperate between each other. Furthermore, Petrobras-related resolutions indicate that while the emergence of global settlements indicates a shift in the way how to cooperate and coordinate enforcement, these schemes are influenced by political and economic considerations. These schemes could escalate into international policy problems with potential systemic effect such as trade sanctions.

As will be discussed in Chapter 6, part of this political game is also negative spillover effects related to the under-enforcement of anti-bribery laws, for example, firms headquartered in non-OECD countries such as China are hardly ever prosecuted, let alone liable to pay sanctions. These new credibility problems emerge largely because of clarity problems. The key questions that arise are: what are these credibility and clarity problems, and how can they be best addressed? These questions are addressed in the following chapter.

References

Acorn, E. (2016) *The Power of Procurement in the Fight against Foreign Bribery*. 2016 OECD Forum Integrity Forum <https://www.oecd.org/cleangovbiz/Integrity-Forum-16-Elizabeth-Acorn.pdf> accessed 31 December 2018.

Bauerschmidt, J. E. (1990) 'Mother of Mercy – Is This the End of RICO – Justice Scalia Invites Constitutional Void for Vagueness Challenge to RICO Pattern' 65 Notre Dame Law Review 1106.

Colangelo, A. J. (2010) 'The Foreign Commerce Clause' (2010) 96 Virginia Law Review 949.

Doyle, Ch. (2016) *Federal Conspiracy Law: A Brief Overview*. Congressional Research Service <https://www.fas.org/sgp/crs/misc/R41223.pdf> accessed 31 December 2018.

Dubber, M. D. and Hörnle, T. (2014) *Criminal Law: A Comparative Approach*. Oxford: Oxford University Press.

Gideon, M. (2013) 'RICO's Extraterritoriality' 50 American Business Law Journal 543.

Hock, B. (2018) 'The Bundling of Foreign Bribery Cases' 2018 TILEC Discussion Paper 12.

Ilzkovotz, F. and Meiklejohn, R. (Eds.) (2006) *European Merger Control: Do We Need an Efficiency Defence?* Cheltenham: Edward Elgar.

Lewi, M. K. (2015) 'When Foreign is Criminal' 55 Virginia Journal of International Law 625.

Oduor, J. et al. (2014) 'Left out of the Bargain: Settlements in Foreign Bribery Cases and Implications for Asset Recovery' Stolen Asset Recovery Initiative <http://star.worldbank.org/star/sites/star/files/9781464800863.pdf> accessed 7 January 2019.

OECD (2012) Typology on Mutual Legal Assistance in Foreign Bribery Cases <http://www.oecd.org/daf/anti-bribery/TypologyMLA2012.pdf> accessed 3 May 2019.

OECD (2017) International Co-operation in Corruption Cases <https://www.oecd.org/corruption/acn/OECD-International-Cooperation-in-Corruption-Cases-2017.pdf> accessed 7 January 2019.

Otey, M. L. (2015) 'Why RICO'S Extraterritorial Reach Is Properly Coextensive with the Reach of Its Predicates' 14 The Journal of International Business & Law 33.

Paoli, L. (2014) *The Oxford Handbook of Organized Crime*. Oxford: Oxford University Press.

Pieth, M., Low, L. A. and Bonucci, N. (Eds.) (2014) *The OECD Convention on Bribery: A Commentary*. Cambridge: Cambridge University Press.

Sullivan, S. (2015) 'The Future of the Foreign Commerce Clause' 83 Fordham Law Review 1955.

7 The effectiveness of extraterritorial anti-bribery enforcement

7.1 Introduction

International extraterritorial regimes should achieve their intended objectives and results. This is important because the effectiveness of state policies and strategies is necessary in order to move toward the better use of public resources, the building of public trust, and ultimately achieve better solutions to problems such as international bribery. This chapter applies the collective action framework and explains in what way and to what extent, extraterritoriality is effective in solving enforcement difficulties of the OECD anti-bribery enforcement regime.

The chapter will show that extraterritoriality facilitates the transition from a "unilateral" to a "multilateral" enforcement regime. This is achieved, for instance, by allowing prosecutors of one country to target foreign corporations and thereby incentivizing the enforcement of the law in home countries of those corporations. Furthermore, extraterritoriality can be also viewed as an institutional outcome of sanctioning corporations in overseas jurisdictions. To resolve collective action problems, this outcome should not only make it easier to hold MNCs liable for bribing foreign public officials but also ensure cooperation and coordination of national enforcement authorities.

As to what extent extraterritoriality contributes, this chapter explains how legal institutions accompanying extraterritorial enforcement make a difference between more and less effective solutions to collective action problems. The effectiveness of these institutions, however, is relative to the demands and capacities of a particular regime. Some regimes lack sufficient participation, whether regarding the regime in general or the enforcement of the law, thus being more concerned with what was discussed in Chapter 2 as the credibility problem. Other regimes struggle with clarity problems such as how to coordinate enforcement. As the OECD anti-bribery enforcement regime moves from its unilateral form to a more multilateral form, the institutional needs of this regime are in transition into a stronger external system of governance.

The rest of this chapter is organized as follows. Section 2 discusses how the effectiveness of enforcement is evaluated. Sections 3 and 4 discuss the effectiveness of extraterritorial enforcement in relation to two alternatives that emerged in practice – the OECD as a "unilateral" regime and the OECD as more of a "multilateral" enforcement regime.

7.2 The effectiveness of international regimes

This work uses the theory of collective action as a normative criterion to assess the effectiveness of extraterritorial enforcement. To assess the effectiveness in this way, the notion of regime effectiveness is understood as the extent to which regimes are able to solve their problems and achieve their objectives (Young, 1999: 109; Young, 2011: 19854; Getz, 2006: 257). This more pragmatic approach is different from more doctrinal and empirical methods that have been used to address effectiveness. The aim of this work is not to assess the successful implementation and enforcement of international law norms (for example, Torpman and Jörgensen, 2005). The approach in this work is also different from those studies that assess whether international rules are complied with (for example, Koh, 1997). Last, in other studies effectiveness is assessed empirically; in the area of anti-corruption, for example, by various empirical generalizations about the frequency of enforcement, the amount of sanctions, and the perceptions of corruption (for example, Margeson, 2014). The following section explains how the effectiveness is assessed in more detail.

7.2.1 The effectiveness of enforcement

From the perspective of collective action, the effectiveness of enforcement depends on both the ability to provide public goods by placing corporations under stringer regulatory scrutiny as well as on a classifying mechanism that ensures the cooperation and coordination of enforcement (Section 2.3.4). The problem is that such classification mechanism is costly to create, and in fact can to some extent undermine the effective provision of enforcement. Cooperation and coordination, for example, might delay the provision of enforcement and introduce strategic considerations of other jurisdictions' legal systems. The existence of this trade-off is the key challenge for the OECD anti-bribery enforcement regime.

How effectively this trade-off is resolved is determined by contextual variables that one uses. These may be, for example, the level of excludability of public goods, the dependence on a public good, the common understanding of problems that a group faces, the presence of leadership, etc. (Ostrom et al., 2002). As has become apparent in the case study of foreign anti-bribery enforcement schemes, the key effect attributed to the US extraterritorial enforcement is that it has activated the enforcement of other countries. From this perspective, we need to observe and compare costs and benefits of two types of regimes that emerged in practice, the OECD as a "unilateral" anti-bribery regime and the OECD as a "multilateral" anti-bribery enforcement regime.

This evolution of the OECD regime is nothing special because international regimes are dynamic structures that evolve from one state of balance into another (Young, 2011: 19855). A hegemonic player, as the US enforcement authorities in the field of international bribery law, can sometimes provide public goods, even if multilateral action does not exist (see, generally, Snidal, 1985; Getz 2006). Moreover, such a hegemon can raise the level of concern among other states about the given problem (Keohane, Haas and Levy, 1993: 397). Once more players participate in the provision of public goods, however, transaction costs between the players increase, and new institutions may be necessary.

This implies that the change in the size of a group is relevant when determining whether the institutional design of a regime is equally effective before and after such change. While self-governance based on trust may be appropriate for small groups, with the increase of economic exchange and in the size of the group, external governance may be more appropriate (see, generally, Masten and Prüfer, 2014). The problem is to design appropriate governance institutions for intermediate-size regimes. According to Dixit, "When an expanding economy reaches the size where external governance becomes just cost-effective, 'it is darkest just before the dawn' for it" (2014: 76). We will see in sections below that the OECD anti-bribery enforcement regime is exactly at such intermediate stage.

7.2.2 The effectiveness potential of extraterritorial regimes

This section discusses the effectiveness potential of two types of anti-bribery enforcement regimes that emerged in practice: the OECD as a unilateral anti-bribery regime and the OECD as a multilateral anti-bribery enforcement regime. By effectiveness potential, what is meant is the ideal functioning of a given type of regime from the perspective of collective action. *Table 7.1* below illustrates the effectiveness potential of these two types of regimes for resolving the credibility problem and the clarity problem.

Table 7.1 refers to the credibility problem and the clarity problem. To remind the reader, the credibility problem reflects a situation in which states are not able to persuade each other to keep their promises and refrain from free-riding (Gibbons and Henderson, 2012: 1351). The credibility problem limits the provision of enforcement as a public good. There are several types of credibility problems such as the lack of will to enforcement foreign anti-bribery laws, low institutional capacity to sanction corporations that bribe, the lack of cooperation and coordination of national enforcement authorities, and enforcement conflicts. Furthermore, there is also the clarity problem associated with administrative-managerial problems within an alliance that aim to produce public goods. If an alliance does not have a mechanism in place in order to clarify the terms of the original promise – issues that cannot be agreed upon in advance – then, they are likely to have clarity problems (Gibbons and Henderson, 2012: 1351).

Table 7.1 The Effectiveness potential of extraterritorial regimes

The Effectiveness Potential of Extraterritorial Enforcement Regimes		
Type of Regime	**Unilateral Enforcement Regime**	**Multilateral Enforcement Regime**
Credibility Problem	wide enforcement reach supported by cooperation of other countries	global enforcement reach supported by cooperation and coordination of other countries
Clarity Problem	well-functioning assistance network based on MLA	cooperation and coordination ensured by direct forms of cooperation such as joint-investigation teams, and supported by coordination rules well-functioning assistance network based on MLA
The Effects of Extraterritoriality	mitigates free-rider problem incentivizes participation	decreasing effect on free-rider problem and participation with increasing membership, new legal and political clashes – more clarity problems

From the perspective of the credibility problem, when it comes to a unilateral regime, a country such as the US can regulate a significant part of the global market. Such a country, as illustrated in *Table 7.1*, may alleviate the credibility problem. However, one hegemonic state alone does not have the economic and institutional capacity to prosecute all of the corporations in the world. Therefore, a unilateral regime cannot provide deterrent sanctions, recovery of stolen assets, and restitution to the full extent. All corporations that seek to improve their competitive position by engaging in bribery can be deterred from bribing only if more countries participate in the provision of enforcement as a public good.

Moreover, the original enforcement can be supported if other countries provide cooperation by means of MLA. For instance, the sharing of evidence and information can decrease the enforcement costs of the hegemon and allow it to increase the provision of public goods.[1] The provision of MLA and similar assistance, however, is a collective action problem in itself. In the case of a unilateral regime, if more countries are willing to assist the hegemon, clarity problems as to how to assist will arise. In such scenario, a mechanism that clarifies the terms of such assistance might be needed to ensure cooperation.

1 See the discussion about MLA in Section 4.9.1 and Section 6.7.1.

In contrast, an enforcement regime can also be multilateral or international, in that multiple countries take part in the enforcement. As far as credibility is concerned, a multilateral enforcement regime can hope more easily to regulate all the corporations in the world. The enforcement reach depends not only on the economic and institutional capacity of multiple actors to prosecute MNCs, but similarly as a unilateral regime depends on the cooperation between relevant actors by means of MLA.

Furthermore, a multilateral enforcement regime needs to deal with clarity problems. In cases of overlapping jurisdiction, the regime ensures that enforcement authorities engage in forms of cooperation that are more direct, such as parallel investigations and joint investigation teams. By doing this, the regime also overcomes clarity problems that arise from differences in national enforcement policies as well as from negotiated settlements. In addition, in some situations, such as in the case of jurisdictional overlap, it is desirable that a regime provides default norms clarifying how to coordinate enforcement.

As to the effects of extraterritoriality, extraterritoriality mitigates, as part of a unilateral regime, the free-rider problem associated with the provision of enforcement as a public good, and incentivizes participation by other countries. Yet, it is recognized both at the academic and policy level that multilateral action potentially has a greater economic and institutional capacity to mitigate global problems than unilateral approaches (Section 2.3.4). However, in the absence of appropriate governance mechanism, extraterritoriality in a multilateral regime could be counterproductive. A high number of selective, uncoordinated, and therefore costly enforcement actions probably generate less positive effects than a smaller number of enforcement actions conducted by a cooperative group of states, or even by a single state.

The following section discusses how in practice, the OECD anti-bribery regime has developed into a hybrid form of a regime that stands somewhere between a unilateral and a multilateral enforcement regime. The practice that emerged is explained in terms of political–economic factors as well as institutional factors related to the credibility and clarity problems.

7.3 The effectiveness of the OECD "unilateral" anti-bribery regime in practice

7.3.1 The rise of foreign anti-bribery enforcement

International regimes can emerge if states show sufficient political concern about an underlying problem (Keohane et al., 1993: 399–401). States have become gradually concerned with international bribery after a series of exogenous changes, mainly the Watergate scandal, the US business lobby, as well as the 9/11 attacks (Section 3.2.1). The FCPA and the OECD Convention have been the most important anti-corruption tools that have followed these exogenous events and facilitated the resolution of the initial collective action problem (Sections 3.2.1 and 3.2.2).

Before 1977, bribery of foreign government officials was permitted. However, following the Watergate scandal, the US adopted the FCPA and international bribery became one of the political priorities in the US. Nevertheless, it took another 20 years before other countries decided to jump into the fray. Moreover, it took even longer before foreign anti-bribery laws were actively enforced. For example, between 1977 and 1988, the DOJ and SEC concluded only 23 enforcement actions (Pines, 1994: 192).

Also, internationally, the US initiated negotiations with other major countries such as Germany, the UK, and Japan about an international treaty criminalizing bribery of foreign public officials. These negotiations materialized only after geopolitical changes related to the end of the Cold War.[2] At the time of the negotiations, the 1998 amendments to the FCPA introduced provisions allowing enforcement authorities to charge foreign firms.[3] The OECD Convention that finally entered into force in 1999 followed these provisions (Tarun, 2006: 12).

The first years of the OECD Convention were followed by a steady acceleration of US foreign anti-bribery enforcement and implementation processes, and by the adoption of other multilateral anti-corruption conventions such as the UNCAC in 2003. However, it was only after another exogenous change – the 9/11 attacks – that the US and other States Parties to the OECD Convention started cooperating more closely on the matters related to transnational crime (Section 3.2.3). Consequently, the first global settlement resulting in penalties as high as hundreds of millions of dollars was *Siemens* in 2008. This should be considered as evidence of an evolution from seeing international bribery as an inchoate concern to a serious law enforcement field.

7.3.2 The OECD as a "unilateral" enforcement regime

The OECD regime is a US-dominated enforcement regime. This regime has relatively high effectiveness potential consisting in (1) unilateral enforcement that covers a wide range of US-based and foreign firms, thus alleviating credibility problems and (2) cooperation and administrative support provided to the US by other countries, thus decreasing enforcement costs. US extraterritorial enforcement contributes to the realization of this enforcement potential by making it easier for national enforcement authorities to hold MNCs accountable for their bribing. US enforcement authorities have legal tools to act even if MNCs hide their illicit activities, for instance by using foreign intermediaries or by operating in so-called secure jurisdictions or tax havens. Furthermore, flexible legal procedures accompanying extraterritoriality create a leverage effect that cuts enforcement costs. Last, while US extraterritorial

2 Many historical overviews of the FCPA refer to new dynamics that came after the fall of the Berlin Wall (see, for example, George and Lacey, 2000).

3 The International Anti-Bribery and Fair Competition Act 1998.

enforcement has extremely wide reach in terms of its institutional capacity, its effect on placing corporations under strict regulatory scrutiny is limited because of political and economic reasons. The following sections explain these findings in more detail.

7.3.2.1 Extraterritoriality: the effect of the credibility problem is alleviated

In line with the President Trump's critique of the FCPA discussed in Chapter 1, much attention has been paid to the lack of enforcement of national foreign bribery laws, as well as to the alleged competitive disadvantage that this lack of enforcement causes to US-based corporations. Yet, the findings of this work indicate differently: in certain markets, the playing field has been largely leveled. *Table 7.2* below illustrates that these that are predominantly sanctioned by the US enforcement authorities are non-US corporations.

In the light of the wide US regulatory web, the lack of economic and institutional capacity to enforce the law in states other than the US is alleviated. *Table 7.2* above illustrates that out of the 40 biggest FCPA and FCPA-related matters, only 13 matters concerned firms with their main headquarters in the US. The US firms were charged with approximately $2252 million in monetary penalties, which is less than 15% of all FCPA and FCPA-related matters. On the other hand, 27 matters concerned firms with their main headquarters in other countries. As these firms were mainly based in Brazil, France, Germany, UK, Switzerland, Netherlands, and Japan, the lack of enforcement in their respective home countries does not matter so much in the end, when ensuring open and competitive markets is concerned.

In other words, low enforcement outside the US is partially offset by the ability of the US enforcement authorities to prosecute corporations headquartered in foreign jurisdictions. In this way, the credibility problem associated with the lack of enforcement as a public good is alleviated. The US enforcement practices that alleviate the credibility problem can be explained by three main arguments.

1 *US authorities have a high institutional capacity to hold MNCs accountable*
 The first reason is institutional. US extraterritoriality and underlying legislation represent an effective basis to match the US institutional capacity to hold MNCs accountable for bribing. In the vast majority of studied enforcement actions, the US authorities held MNCs legally responsible for the activities of their foreign subsidiaries and agents. The US enforcement authorities use a number of effective tools such as referring to the de facto vicarious liability of issuers over their foreign subsidiaries, complicity and conspiracy charges, and bundling of allegations in out-of-court settlements. Moreover, they further strengthen the effectiveness of prosecution by using various statutes that factually cover foreign bribery. These techniques discussed in Chapters 5 and 6 indicate that global corporate networks do not fully prevent corporations from facing bribery charges.

Table 7.2 Nationality of MNCs under the US anti-bribery laws[a]

<table>
<tr><th colspan="4">Nationality of MNCs under the US anti-bribery laws and penalties (2008–2018)</th></tr>
<tr><th>France</th><th>Germany</th><th>Switzerland</th><th>United States</th></tr>
<tr><td>Alstom - $772m (2014)
Société Générale – $585.6m (2018)
Total - $398m (2013)
Technip - $338m (2010)
Alcatel- Lucent SA- $137m (2010)</td><td>Siemens AG - $800m (2008)
Daimler AG - $185m (2010)
Magyar/Deutsche Telekom - $95m (2011)</td><td>Weatherford - $252m (2013)
Panalpina, - $82m (2010)
Credit Suisse (SUI/Hong Kong) - $76.9m (2018)
ABB Ltd - $58m (2010)</td><td rowspan="5">KBR/Halliburton - $579m (2009)
Och-Ziff $412m (2016)
Alcoa $384m (2014)
JPMorgan $264m (2016)
Avon $135m (2014)
HP $108m (2014)
Johnson&Johnson$70m (2011)
Legg Mason $67m (2018)
Pfizer Inc $60m (2012)
Bio-Rad $55m (2014)
Archer Daniel Midlands Company $54m (2013)
Polycom $36.6m (2018)
Zimmer Biomet $30.5m (2017)</td></tr>
<tr><th>Netherlands</th><th>Japan</th><th>Brazil</th></tr>
<tr><td>VimpelCom - $795m (2016)
Snamprogetti/ENI (NL/Italy) - $365m (2010)
SBM Offshore - $238m (2017)</td><td>Panasonic - $280.6m (2018)
JPG - $219m (2011)
Marubeni - $55m (2012)</td><td>Odebrecht/ Braskem -$3390m (2016)
Petrobras - $1786.6m (2018)
Embraer - $205.5m (2016)</td></tr>
<tr><th colspan="3">UK/Sweden/Singapore/Israel/Chile</th></tr>
<tr><td colspan="3">Telia (Sweden) - $965.6m (2017)
Teva (Israel) - $519.3m (2016)
Keppel (Singapore) – $422.2m (2017)
BAE (UK) - $400m (2010)
Rolls-Royce (UK) - $195.5m (2016)
SQM (Chile) - $30.5m (2017)</td></tr>
<tr><td colspan="3">27 matters against Non-US-based firms
imposed $13.6 billion
after offsetting $3.4 billion</td><td>13 matters against US-based firms
$2.3 billion</td></tr>
</table>

a Sanctions presented in *Table 7.2* include sanctions awarded by the US enforcement authorities. This also includes sanctions that were not actually paid to the US treasury if they were offset from sanctions awarded outside the US. It means that in *Telia*, for example, $965.6 million is included despite the fact that the DOJ and the SEC credited sums paid to the Dutch and Swedish enforcement authorities. Such offsetting can be also seen in *Rolls-Royce*, *VimpelCom*, *Embraer*, *Odebrecht/Braskem*, *Societe Generale*, *Petrobras*, and *Keppel*. However, sanctions that were awarded by non-US enforcement authorities are not included. In *Siemens*, for example, offsetting of penalties was not taking place, hence only $800 million is provided, despite the fact that German enforcement authorities collected another $800 million. Furthermore, settlements in *Bonny Island* scheme are counted separately.

2 *US extraterritoriality increases the efficiency of enforcement*

Second, extraterritoriality, together with the use of DPAs and other flexible procedures, increases the economic capacity of US enforcement. The DOJ and the SEC structured a number of anti-bribery enforcement actions so to include hundreds of unrelated projects into a single proceeding and negotiated prosecution agreements with MNCs.[4] Corporations have regularly admitted liability for bribery charges that they would likely defend if brought in isolation, for example because of a lack of jurisdiction. When faced with the alternative prospect of multiple actions, corporations usually prefer to buy these settlement bundles. The possibility of a definitive, and hopefully lower sanction in a single settlement is more attractive than the prospect of an accumulation of sanctions from multiple, expensive prosecutions. Moreover, the possibility of debarment if sentenced by a court with anti-bribery charges is always a consideration.

In effect, these DPAs and procedural techniques such as allegation bundling increase the efficiency of enforcement by increasing the scope of US enforcement actions. In other words, the use of plea-bargaining, together with extraterritoriality, enables the US enforcement authorities to better handle the issue of bribery by either, countering the same amount of bribery while using less resources, or managing to fight bribery to a larger extent using the same resources.[5]

3 *The global character of markets makes unilateral enforcement relatively less prone to protectionism*

Third, while the US enforcement authorities may consider a number of political–economic factors when enforcing foreign anti-bribery laws, and enforce the law in ways that protect firms that are considered "national champions," in practice, the structure of global markets makes it increasingly difficult. In global markets, MNCs are not bound by political boundaries, and, as Nichols argues, there are complex capital relationships between firms subjected to US anti-bribery laws and firms that are not subjected to these laws. For example, enforcement actions against MNCs with headquarters in the US influence many foreign firms that own US firms (Nichols, 2016: 224–226).

What is more, extraterritorial enforcement has incentivized private self-regulation, aiming to change "bad" foreign business partners into more compliant ones. In the field of merger and acquisitions, as well as in the due diligence of suppliers, businesses under US anti-bribery laws

4 For example, *Alstom* and *Teva* illustrate foreign anti-bribery bundling (Section 6.6.2).

5 Efficiency is "the extent to which the program has converted or is expected to convert its resources/inputs [...] economically into results in order to achieve the maximum possible outputs, outcomes, and impacts with the minimum possible inputs" (World Bank, 2007: xxviii).

regularly check their business partners' compliance with US laws in order to mitigate the risk of being accountable for the partners' bribery.

Political motives can be assumed in a number of enforcement actions. Nevertheless, because of global business chains and technological interconnections, it is increasingly difficult to claim that certain enforcement actions are purely protectionist, let alone claim that the mere existence of national enforcement disadvantages firms headquartered in certain countries. In general terms, more enforcement within a unilateral enforcement regime alleviates the credibility problem, and thereby ensures more open and competitive markets.

7.3.2.2 Extraterritorial enforcement remains regional: political and institutional limits

While US extraterritorial enforcement alleviates some credibility problems, there are both political–economic and institutional limits to what the US enforcement authorities can achieve in terms of effectiveness. In fact, the MNCs charged by US enforcers are mostly headquartered in six or seven countries. *Table 7.2* (Section 7.3.2) shows that out of the 40 biggest FCPA and FCPA-related matters, Brazilian-based firms were sanctioned $5382 million in penalties in total, which is 39.6% of all penalties imposed on non-US firms. French-based firms come in second with $2231 million, which is slightly 16.4% of all penalties imposed non-US firms.[6] The Dutch-based and German-based firms come in third and fourth, with $1398 million and $1080 million, respectively, which represents 10.3% and 7.9% of all penalties imposed non-US firms.

However, firms headquartered in some countries such as China and India are hardly ever prosecuted, let alone liable to pay sanctions.[7] Clearly, US national enforcement cannot, or does not aim to, change the way business is done in every market even if said business is based on foreign bribery. Despite the fact that US enforcement alleviates some credibility problems, it nevertheless seems to discriminate among firms, especially when it comes to where certain firms are based. Therefore, without the active participation of other countries, some markets will remain under-regulated.

6 Note that US-based firms were sanctioned $2255 million.

7 Note that there have been some Chinese and Indian subsidiaries of MNCs that resolved foreign anti-bribery enforcement actions, but large corporations headquartered in China and India have still not had to resolve any significant enforcement action. See, for example, in December 2018, Polycom resolved a $36.6 million allegations of international bribery by its Chinese subsidiary with the SEC and the DOJ. United States, Polycom Inc, Declination with Disgorgement (20 December 2018) <https://www.justice.gov/criminal-fraud/file/1122966/download> accessed 28 April 2019. But see the New Initiative to Combat Chinese Economic Espionage (Section 10.2.1).

The question, then, is: Why do US authorities charge foreign firms headquartered in certain countries more often than other firms, including firms headquartered in the US? This study suggests four main explanations.

1 *US foreign policy considerations – the competitiveness of US businesses*

The first explanation for why major foreign firms have been charged more often than major US-based firms is political–economic. Many of the charged firms are competitors to US-based firms, either in the US markets or in other markets. Hence, the US has a good reason to level the playing field in those markets because the France, UK, Germany, and Switzerland have improved their enforcement record only recently, and other countries such as Japan are still without foreign anti-bribery enforcement. At the same time, it was in the US interest to get the attention of underperforming jurisdictions and incentivize them to be more active in their anti-bribery approaches. Indeed, countries such as Brazil, France, the Netherlands, Germany, the UK, and Switzerland have adopted relevant legal instruments to sanction foreign bribery and have started to cooperate with the US via MLA as well as by using more informal and direct methods of cooperation.

2 *US foreign policy considerations – the privileged protection of US investors*

Another political–economic reason, and strong incentive, to sanction non-US corporations is the presence of US-related investments in foreign firms. Petrobras securities, for example, are listed for trading in the NYSE. Because of the Petrobras corruption as well as because of the consequences of the enforcement actions, these investors that purchased Petrobras securities were harmed and brought a class action against Petrobras in the US.[8] The fact that Petrobras was allowed to offset the civil penalty of $933 million from a $2.95 billion resolution that it agreed to pay to its investors in the US shows clear link between the resolution with the US authorities and the resolution with the US-related investors.[9] The possibility to offset quasi-criminal sanction and from private settlements, in fact, implies a preferential treatment of the US investors as opposed to other securities investors in Brazil and European exchanges. Petrobras was put in the position to discriminate between its investors.

3 *Sanctioned non-US corporations had weak compliance systems*

The third explanation is institutional – foreign firms did not have experience with anti-bribery compliance. It is a fact that many non-US firms headquartered in OECD countries invest in the US market. They

8 In re Petrobras Securities Litigation, No. 14-cv-9662 (Agreement of Settlement, 1 February 2018).

9 DOJ, *Petroleo Brasileiro S.A. – Petrobras Agrees to Pay More than* $850 million for FCPA Violations (Press Release, 27 September 2018) <https://www.justice.gov/opa/pr/petrleo-brasileiro-sa-petrobras-agrees-pay-more-850-million-fcpa-violations> accessed 17 January 2019.

are listed on US stock exchanges, have US subsidiaries, and operate via US agents. Therefore, they have to comply with US anti-bribery laws. However, while the US-based firms had been building experience with FCPA compliance since 1977, a number of foreign corporations were not prepared for the relatively sudden increase in the enforcement of the FCPA near the year 2008. Firms such as Siemens, Daimler, Alstom, and BAE were endemic bribers that lacked effective anti-bribery compliance measures and were charged at a time of rapidly growing US enforcement. As can be seen for example in *Alstom*, the lack of experience in compliance with US standards and negotiating with the US enforcement authorities over settlements, resulted in the criminal penalty of $772 million. These factors made many non-US corporations an easy target for the US enforcement authorities.

4 *Corporations headquartered in certain major countries are not prosecuted*

The last point that needs to be addressed is why the US authorities have not focused on corporations with headquarters in countries such as China. The lack of institutional capacity for US enforcement is not the main reason, because US foreign bribery laws apply to many of these corporations. For instance, large Chinese corporations have to comply with US law because they are increasingly listed in the US, they are buying American firms, or they are even attempting to acquire US self-regulatory business bodies such as the Chicago Stock Exchange.[10] However, whilst Chinese, Indian, and other non-US corporations, should, in theory, bear a similar risk of prosecution under US laws as those borne by their French or Brazilian competitors, in practice, they do not.[11] This is because of three main reasons.

A first explanation lies in the lack of cooperation, both informal and more formal, between the US enforcement authorities and the enforcement authorities in those counties – China and India, among others. It was discussed above that assistance by means of MLA decreases enforcement resources and allows the US authorities to be more effective in prosecuting corporations. While this book provides evidence about said assistance from countries such as Germany and the Netherlands, there is no evidence that these other large countries are involved in such cooperation. Therefore, the lack of cooperation decreases the institutional capacity as well as the economic capacity of the US enforcement authorities to prosecute said corporations.

10 Massa, A. and Louis, B. (2016) *Obscure Chinese Firm Dives Into $22 Trillion U.S. Market.* Bloomberg <http://www.bloomberg.com/news/articles/2016-02-05/obscure-chinese-firm-dives-into-22-trillion-u-s-stock-market> accessed 23 January 2019.

11 See, generally, Fox, T. (2011) *Welcome to the FCPA: Chinese Companies and Reverse Mergers* (*LexisNexis Legal Newsroom,* 2011) <https://www.lexisnexis.com/legalnewsroom/securities/b/securities/archive/2011/02/02/welcome-to-the-fcpa-chinese-companies-and-reverse-mergers.aspx?Redirected=true> accessed 23 January 2019.

Second, those corporations that have not been prosecuted might have learned how to do business transnationally, without using bribery. While this may be the case in some markets, overall, the likelihood that companies from China and India may win business by paying bribes is considered more probable than the likelihood of companies from the US and other countries such as Germany and the UK.[12] Therefore, it is not likely that those discussed corporations that are not prosecuted would be generally more compliant than the foreign corporations that have been prosecuted.

Last, the US enforcement authorities may simply lack the economic incentives to prosecute corporations headquartered in certain countries because of the possible political and economic consequences that said prosecution might have. This *ex-ante* threat of political–economic consequences is closely linked to the credibility problems of a more international anti-bribery enforcement regime. These credibility problems, including both the threat of large enforcement conflicts and their factual emergence, are discussed in Section 7.4 below.

7.3.3 Concluding remarks

To conclude, the unilateral enforcement regime based on US extraterritorial enforcement largely fulfills its enforcement potential. This is because the regime has a high institutional capacity. Its institutional design increases the efficiency of enforcement, and the global character of markets makes it likely that such enforcement fosters market competition. Moreover, there is evidence of a relatively large assistance network by means of MLA that increases the institutional and economic capacity of enforcement. On the other hand, the effectiveness potential is not fulfilled when it comes to the prosecution of corporations headquartered in certain major countries. While a number of these corporations shall comply with US anti-bribery laws, they are not, in practice, prosecuted should they decide not to comply with these laws. The lack of a stable assistance network between the US and certain major economies, as well as the political–economic constraints to prosecute foreign corporations headquartered in these economies, explain why this potential is unfulfilled.

7.4 An evolution to a shaky multilateral enforcement regime

The OECD anti-bribery enforcement regime is in a transition from its unilateral form dominated by the US, into a multilateral or international, in that multiple countries take part in the enforcement regime. While the

12 Transparency International, *The 2011 Bribe Payers Index* <http://www.transparency.org/bpi2011> accessed 9 February 2019.

effectiveness potential of multilateral enforcement regimes is higher than that of unilateral regimes, the potential is not necessarily fulfilled. As will be argued, the OECD as a multilateral enforcement regime alleviates credibility problems but is nevertheless accompanied by clarity problems and new credibility problems that arise from the transition.

7.4.1 Credibility problems of multilateral enforcement

The OECD as a multilateral enforcement regime struggles to reach its full potential because the transition of the regime's equilibrium from unilateral steady-stage to another stage is accompanied by new credibility problems.[13] *Table 7.3* below summarizes the role of credibility problems in this transition.

In the left column, *Table 7.3* summarizes how the credibility problem of the unilateral enforcement regime is resolved, and why extraterritoriality nevertheless discriminates among firms, especially when it comes to where certain firms are based. In the right column, *Table 7.3* illustrates the transition to the multilateral enforcement regime. In the multilateral enforcement regime, the original credibility problems are resolved in some markets due to more countries being active in the enforcement of foreign anti-bribery laws, and due to the assistance network that have brought a decrease in enforcement costs. However, it is also illustrated that also in the multilateral regime the old collective action problem persists in some markets. Moreover, new – second-order – credibility problems have appeared in markets where the original collective action problem was resolved (Section 2.3.4). As will be explained in the following section, occasional large enforcement conflicts and regular minor enforcement conflicts limit the effectiveness of the multilateral enforcement regime. Not only can an alternative to these conflicts be found via direct cooperation, but more often than not, by the non-enforcement of foreign bribery laws. By these reasons, the effectiveness potential of the OECD multilateral enforcement regime is, in many respects, unfulfilled.

7.4.2 The Regionalism of multilateral anti-bribery enforcement and new credibility problems

7.4.2.1 Extraterritoriality: the persistence of regionalism

While the OECD enforcement regime currently includes several states that enforce actively their foreign anti-bribery laws, it still remains a regional instrument only, with a regional response. We discussed above that the headquarters of the charged MNCs are mostly in six or seven countries, and that some markets remain under-regulated. Even with the increase of institutional and economic capacity of the OECD enforcement regime, however, corporations with headquarters in certain non-OECD countries are still not

13 See Table 7.1: The Effectiveness potential of extraterritorial regimes (Section 7.2.2).

Table 7.3 The formation of a multilateral enforcement regime – the credibility problem

The Credibility Problem in Practice *The OECD enforcement regime is dominated by the US but evolves into a multilateral enforcement regime*	
Unilateral Enforcement Regime *US Extraterritorial Enforcement* →	**Multilateral Enforcement Regime** *Increasingly Multilateral Enforcement*
Extraterritoriality alleviates the credibility problem + high institutional capacity + institutional design increases the efficiency of enforcement + relatively large assistance network **Extraterritoriality remains regional** - sanctioned corporations are headquartered only in several major economies - political and institutional constraints to prosecute foreign corporations headquartered in certain countries, e.g. ex ante threat of enforcement conflicts - no evidence of a stable assistance network between the US and certain major countries	**The original credibility problem is increasingly resolved** + high institutional and economic capacity + - extraterritorial reach increases but still remains regional – more political constraints, less institutional limitations + - relatively large assistance network but problems with certain major countries **New Credibility Problems** - the increased potential of large enforcement conflicts - uncoordinated follow-up enforcement - + mixed evidence of more direct cooperation

prosecuted. These are credibility problems that undermine the provision of enforcement as a public good. To a great extent, these problems have similar causes as the ones that undermine the unilateral enforcement regime:

1 Enforcement authorities that enforce their foreign anti-bribery laws actively lack the economic incentives to prosecute corporations headquartered in certain countries because of the possible political and economic consequences that said prosecution might have. These issues are largely linked to the *ex-ante* threat of large enforcement conflicts.
2 The lack of cooperation, both informal and more formal, between enforcement authorities that enforce their foreign anti-bribery laws actively and the enforcement authorities where the corporations that are usually not prosecuted are headquartered.

What is more, these credibility problems also partially persist within the OECD anti-bribery enforcement regime because corporations headquartered in certain large countries that ratified the OECD Convention are rarely prosecuted. This indicates that further expansion of the OECD anti-bribery regime would not limit the regional nature of its enforcement. In fact, such expansion could limit the effectiveness of enforcement by increasing the diversity of the OECD anti-bribery regime, and by making it difficult to design an effective governance institution within the regime.[14] The following part discusses the emergence of new credibility problems – large enforcement conflicts.

7.4.2.2 The threat of large enforcement conflicts

With the increasing enforcement of foreign anti-bribery laws, the OECD anti-bribery regime faces the threat of enforcement conflicts. When the stakes are high, and the countries that enforce foreign anti-bribery laws are large, the issue of enforcement turns into a highly political game. In effect, the provision of enforcement can be prevented because of high transaction costs, as well as jurisdictional conflicts that may escalate into international policy problems.[15]

Open conflict, however, is rare. Within the OECD enforcement regime, states whose firms used to face US enforcement were often reluctant to cooperate with the US because of both political and economic reasons. Under the US enforcement pressure, these states started to engage and have become active in negotiating multijurisdictional settlements. As was seen in *SBM Offshore*, not all multijurisdictional settlements lead to coordinated enforcement. But enforcement conflicts, such as these in Brazil, are diminishing with time, once particular national enforcement authorities learn how to work together.

This way of ensuring cooperation and coordination makes the OECD international regime "shaky." This, in some cases, leads to a situation that resembles a trade negotiation between multiple enforcement authorities that impose tariffs on each other's national corporate champions. Moreover, schemes such as *Petrobras* allow the US enforcement authorities to discriminate foreign investors of the sanctioned corporations by allowing these corporations to deduct prospective class action payments to US investors from penalties awarded by the US enforcement authorities.

While open enforcement conflicts are rare, the threat of these conflicts leads to negative spillover effects related to the provision of enforcement. As an alternative to political and economic conflicts, national enforcement authorities may decide not to prosecute certain types of businesses. In a number of markets, the US and other enforcement authorities are endowed with sufficient institutional capacity to prosecute foreign corporations, but they lack the economic and political incentives to do so. Hence, as in the "unilateral" enforcement regime, lack of enforcement remains a problem also at the multilateral level.

14 This relates to the clarity problems of multilateral enforcement that are discussed (Section 7.4.3).

15 See Taylor (2006: 49–51), discussing the threat of trade sanctions in the context of extraterritorial enforcement of competition law.

7.4.2.3 The role of small countries: assistance and minor conflicts

Not every enforcement authority is capable of mounting global bribery prosecution against an international corporation. First, small countries have less jurisdictional links to MNCs than large countries have. For example, large stock exchanges that establish such links are only in a small number of major economies. Second, small countries do not have the resources to consolidate hundreds of bribery schemes into a single proceeding, hence, they are less efficient than large countries.[16] Even if they have legislation that is similar to US legislation, and dispose of a reasonable enforcement budget, they cannot use the leverage effect of extraterritoriality in the same way as the US can.[17] Another economic consideration is that it is more likely that MNCs leave markets of small countries that impose high sanctions for foreign bribery, than that MNCs leave the US market, or stop doing business with US-based corporations. Because of these capacity limits and economic implications, it cannot be expected that small economies will deal with major bribery schemes in all of their complexity.

However, the contributory rather than leadership role of small countries should not be underestimated. Their active participation through the international network reinforces the negotiating position of authorities and makes enforcement more complete. In a number of cases, small countries not only provided MLA to enforcement from larger economies, but also applied their domestic anti-corruption laws together with, or in reaction to, US enforcement. For instance, Poland in *HP* engaged in a follow-up prosecution of natural persons – Polish citizens – and made the US enforcement action more complete. Furthermore, and perhaps more importantly, these joint schemes empower these nations in signaling their intolerance of bribery.

Yet, in a number of cases, small countries acted as a de facto "private plaintiff." Such plaintiffs then use the enforcement actions of other countries in order to receive money into their public treasury or to improve the reputation of their enforcement authorities. As discussed above, these activities can be seen both within the OECD anti-bribery enforcement regime, see, for instance, Greece in *Siemens* (Section 5.5.2), and outside the OECD framework, Nigeria being the most frequent follow-up enforcer.[18] While follow-up enforcement may increase transactions and compliance costs, they have only a minor negative impact from the perspective of collective action. A relatively low volume of these activities can hardly disincentivize major states from the enforcement of foreign anti-bribery laws.

16 See, generally, Rauxloh (2012: 37–38) discussing the advantages and disadvantages of plea bargaining.

17 It is important to note that neither the US, nor smaller countries such as the Czech Republic, Slovakia, or Slovenia, conducted many small foreign anti-bribery enforcement actions.

18 See, for example, *Siemens* (Section 5.5) and *Bonny Island* (Section 5.6).

7.4.3 Clarity problems and multilateral enforcement

The extraterritorial enforcement of foreign anti-bribery laws relates to the two main types of clarity problems that undermine the effectiveness of the OECD enforcement regime. First, the enforcement policy of the OECD regime remains vague. Second, the complex character of the legal institutions that are available to national enforcement authorities ought to be taken into consideration. Why these clarity problems arise and how they undermine the provision of enforcement as well as the cooperation and coordination of enforcement is discussed in the following sections. Furthermore, the following sections also discuss how extraterritorial enforcement relates to these clarity problems.

7.4.3.1 The clarity problem and the provision of enforcement

1 *The clarity problem is connected with the lack of awareness about how extraterritoriality contributes to the effectiveness of enforcement*

The lack of understanding of what is involved in the enforcement of foreign anti-bribery laws, how such enforcement is being carried out, and ultimately how it should be carried out, including the differences between the members' enforcement policies and legal principles, limits the provision of enforcement as a public good. In this context, extraterritoriality has improved enforcement capacity and proved to remedy to non-enforcement of foreign anti-bribery laws.

From this perspective, the lack of awareness about the usage of certain elements of US enforcement practices and US laws, whether they be specific to foreign bribery or more general, may limit placing corporations under strict regulatory scrutiny. In other words, because the discussed benefits of extraterritoriality are not always recognized, or understood, by some countries, the OECD enforcement regime cannot fully benefit from them. Specific legal principles and legal tools linked with extraterritorial enforcement limit the possibilities for MNCs to hide their illicit activities by, for instance, operating in secure jurisdictions. Therefore, the lack of awareness about these principles and tools prevents other countries from improving their enforcement activity.

2 *The clarity problem is associated with the lack of knowledge about the substantive fragmentation of anti-corruption laws*

The OECD anti-bribery enforcement regime establishes relatively coherent legal standards criminalizing foreign bribery, including the offense of bribery of foreign public officials. Nevertheless, a much broader legal background influences the enforcement of foreign anti-bribery laws. This leads to what we call "substantive fragmentation." Because these relevant laws vary from one country to the other, substantive fragmentation takes a different guise in every country. Accordingly, it can only be understood with localized legal knowledge. The lack of understanding of how to use this fragmentation to address the complexity of international bribery schemes undermines the provision of enforcement as a public good.

Bribing by MNCs is often closely related to books and records violations, security offenses, tax fraud, and money laundering. Furthermore, a number of factual links can be identified between foreign anti-bribery enforcement and national security measures. For example, a number of non-US corporations that were sanctioned for bribing foreign public officials, such as Siemens and BAE, are the subject to US special security agreements.[19] In these agreements, the US authorities may require corporations that win governments bids that raise national security concerns to appoint certain government officers in a board of directors.

The lack of shared knowledge about substantive fragmentation, as it may arise in the various enforcing countries, limits placing corporations under strict regulatory scrutiny. For example, by constructing legally relevant bribery cases on the basis of multiple bribery-related charges, US enforcement authorities proved to be relatively effective in charging MNCs for foreign bribery. In other countries, this creative approach to enforcement might be lacking, and beyond that enforcers might not fully grasp how corruption and bribery related to other societal problems and other possible relevant laws. In other words, because benefits of a creative exercise of prosecutorial authority that relies on substantive fragmentation are not always recognized, or understood, in other countries, the OECD enforcement regime cannot fully benefit from them. The effectiveness of enforcement is hereby hampered.

7.4.3.2 Clarity problems and cooperation and coordination

Extraterritoriality can be also viewed as an institutional outcome that, on the one hand, helps to overcome the collective action problem. Yet, this institutional outcome can, at some point of time, undermine collective action. The problem with extraterritoriality, as it functions within the OECD anti-bribery enforcement regime, is that it is associated with clarity problems that prevent cooperation and coordination between national enforcement authorities. This is undesirable because, as was discussed in Chapter 2, the provision of public good increases when the enforcement is cooperative. Sections below explain what these clarity problems are and why they persist.

1 *Plurality of national enforcement policies and regulatory convergence*

The core feature of extraterritorial enforcement of foreign anti-bribery laws is that it allows national enforcement authorities to sanction corporations in foreign jurisdictions. By its nature extraterritoriality implies

19 See, generally, US Department of Defense (2015) Biennial Report to Congress on Improving Industrial Security <http://www.dss.mil/documents/about/February_2015_Biennial_Repor_%20to_Congress_9MARCH2015.pdf> accessed 11 February 2017.

regulatory clashes between multiple countries.[20] These clashes are reflected in national enforcement policies and national laws. The lack of understanding of this regulatory heterogeneity and the incompatibility of some approaches limits cooperation and coordination between national enforcement authorities.

The existence of these more general clarity problems is nothing new. We see these same problems being raised within the legal discourse about the differences and similarities between common law and the civil law systems. Whether they are concerned with the spirit of the people (Legrand, 1996), legal traditions (Glenn, 2010), or more formalistic methods of comparison based on, for instance, the isolated study of legal rules in the society (Nelken and Feest, 2001), comparative studies have covered an immense number of legal topics. In the case of international bribery law, the scope of these principal clashes starts from the rule of law and due process, through to the protection of privacy, and finishing at different views on the use of corporate liability rather than the liability of natural persons.

The task of the formal OECD monitoring mechanism is to tackle the heterogeneity of national anti-bribery measures based on its principle of functional equivalence, rather than to decide upon these types of principal conflicts. Despite the fact that the principle of functional equivalence allows for heterogeneity, because of institutional reasons and normative constraints, we see a number of examples indicating that US law and the laws of other OECD countries have been converging.[21] It is more likely than not that this legal convergence will also be followed by the convergence of national enforcement policies.

There are many examples of the said convergence. DPAs are being introduced as novel concept in many jurisdictions, including UK law[22] and French law.[23] Furthermore, there are many other convergences where concepts that would traditionally be seen as common law concepts are adopted in civil law countries. For instance, in countries such as the Czech Republic and Slovakia, the concept of the criminal liability of

20 See Section 3.3.3 for the discussion about the heterogeneity of national foreign anti-bribery approaches.

21 See Section 3.3 for the discussion about functional equivalence. See, generally, Teubner (1983: 277) claiming that the legal system should neither "develop its own purposive program nor to decide goal conflicts between competing policies. It is to guarantee coordination processes and to compel agreement."

22 UK introduced DPAs and used them for the first time in *ICBC Standard Bank*, an enforcement action concluded in 2015.

23 France adopted Sapin II and concluded its first DPA (*Société Générale*) in 2018. LOI n° 2016-1691 du 9 décembre 2016 relative à la transparence, à la lutte contre la corruption et à la modernisation de la vie économique (Sapin II), available at https://www.legifrance.gouv.fr/affichLoiPubliee.do?idDocument=JORFDOLE000032319792&type=general&legislature=14, accessed 11 January 2019.

legal persons was introduced only recently.[24] The US concept of whistleblowing and the protection of whistleblowers have been increasingly used in EU countries.[25] The EU has introduced a new system of integrated non-financial reporting; under this system, large corporations should report on anti-corruption and bribery issues as of the financial year 2017.[26] These convergences indicate that some clarity problems are diminishing.

2 *Extraterritorial enforcement processes: the lack of transparency and predictability*

While foreign anti-bribery laws are converging, extraterritorial enforcement is based on enforcement measures that are largely political. Most importantly, the effectiveness of enforcement is largely based on negotiated settlements concluded in the shadow of the law. Foreign anti-bribery laws in these situations represent a mere menu of threats enforcement authorities may use, such as debarment and high sanctions. The menu, however, does not indicate "what options are exercised or what threats are used" (Stuntz, 2004: 2568–2596). The effectiveness of extraterritoriality naturally comes with costs in terms of transparency, predictability of enforcement, and other elements that can be associated with the rule of law.

Despite releasing national policy documents, the mix of possible enforcement patterns and policies, both within and outside the OECD enforcement regime, is indefinable. Choi and Davis, for example, argue that the FCPA enforcement is not very predictable, because the enforcement actions of US authorities are explained by four rationales: legality, self-interest, altruism, and coordination (Choi and Davis, 2014). These rationales interact and cause clarity problems that can be hardly resolved (Hock, 2014).

Consequently, the OECD anti-bribery enforcement regime faces clarity problems because it has not developed a governance mechanism that allows its members to resolve clarity problems associated with extraterritorial enforcement processes. From the collective action perspective, as explained in Chapter 2, national enforcement authorities, therefore, struggle to:

1 observe and share information about the behavior of each member; and
2 define desirable and undesirable enforcement behavior (Section 2.2.2).

24 For example, in the Czech Republic, legislation introducing the concept of the criminal liability of legal persons is effective since 1 January 2012. Zákon č. 418/2011 Sb., o trestní odpovědnosti právnických osob a řízení proti nim.

25 In the US, see the Federal False Claims Act of 1986 and the Sarbanes-Oxley Act of 2002. In Europe, see Worth (2013).

26 European Parliament and Council Directive 2014/95/EU of 22 October 2014 amending Directive 2013/34/EU as regards disclosure of non-financial and diversity information by certain large undertakings and groups [2014] OJ L 330.

These two challenges relate to extraterritorial enforcement processes, such as settlement negotiations, rather than concrete foreign anti-bribery norms as they stand in statutes.

Regarding the first challenge, clarity problems persist because of the lack of transparency regarding information about the behavior of members as well as the lack of awareness about the discussed extraterritorial enforcement processes. The availability of data is limited regarding, for instance, the following questions: What state initiated the cooperation, with which states, and why? Did the states that were asked to cooperate provide cooperation? And why have some of them refused to cooperate? Answering these questions will help develop better tuned and more achievable anti-bribery enforcement policies in an alliance whose members differ significantly in terms of their economic capacity as well as in their legal and political approaches to foreign anti-bribery enforcement.

Regarding the second point, the regime is not able to explicitly signal what is considered to be desirable enforcement behavior. This is because the monitoring framework of the regime is not able to cover extraterritorial enforcement processes. Most importantly, clarity problems persist because of the lack of specificity in defining what is achievable in terms of enforcement for particular countries, in the light of their economic capacity. How these clarity problems could be mitigated, for example, by evaluating countries according to a broader range of enforcement activities, is discussed in the next chapter (Section 8.4.4).

3 Enforcement conflicts and appropriate jurisdiction

Alongside the lack of a common enforcement policy, unified legal principles, and transparency and predictability, jurisdictional conflicts form another type of clarity problem.[27] The worst are conflicts where large countries enforce foreign anti-bribery laws without coordinating their respective actions, and conflicts where no authority claims jurisdiction in order to prosecute international bribery.[28] Whether a potential conflict is identified before the prosecution of an MNC, at the time of the conclusion of a foreign bribery resolution, or after the conclusion, a governance mechanism is needed in order to mitigate these conflicts. Without such governance mechanism, there is a danger that the resolutions of these jurisdictional and enforcement problems would be opportunistic and without clear prospect of enforcement cooperation. More practical problems associated with enforcement conflicts and how to resolve them are discussed in the following chapters.

27 See Figure 2.4: Extraterritoriality implies clarity problems (Section 2.4.2).

28 The key example of the lack of coordination that resulted into an enforcement conflict is *SBM Offshore/Petrobras* (Section 6.7.3).

7.5 Conclusion

The concept of effectiveness of enforcement stands at the heart of this chapter. The first challenge for the OECD anti-bribery enforcement regime is that the problem it aims to solve is too complex: How can MNCs be held criminally liable for bribing foreign public officials? Second, the aim of foreign anti-bribery law enforcement is defined too broadly, and the fragments of a common enforcement policy that can be found in the OECD Convention and other documents alone cannot overcome problems caused by fragmented enforcement policies. Last, the principle of functional equivalence of the OECD Convention allows for the choosing of various means to achieve these rather blurred ends. This often involves clarity clashes that increase the probability that states promote their own self-interests – for example by making a choice to prefer some norms and principles over other norms and principles – at the expense of the greater aims of the regime.

Extraterritoriality has two main roles. First, extraterritoriality is a force that shifts the trajectory from a collective action problem characterized by no-enforcement, and the problem of opportunism characteristic of unilateral enforcement, toward a new, multilateral system of enforcement. In other words, extraterritoriality is a political–legal phenomenon that facilitates the transition to a potentially more effective solution to collective action problems, for instance, by incentivizing enforcement and participation. Second, extraterritorial enforcement determines a regime that is path-dependent and, at some point, limits further development of the regime by locking-in old institutions. While the regime is growing in size, substantive and procedural legal institutions representing solutions to old problems are not sufficient for addressing new credibility and clarity problems that arise. While some extraterritoriality will always be needed to address the complexity of global problems, in time, it will need to evolve from its "corrective-political" function into a legal technique that is part of a broader cooperative network. The following chapter provides a number of suggestions how the OECD anti-bribery enforcement regime can mitigate existing credibility and clarity problems.

References

Choi, S. J. and Davis, K. E. (2014) 'Foreign Affairs and Enforcement of the Foreign Corrupt Practices Act' 11 Journal of Empirical Legal Studies 409.

Dixit, A. K. (2014) *Lawlessness and Economics: Alternative Modes of Governance*. Princeton, NJ: Princeton University Press.

George, B. C. and Lacey, K. A. (2000) 'A Coalition of Industrialized Nations, Developing Nations, Multilateral Development Banks, and Non-Governmental Organizations: A Pivotal Complement to Current Anti-Corruption Initiatives' 33 Cornell International Law Journal 547.

Getz, K. A. (2006) 'The Effectiveness of Global Prohibition Regimes: Corruption and the Antibribery Convention' 45 Business & Society 19853.

Gibbons, R. and Henderson, R. (2012) 'Relational Contracts and Organizational Capabilities' 23 Organization Science 1350.

Glenn, P. H. (2010) *Legal Traditions of the World: Sustainable Diversity in Law.* Oxford: Oxford University Press.

Hock, B. (2014) 'Intimations of Global Anti-Bribery Regime and the Effectiveness of Extraterritorial Enforcement: From Free-Riders to Protectionism?' TILEC Discussion Paper No. 2014-009 <https://ssrn.com/abstract=2395156> accessed 26 January 2019.

Keohane, R. O., Haas, P. M. and Levy, M. A. (1993) 'Improving the Effectiveness of International Environmental Institutions' In R. O. Keohane, P. M. Haas and M. A. Levy (Eds.) *Institutions for the Earth: Sources of Effective International Environmental Protection* (pp. 397–426). Cambridge, MA: The MIT Press.

Koh, H. H. (1997) 'Why Do Nations Obey International Law?' (1997) 106 Yale Law Journal 2599.

Legrand, P. (1996) 'European Legal Systems are not Converging' 45 International & Comparative Law Quarterly 52.

Margeson, G. N. (2014) An Analysis of the Effectiveness of the Foreign Corrupt Practices Act in Combating Corruption. The University of Texas at Austin, Report <https://repositories.lib.utexas.edu/bitstream/handle/2152/26501/MARGESON-MASTERSREPORT-2014.pdf?sequence=1&isAllowed=y> accessed 4 May 2019.

Masten, S. E. and Prüfer, J. (2014) 'On the Evolution of Collective Enforcement Institutions: Communities and Courts' 43 Journal of Legal Studies 359.

Nelken, D. and Feest, J. (2001) *Adapting Legal Cultures.* Oxford: Hart Publishing.

Nichols, P. M. (2016) 'The Neomercantilist Fallacy and the Contextual Reality of the Foreign Corrupt Practices Act' 53 Harvard Journal on Legislation 203.

Ostrom, E. et al. (2002) *The Drama of the Commons.* Wahington, DC: National Academy Press.

Pines, D. (1994) 'Amending the Foreign Corrupt Practices Act to Include a Private Right of Action' 82 California Law Review 185.

Snidal, D. (1985) 'The Limits of Hegemonic Stability Theory' 39 International Organization 579.

Stuntz, W. J. (2004) 'Plea Bargaining and Criminal Law's Disappearing Shadow' (2004) 117 Harvard Law Review 8.

Tarun, R. W. (2006) Basics of the Foreign Corrupt Practices Act. Latham & Watkins <https://www.lw.com/upload/pubContent/_pdf/pub1287_1.pdf> accessed 20 July 2019,

Teubner, G. (1983) 'Substantive and Reflexive Elements in Modern Law' 17 Law & Society Review 239.

Torpman, J. and Jörgensen, F. (2005) 'Legal Effectiveness: Theoretical Developments on Legal Transplants' 91 Archives for Philosophy of Law and Social Philosophy 515.

World Bank (2007) Sourcebook for Evaluating Global and Regional Partnership Programs Indicative Principles and Standards.

Worth, M. (2013) Whistleblowing in Europe. Transparency International <https://whistlenetwork.files.wordpress.com/2014/01/whistleblowing-in-europe-report-november-2013.pdf> accessed 4 May 2019.

Young, O. R. (1999) *Governance in World Affairs.* Ithaca, NY: Cornell University Press.

Young, O. R. (2011) 'Effectiveness of International Environmental Regimes: Existing Knowledge, Cutting-Edge Themes, and Research Strategies' 108 Proceedings of the National Academy of Sciences of the United States of America 254.

8 How should the OECD anti-bribery enforcement regime foster collective action?

8.1 Introduction

This chapter provides suggestions so that states and the OECD may consider how extraterritoriality contributes to solving collective action problems, and adopt a policy to foster collective action. The main issue is that the OECD anti-bribery enforcement regime developed a mechanism to resolve initial collective action problem associated with the lack of enforcement. However, the alleviation of the old collective action problem has been accompanied by new collective action problems that limit the effectiveness of the OECD enforcement regime.[1] While institutional limitations to provide enforcement as a public good still play a role, it is mainly the lack of cooperation and coordination between national enforcement authorities that needs to be incentivized. This, however, requires more robust governance mechanism.

The rest of this chapter is organized as follows. Section 2 explains why more robust governance mechanism is desirable and indicates limits of the OECD in delivering such mechanism. Sections 3 and 4 suggest how to address credibility and clarity problems of the OECD anti-bribery enforcement regime.

8.2 Desirable and undesirable heterogeneity: when external governance is just effective

Collective action problems of the OECD anti-bribery enforcement regime are closely associated with the heterogeneity of national enforcement policies and legal approaches to international bribery (Section 3.3.3). When concerned primarily with large and divergent groups, said heterogeneity is problematic and the discussed credibility and clarity problems arise. Each regime's type, however, is a unique system with different organizational–institutional demands and such heterogeneity may be a better option in relatively small groups based on informal, decentralized, and self-enforcing

1 See Table 7.3: The formation of a multilateral enforcement regime – the credibility problem.

governance mechanism.[2] In the transition from one type of regime to another type, appropriate measures to address collective action problem are changing. Path-dependence of old institutions, political challenges, and the lack of clarity about how to design new institutions in the transition can block a regime to ever evolve into its more effective form.

The OECD anti-bribery enforcement regime is a regime in transition. In this regime, heterogeneity proved to be acceptable when the OECD regime struggled with a lack of capacity and willingness to enforce foreign anti-bribery laws. This also proved to be acceptable when states cooperated within relatively small networks. Through direct and informal means, the US, UK, French, Brazilian, German, Dutch, and Swiss enforcement authorities successfully mitigated potential enforcement conflicts while still providing enforcement. As the enforcement of foreign anti-bribery laws is increasing, however, many states that are involved in, and relevant for, foreign anti-bribery enforcement, are not part of such direct and informal networks.

The OECD anti-bribery enforcement regime is in the darkest point that precedes the dawn, a stage where external governance is just effective (Dixit, 2014: 76). As explained in previous chapters, the OECD Convention addresses jurisdictional conflicts through a coordination mechanism based on a consultation procedure (Section 4.9.2).

This exemplifies how the regime is not able to clarify some enforcement processes and monitor them in sufficient detail. While the regime should attempt to mitigate some of these clarity problems, principally the OECD Convention does not provide, and should not be expected to, provide grounds for the WGB or any other body to define a common enforcement policy. The agreement needs to be reached between its Signatories.

While more robust governance mechanism is needed to control undesirable heterogeneity, a certain degree of informality, flexibility, and therefore heterogeneity, is still necessary. Strong centralization and the harmonization of national foreign anti-bribery laws do not, at this point, offer a practical solution to new credibility and clarity problems. To solve these problems, new institutions are needed but any additional centralization and harmonization should be preceded by, and be the result of, direct cooperation within more informal and practically oriented enforcement networks. Furthermore, some degree of heterogeneity is also desirable because of the need to face the lack of understanding we have about the complexity of transnational economic crime, or indeed to hold MNCs liable for bribery effectively. From this perspective, pre-defined, harmonized, and centralized tools that deal with jurisdictional overlaps and potential enforcement conflicts, can, at this stage, limit the provision of existing enforcement.

2 In other words, inclusiveness is not necessarily beneficial. For example, in large groups, clarity problems might be so costly that a multilateral response to international bribery becomes overall less effective than a unilateral response. For example, Dixit (2014: 46) argues that it is unsure whether large groups with external governance are better than self-governing small groups with optimal size.

Following sections allude how the most important credibility and clarity problems that undermine collective action can, and should, be addressed by the OECD anti-bribery enforcement regime.

8.3 Addressing credibility problems

The OECD has evolved into a shaky multilateral enforcement regime that partially fulfills its enforcement potential. Besides the lack of concern and political will, the threat of large enforcement conflicts is another reason why the original credibility problem, associated with the lack of enforcement, persists (Section 7.4.2). In effect, while the institutional capacity of the OECD anti-bribery enforcement regime has increased, extraterritorial enforcement has remained regional because the regime members failed to sanction MNCs headquartered in major non-OECD countries (Section 7.3.2). Moreover, the threat of enforcement conflicts disincentivizes new states to start enforcing their foreign anti-bribery laws. Last, the threat also prevents assistance by means of MLA, hence increases enforcement costs and decreases the effectiveness of prosecution.

The partial persistence of the old credibility problem and the emergence of new credibility problems inside the OECD regime suggest that bringing new signatories to the OECD Convention should not be a policy priority. As discussed above, credibility problems are, to a great extent, consequential on a number of clarity problems, such as the determination of appropriate jurisdiction, associated with larger groups (see, generally, Section 4.9.2). Adding new signatories to the OECD Convention would increase the size and diversity of the regime, hence make it even more difficult for states to cooperate and coordinate their enforcement.

To retain, and potentially increase, the provision of enforcement as a public good, the increased size of the regime has to be accompanied by an external governance mechanism such as an international arbitration body or an international tribunal. These alternatives to the OECD anti-bribery enforcement regime are, as will be discussed in Chapter 9, not feasible at this point. Therefore, the OECD should rather focus on improving the current cooperation and coordination through providing more clarity. Even this, however, requires new institutions.

8.4 Addressing clarity problems

Benefits available from tackling international bribery can be realized more effectively by instituting a governance system that reflects the size of a regime (Section 7.2.1). Designing appropriate governance institutions for intermediate-size regimes is, however, challenging (see, for example, Hadfield and Weingast, 2012; Dixit, 2014). Because the OECD anti-bribery enforcement regime has become such intermediate-size, decentralized, enforcement regime with no authority to solve disputes between group members, it faces clarity problems (Section 7.4.3). In such stage, a regime, in order to be effective, must find a mechanism to define acceptable and unacceptable behavior (Section 2.3.4).

For the OECD anti-bribery enforcement regime, the key issue is to distinguish between acceptable and unacceptable forms of foreign anti-bribery enforcement. The OECD regime should internalize the complexity of extraterritoriality so as to evolve from its "corrective-political" function that primarily focuses on the mitigation of the original credibility problems associated with the lack of enforcement, into a legal technique that is part of a broader cooperative network. This section provides several suggestions regarding how the OECD regime can, and should, incentivize such transformation.

8.4.1 More awareness is needed about how extraterritoriality contributes to effectiveness

The awareness-spreading about how US extraterritorial enforcement techniques contribute to effectiveness will improve the provision of enforcement as a public good (Section 7.4.3). In this context, policy-makers and other relevant stakeholders should recognize the fact that in reality, the counterfactual to extraterritoriality is non-enforcement. From this perspective, other countries should consider adopting some elements of US enforcement practices and US laws, whether they be specific to international bribery or more general. In practice, we see a number of knowledge-sharing activities that bring law enforcement practitioners from all regions of the word together, such as the Global Network of Law Enforcement Practitioners against Corruption.[3] These activities may not only spread the awareness about the effectiveness of extraterritoriality but may also contribute to the convergence of national anti-bribery enforcement policies.

8.4.2 Concurrence of substantive laws as an opportunity for more effective enforcement

Foreign anti-bribery enforcement derives its effectiveness from the application of multiple "functionally equivalent" laws (Section 7.4.3). The lack of understanding and recognition of how to use the substantive fragmentation of anti-corruption laws in order to address the complexity of foreign bribery schemes is a clarity problem. This clarity problem limits the provision of enforcement as a public good. In this context, because the abovementioned benefits of a creative exercise of prosecutorial authority that relies on substantive fragmentation are not always recognized, or understood, in some countries, the OECD enforcement regime cannot fully benefit from them. In order to derive advantages from this substantive fragmentation, more research on the interaction between international bribery and other problems such as global financial

3 OECD Global Network of Law Enforcement Practitioners against Corruption <https://www.oecd.org/corruption/acn/lawenforcement/> accessed 28 January 2019.

stability, international security and terrorism, and tax fraud, is needed. Further, the cross-fertilization of existing regimes regulating international economic criminality may open new and more effective avenues of cooperation between national enforcement authorities. Moreover, such cross-fertilization may also contribute to the coordination of extraterritorial enforcement activities (for the discussion about these alternatives, see Chapter 9).

8.4.3 Plurality of national enforcement policies: awareness about the costs effectiveness is needed

Extraterritorial enforcement of foreign anti-bribery laws reflects moral, economic, and political differences between the countries' approaches to the problem of international bribery. It is not the role of the OECD to address these more general clarity problems. Nevertheless, policy-makers and other relevant stakeholders should be aware that the effectiveness of enforcement comes with opportunity costs that enforcement authorities have to face. For example, it is an opportunity cost to prefer the effectiveness of prosecution to due process and legal certainty. These costs relate to the non-application of other possible policies and principles, by giving preferences to some rights, obligations, and values, over others.

Policy-makers should be aware of the plurality of enforcement policies and related opportunity costs. The OECD anti-bribery enforcement regime needs more discussion and research about this plurality, for example, the clash between the prosecution of individuals and the prosecution of corporations. Enforcement authorities that prioritize the prosecution of individuals can be more likely seen as less effective than these that predominantly prosecute corporations. Individuals will more likely than corporations challenge national enforcement authorities in front of courts. In effect, enforcement authorities that focus on individuals will likely face more procedural obstacles to conclude their enforcement actions than these that are concluding DPAs with corporations.

8.4.4 Extraterritorial enforcement processes: more transparency and specificity is needed

Another crucial challenge is how can cooperation between national enforcement authorities be incentivized in a regime based on the plurality of national enforcement policies? First, the OECD anti-bribery enforcement regime faces clarity problems because it has not developed a governance mechanism that allows members to observe and share information about extraterritorial enforcement processes (Section 7.4.3). It is true that the WGB operates a robust peer-review mechanism in which reviewers from state parties become highly familiar with the legal system and some of the enforcement practices of other state parties, however, this is not done at the operational level, for example in the enforcement practice of national enforcement authorities.

The regime needs to ensure that more information about the behavior of members is available by understanding "work as it is being done," and integrating these findings into explicit agreements about "how work is going to be done before it is performed" – as was illustrated by the Toyota case (Section 2.3.4). This requires more transparency and awareness about the discussed extraterritorial enforcement processes. More data and research are needed regarding, for instance, what state initiated the cooperation, with which states, and why? This work contributes to the clarification of some of these interactions. Yet, the availability of data is limited.

Furthermore, the OECD anti-bribery enforcement regime faces clarity problems because it has not developed a governance mechanism that defines desirable and undesirable enforcement behavior with sufficient precision. In this context, a more robust monitoring framework of enforcement and enforcement-related activities would mitigate the lack of information about the behavior of the OECD members. What is more, it would also signal what is considered to be desirable enforcement behavior.

Most importantly, more specificity is needed in defining what is achievable in terms of enforcement for particular countries, taking into account their economic and institutional capacity. Even if this is politically tinged, some elementary distinction between the role of small and big countries is necessary in order to build trust and incentivize cooperation (Section 7.4.2). For example, small countries, despite their lack of primary enforcement activity, may, in fact, be relatively effective from the perspective of collective action if they, for example, pro-actively provide evidence and other forms of assistance to foreign enforcement authorities. However, they may lack incentives because their contribution to the effectiveness of enforcement may not be sufficiently recognized and acknowledged by others. Hence, countries should not only be evaluated according to their success in prosecuting MNCs but according to a broader range of criteria (Lord, 2016: 163 et seq.). Splitting the roles and comparing between the countries within the OECD regime, at least to some extent, is desirable.

8.4.5 Jurisdictional conflicts and appropriate jurisdiction

Last, problems associated with jurisdictional conflicts need to be discussed. These conflicts center around the question of appropriate jurisdiction (Section 4.9.2). To determine appropriate jurisdiction, one needs to ask a number of legal questions. The most relevant questions are the following:

1 *What national law should apply, for example, US law or German law, and what authority should enforce relevant legal norms?*

Regarding the first problem, the jurisdiction over foreign bribery cases is often based on the principle of objective territoriality, known as the "effects" doctrine. The effects doctrine increases a possibility of legal conflicts between states, whether conflicting laws or authorities because it allows enforcement authorities to assert jurisdiction over a wide range of entities. Furthermore, these clarity problems also relate to the principle of adjudicatory jurisdiction that determines the body that decides on matters. In legal systems that provide foreign anti-bribery enforcement regularly, the body that, in fact, decides on matters, is an enforcement authority, rather than the court by concluding an out-of-court settlement.[4] This, as will be discussed in Section 8.4.5.1 further complicates the resolution of these conflicts.

2 *What norms of the relevant national legal order should apply? For example, how national laws solve the conflict between privacy law and foreign anti-bribery law*

Some clarity problems are more profound because of clashes between two or more substantive regimes. This is referred to as the absolute conflict of laws, where parties are not able to comply with conflicting laws of two states simultaneously (Colangelo, 2016: 721). One example is the question of how to resolve competing demands arising from US foreign anti-bribery investigations and EU data protection laws. A frequently discussed challenge is one, where in the context of a FCPA violation, a defendant decides to implement an internal investigation in the EU. In the context of such internal investigation, US enforcement authorities required MNCs to collect and preserve evidence. Such requirement includes the collection of personal data such as contracts, emails, and contacts that are protected by EU privacy laws, and their collection is subject to a declaration by a relevant national data protection authority. These demands may differ, leading to situations where a corporation, in an attempt to be credited with full cooperation by US enforcement authorities during a plea-bargaining phase, may in some cases violate EU data protection laws.[5]

3 *How should "idem," whether cases are identical and actually conflict, be determined, and what, if any, proceeding should be dropped if cases are identical?*

A last example of a clarity problem is the question of whether two parallel prosecutions actually overlap.[6] It was discussed in Chapter 5 that the lack of transparency in foreign anti-bribery enforcement, the use of multiple functionally equivalent charges, and the complexity of foreign bribery schemes, provide a challenge for determining what constitutes a

4 It must be noted that extraterritorial enforcement closely ties the question of adjudicative jurisdiction with that of the jurisdiction to enforce the law. Zerk (2010: 26) argues that the effects doctrine "refers to a sometimes contested application of the objective territoriality principle which says that each state has the right to regulate conduct abroad which is directly capable of producing serious (or 'substantial') effects (usually economic effects) within the territory of the regulating state."

5 Carol A. F. Umhoefer, *How EU Data Protection Laws Impact Cross-Border FCPA Investigation* (DLA Piper, 24 September 2014) <https://www.dlapiper.com/en/us/insights/publications/2014/09/the-global-anticorruption-perspective-q3-2014/how-eu-data-protection-laws-impact/> accessed 28 January 2019.

6 See Section 4.9.4 for the discussion about the *ne bis in idem* principle.

single foreign bribery case.[7] This implies a challenge to determine how and to what extent two parallel enforcement actions overlap.

Following sections allude how jurisdictional conflicts and the issue of appropriate jurisdiction should be addressed by the OECD anti-bribery enforcement regime.

8.4.5.1 The OECD coordination mechanism reflects reality

The OECD regime offers a limited solution to the above-discussed clarity problems. Under the current regime, countries should negotiate, behind the walls of the OECD, in view to determine the appropriate jurisdiction.[8] The negotiation procedure is related to international comity, an institution that has proved useful in other legal fields, including tax, insolvency, competition, and environmental regulation.[9] For example, in competition law, bilateral agreements between the US and the EU have, to some extent, increased co-operation between enforcement authorities.[10] While no such specific agreements have been concluded regarding foreign anti-bribery enforcement, the US and other countries have concluded guidelines for handling criminal cases affecting two or more countries (see Section 4.9.3).[11]

The problem with the doctrine of international comity is its discretionary character and the relative simplicity. International comity is based on static commitments that proved to be insufficient for the resolution of jurisdictional problems in which more countries believe that their interests are predominant (in the competition law context, see Ezrachi, 2012: 115–118). As was seen, for example, in *Petrobras*-related enforcement actions, this is also a problem in the case of international bribery. For example, because of a lack of information and agreement regarding what acts of bribery are included in DPAs, the doctrine of international comity, presumably, only has a limited effect on resolving and preventing jurisdictional conflicts.

7 See Section 5.2 for the discussion about methodological challenges regarding the construction of a foreign bribery case.

8 See Article 4.3 of the OECD Convention.

9 OECD, 'Challenges of International Co-operation in Competition Law Enforcement' (2014) 11–13 <https://www.oecd.org/daf/competition/Challenges-Competition-Internat-Coop-2014.pdf> accessed 29 January 2019.

10 See Taylor (2006: 106–143) who discusses cooperation and coordination mechanisms in competition law, including a link between trade sanctions and extraterritorial enforcement of competition law.

11 UK (2007) Attorney General's Domestic Guidance for Handling Criminal Cases Affecting both England, Wales or Northern Ireland and the United States of America <https://www.publications.parliament.uk/pa/ld200607/ldlwa/70125ws1.pdf> accessed 5 May 2019. See also Crown Prosecution Service (2013) Director's Guidance on the Handling of Cases where the Jurisdiction to Prosecute is Shared with Prosecuting Authorities Overseas <http://www.cps.gov.uk/publications/directors_guidance/director_s_guidance_on_concurrent_jurisdiction.html> accessed 5 May 2019.

Nevertheless, from the perspective of collective action, Article 4(3) of the OECD Convention provides a platform for states to mitigate some clarity problems, and hence provides a regional system of international comity, based on the OECD Convention. While such solution can have only limited impact, it is reasonable and useful.[12] As will be discussed below such solution could be accompanied by a set of soft factors to be taken into consideration when determining appropriate jurisdiction.

A consultation procedure that is similar to the one provided by the OECD Convention is recognized by EU law, for example, in the area of combating terrorism and in the area of fight against organized crime.[13] The consultation procedure under EU law is different from international anti-bribery law in two ways. First, EU law is more specific than the OECD Convention. For example, Article 9 of the Framework Decision on combating terrorism, indicates that the aim of consultation procedure is to centralize proceedings in one Member State. To do so, the Member States shall take into account four factors: territoriality of acts, nationality of perpetrator, the origin of the victims, and the territory where the perpetrator was found.[14] These are rather broad indicators that have limited practical usage in complex transnational cases where the location of relevant acts, perpetrators, and victims is difficult to determine with sufficient clarity.

Second, some EU agencies, such as Eurojust, an agency of the EU dealing with judicial cooperation in criminal matters, provide additional guidance and support in determining appropriate jurisdiction. Notably, Eurojust issued guidelines assisting national enforcement authorities in determining appropriate jurisdiction. The guidelines specify the basic process of initiating cooperation and coordination as well as they provide criteria that should be taken into account when making a decision about appropriate jurisdiction.[15] National enforcement authorities should take into account, for example, the possibility of obtaining witnesses, interests of victims, sentencing powers, length of proceedings, and proceeds of crime.[16] Similar guidance on appropriate jurisdiction would be useful in mitigating clarity problems in the area of foreign anti-bribery enforcement. Such guidance should take into account specificities of the OECD anti-bribery enforcement regime, including extraterritorial techniques and processes.

12 See Section 4.9.3 for the general discussion about the doctrine of international comity.

13 See, for example, Framework Decision 2002/475/JHA of 13 June 2002 on combating terrorism.

14 Framework Decision 2002/475/JHA of 13 June 2002 on combating terrorism. Framework Decision 2008/841/JHA of 24 October 2008 on the fight against organized crime.

15 Eurojust (2016) Guidelines for deciding 'which jurisdiction should prosecute?' <http://www.eurojust.europa.eu/doclibrary/Eurojust-framework/Casework/Guidelines%20for%20deciding%20which%20jurisdiction%20should%20prosecute%20(2016)/2016_Jurisdiction-Guidelines_EN.pdf> accessed 30 January 2019.

16 Ibid 1–4.

Moreover, Eurojust also offers procedural support. Within its mandate, the Eurojust can help facilitate consultation and proactively detect parallel proceedings. It can also issue recommendations and non-binding opinions about appropriate jurisdiction. At its coordination meetings, Eurojust can also encourage joint investigation teams (JITs) as a tool to prevent and resolve jurisdictional conflicts.[17] While EU agencies such as Europol cannot authoritatively decide over appropriate jurisdiction, they provide more specificity and procedural guidance that could inspire the OECD and its Signatories. The OECD anti-bribery enforcement regime needs more discussion about who and how should enforce foreign anti-bribery laws in a particular case.

8.4.5.2 Conflicts of norms and ne bis in idem

The discussed soft-law guidelines and procedural support in initiating enforcement cooperation contribute to the provision of predictable resolutions of jurisdictional conflicts. Some could argue that soft-law approaches are not enough and that the OECD anti-bribery enforcement regime needs more direct and explicit *ex-ante* norms on appropriate jurisdiction. Yet, *ex-ante* norms will not provide any additional clarity. Rules regarding conflict of laws, conflict of norms, and the *ne bis in idem* principle would decrease predictability and increase arbitrariness of enforcement.

From the perspective of collective action, ex-ante binding criteria determining appropriate jurisdiction are arbitrary. This is because the OECD anti-bribery enforcement regime provides enforcement based on substantive, procedural and normative fragmentation. This fragmentation is accompanied by what is in theory described as *sui generis* conflicts (Michaels and Pauwelyn, 2012: 374–376). By *sui generis* conflicts, what is meant are complex conflicts between norms – for example, one indicating to report certain fact and other making such reporting illegal – applicable laws and competent forums (see, generally, Fontanelli, 2011).[18] The fragmentation of foreign anti-bribery law and *sui generis* conflicts make classic rules on conflicts of norms, including principles of specialty, superiority, and posterity ineffective. They make ineffective also rules on conflict of laws (Michaels and Pauwelyn, 2012: 374–376).

Furthermore, as was discussed in Chapter 5, each national enforcement authority can qualify the acts of a given corporate group differently, using a number of different procedures, and thus create uncertainty about what acts are actually being prosecuted.[19] Because there is the lack of transpar-

17 Ibid 4.

18 See, generally, the discussion in Filippo Fontanelli, 'Tomer Broude and Yuval Shany (eds). Multi-Sourced Equivalent Norms in International Law. Oxford: Hart Publishing, 2011. Pp. 344. $120. ISBN: 9781849461450' (2012) 23 European Journal of International Law 597.

19 See Section 5.2 for the discussion about methodological challenges regarding the construction of a foreign bribery case.

ency about what acts DPAs include and how national enforcement authorities build their cases, *ex-ante* defined rules and principles such as *ne bis in idem* are likely to be ineffective without prior direct cooperation in investigation and prosecution. One needs to know what "idem" is in order to apply the *ne bis in idem* principle.

8.5 Conclusion

The OECD anti-bribery enforcement regime is in the darkest point that precedes the dawn, a stage where external governance is just effective. In this stage, the regime struggles to clarify some enforcement processes and monitor them in sufficient detail. This chapter provides the following suggestions so that states and the OECD may consider how extraterritoriality contributes to solving collective action problems.

1 More awareness about how extraterritoriality contributes to the effectiveness of prosecution is needed.
2 Policy-makers and national enforcement authorities should better understand and utilize the concurrence of substantive laws because it creates an opportunity for more effective enforcement.
3 While the plurality of national enforcement policies should be generally accepted, the opportunity costs of the effectiveness of enforcement should be acknowledged and considered by policy-makers. More specificity in terms of the clash between individual and corporate enforcement is needed.
4 More transparency and data regarding extraterritorial processes are needed. For instance, what state initiated the cooperation, with what states, and why? Did the states that were asked to cooperate provided cooperation, and why did some of them refuse to cooperate?
5 A more robust monitoring framework of enforcement and enforcement-related activities will mitigate the lack of information about the behavior of the members, but also more explicitly signal what is considered to be desirable enforcement behavior. More specificity is needed in defining what is achievable in terms of enforcement for particular countries, reflecting their economic capacity.
6 The OECD coordination mechanism reflects the reality of what the OECD can do, in legal terms, in order to incentivize cooperation and coordination. This mechanism should be accompanied by soft-law guidelines and procedural support, similar to these that are provided by some EU agencies such as Europol. Enforcement conflicts can hardly be solved *ex ante* by precise rules on conflict of norms or conflict of laws. *Ex post* solutions such as the *ne bis in idem* principle are also rather ineffective.

These relatively modest suggestions are given by the fact that while more robust governance mechanism is needed to control undesirable heterogeneity that exists within the regime, a certain degree of informality, flexibility, and therefore heterogeneity, is still necessary. Strong centralization and the harmonization of national foreign anti-bribery laws do not, at this point, offer a practical solution to new credibility and clarity problems that are arising from increasing extraterritorial enforcement. The real challenge associated with the resolution of clarity problems is that new institutions addressing the lack of cooperation and coordination should not diminish the institutional capacity of a regime. One should not forget that the existing extraterritorial regime and accompanied jurisdictional conflicts are an alternative to a regime without enforcement.

The following chapter discusses existing and hypothetical alternatives to the OECD anti-bribery enforcement regime.

References

Colangelo, A. J. (2016) 'Absolute Conflicts of Law' (2016) 91 Indiana Law Journal 719.

Dixit, A. K. (2014) *Lawlessness and Economics: Alternative Modes of Governance*. Princeton, NJ: Princeton University Press.

Ezrachi, A. (2012) *Research Handbook on International Competition Law*. Cheltenham: Edward Elgar.

Fontanelli, F. (2011) 'Tomer Broude and Yuval Shany (eds). Multi-Sourced Equivalent Norms in International Law. Oxford: Hart Publishing, 2011. Pp. 344. $120. ISBN: 9781849461450' 23 European Journal of International Law 597.

Hadfield, G. K. and Weingast, B. R. (2012) 'What Is Law? A Coordination Model of the Characteristics of Legal Order' 4 Journal of Legal Analysis 471.

Lord, N. (2016) *Regulating Corporate Bribery in International Business*. London: Routledge.

Michaels, R. and Pauwelyn, J. (2012) 'Conflict of Norms or Conflict of Laws?: Different Techniques in the Fragmentation of Public International Law' 22 Duke Journal of Comparative & International Law 349.

Taylor, M. D. (2006) *International Competition Law: A New Dimension for the WTO?* Cambridge: Cambridge University Press.

Zerk, J. A. (2010) 'Extraterritorial Jurisdiction: Lessons for the Business and Human Rights Sphere from Six Regulatory Areas' (Harvard University, John F. Kennedy School of Government <https://www.hks.harvard.edu/sites/default/files/centers/mrcbg/programs/cri/files/workingpaper_59_zerk.pdf> accessed 25 February 2019.

9 Beyond the OECD

International court and other alternatives

9.1 Introduction

The OECD anti-bribery enforcement regime and its extraterritoriality have been effective in overcoming initial collective action problems associated with the lack of enforcement. Yet, the regime still struggles to move into a broader cooperative network with trust and clearly established enforcement processes. This is not the failure of the OECD. As other enforcement regimes that are in the move from a unilateral form to a multilateral form, the OECD enforcement regime needs a stronger external system of governance (see Chapter 2). The external system of governance, however, is what states yet need to transferred onto the OECD.

This chapter discusses governance alternatives existing in other legal fields, including human rights, intellectual property (IP), eCommunications, AML, and tax. The chapter explains why and when an enforcement system supervised by an international tribunal such as the International Criminal Court (ICC), the World Trade Organization (WTO) model, and more decentralized solutions could work, and why, and when, they could not work.

A decentralized model with the delegation of some enforcement tasks to an external body is the most appropriate governance alternative. A more centralized anti-bribery model should be based on the shared competence between the OECD, or other international organization, and state members. The coordination and cooperation between an international organization and its members should be facilitated by a transgovernmental network such as BEREC in the field of eCommunications.

Moreover, this chapter indicates that the problem of international bribery should be understood in line with other economic crimes. Policy-makers and national enforcement authorities should build more bridges between the anti-bribery regime and complementary enforcement regimes such as these in the area of AML and taxation. An important role in building such bridges have transgovernmental networks. Furthermore, this chapter also discusses the impact of private actors on collective action and indicates how private and public actors can and should cooperate to mitigate collective action problems.

9.2 International anti-corruption court

This section and the following sections provide a snapshot of governance alternatives to the OECD anti-bribery enforcement regime. The main focus is on the role of international tribunals and other bodies with powers to interpret the law, apply the law and to settle disputes.

The idea of the establishment of an anti-corruption court is not new. At the time of the adoption of the first anti-corruption conventions, a number of scholars discussed how such tribunal could be established within the WTO (Nichols, 1997; Abbott and Snidal, 2002) or that states should be held accountable for tolerating corruption and bribery under international human rights mechanisms (Balakrishnan, 1999). More recently, a number of scholars and professionals reopened this discussion (Pearson, 2013; Spalding, 2014; Wolf, 2014; Peters, 2018). Most radical suggestions in this discussion (Wolf, 2014) include the establishment of an International Anti-Corruption Court based on the ICC model.[1]

The establishment of a centralized anti-corruption body should be set in a broader discussion about the evolution of international courts and their ability to advance the rule of international law (Shany, 2009). The ICC model with its Office of Prosecutors exercise a very broad jurisdiction over crimes such as genocide. The Office of Prosecutors, as an independent organ of the ICC, prosecutes cases only if national enforcement authorities are not willing to do so. The most centralized model of an anti-bribery court would then allow such court to take their own action instead of state in cases of states' reluctance to adjudicate.

The idea of centralized body with the power to fairly and impartially deal with corrupt businesses and oligarchs is appealing. Centralized enforcement bodies such as the ICC are in many respects successful in producing impartial and fair decisions. Yet, their key problem is that their ability to resolve conflicts against the true wishes of all parties involved is extremely limited (Shany, 2009). Beyond the most serious crimes such as war crimes, international courts and tribunals lack the state cooperation, including the enforcement of the tribunal's orders, in politically sensitive cases (Shany, 2009: 74).

Typologically, international bribery and corruption is exactly the area in which international courts such as the ICC will struggle to seek the state cooperation. Even the OECD anti-bribery enforcement model with its decentralized system, soft arrangements, and narrower focus did not persuade some major stakeholders to join. From this perspective, it is difficult to imagine that the problem of corrupt relationships between large MNCs and corrupt government officials will be solved by a voluntary submission of these

1 See also the discussion at the Global Anticorruption Blog, among many others see Whiting, A. (October 4, 2018) Is an International Anti-Corruption Court a dream or a distraction? <https://globalanticorruptionblog.com/2018/10/04/guest-post-is-an-international-anti-corruption-court-a-dream-or-a-distraction/> accessed 17 March 2019.

stakeholders under the jurisdiction of an international court. Moreover, even if a centralized body with adjudicatory powers was established, the lack of true agreement of all stakeholders would lead to a range of new credibility problems such as the legitimacy and efficiency of such model. Moreover, an international anti-bribery tribunal might ultimately undermine existing enforcement structures and result in less collective action. This leaves us with tribunals with much narrower competence.

9.3 WTO model: a body deciding state disputes

International courts, such as the World Trade Organization Appellate Body (WTO AP), proved effective in sustaining regimes with specific objectives such as economic integration and trade liberalization. Shany (2009: 82) discusses that the expansion of judiciary powers of these courts is possible thanks to "a very delicate equilibrium between the states parties and other stakeholders participating in a specific legal regime, and between the states and other stakeholders and the regime's institutions." This specificity seems to explain why this new judiciary appeared in economic regimes rather than in the traditional piece building projects.

The WTO-type dispute settlement model is more promising in improving anti-bribery collective action than the ICC model. Consider how the WTO deals with the enforcement of IP protections. IP has important trade-related aspects. Measures and procedures to enforce these rights can become barriers to legitimate trade. This is the reason why the WTO Member States agreed to the Agreement on Trade-Related Aspects of Intellectual Property Rights (TRIPS). For example, Article 3 of the TRIPS provides that Member States shall not treat the nationals of other Member States less favorably than their own nationals with regard to the protection of IP. If states fail to do so, other states can use the WTO dispute settlement mechanisms. The dispute settlement is compulsory and provides legally binding decisions and sanctions.

The WTO treatment of IP can also inspire the movement in the area of foreign anti-bribery law because international bribery transactions show similar links to international trade as IP transactions. Nichols (1997) argues that similarly to IP, an international bribery requirement is a non-tariff barrier to trade in goods and service that undermines WTO objectives such as global welfare. More recently, Spalding (2014) argues that amendments to the WTO agreements could create the first anti-bribery forum in which major state could bring complaints against each other for failure to enforce their foreign anti-bribery laws.

Yet, the WTO has never aimed at combating international bribery. Abbott and Snidal (2002) provide that this is because the WTO, as a hard law regime has reduced its effectiveness in handling sensitive issues such as corruption. The WTO lacks a normative leadership to go beyond their bargaining quo-pro-quo mode of operation. Why then was IP included and international bribery excluded from the WTO agreements? Morrison (2002: 206–207) argues that IP agreements are agreed purely because they are valued maximizing for the exchanging parties.[2] Societally beneficial implications are rather side effects. International bribery is different as it requires much deeper moral condemnation and deeper economic argument against international bribery. One does not bargain with oligarchs and corrupt politicians whether to punish, or not, international bribery. International bribery needs to be prohibited even if such prohibition is in the given case inefficient (Morrison, 2002).

The WTO can be an appropriate venue for international anti-bribery movement only if it can compromise its quo-pro-quo mode of operation with stronger normative leadership. Maybe paradoxically, the OECD anti-bribery enforcement regime was able to provide more normative leadership because of its soft nature. Relatively soft arrangements in terms of who and how should have jurisdiction over transnational cases of bribery allow for more heterogeneity of measures and enforcement responses than the WTO model. This heterogeneity was necessary in the 1990s when no state was sanctioning major cases of international bribery. The OECD success and the WTO non-engagement show again that institutional requirements for collective actions are changing, and we need to be patient with centralizing the mode of governance.

The fact that the OECD anti-bribery enforcement regime does not provide any binding dispute settlement mechanism proved to be beneficial at the time when the enforcement of foreign anti-bribery laws was very low. Nevertheless, now is the time for stronger external governance mechanism. In order to create one, we should consider models that are softer than the WTO but harder than the OECD.

9.4 Decentralized enforcement models: eCommunication

Decentralized enforcement models are more politically acceptable than a centralized anti-corruption court. Indeed, numerous studies show how the need to deal with credibility and clarity problems accounted for the willingness of states to delegate some of their authority to a supranational organization (Pollack, 2003). This is very common in Europe where a centralized enforcement model, such as State aid, is the exception. In general, and as a default rule, the Member States apply and enforce EU law. In a number of regulatory areas, the EU and its Member States are in a similar relationship as the OECD and its signatory states. There are no fully harmonized rules, but instead, general obligations deriving from an international treaty. States implement and enforce the rules in accordance with their own legal traditions, as well as their own substantive and procedural rules.

2 Please note, however, that while these agreements can be value maximizing, distributional effects are an issue. Critiques might argue that developed countries enjoy much more benefits than developing countries.

9.4.1 Toward more centralization: the eCommunication model

Regulatory processes within the EU regulatory models imply a number of credibility and clarity problems that are similar to those faced by the OECD anti-bribery enforcement regime. In the field of eCommunications, as Visser (2013: 157) argues, the convergence of the telecommunications sector requires a single regulatory framework.[3] Yet, the Member States differ in their regulatory capacities, resources, and expertise. Moreover, there is limited EU case-law on electronic communication networks and services, and political pressure and regulatory capture may lead to the pursuit of national self-interest (Visser, 2013: 157; Cole, 2010). These credibility and clarity problems can also be seen in the field of foreign anti-bribery regulation (see Chapter 6).

To deal with these problems, the Member States delegated some enforcement tasks to EU bodies such as the EU Commission. For example, in the EU regulation of public utilities such as electricity and telecommunications, the EU and its Members States share competence, meaning that they both can adopt legally binding acts in the given area. While EU regulatory models do not include a fully centralized regulatory authority, EU bodies usually oversight national regulatory bodies in order to ensure coherence and protect fundamental EU rationales such as the functioning of internal market (Sauter, 2016). The centralized oversight clarifies enforcement processed and allows the regime to operate like a coordinated network. The eCommunications regulatory model has produced flexible rules and resulted in the fall of telecoms' services prices by approximately 30%.[4]

Under the current eCommunication framework, NRAs (National Regulatory Authorities) are obliged under EU law to consult their draft regulatory measures prior to their adoption. The EU Commission can then assess the compliance of the measures with EU law and assess whether they create a barrier to internal market. After an in-depth investigation, the EU Commission can withdraw its reservations, issue a veto if, for example, the definition of a relevant market is concerned, or issue a recommendation to amend the measures.[5]

3 Paragraph 5 of the European Parliament and Council Directive 2002/21/EC of 7 March 2002 on a common regulatory framework for electronic communications networks and services (Framework Directive) [2002] OJ L 108 (hereinafter Electronic Communication Directive). Please note that this area is constantly changing. The so-called Telecom reform package that includes five Directives has been replaced by the European Parliament and Council Directive 2018/1972 of 11 December 2018 on establishing the European Electronic Communications Code.

4 European Commission (24 April 2018) *Telecom Rules* <https://ec.europa.eu/digital-single-market/en/telecoms-rules> accessed 23 March 2019.

5 European Commission (7 January 2019) *Consultation procedures in telecom* <https //ec.europa.eu/digital-single-market/en/consultation-procedures-telecom> accessed 23 March 2019.

The interaction between NRAs and the EU Commission can be illustrated by the case related to the operation of Magyar Telekom in Hungary.[6] In December 2018, the EU Commission issued a recommendation on the Hungarian regulator's draft regulation. The regulation provided the method of calculation of the return investment granted to Magyar Telekom for the provision of its network lines. Because Magyar Telekom enjoyed a dominant position, the Hungarian regulator proposed to oblige the company to provide access to its network against the payment of a fee.

However, the method of calculation of the access fee used a size premium mark-up. The mark-up, according to the EU Commission, could lead to excessive access prices and was not consistent with eCommunication regulatory framework.[7] The Commission, therefore, recommended to the Hungarian NRA to amend or withdraw the remedies relating to price regulation of the leased lines in Hungary. The EU Commission wanted to avoid overestimating the cost of equity, in particular by ensuring that the size premium mark-up is not included in the calculation.[8] If the relevant NRA does not implement such recommendations, the process can end up in front of the Court of Justice of the European Union (CJEU). To prevent disputes and undesirable heterogeneity of regulatory measures, the Member States and the EU established an intermediary network organization.

9.4.2 A classification mechanism: BEREC

The success of a decentralized enforcement regime depends largely on its ability to adapt its institutional design to new conditions. In the field of eCommunication, NRAs ensure more clarity and coordination by delegating some enforcement tasks to EU bodies. Yet, this may lead to clashes between NRAs and the EU. The eCommunications regime has addressed the interface between the NRAs and EU institutions by establishing classifying bodies. The first network – the European Regulatory Group – was an informal network that provided reflection, discussion, and advice, in order to ensure more consistency in the application and enforcement of the law. The second network, that replaced the first, is the Body of European Regulators for Electronic Communication (BEREC),[9] an EU agency providing technical input and opinions.

6 Case HU/2018/2107: wholesale high-quality access provided at a fixed location in Hungary.

7 European Commission (17 December 2018) *EU Commission issues recommendation concerning the wholesale high quality access market in Hungary* <https://ec.europa.eu/digital-single-market/en/news/eu-commission-issues-recommendation-concerning-wholesale-high-quality-access-market-hungary> accessed 23 March 2019.

8 Commission Recommendation of 17.12.2018 in Case HU/2018/2107: wholesale high-quality access provided at a fixed location in Hungary.

9 European Parliament and Council Regulation 1211/2009 of 25 November 2009 establishing the Body of European Regulators for Electronic Communications (BEREC) and the Office [2009] OJ L 337/1.

In December 2018, BEREC was reformed and obtained new regulatory tasks.[10] BEREC comprises the Board of Regulators composed of one member from each Member State.[11] The Board of Regulators acts independently and objectively regardless of any particular national or personal interest.[12] BEREC should ensure consistent application of the regulatory framework and promote an effective internal market.[13] To fulfill its mission, it can, for example, issue guidelines, report on technical matters, keep registers and databases, and deliver opinions on draft regulations. The EU Commission and the NRAs are not bound by these measures but they need to take utmost account of any measures adopted by BEREC.

It must be noted that the eCommunication regime is often compared to the EU competition law model, including its European Competition Network that has developed even more sophisticated tools to address consistency (Monti, 2016). However, this may be due to the fact that the EU competition law model is overall much more centralized than the eCommunication model, because the EU Commission has the authority, for example, to relieve the NCA of their cases, which implies more consistency and coordination.[14]

9.4.3 Concluding remarks

To conclude, there has been repeating calls for an establishment of a central body with strong competences and wide jurisdiction over international bribery, this solution is neither feasible nor desirable. Rather, decentralized enforcement models such as the one that exists in the area of EU economic governance are more promising. These models are characterized by more centralization in a way that some regulatory tasks are delegated onto EU bodies. There is an extensive discussion among scholars about why, how, and when the Member States delegate their authority, which body regulates, and which regulatory model is more effective in a given regulatory area (among many others, see Eberlein and Grande, 2005; Dehousse, 2016; Mathieu, 2016). Moreover, these models are coordinated by transnational regulatory networks such as BEREC that can be understood as a classifying institution (see Chapter 2). This discussion can inspire scholars in the field of foreign anti-bribery law. The following section investigates the role of transnational networks in ensuring collective action.

10 European Parliament and Council Regulation 2018/1971 of 11 December 2018 establishing the Body of European Regulators for Electronic Communications (BEREC) and the Agency for Support for BEREC (BEREC Office).

11 Article 7.1 of the Regulation 2018/1971. Not that the Commission shall participate in all deliberations of the Board of Regulators without the right to vote (Article 7.4).

12 Article 8 of the Regulation 2018/1971.

13 BEREC, What is BEREC? <https://berec.europa.eu/eng/about_berec/what_is_berec/> accessed 18 March 2019.

14 See Council Regulation (EC) 1/2003 of 16 December 2002 on the implementation of the rules on competition laid down in Articles 81 and 82 of the Treaty [2003] OJ L 1/1, art 11(6).

9.5 Transnational regulatory networks

The BEREC and the European Regulatory Group are two examples of so-called transgovernmental, or more generally, transnational regulatory networks.[15] The OECD characterizes these networks as:

> [R]egulatory co-operation based on loosely-structured, peer to peer ties developed through frequent interactions rather than formal negotiation involving specialized domestic officials (typically regulators) directly interacting with each other (for instance though structured dialogues or memorandum of understanding) often with minimal supervision by foreign ministries.
>
> (OECD, 2013: 156)

Whether it is their flexibility and speed in addressing policy and practical problems, or the ability to directly cooperate by, for example, exchanging experience and information, a number of these networks have contributed to the effective solving of cooperation and coordination problems.

In a decentralized regime such as the OECD anti-bribery enforcement regime, transnational regulatory networks could be a bridge from an enforcement that lacks coordination, and to some extent legitimacy, to a regime with a stronger external system of governance. One key advantage is that transnational regulatory networks depoliticize sensitive issues, for example, through different working group they organize, and supposedly increase the independence of national enforcement authorities. Slaughter (2000: 120) provides that "disaggregating the state into its functional components makes it possible to create networks of institutions engaged in a common enterprise even as they represent distinct national interests." Ultimately, there is a higher chance to establish an external governance mechanism because such common enterprise agrees more easily on a common enforcement rationale, clarify enforcement processes, and build more trust.

Furthermore, in regimes that are already more coordinated, transnational networks are needed to ensure regulatory coherence and enforcement coordination. In the above-discussed case of eCommunication regulation, the EU Commission is in a position of an intellectual leader, jointly and indirectly coordinating regulatory processes with BEREC (Sauter, 2016: 223–234). In this way, BEREC mitigates potential clarity problems between the EU Commission and the Member States as well as between the Member States themselves.[16]

15 Please note that there is not one consistent definition of transnational regulatory networks (see Verdier, 2009).

16 Similarly, in the anti-trust area, thanks to meetings between anti-trust case handlers and policy officials, the International Competition Network created momentum for increasing effectiveness in international anti-trust cooperation, including the cooperation and coordination of specific cases (Ezrachi, 2012: 121–135).

9.5.1 Transgovernmental anti-corruption networks

The OECD has been active in launching multiple partnerships to support knowledge-sharing activities that bring law enforcement practitioners and other anti-corruption actors together. The OECD is collaborating with international anti-corruption fora and networks such as the G20 Anti-Corruption Working Group (ACWG).[17] The ACWG was established in 2010 to provide high-level recommendations on how to fight international corruption. The key contribution of the ACWG has been its ability to coordinate national and international anti-corruption players. The group includes not only 19 countries and the EU but also works with the World Bank Group, the IMF, the FATF, the Business 20, and other anti-corruption actors.[18] The ACWG organizes a number of anti-corruption initiatives such as expert meetings and conferences, but in its nature remains a high-level initiative.

The G20 initiatives are complemented by anti-corruption programs that are more focused. The OECD launched a number of joint initiatives with regional partners to support business integrity and national governments in their anti-corruption efforts. For example, the OECD Working Group on Bribery organizes the Anti-Corruption Network for Eastern Europe and Central Asia. This informal network supports the exchange of experience among law enforcement practitioners, exchange of information, and the promotion of regional anti-corruption activities.[19] Furthermore, the OECD is partnering with the African Development Bank on the OECD/AfDB Join Initiative that through its 21 country members aims, for example, to increase the capacity for effective enforcement.[20] Similar projects also operate in other regions including in Asia-Pacific, Latin America Caribbean, and Middle East North Africa. Moreover, the OECD launched a number of national anti-corruption projects such as these in Greece and Ukraine.[21]

Clearly, the OECD is very successful in supporting anti-bribery collective action through informal networks. There is a good potential that some of these networks will once, in one form or the other, help develop a stronger external system of governance.

17 G20 is an informal network of the most powerful states and the EU. G20 represents around 90% of the world's GDP. Its main objectives are related to enhancing international economic cooperation, financial stability, and long-term economic growth. See European Parliament, 'The European Union's Role in international Economic Fora: Paper 1: The G20' (Directorate General for Internal Policies, April 2015, 8 <http://www.europarl.europa.eu/RegData/etudes/STUD/2015/542207/IPOL_STU(2015)542207_EN.pdf> accessed 27 March 2019.

18 Bundesministerium der Justiz und für Verbraucherschutz, *The G20 Anti-Corruption Working Group* <https://www.bmjv.de/DE/Themen/G20/G20_node.html> accessed 25 March 2019.

19 OECD Global Network of Law Enforcement Practitioners against Corruption <https://www.oecd.org/corruption/acn/lawenforcement/> accessed 24 March 2019.

20 OECD/AfDB Initiative <http://www.oecd.org/corruption/businessintegrityandantibriberyeffortsinafricaoecdafdbinitiative.htm> accessed 25 March 2019.

21 OECD, Bribery and Corruption <http://www.oecd.org/corruption/> accessed 25 March 2019.

9.5.2 More direct cooperation and coordination – AML

The extraterritorial enforcement of foreign anti-bribery laws is part of a broader transnational legal process. International bribery is often closely linked to books and records violations, security offenses, tax fraud, and money laundering. While this so-called substantive legal fragmentation makes the coordination of foreign anti-bribery enforcement more challenging, and some may thus argue that more harmonization is needed, it is also an opportunity for the OECD anti-bribery enforcement regime (see Section 7.4.3).

The substantive fragmentation is an opportunity because besides anti-corruption-specific networks, the OECD and its Member States have created a number of networks in AML, tax, and other bribery-related fields. These networks can not only increase the institutional capacity to sanction international bribery but also improve the cooperation and coordination of anti-bribery enforcement. If, for example, a high level of cooperation and coordination already exists in an anti-money laundering network, cooperation and coordination with regard to foreign bribery may be increased by extending the agenda of the anti-money laundering network to issues related to international bribery.

In other words, building bridges between supplementary substantive regimes provides an opportunity to create a better basis for direct cooperation and coordination in anti-bribery enforcement. One example is the system based on the activities of the Financial Action Task Force (FATF), an intergovernmental body that sets standards related to legal, regulatory, and operational measures for combating money laundering and the financing of terrorism. FATF has 36 member jurisdictions, in addition to the EU and the Gulf Co-operation Council. According to FATF Recommendation 29:

> [C]ountries should establish a financial intelligence unit (FIU) that serves as a national centre for the receipt and analysis of: (a) suspicious transaction reports; and (b) other information relevant to money laundering, associated predicate offences and terrorist financing, and for the dissemination of the results of that analysis.[22]

A predicate offense of money laundering is international bribery.

The materialization of the FATF Recommendation 29 is the so-called Egmont Group, an informal network of financial intelligence units for the stimulation of international cooperation in money laundering and the financing of terrorism. The Egmont Group meets regularly in order to facilitate information exchange, training and the sharing of information. As to the results, the Egmont Group

22 FATF, 'International Standards on Combating Money Laundering and the Financing of Terrorism & Proliferation, The FATF Recommendations' (FATF, October 2018) recommendation 29 <http://www.fatf-gafi.org/media/fatf/documents/recommendations/pdfs/FATF%20Recommendations%202012.pdf> accessed 25 March 2019.

provides a number of examples of international bribery activities being detected by the financial intelligence units. This increases a common understanding of the scope of the illegal activity and creates a space for establishing a JIT or coordinated enforcement strategy between parallel investigations and prosecutions.

The AML measures and tools should also be used in the fight against international bribery. While the FATF and the OECD are separate organizations, the FATF Secretariat is housed administratively at the OECD and cooperate closely on various issues. In cooperation with the ASWG and the OECD, for example, the FATF published the best practices paper on the use of the FATF recommendations to combat corruption. The paper acknowledges that relevant AML and anti-corruption experts are not always fully aware of the broad range of tools and information available to support them in corruption prevention and detection, as well as with investigations, prosecutions, international cooperation, and recovery of the proceeds of corruption (FATF/OECD, 2013: 4). This indicates that there is a need to look deeper into possible linkages between the AML regime and the OECD anti-bribery regime.

9.5.3 Beneficial owners, automatic exchange of information, and tax regulation

Economic crimes such as international bribery and tax evasion are based on similar principles, mainly the use of complicated systems of corporate veils and shell companies in order to hide the identity of true owners. This is the reason why obtaining beneficial ownership information, such as who in fact owns a bank account, is extremely relevant not only for tax collection but also for law enforcement, whether it be in relation to tax fraud, money laundering, or foreign anti-bribery enforcement (see, generally, Knobel and Meinzer, 2014). Cases such as the "Panama Papers", which involved millions of leaked documents containing private financial information, many pointing toward multiple economic crimes including international bribery, confirm that owners should be able to justify the origins of their funds (see Deloitte, 2016).

We should build bridges between international bribery and other economic crimes that are based on financial secrecy. In recent years, financial secrecy was addressed by new political and legal mechanisms, including those related to the exchange of tax information, the freezing and confiscation of assets, and bank secrecy.[23] One of the most important developments is the adoption of the Common Reporting Standard, a global standard of automatic exchange of tax information that was developed by the OECD together with

23 See EU Commission, *Confiscation and Freezing of Assets* <https://ec.europa.eu/info/law/cross-border-cases/judicial-cooperation/types-judicial-cooperation/confiscation-and-freezing-assets_en> assessed 27 March 2019.

G20 countries.[24] As of March 2019, more than 100 jurisdictions committed to the standard and there were more than 3600 bilateral exchange relationships.[25] The implementation of the Common Reporting Standard is strengthened by the monitoring and peer-reviewed activities of the Global Forum on Transparency and Exchange of Information for Tax Purposes, a multilateral framework including 154 members, mostly national states, and 18 observers.[26]

This information-sharing mechanism in relation to tax matters could improve anti-bribery collective action. The Common Reporting Standard includes, among other things, the automatic exchange of key indicators such as profits, taxes paid, and assets of MNCs. These indicators allow national tax authorities to undertake a risk assessment more effectively and better decide what should be subject to a tax audit.[27] Having the necessary expertise and an increasing amount of information, tax authorities are in a great position to identify and track suspicious payments, and consequently, also international bribery. According to Beach (2016):

> [W]hen a company pays a bribe or a kickback, the firm must either attempt to pass off a bribe as a legitimate business expense or else submit a return inconsistent with other financial records. Either move could raise red flags by causing discrepancies between account books and tax liability.

From this perspective, most of the large foreign anti-bribery enforcement schemes analyzed in this book are also *de facto* tax frauds.

In sum, sharing of standardized information on tax matters and close cooperation between financial intelligence units are two examples of how informal and direct interactions can increase collective action by limiting clarity

24 OECD, 'Standard for Automatic Exchange of Financial Account Information in Tax Matters' (OECD Publishing, 21 July 2014) <http://www.oecd.org/ctp/exchange-of-tax-information/standard-for-automatic-exchange-of-financial-account-information-for-tax-matters-9789264216525-en.htm> accessed 27 March 2019. The standard is based on Article 6 of the Convention on Mutual Administrative Assistance in Tax Matters, 25 January 1988, *in force* 1 April 1995 (amended 1 June 2011). The Convention was developed by the OECD and the Council of Europe.

25 See OECD, *Global Forum on Transparency and Exchange of Information for Tax Purposes* (Activated Exchange Relationships) <http://www.oecd.org/tax/automatic-exchange/international-framework-for-the-crs/exchange-relationships/#d.en.345426> accessed 27 March 2019.

26 The observers are, for example, the World Bank Group, United Nations, International Monetary Fund, etc., for a complete list of observers see OECD, *Global Forum on Transparency and Exchange of Information for Tax Purposes* (Global Forum Observers) <http://www.oecd.org/tax/transparency/about-the-global-forum/members/globalforumobservers.htm> accessed 27 March 2019.

27 See OECD, *Global Forum on Transparency and Exchange of Information for Tax Purposes* (About Automatic Exchange) <http://www.oecd.org/tax/automatic-exchange/about-automatic-exchange/> accessed 17 February 2017.

problems. It is promising that more integrated and holistic approaches to tackle economic are high on the political agenda. Further research should explore what complementary networks are already available, how they can be integrated, and to what extent bribery-specific networks are needed.[28] We should also discuss how, and by whom, complementary networks can, and should, be coordinated (see, generally, Eberlein and Newman, 2008).

9.6 Self-regulation and corporate compliance

Institutions and organizations that govern the life of billions of people are not only the result of traditional legislative processes led by nation states. Private actors such as business associations are increasingly the sources of a more informal and flexible international lawmaking (Pauwelyn, Wessel and Wouters, 2012). This is positive because private orders usually enjoy more expertise, flexibility, resources, and better knowledge of the actors they regulate. Private ordering might, however, pay inadequate attention to public interest, misuse market power, and engage in other undesirable activities (Gomtsian et al., 2018: 90–95; Hock and Gomtsian, 2018: 188–189). Big questions are when, how, and to what extent, public orders should attempt to limit the power of private orders. This discussion is also relevant in foreign anti-bribery law.

In action, public ordering and private ordering interact. When international bribery is concerned, this interaction is an opportunity because private modes of governance can further improve anti-bribery collective action. The following sections allude to what extent private anti-bribery enforcement is feasible and discuss the role of compliance industry in solving collective action problems associated with the enforcement of foreign anti-bribery regulation.

9.6.1 Business case for fighting international bribery

Corporate bribery is costly for businesses even if they do not have to pay fines. Market competition infiltrated by international bribery generates a suboptimal business equilibrium in which overall business profits are lower than in a market based on economic efficiency. For instance, bidding for a tender for oil and gas exploration usually involves only several big bidders. If nobody bribes, all corporations could compete on merit, rather than pay for building corrupt relationships.[29] Moreover, international bribery implies bad

28 For the overview of organizations fighting international corruption and bribery see United against Corruption, *Anti-Corruption Links* (United Nations Campaign) <http://www.anticorruptionday.org/actagainstcorruption/ar/resources/index.html> accessed 27 March 2019.

29 The assumption is that corporations have reasonable chances to win a bid. If a corporation cannot reasonably compete on merits, it would never stop bribing if this is the only way how to win.

business culture that infiltrates a corporation internally. Research shows that MNCs lose billions of dollars annually because of private corruption, for example, when MNC's suppliers bribe their employees (United Nations, 2010). These costs, next to the cost of potential government sanctions, incentivize businesses to prevent international bribery.

While MNCs are often the source of various global problems, many consider MNCs as the solution (Martinez-Diaz and Woods, 2009). Firms could, for example, conclude an agreement not to bribe. More generally, similar agreements based on purely private, informal, promises, or formal business associations has been a common practice for centuries. For example, since the 10th or 11th century onwards, merchant guilds emerged and established administrative bodies outside the rulers' territories in order to ensure the enforcement of contracts, as well as to ensure the protection of its members against crime (Greif, Milgrom and Weingast, 1994). In modern times, groups of alien businesses have been conventionally creating their own orders in order to protect their interests, without relying on formal laws.

The model of business associations aiming to mitigate international bribery has certainly potential to increase the sense of trust between corporations, provide more transparency by disclosing members' assets, and information on how they are doing business, and with whom. In practice, however, anti-bribery business associations, remain relatively weak, and are not sufficient for the prevention of international bribery.

In fact, corporations had not shown any noteworthy signs of anti-bribery collective action before the FCPA was adopted and later enforced. Historically, international bribery was the leading business norm in many markets, such as in the oil and gas industry in Africa (see Demas, 2011). Such business norm may be so strong that even if corporations want to change the pattern, they do not, because they are caught in what economists call a prisoner's dilemma situation. It means that despite the fact that in the long-term, not bribing would be the best strategy for them and society, they nevertheless decide to take part in acts of bribery. The lack of trust and information incentivizes businesses to bribe because non-bribers would most probably lose business due to a competitive advantage provided to businesses that do bribe (Klitgaard, Ronald and Lindsey, 1999: 31).

Moreover, agreeing to mitigate bribery in foreign markets might stimulate the temptation of businesses to collude in order to increase their market power. Scholars provide that systemic bribery, for example, might decrease competition between bidders, facilitate collusion in price and thereby lead to its increase (Piga, 2011). In fact, if corporations agree not to bribe, they might do so in order to capture a market and impose monopoly prices. Moreover, they can even capture the state by changing laws and directing government decision-making. International bribery, collusion, and state capture are interconnected problems, especially in developing countries with weak governance structures that can hardly be mitigated by businesses or their associations alone.

9.6.2 Public–private interaction and effective compliance

Collective action problems associated with the enforcement of foreign anti-bribery laws are not only a problem of public actors. This is because businesses are expected to design effective compliance programs to prevent international bribery, and self-report detected violations to enforcement authorities. In *Eli Lilly*, for example, the SEC stated that:

> [W]hen a parent company learns tell-tale signs of a bribery scheme involving a subsidiary, it must take immediate action to assure that the FCPA is not being violated, [...]. We strongly caution company officials from averting their eyes from what they do not wish to see.[30]

This system of enforcement has stimulated the emergence of a compliance industry led by the US consultants, audit firms, and law firms. After all, under the American system, prosecutors rely heavily on results of internal investigation provided by consultancy firms.

The need to establish anti-bribery compliance function is accompanied by attempts to standardize such function. Businesses that need to comply with foreign anti-bribery laws are incentivized to verify whether their suppliers, business partners, and clients do business ethically. An independent certification, based on for example the ISO 37001 anti-bribery standard, makes it easier for corporations to signal their compliance to other businesses, and help them to recognize compliance of other businesses with the same standard.[31]

These self-regulatory processes increase the reach of foreign anti-bribery enforcement. Doing business with parties coming from, or doing business in, countries with different business and cultural standards, should be subject to proper due diligence and contractual guarantees. For example, *Alcatel-Lucent* illustrates that if corruption risks are too high, investing corporations may stop using certain foreign marketing agents and sale representatives, and even leave certain markets.[32] Furthermore, the standard is also spread through mergers and acquisition. In *TSKJ*, Saipem acquired Snamprogetti from ENI (see Section 5.6). ENI, the predecessor corporations, was required to pay fine associated with foreign bribery of Snamprogetti. This is because Saipem concluded an indemnification agreement before the acquisition.[33]

30 Securities and Exchange Commission, *SEC Charges Eli Lilly and Company with FCPA Violations* (Press Release 20 December 2012) <https://www.sec.gov/News/PressRelease/Detail/PressRelease/1365171487116> accessed 15 April 2019.

31 See International Organization for Standardization, ISO 37001 – Anti-bribery management systems <https://www.iso.org/iso-37001-anti-bribery-management.html> accessed 15 April 2019.

32 *United States vs. Alcatel-Lucent France, S.A., et al., No. 10-cr-20906* (27 December 2010).

33 Saipem, *Annual Report 2013, 122* <http://www.saipem.com/en_IT/static/documents/2738BilSaipem13Ing_F.pdf> accessed 16 April 2019.

In effect, corporations that have to comply directly with US law, are incentivized to further spread the FCPA compliance standards to corporations that do not have to comply directly with the FCPA.[34] Still, anti-bribery private-ordering has limitations. Dixit (2015: 46) provides that:

> [T]he community institution operating on the supply side of bribery that I have proposed here cannot by itself eliminate or even greatly reduce it. But it can significantly strengthen the effectiveness of the government's formal system of detection and punishment that operates mostly on the demand side.

The effectiveness of a private anti-corruption movement, without incentives provided by hard-law enforcement, is a theoretical issue, rather than a practical one. The private self-regulation in this field, nevertheless, can significantly improve the provision of enforcement as a public good (for more general discussion about private policing, see Button, 2019).

To conclude, the current regime invites private orders to self-regulate. The regime relies on the authority of the US prosecutors that enjoy wide discretion when negotiating settlements with corporations. The power of US prosecutors somehow counter-balance the power of the private sector to self-regulate in this area. In majority of other OECD countries, prosecutors, however, are not so powerful and it is not clear whether, and how, additional public guarantees should be provided. The anti-bribery compliance function, and the compliance industry that supports this function, should not exist just for the sake of more self-regulation and capacity building, or even worse, for the sake of the compliance industry itself and as a marketing tool. It is legitimate to ask why in cases such as *Avon*, legal and compliance fees related to the foreign anti-bribery enforcement scheme are more than double the incurred penalties.[35]

9.7 Conclusion

Current decentralized extraterritorial enforcement is an institutional outcome that has helped overcome the collective action problem. In order to move into a broader cooperative network with trust and clearly established enforcement processes, the regime needs more teeth. A decentralized model with the delegation of some enforcement tasks to an external body is the most appropriate governance alternative. The OECD anti-bribery enforcement

34 This goes in line with Article 8 of the OECD Convention, and Section X of the 2009 Recommendation that requires its Signatories to incentivize businesses by their laws and policies to take appropriate precautionary measures.

35 For more info about the costs of the compliance, see generally, *Economist*, *The Anti-Bribery Business* (9 May 2015) <http://www.economist.com/news/business/21650557-enforcement-laws-against-corporate-bribery-increases-there-are-risks-it-may-go> accessed 16 April 2019.

regime can be inspired by some solutions of governance problems existing at the EU level. For example, the eCommunication model has come through a phase in which national enforcement was leading, to a system where the EU Commission must be notified by the NRAs about their decisions and can, under certain circumstance, veto these decisions.[36] What is needed is a more centralized anti-bribery model based on the shared competence between the OECD, or other international organization, and state members. The coordination and cooperation between an international organization and its members should be facilitated by a transgovernmental network that already exists in the international anti-corruption area as well as in substantively related areas such as international tax law and AML.

Moreover, the American system of enforcement is so effective because it relies heavily on the private sector that is required to self-regulate. This is positive because private orders usually enjoy more expertise, flexibility, and resources. Yet, such system cannot be implemented in countries in which the discretion of prosecutors is relatively low. It is not clear to what extent prosecutors should rely on private self-regulation in this area, and trust in self-policing of corporations.

Last, other governance alternatives are neither desirable nor feasible. An international anti-corruption court does not lead to a more effective enforcement regime; rather it is a solution of problems that may emerge in the future. The OECD enforcement regime and other countries in the world need much more detailed understanding and agreement about the rationales of the fight against international bribery. An international anti-corruption court represents an *ex-post* solution to legal but not political problems, including the above-discussed policy fragmentation. Moreover, even if a centralized body with adjudicatory powers was established, the lack of true agreement of all stakeholders would lead to a range of new credibility problems such as the legitimacy and efficiency of such model. Even in established systems with bodies that solve disputes between states, the sensitive issues are very political. For instance, the US has been blocking the appointment of the WTO Appellate Body members (Hillman, 2018). As much politically sensitive cases of international bribery are, there should be caution in suggesting to bring them the Appellate Body or an international anti-bribery tribunal. These solutions might ultimately undermine existing enforcement structures and result in less collective action.

References

Abbott, K. W. and Snidal, D. (2002) 'International Action on Bribery and Corruption: Why the Dog Didn't Bark in the WTO' In D. M. Kennedy and J. D. Southwick (Eds.), *The Political Economy of International Trade Law* (pp. 177–204). Cambridge: Cambridge University Press.

36 Article 7 of the Electronic Communication Directive.

Balakrishnan, R. (1999) 'Corruption, Legitimacy and Human Rights: The Dialectic of the Relationship' 14 Connecticut Journal of International Law 495.

Beach, K. (2016) *The Internal Revenue Service's (Potential) Role in Combating Foreign Bribery* (The Global Anticorruption Blog) <https://globalanticorruptionblog.com/2016/02/05/the-irs-should-supplement-fcpa-investigations/> accessed 27 March 2019.

Brenninkmeijer, A., Moonen, G., Debets, R. and Hock, B., (2018) 'Auditing Standards and the Accountability of the European Court of Auditors (ECA)' 14 Utrecht Law Review 1.

Button, M. (2019) *Private policing*. Abingdon: Routledge.

Cole, M. (2010) *Pursuing European Regulatory Cooperation and Consistency*. Global Competition Review 24–25 <https://www.cov.com/~/media/files/corporate/publications/2010/02/pursuing-european-regulatory-cooperation-and-consistency.pdf> accessed 18 March 2019.

De Visser, M. (2013) 'The Reform of EU Electronic Communications Law: Revolution or Evolution?' In P. Larouche and P. Cserne (Eds.) *National Legal Systems and Globalization: New Role, Continuing Relevance* (pp. 155–181). The Hague: Asser Press.

Dehousse, R. (2016). 'The Politics of Delegation in the European Union' In D. Ritleng (Ed.) *Independence and legitimacy in the institutional system of the European Union* (pp. 57–82). Oxford: Oxford University Press.

Deloitte (2016) *In the Wake of the "Panama Papers"* <http://www2.deloitte.com/content/dam/Deloitte/us/Documents/finance/us-fas-panama-papers-leak.pdf> accessed 27 March 2019.

Demas, R. R. (2011) 'Moment of Truth: Development in Sub-Saharan Africa and Critical Alterations Needed in Application of the Foreign Corrupt Practices Act and Other Anti-Corruption Initiatives' 26 American University International Law Review 315.

Dixit, A. D. (2015) 'How Business Community Institutions Can Help Fight Corruption' 29 The World Bank Economic Review.

Eberlein, B. and Grande, E. (2005) 'Beyond Delegation: Transnational Regulatory Regimes and the EU Regulatory State' 12 Journal of European Public Policy 1.

Eberlein, B. and Newman, A. L. (2008) 'Escaping the International Governance Dilemma? Incorporated Transgovernmental Networks in the European Union' 21 Governance 1.

Ezrachi, A. (2012) *Research Handbook on International Competition Law*. Cheltenham: Edward Elgar.

FATF/OECD (2013) *The Use of the FATF Recommendations to Combat Corruption* <http://www.fatf-gafi.org/media/fatf/documents/recommendations/BPP-Use-of-FATF-Recs-Corruption.pdf> accessed 25 March 2019.

Gomtsian, S., Balvert, A., Hock, B., and Kirman, O. (2018) 'Between the Green Pitch and the Red Tape: The Private Legal Order of FIFA' 43 Yale Journal of International Law, 43, 1.

Greif, A., Milgrom, P. and Weingast, B. R. (1994) 'Coordination, Commitment, and Enforcement: The Case of the Merchant Guild' 102 Journal of Political Economy 745.

Hillman, J. A. (2018) 'How to Make Trade War Even Worse'. *New York Times* <https://www.nytimes.com/2018/12/17/opinion/trade-war-china-wto.html> accessed 16 April 2019.

Hock, B. and Gomtsian, S. (2018) 'Private Order Building: The State in the Role of the Civil Society and the Case of FIFA' 17 The International Sports Law Journal 186.

Klitgaard, R. E., Ronald, M. A. and Lindsey, P. H. (1999) *Corrupt Cities: A Practical Guide to Cure and Prevention*. Oakland, CA: ICS Press.

Knobel, A. and Meinzer, M. (2014) *Automatic Exchange of Information: An Opportunity for Developing Countries to Tackle Tax Evasion and Corruption* (Tax Justice Network, June 2014) <http://www.taxjustice.net/wp-content/uploads/2013/04/AIE-An-opportunity-for-developing-countries.pdf> accessed 27 March 2019.

Martinez-Diaz, L. and Woods, N. (2009) *Networks of Influence? Developing Countries in a Networked Global Order*. Oxford: Oxford University Press.

Mathieu, E. (2016). *Regulatory Delegation in the European Union: Networks, Committees and Agencies*. London: Palgrave Macmillan.

Monti, G. (2016) 'Independence, Interdependence and Legitimacy: The EU Commission, National Competition Authorities, and the European Competition Network' In D. Ritleng (Ed.) *Independence and Legitimacy in the Institutional System of the European Union* (pp. 180–205). Oxford: Oxford University Press.

Nichols, P. M. (1997) 'Outlawing Transnational Bribery through the World Trade Organization' 28 Law & Policy in International Business 2.

OECD, *International Regulatory Co-operation: Addressing Global Challenges* (OECD Publishing 2013).

Pauwelyn, J., Wessel, R. A. and Wouters, J. (2012) *Informal International Lawmaking*. Oxford: Oxford University Press.

Pearson, Z. (2013) 'An International Human Rights Approach to Corruption' In P. Larmour and N. Wolanin (Eds.) *Corruption and Anti-Corruption* (pp. 30–61). Canberra: ANU E Press.

Piga, G. (2011) 'A Fight Chance Against Corruption in Public Procurement?' In S. Rose-Ackerman and T. Søreide (Eds.) *International Handbook on the Economics of Corruption* (pp. 141–181). Cheltenham: Edward Elgar.

Pollack, M. (2003) *The Engines of European Integration. Delegation, Agency and Agenda Setting in the EU*. Oxford: Oxford University Press.

Sauter, W. (2016) *Coherence in EU Competition Law*. Oxford: Oxford University Press.

Slaughter, A-M. (2000) 'The Real World Order' In P. O'Meara, H. D. Mehlinger, and M. Krain (Eds.) *Globalization and the Challenges of a New Century* (pp. 122–122). Bloominghton: Indiana University Press.

Spalding, A. B. (2014) 'Corruption, Corporations, and the New Human Right' 91 Washington Law Review 1365.

United Nations Global Compact (2010) *Fighting Corruption in the Supply Chain: A Guide for Customers and Suppliers* <http://www.unglobalcompact.bg/wp-content/uploads/2014/05/131.pdf> accessed 14 April 2019.

Verdier, P-H. (2009) 'Transnational Regulatory Networks and Their Limits' 34 Yale Journal of International Law 1.

10 Conclusion

International bribery and other global problems such as global warming and international cartels feature collective action problems between states. While most of the states want to benefit from the mitigation of global problems, many free-ride on the activity of others. One may say, every other country in the world is polluting, bribing, tolerating international cartels, why shouldn't we? Consequently, states too often fail to act at all, and everybody loses.

Yet, hegemonic countries and international actors sometimes attempt to resolve collective action problems and play the role of a policemen of the world. They use extraterritorial enforcement in order to regulate both domestic and foreign entities in far-away jurisdictions. Some forms of extraterritoriality are less expansive. For example, the EU Regulation on Credit Rating Agencies provides that credit ratings issued by an agency established outside the EU can only be relied upon by financial institutions established in the EU if the credit rating is endorsed by an EU agency, or if the foreign agency in question is certified by the EU.[1]

Other forms of extraterritoriality are more expansive. Especially, the US has pioneered expansive forms of extraterritoriality in the area of corporate liability for economic crimes based on, for example, the FCPA, money laundering statutes, and the RICO. Nevertheless, the EU Commission also has experience with sanctioning US hi-tech champions by billions of Euros for misusing dominant position and hurting consumers (see Petrucci, 2018).

Many of these extraterritorial practices are controversial and there is huge discussion about whether, how, and when extraterritoriality is desirable (Section 1.2.2). This book uses a collective action perspective to shed new light on the question how extraterritoriality functions and to what extent extraterritorial enforcement is desirable. How, and when, extraterritoriality can produce public goods? And, how do we incentivize jurisdictions that enforce their laws to cooperate and coordinate their actions?

1 Regulation (EC) 1060/2009 of 16 September 2009 on Credit Rating Agencies [2009] OJ L302/1. Scott (2014: 90) argues that this is typical for the EU where "the application of a measure is triggered by a territorial connection but in applying the measure the regulator is required, as a matter of law, to take into account conduct or circumstances abroad."

10.1 Foreign anti-bribery enforcement as a collective action problem

The regulation of international bribery is a collective action problem. Be it its effects on economic growth, incentives to invest, or value for money, bribery undermines overall productivity and public welfare, and is thus considered to hinder the achievement of public goods (Section 2.3.3). Yet, despite the undesirability of international bribery, a collective action problem plagues anti-bribery policy. Each state, acting on its own, has an incentive to not adopt and enforce foreign anti-bribery laws and cooperate with other countries on such enforcement.

Notwithstanding the myriad of competing views about extraterritorial enforcement in the area of international anti-bribery law, enforcement is crucial for mitigating bribery. First, extraterritorial enforcement is a technical matter because it is necessary to reach corrupt firms that are hiding in secure jurisdictions and tax havens. Second, reducing international bribery is associated with the establishment of open and competitive markets, poverty alleviation and economic growth. These are globally shared values that justify foreign anti-bribery enforcement in principle, despite the competition of state, business, and other interests underlying these aims (Rose-Ackerman, 2011: 78–79). Hence, the provision of foreign anti-bribery enforcement is a public good because placing as many corporations as possible under strict regulatory scrutiny facilitates, assumedly, the achievement of aims of international anti-bribery policy.

10.2 More collective action: who else is coming on board?

The initial collective action problem associated with the lack of enforcement has been resolved in significant part of the world. Around 2008, the US enforcement authorities have started charging MNCs for international bribery, issuing penalties as high as billions of dollars (Section 3.2; see Table 7.2). The US enforcement operates through the OECD anti-bribery enforcement regime that has facilitated the cooperation and coordination between the US and other countries such as Germany, France, the Netherlands, Brazil, and the UK (Section 6.7.3 and Table 6.1). This is an improvement. But what next?

10.2.1 Signs of further expansion: Russia and the US–China trade war

In some markets, national enforcement authorities lack economic incentives to prosecute certain corporations. The OECD enforcement regime discriminates among firms, especially when it comes to firms based in countries such as Russia, China, and India.[2] The lack of US enforcement

2 Note that there have been some Chinese and Indian subsidiaries of MNCs that resolved foreign anti-bribery enforcement actions, but large corporations headquartered in China and India have still not had to resolve any significant enforcement action.

against these corporations cannot be fully explained by the lack of institutional capacity of the regime (for the analysis of enforcement patterns, see Chapter 6). The threat of large enforcement conflicts and the lack of enforcement assistance between the OECD Convention signatory counties and certain major economies are important sources of this discrimination (Section 7.3.2).

Yet, changes in the US trade policy that came with the Trump's administration indicate the US enforcement authorities may incline to focus also on corporations headquartered in Russia and outside the OECD regime. In March 2019, the first major Russian-based corporation was charged with $850 million for international bribery in Uzbekistan.[3] Moreover, In November 2018, the DOJ has announced the New Initiative to Combat Chinese Economic Espionage.[4] The initiative primarily focuses on Chinese trade theft cases. For example, the DOJ filed charges against Fujian Jinhua Integrated Circuit, a Chinese-state owned company, and its Taiwanese partner and three individuals with stealing trade secrets from an American technology company. According to Attorney General Jeff Sessions, the companies could face sanctions worth more than $20 billion.[5] Similarly, the DOJ charged Huawei, Chinese telecom manufacturer for theft of trade secrets, wire fraud, and obstruction of justice.[6] Some of these cases also allegedly include international bribery.

One of the key priorities of the Chinese initiative is to identify FCPA cases involving companies that compete with American businesses.[7] Assistant Attorney General Benczkowski indicated that the DOJ will prioritize international bribery cases that include Chinese companies and individuals in order to improve the competitiveness of American corporations:

> [W]e know that Chinese companies and individuals also have bribed government officials in other countries in order to win contracts. The Criminal Division is committed to fully enforcing the Foreign Corrupt

3 United States Department of Justice, *Mobile TeleSystems PJSC and Its Uzbek Subsidiary Enter into Resolutions of $850 Million with the Department of Justice for Paying Bribes in Uzbekistan* (Press Release 7 March 2019) <https://www.justice.gov/opa/pr/mobile-telesystems-pjsc-and-its-uzbek-subsidiary-enter-resolutions-850-million-department> accessed 18 April 2019.

4 United States, *Attorney General Jeff Sessions Announces New Initiative to Combat Chinese Economic Espionage* (1 November 2018) <https://www.justice.gov/opa/speech/attorney-general-jeff-sessions-announces-new-initiative-combat-chinese-economic-espionage> accessed 28 April 2019.

5 United States, *Attorney General Jeff Sessions Announces New Initiative to Combat Chinese Economic Espionage* (1 November 2018) <https://www.justice.gov/opa/speech/attorney-general-jeff-sessions-announces-new-initiative-combat-chinese-economic-espionage> accessed 28 April 2019.

6 United States, Chinese Telecommunications Device Manufacturer (28 January 2019) <https://www.justice.gov/opa/pr/chinese-telecommunications-device-manufacturer-and-its-us-affiliate-indicted-theft-trade> accessed 28 April 2019.

7 United States (2018) Attorney General Jeff Session's China Initiative Fact Sheet <https://www.justice.gov/opa/speech/file/1107256/download> accessed 28 April 2019.

> Practices Act. Bringing these offenders to justice will help create a level playing field for American companies in foreign markets.[8]

These strategies, and charges already brought under the Economic Espionage Act[9], provide signs of further expansion of the US foreign anti-bribery enforcement.

10.2.2 *Extraterritoriality and small countries*

Extraterritorial enforcement is not for everybody. The high institutional capacity of US foreign anti-bribery enforcement goes along with its economic capacity. Technological and economic globalization allows the US enforcement authorities to prosecute corrupt corporations and their bribery schemes in their complexity. In large enforcement schemes that include endemic bribery (Section 5.4.1 and 5.5), the US authorities, for example, bundle hundreds of bribery allegations into one settlement. Leverages like this make the enforcement by large economies more efficient, as opposed to small economies (7.3.2.). Even if small economies have extraterritorial legislation and are equipped with a reasonable enforcement budget, they cannot deal with large cases of international bribery at the same level of complexity as large economies can (Section 7.4.2).

Still, the role of relatively smaller economies is extremely important in allowing the US, and a limited number of other strong economies, to prosecute MNCs. This is yet another area in which the OECD makes a difference. While extraterritorial enforcement is not for everybody, the OECD is effective in facilitating enforcement assistance and cooperation. The difference in enforcement roles of relatively smaller countries and enforcement leaders should, nevertheless, be addressed more explicitly by the OECD regime.

To sum up: while dominated by the US, the OECD anti-bribery enforcement regime is evolving into a multilateral enforcement regime. Many jurisdictions have started cooperating with the US, and some non-US jurisdictions have even started concluding their own enforcement actions. While these developments are positive, this transition features new collective action problems.

10.3 External governance as a response to new collective action problems

The OECD anti-bribery enforcement regime is based on functional equivalence of measures (Section 3.3). The equivalence allows for the heterogeneity of national enforcement policies and legal approaches to foreign anti-bribery

8 United States, Attorney General Brian A. Benczkowski of the Criminal Division Delivers Remarks Regarding Chinese Economic Espionage (1 November 2018) < https://www.justice.gov/opa/speech/assistant-attorney-general-brian-benczkowski-criminal-division-delivers-remarks-regarding> accessed 28 April 2019.

9 The Economic Espionage Act of 1996, 18 U.S.C. §1831 et seq.

enforcement. Such heterogeneity is acceptable when concerned primarily with relatively small groups based on informal, decentralized, and self-enforcing governance mechanism. With the increasing number of states that are active, however, the heterogeneity makes cooperation and coordination more challenging, limits the enforcement reach of the OECD regime, increases the cost of enforcement as well as the possibility of political and legal clashes (see Spahn, 2012; Turk, 2013; Section 7.4.3).

With the emerging multilateral enforcement, the OECD anti-bribery enforcement regime is heading toward a stage in which external governance is just effective (see Dixit, 2014: 76). This is a difficult position to be in. In this stage, differences between national enforcement laws and policies are increasingly problematic. Yet, it is still not clear when, and how, to establish a stronger governance mechanism that would deal with negative effects associated with such differences (for policy suggestions, see Chapter 8).

An external system of governance is what states yet need to create, for example by transferring some of their authority onto the OECD, or other international body (Section 9.1). While some authors re-opened discussions about an international anti-corruption court, this solution does not lead to a more effective enforcement regime; rather it is a solution of problems that may emerge in the future (Section 9.2). More effective would be a decentralized model in which nation-states share some enforcement tasks with an external body. Furthermore, in such model, a transgovernmental network can be used as an intermediary between an international organization and its members, shall their cooperation and coordination need to be facilitated (Section 9.4).

10.4 Transnational law: effectiveness and the rule of law – public and private

Extraterritorial enforcement of national laws is part of transnational legal processes that fall outside the traditional understanding of formal law. These processes have been conventionally depicted as accompanying a rise of the private sector, including private rule-making bodies that produce mutable, informal, and hence more effective institutions, as compared to the decreasing role of the regulatory state (see, generally, Fischer-Lescano and Teubner, 2004; Berman, 2007; Delimatsis, 2011). However, as illustrated in this project, extraterritorial enforcement practices of national enforcement authorities, including police, prosecutors, and financial regulators, are similarly mutable and informal. This indicates that certain elements of the state are gaining, rather than losing, global regulatory power (Andreas and Nadelman, 2006; Riles, 2008).

This informality and flexibility allows enforcement authorities to compromise the rule of law in the name of effective enforcement. While this book provides a narrow perspective on such informality and flexibility, it recognizes the need for more inclusive economic and political institutions. In a unilateral regime, extraterritoriality may be an effective alternative to a non-existing enforcement. Within a multilateral enforcement regime, however, the cooperation and coordination of enforcement are crucial for extraterritoriality to remain effective.

Cooperation and coordination are extremely challenging to sustain without certain level of the rule of law and accountability, virtues largely suppressed within regimes based on a unilateral form of extraterritoriality. This means that certain legal attributes such as publicity, clarity, stability, and consistency are in fact important conditions of effectiveness. From the perspective of collective action, these attributes increase the effectiveness of enforcement by facilitating the creation of common knowledge and normative classification of acceptable and unacceptable behavior (Section 2.2.2). A million-dollar question is then how to resolve the clash between ruthless and protectionist, but effective, extraterritorial enforcement and the way such enforcement can be accepted and supported by all relevant stakeholders, including foreign states, citizens, and businesses, that are influenced by such enforcement.

A hegemon can become more democratic only if these who are concerned care. In the area of foreign anti-bribery enforcement, for instance, the EU, its member states, and other countries should provide counterbalance to the US enforcement. European corporations have been sanctioned for international bribery in the US mainly because European regulators were unable or unwilling to do so. One may ask, for example, why cartels are considered the problem for the EU's internal market and international bribery is not considered to be the problem. Once the EU and other countries engage in enforcement and initiate closer dialogue with the US, the system has a good chance to develop into more cooperative enforcement network. I leave this for further research.

The key task for the future research is to learn more about the link between the effectiveness and the rule of law, accountability, and other elements of good legal order. The collective action perspective tends to simplify these clashes in the name of pragmatism. It is positive, at the end of the day, to provide recommendations and suggestions that are pragmatic. To gain more detail and depth, however, further interactions between economic governance approaches and approaches that attempt to complicate the matter, rather than simplify, will be useful. More integrated agendas that attempt to abstract trade-offs caused by extraterritoriality are, for example, the focus of global administrative law (see, for example, Krisch and Kingsbury, 2006; Zumbansen, 2013).

Further research should also acknowledge that ruthlessness and protectionism in-built in extraterritorial enforcement are based on similar desires that are observed in the private sector. Even though extraterritorial enforcement and private ordering feature common elements, their relationship is unexplored. This observation has methodological, substantive, and jurisdictional implications. When it comes to methodology, the nature of extraterritorial enforcement invites researchers to explore extensive literature on private ordering and use findings of this literature in order to analyze extraterritorial regimes (see relevant references in Section 2.2.2).

When it comes to the substance, foreign anti-bribery enforcement does not function independently from other substantive regimes that aim to mitigate transnational economic crime. The use of complicated systems of corporate veils and shell companies to hide the identity of true owners is a common feature of economic crimes. A deeper understanding of these principles, the underlying legislation that accompanies them, and the interaction between the problem of international bribery and other problems such as global financial stability, international security, industrial espionage, and tax fraud, is needed. A future study could, for example, compare other extraterritorial regimes that are related to the problem of international bribery in order to determine how key elements of extraterritoriality function in different institutional and organizational settings. Another study could also focus on how the fragmentation of laws on transnational economic crime can be used to achieve more cooperation and coordination in foreign anti-bribery enforcement.

Last, one needs to consider who should be in charge. Further studies should focus on the interaction between a broader range of anti-bribery actors, especially public actors and private actors, including standard-setting bodies such as the International Organization for Standardization, businesses, and compliance industry. This is important because the American system of enforcement is so effective because it relies heavily on the self-enforcement of private sector. Businesses are expected to have effective compliance programs and self-report problems to relevant authorities.

With the growth of compliance industry, it is difficult to ignore the resources and expertise of private investigations. In many instances, businesses can investigate and resolve corruption incidents more efficiently than public actors. In doing so, they will press for more privatization and standardization of policing. Yet, the thriving trade in self-policing their own incidents of corruption raises questions about the extent of social control that private actors possess (see, in different context, Ellickson, 2016). Corporations can be more effective and efficient in supplying certain policing tasks, but the question is whether the private fight for a good ethical standing will pass part of its revenues to society at large. Overall, corporations should primarily aim to do good clean business, and national enforcement authorities should aim to be the best in investigating and prosecuting. These two tasks overlap, but they are not the same.

References

Andreas, P. and Nadelmann, E. (2006) *Policing the Globe: Criminalization and Crime Control in International Relations*. New York: Oxford University Press.

Berman, P. S. (2007) 'Global Legal Pluralism' 80 Southern California Law Review 1155.

Delimatsis, P. (2011) 'The Fragmentation of International Trade Law' 45 Journal of World Trade 87.

Dixit, A. K. (2014) *Lawlessness and Economics: Alternative Modes of Governance*. Princeton, NJ: Princeton University Press.

Ellickson, R. C. (2016) 'When Civil Society Uses an Iron Fist: The Roles of Private Associations in rulemaking and Adjudication' 18 American Law and Economics Review 2.

Fischer-Lescano, A. and Teubner, G. (2004) 'Regime-Collisions: The Vain Search for Legal Unity in the Fragmentation of Global Law' 25 Michigan Journal of International Law 999.

Krisch, N. and Kingsbury, B. (2006) 'Introduction: Global Governance and Global Administrative Law in the International Legal Order' 17 European Journal of International Law 1.

Petrucci, C. (2018) *Both EU and US Want to Protect Competition – So Why Do They Disagree about Google's €4.32 Billion Fine? <https://theconversation.com/both-eu-and-us-want-to-protect-competition-so-why-do-they-disagree-about-googles-4-32-billion-fine-100283> accessed 20 April 2019.*

Riles, A. (2008) 'The Anti-Network: Private Global Governance, Legal Knowledge, and the Legitimacy of the State' 56 American Journal of Comparative Law 605.

Rose-Ackerman, S. (2011) 'Anti-Corruption Policy: Can International Actors Play a Constructive Role?' (2011) 440 Yale Law & Economics Research Paper.

Spahn, E. K. (2012) 'Multijurisdictional Bribery Law Enforcement: The OECD Anti-Bribery Convention' 53 Virginia Journal of International Law 1, 43.

Turk, M. C. (2013) 'A Political Economy Approach to Reforming the Foreign Corrupt Practices Act' 33 Northwestern Journal of International Law & Business 325.

Zumbansen, P. (2013) 'Administrative law's Global Dream: Navigating Regulatory Spaces between "National" and "International"' 11 International Journal of Constitutional Law 2.

Table of cases and settlements

Securities and Exchange Commission (US)

SEC vs. ABB Ltd., No. 10-cv-1648 (29 September 2010)
SEC vs. Alcoa Inc., No. 3-15673 (9 January 2014)
SEC vs. Alcatel-Lucent S.A., No. 10-cv-24620 (27 December 2010)
SEC vs. Aon Corporation, No. 11-cv-2256 (20 December 2011)
SEC vs. Archer-Daniels-Midland Company, No. 13-cv-2279 (20 December 2013)
SEC vs. Avon Products Inc., No. 14-cv-9956 (17 December 2014)
SEC vs. Biomet Inc., No. 12-cv-454 (26 March 2012)
SEC vs. Bio-Rad Laboratories Inc., No. 3-16231 (3 November 2014)
SEC vs. Daimler AG, No. 10-cv-473 (22 March 2010)
SEC vs. Eli Lilly and Company, No. 12-cv-2045 (20 December 2012)
SEC vs. ENI, S.p.A. and Snamprogetti Netherlands B.V., No. 10-cv-2414 (7 July 2010)
SEC vs. Halliburton Company and Kbr Inc., No. 4:09-cv-399 (11 February 2009)
SEC vs. Hewlett-Packard Company, No. 3-15832 (9 April 2014)
SEC vs. Innospec Inc., No. 10-cv-448 (18 March 2010)
SEC vs. Johnson & Johnson Corporation, No. 11-cv-686 (8 April 2011)
SEC vs. Magyar Telekom Plc and Deutsche Telekom A.G., No. 11-cv-9646 (29 December 2011)
SEC vs. Panalpina Inc., No. 10-cv-4334 (4 November 2010)
SEC vs Petróleo Brasileiro S.A. – Petrobras, No. 3-18843 (27 September 2018)
SEC vs. Pfizer Inc., No. 12-cv-1303 (7 August 2012)
SEC vs. Ralph Lauren Corporation, Non-Prosecution Agreement (22 April 2013)
SEC vs. Royal Dutch Shell Plc, No. 3-cv-1410 (4 November 2010)
SEC vs. Siemens Aktiengesellschaft, No. 08-cv-2167 (15 December 2008)
SEC vs. Sociedad Quimica Y Minera De Chile, No. 3-17774 (13 January 2017)
SEC vs. Smith & Wesson Holding Corporation, No. 3-15986 (28 July 2014)
SEC vs. Technip, No. 10-cv-2289 (28 June 2010)
SEC vs. Total S.A., No. 3-15338 (29 May 2013)
SEC vs. Tyco International Ltd, No. 12-cv-1583 (24 September 2012)
SEC vs. Weatherford International Ltd, No. 13-cv-3500 (26 November 2013)
SEC vs. Wyeth LLC, No. 12-cv-1304 (7 August 2012)

Department of Justice (US)

US vs. ABB Ltd., No. 10-cr-664 (29 September 2010)

US s vs. ABB Ltd. – Jordan, No. 10-cr-665 (29 September 2010)

US vs. Alcatel-Lucent, S.A., No. 10-cr-20907 (27 December 2010)

US vs. Alcatel-Lucent France, S. A., No. 10-cr-20906 (27 December 2010)

US vs. Alcoa World Alumina LLC, No. 14-cr-7 (9 January 2014)

US vs. Alstom S.A., No. 14-cr-246 (22 December 2014)

US vs. Alfred C. Toepfer International Ukraine Ltd, No. 13-cr-20062 (20 December 2013)

US vs. Avon Products Inc., No. 14-cr-828 (17 December 2014)

US vs. BAE Systems Plc, No. 10-cr-035 (4 February 2010)

US vs. Biomet Inc., No. 12-cr-80 (26 March 2012)

US vs. Bio-Rad Laboratories Inc., Non-Prosecution Agreement (3 November 2014)

US vs. Bridgestone Corporation, No. 11-cr-651 (15 September 2011)

US vs. Control Components, No. 09-cr-162 (5 July 2018)

US vs. Credit Suisse, Non-Prosecution Agreement (22 April 2013)

US vs. Daimler AG, No. 10-cr-63 (24 March 2010)

US vs. Deutsche Telekom AG, Non-Prosecution Agreement (29 December 2011).

US vs. Hawilla, Traffic Sports USA, INC., and Traffic Sports International, INC., No. 14-cr-609 (12 December 2014)

US vs. Hawit et al., No. 15-cr-252 (25 November 2015)

US vs. Hewlett-Packard Mexico, S. De R.L. De C.V., Non-Prosecution Agreement (9 April 2014)

US vs. Hewlett-Packard Polska, SP. Z O.O., No. 14-cr-202 (9 April 2014)

US vs. Innospec Inc., No. 10-cr-061 (17 March 2010)

US vs. vs. Jeffrey Tesler No. 09-cr-98 (11 March 2011)

US vs. JGC Corporation, No. 11-cr-260 (6 April 2011)

US vs. Joel Esquenazi, et al., No. 09-cr-21010 (4 December 2009)

US vs. Johnson & Johnson (Depuy), No. 11-cr-99 (8 April 2011)

US vs. Kellogg Brown & Root Llc, No. 9-cr-71 (11 February 2009)

US vs. Keppel Offshore & Marine Ltd., No. 17-cr-697 (22 December 2017)

US vs. Magyar Telekom, Plc, No. 11-cr-597 (29 December 2011)

US vs. Marubeni Corporation, No. 12-cr-22 (17 January 2012)

US vs. Mobile Telesystems PJSC, No. 19-cr-167 (6 March 2019)

US vs. Nexus Technologies, No. 08-cr-522 (28 October 2009)

US vs. Odebrecht S.A., No. 16- cr-00643 (21 December 2016)

US vs. Panalpina Inc., No. 10-cr-765 (4 November 2010)

US vs. Panalpina World Transport (Holding) Ltd., No. 10-cr-769 (4 November 2010)

US vs. Panasonic Avionics Corporation, No. 18-cr-118 (30 April 2018)

US vs. Pfizer H.C.P. Corp., No. 12-cr-169 (7 August 2012)

US, Polycom Inc., Declination with Disgorgement (20 December 2018)

US vs. Pride International Inc., No. 10-cr-766 (4 November 2010)

US vs. Ralph Lauren Corporation, Non-Prosecution Agreement (22 April 2013)

US vs. Rolls-Royce PLC, No.2:16-cr-00247 (20 December 2016).

US vs. SGA Societe Generale Acceptance, N.V. No. 18-cr-274 (5 June 2018)
US vs. Siemens Aktiengesellschaft, No. 08-cr-367 (15 December 2008)
US vs. Siemens S.A. (Argentina), No. 08-Cr-368 (15 December 2008)
US vs. Siemens S.A. (Venezuela), No. 08-Cr-370 (15 December 2008)
US vs. Sociedad Quimica Y Minera De Chile, No. 17-cr-13 (13 January 2017)
US vs. Société Générale S.A., No. 18-cr-00253 (4 June 2018)
US vs. Snamprogetti Netherlands B.V., No. 10-cr-460 (7 July 2010)
US vs. Technip S.A., No. 10-cr-439 (28 June 2010)
US vs. Telia Company AB, No. 17-cr-581 (21 September 2017)
US vs. Teva Pharmaceutical Industries, No. 16-cr-20968 (22 December 2016)
US vs. Total S.A., No. 13-cr-239 (29 May 2013)
US vs. Tyco Valves and Controls Middle East, No. 12-cr-418 (24 September 2012)
US vs. VimpelCom LTD., No. 16-crm-137 (18 February 2016)
US vs. Weatherford International Ltd., No. 13-cr-733 (26 November 2013)
US vs. Weatherford Services Ltd., No. 13-cr-734 (26 November 2013)
US vs. Webb et al., No. 15-cr-252 (20 May 2015)
US vs. ZAO Hewlett-Packard, No. 14-cr-201 (9 April 2014)

Serious Fraud Office (UK)

Serious Fraud Office vs. Mabey & Johnson Ltd., Plea (25 September 2009)
Serious Fraud Office vs. MW Kellogg Ltd., Civil settlement (16 February 2011)
Serious Fraud Office vs. MacMillan Publishers Ltd., Civil settlement (22 July 2011)
Serious Fraud Office vs. Oxford Publishing Ltd., Civil settlement (3 July 2012)
Serious Fraud Office vs. Miltiades Papachristos and Dennis Kerrison, [2014] EWCA Crim 1863 (9 September 2014)
Serious Fraud Office vs. Standard Bank Plc, Approved Judgement of the Crown Court at Southwark, No: U20150854 (30 November 2015)

Germany

Bundesgerichtshof, Judgement of 29 August 2008 (2 StR 587/07)
Staatsanwaltschaft München vs. Siemens Aktiengesellschaft (Bußgeldbescheid) (3 December 2008)
LG München I, 6 Kls 570 Js 50263/09, openJur 2016, 154 (Beschluss) (in re: MAN AG, 10 December 2009)

Other Cases

Cedeno vs. Intech Group, Inc., 733 F.Supp. 2d 471 (S.D.N.Y 2010)
Croatia v. MOL Hungarian Oil and Gas Plc, PCA Case 2014–15
Crown Office & Procurator Fiscal Service vs. International Tubular Services (17 December 2014)
European Community vs. Rjr Nabisco Inc et al., No. 11-2475 (2nd Cir. 2014)
Financial Services Authority vs. Aon Limited (6 January 2009)

Financial Services Authority vs. Barclays Bank Plc (21 July 2011)

Financial Services Authority vs. Willis Limited (21 July 2011)

Hilton vs. Guyot, 159 U.S. 113 (1895)

In re Petrobras Securities Litigation, No. 14-cv-9662 (Agreement of Settlement, 1 February 2018)

Kiobel vs. Royal Dutch Petroleum Co., 569 (2013)

Morrison vs. Nat'l Austl. Bank, 561 U.S. 247 (2010)

Pinkerton vs. United States, 328 U.S. 640 (1946)

Regina vs. Bae Systems Plc, Note for Opening (22 November 2010)

RJR Nabisco, Inc. et al. vs. European Community et al., 579 U.S. (2016)

Regina vs. Innospec Limited, [2010] EW Misc 7(EWCC) (26 March 2010)

Regina v Rolls-Royce plc, Rolls-Royce Energy Systems, Inc. Statement of Facts (17 January 2017)

SEC vs. Elek Straub, Andras Balogh and Tamas Morvai., No. 11-civ-9645 (S.D.N.Y. 2013)

United States vs. Winter, 509 F.2d 975 (5th Cir.1975)

United States vs. Macallister, 160 F.3d 1304 (11th Cir. 1998)

United States vs. Chao Fan Xu, 706 F.3d 965 (9th Cir. 2013)

World Duty Free Co. vs. Republic of Kenya ICSID Case No. Arb/00/007 (2006)

International agreements

1959 European Convention on Mutual Assistance in Criminal Matters, Strasbourg, 20 April 1959, *in force* 12 June 1962, ETS No. 030

1965 Convention on the Settlement of Investment Disputes between States and Nationals of Other States, Washington, DC, 18 March 1965, *in force* 14 October 1966, 575 UNTS

1988 Convention on Mutual Administrative Assistance in Tax Matters, 25 January 1988, *in force* 1 April 1995, amended 1 June 2011

1996 Inter-American Convention against Corruption, 29 March 1996, *in force* 6 March 1997, 35 ILM 724

1997 Convention on the Fight against Corruption Involving Officials of the European Communities or Officials of Member States of the European Union, [1997] OJ C 195

1997 OECD Convention on Combating Bribery of Foreign Public Officials in International Business Transactions, Paris, 17 December 1997, *in force* 15 February 1999, 37 ILM 1

1999 Council of Europe Criminal Law Convention on Corruption, Strasbourg, 27 January 1999, *in force* 1 July 2002, Eur. T.S. No. 173

2000 European Union Convention on Mutual Legal Assistance, [2000] OJ C 197

2000 United Nations Convention against Transnational Organized Crime, New York, 15 November, *in force* 29 September 2003, 2225 UNTS

2003 Agreement on Mutual Legal Assistance between the European Union and the United States of America, [2003] OJ L 181

2003 African Union Convention on Preventing and Combating Corruption, Maputo, 11 July 2003, *in force* 5 August 2006, 43(1) ILM 5

2003 United Nations, Convention Against Corruption, New York, 31 October 2003, *in force* 14 December 2005, 2349 U.N.T.S. 41, 43 I.L.M. 37

2007 Treaty on the Functioning of the European Union, TFEU

Statutes

United States

1789 Alien Tort Claims Act 1789
1890 Sherman Antitrust Act 1890
1909 New York State Penal Law 1909
1934 Securities Exchange Act 1934
1952 Travel Act 1952
1970 Bank Secrecy Act 1970
1970 Racketeer Influenced and Corrupt Organizations 1970
1976 Arms Export Control Act 1976
1977 Foreign Corrupt Practices Act 1977
1986 Money Laundering Control Act 1986
1986 Federal False Claims Act 1986
1988 Omnibus Trade and Competitiveness Act 1988
1996 Economic Espionage Act 1996
1998 International Anti-Bribery and Fair Competition Act 1998
2001 US Patriot Act 2001 (Uniting and Strengthening America by Providing Appropriate Tools Required to Intercept and Obstruct Terrorism)
2002 The Sarbanes-Oxley Act 2002

United Kingdom

1861 Accessories and Abettors Act 1861
1889 Public Bodies Corrupt Practices Act 1889, c. 69
1906 Prevention of Corruption Act 1906, c. 34
1977 Criminal Law Act 1977, c. 45
1985 Companies Act 1985, c. 6
2000 Financial Services and Markets Act 2000
2002 Proceeds of Crime Act 2002, c. 29
2002 Police Reform Act 2002, c. 30
2003 Crime (International Cooperation) Act 2003, c. 32
2010 Bribery Act 2010, c. 23
2013 Crime and Courts Act 2013, c. 22

Germany

1949 Grundgesetz (Constitution)
1987 Strafprozeßordnung (StPO) (Code of Criminal Procedure)
1987 Gesetz über Ordnungswidrigkeiten (OWiG) (Administrative Offences Act)
1994 Gesetz über die internationale Rechtshilfe in Strafsachen (IRG)
1998 Gesetz zur Bekämpfung Internationaler Bestechung (IntBestG) (Transposition Act)
1998 Strafgesetzbuch (StGB) (Criminal Code)
2002 Bürgerliches Gesetzbuch (BGB) (Civil Code)
2017 Geldwäschegesetz (Money Laundering Act)

France

2016 LOI n° 2016-1691 du 9 décembre 2016 relative à la transparence, à la lutte contre la corruption et à la modernisation de la vie économique (Sapin II)

Recommendations, guidelines, and reports of public authorities and international organizations

1976 International Traffic in Arms Regulation, 22(1)(M) C.F.R. §120–130, US Department of State
1977 ICC Rules on Combating Corruption (2011 edition), International Chamber of Commerce
1981 Impact of Foreign Corrupt Practices Act on U.S. Business, United States General Accounting Office
1990 Guidelines on the Role of Prosecutors, U.N. Doc. A/Conf.144/28/Rev.1 at 189, United Nations
1994 Recommendation of the Council on Bribery in International Business Transactions, OECD
1997 Commentaries on the Convention on Combating Bribery of Foreign Public Officials in International Business Transactions, OECD
1997 Revised Recommendation of the Council on Combating Bribery in International Business Transactions, OECD
1997 U.S. Attorneys' Manual, 9–27.000 – Principles of Federal Prosecution, United States
1997 U.S. Attorneys' Manual, 9–28.000 – Principles of Federal Prosecution of Business Organizations, United States
1999 United Kingdom Review of Implementation of the Convention and 1997 Recommendation, OECD Working Group on Bribery
1999 United States Review of Implementation of the Convention and 1997 Recommendation, OECD Working Group on Bribery
1999 Foreign Corrupt Practices Act Opinion Procedure Regulation, DOJ
1999 Germany Review of Implementation of the Convention and 1997 Recommendation, OECD Working Group on Bribery
2000 Recommendation Rec(2000)19 of the Committee of Ministers to Member States on the Role of Public Prosecution in the Criminal Justice System, Council of Europe
2002 United States: Phase 2 Report on the Application of the Convention on Combating Bribery of Foreign Public Officials, OECD Working Group on Bribery
2003 United Kingdom Phase I bis: Review of Implementation of the Convention, OECD Working Group on Bribery

2008 Phase 2bis Report on Implementing the OECD Anti-Bribery Convention in the United Kingdom, OECD Working Group on Bribery
2007 Attorney General's Domestic Guidance for Handling Criminal Cases Affecting Both England, Wales or Northern Ireland and the United States of America, United Kingdom
2007 Guide to Criminal Prosecution in the United States, Organization of American States
2009 Recommendation of the Council for Further Combating Bribery of Foreign Public Officials in International Business Transactions, OECD
2009 Typologies on the Role of Intermediaries in International Business Transactions, Working Group on Bribery
2009 Recommendation of the Council on Tax Measures for Further Combating Bribery of Foreign Public Officials in International Business Transactions, OECD
2009 Corporate Crime: DOJ Has Taken Steps to Better Track Its Use of Deferred and Non-Prosecution Agreements, but Should Evaluate Effectiveness, United States Government Accountability Office
2010 Phase 3 Report on Implementing the OECD Anti-Bribery Convention in the United States, OECD Working Group on Bribery
2010 United Kingdom Phase 1ter: Report on the Application of the Convention on Combating Bribery of Foreign Public Officials in International Business Transaction and the 2009 Revisited Recommendation on Combating Bribery in International Business Transactions, OECD Working Group on Bribery
2011 Joint Investigation Teams Manual, Council of the European Union
2011 Convention on Combating Bribery of Foreign Public Officials in International Business Transactions and Related Documents, OECD
2011 Phase 3 Report on Implementing the OECD Anti-Bribery Convention in Germany, OECD Working Group on Bribery
2011 US Sentencing Guidelines, United States Sentencing Commission
2011 The Bribery Act 2010 Guidance, United Kingdom – Ministry of Justice
2012 International Standards on Combating Money Laundering and the Financing of Terrorism & Proliferation, The FATF Recommendations, FATF
2012 United States: Follow-up to the Phase 3 Report & Recommendations, OECD Working Group on Bribery
2012 Phase 3 Report on Implementing OECD Anti-Bribery Convention in the United Kingdom, OECD Working Group on Bribery
2012 Resource Guide to the US Foreign Corrupt Practices Act, Criminal Division of the DOJ the Enforcement Division of the SEC
2013 Director's Guidance on the Handling of Cases where the Jurisdiction to Prosecute is Shared with Prosecuting Authorities Overseas, the Crown Prosecution Service

2013 The Russian Federation Phase 2: Report on Implementing the OECD Anti-Bribery Convention in the Russian Federation, OECD Working Group on Bribery
2013 Germany: Follow-up to the Phase 3 Report & Recommendations, OECD Working Group on Bribery
2014 An Analysis of the Crime of Bribery of Foreign Public Officials, OECD Foreign Bribery Report
2014 Monitoring of County Compliance under the OECD Anti-Bribery Convention: Compilation of Responses from the Public Consultation on the Parameters for Phase 4, OECD
2014 United Kingdom: Follow-up to the Phase 3 Report & Recommendations, OECD Working Group on Bribery
2014 Opinion Procedure Release, No. 14-02, DOJ
2014 Standard for Automatic Exchange of Financial Account Information in Tax Matters, OECD
2014 Deferred Prosecution Agreements Code of Practice, Crime and Courts Act 2013, SFO and CPS
2015 FIFA Statutes: Regulations Governing the Application of the Statutes Standing Orders of the Congress, FIFA
2016 Guidelines for Deciding 'Which Jurisdiction Should Prosecute?' Eurojust
2016 ISO 37001:2016 Anti-Bribery Management Systems, International Organization for Standardization
2016 The Fraud Section's Foreign Corrupt Practices Act Enforcement Plan and Guidance, DOJ
2017 International Co-operation in Corruption Cases, OECD
2018 Phase 4 Report on Implementing the OECD Anti-Bribery Convention in Germany
2018 Policy on Coordination of Corporate Resolution Penalties, DOJ

Index

Note: **Bold** page numbers refer to tables and *italic* page numbers refer to figures.

Abbott, K.W. 228, 229
accounting fraud 45, 112
accounting provisions *see* books and records
African Union Convention 46
Alba 161
Alcoa World Alumina and Chemicals (AWAC) 161–2
Alstom 171–3, 180
alternative charges 142, 151, 160; German law 159–60; UK law 157; US law 151
anti-bribery standard 3, 6, 41, 241; private 45
anti-corruption: court 228–9, 243; domestic law 40; networks 235; policy 8, 25–6; private 242; treaties 45–6
anti-trust 40, 145; law 157; *see also* competition
AON 179
Archer Daniels Midland Company (ADM) 166
asset recovery *see* recovery of stolen assets
associated person 66, 81–2, 84
awareness: about extraterritoriality 208, 212, 218; about the plurality of enforcement policies 219; on the negative effects of international bribery 43

BAE scheme 120–1, 140–5, 157, 179
Bank Secrecy Act 156
banks: illegal payments through 126–7; secrecy 98, 178, 237; Swiss 129, 139
beneficial ownership 237
BEREC 227, 234; classification mechanism 232–3
Berman, P. S. 79, 250
bid-rigging 157; *see also* public procurement
Bonny Island scheme 120, *132*, 130–40
books and records: accurate 41, 122; provisions 125, 126, 165–7; violations 164, 236
Brazil 183–7, **184**, **198**; multijurisdicitonal settlements **184**; *see also* FCPA
Brazilian Football Confederation (CBF) 152
breach of trust 123, 159
bribe 75–79; anything of value 41, 63
briber 60–1
bribery: active 19; authorization 63, 67; commercial 73, 112, 154, 159; definition 19;harmful 22–5; of foreign public official 44, 196; offense of 59; passive 19, 55; *see also* foreign bribery; international bribery
Bribery Act 55, 65–6, 73, 77, 83, 116, 157–8; section 7 84
Bribery Act Guidance 66, 77–8
bribery case 93–6; aprroaches to study 111–13; bundle 109
bribery, indirect 61–70, 161
Bundeskriminalamt, German Federal Criminal Police Office 89
bundle *see* bribery case
Bürgerliches Gesetzbuch (BGB) 54
business: association 24, 239–40; international transactions 4, 13, 19–20, 24; lobby 3, 195; partners 84, 187, 188, 199–200, 241

Canada 173
centralized authority 16, 26, 30, 228
Choi, S. J. 211
civil law 64, 69, 101, 210
civil recovery orders 55, 117, 158, 160
clarity problem 27–8; adressing 217–25; cooperation and coordination 212; effectiveness **194**, 193–5; functional equivalence 51; heterogeneity 215–17; multilateral enforcement 208–9; *see also* credibility problem
class action 139, 187, 201, 206
Colangelo, A. J. 7, 102, 149, 221
collective action 1, 4; and classifying mechanism 28–30; and public good 22–8; problem 4, 10, 14, 16–19; theory 14–18; two orders of 28–30
collusion 185, 240
common law 85, 101, 210
competition: fair and equal 34; political and economic 13, 23; *see also* EU competition law
competitive disadvantage 1, 42, 197
compliance industry 239, 241–2, 252
compliance program 8, 78, 91–2, 141, 166, 168, 241, 252
compliance, corporate 239–42
complicity 67–70
CONCACAF 152
conflict of interests 7
conflict of laws 224
CONMEBOL 152
consent jurisdiction 163–5
conspiracy 67–70; indirect bribery 105; jurisdiction 119; Racketeer Influenced and Corrupt Organization Act (RICO) *see* Racketeer Influenced and Corrupt Organization Act (RICO); US enforcement 169–74
cooperation and coordination 96–104, 138–39, 209–14; *Bonny Island* scheme 127–9; enforcement 33, 35; mechanism 17; national enforcement authorities 9, 27; patterns of enforcement 187; problems 9; Siemens 127–29; *see also* collective action; clarity problem; credibility problem; enforcement; regime corporate liability 10, 61, 64, 69, 85, 91, 119, 210; *see also* liability of legal persons
corruption: definition 19; domestic 6–7; foreign 6–7; harmful 22–25
Council of Europe (CoE) 26, 98
Council of Europe Criminal Law Convention on Corruption 46
credibility problem 27–28; adressing 217; alleviated 197; effectiveness193–95, **194**; in practice **205**; multilateral enforcement 204; new 207;*see also* clarity problem
criminal enterprise 154, 158, 160

Daimler 163–64, 177
Davis, K. E. 23, 211
debarment 55, 93, 164, 199, 211
deferred prosecution agreement *see* settlement
Department of Justice (DOJ): agency principle 64; *Bonny Island* scheme **136**; enforcement policy 90–91;independence 88; policy of coordination of corporate resolutions 100; Siemens **124**
Deutsche Telekom (DT) 149, 163
discretion, prosecutorial 78, 86, 89, 90–2
Dixit, A. K. 16, 17, 193, 216, 217, 242, 250
double jeopardy 101–2; *see also ne bis in idem*
due diligence 168, 188, 199, 241; *see also* compliance programs

eCommunication model 230–3
eCommunications 227
economic crime, transnational 103, 151, 158–9, 252
economic growth 7, 13, 23, 24, 26, 247
economics 18, 27
effectiveness *see* clarity problem; credibility problem; extraterritoriality; MLA; regime
efficiency: allocative 5; corruption 23; enforcement 199, **205**, 249; markets 15, 24; procedural 151, 160, 169–70
enforcement: as public good 22–8; centralized 87; decentralized 53, 89; matter 110–11, 197; multilateral 32–4; unilateral 28, 32–3, 196–203
enforcement authorities 6; national 8, 58; non-US 22
enforcement conflict 34; and appropriate jurisdiction 212; rare 187; threat of large 206; *see also* jurisdictional conflict

enforcement scheme: definition 110; in Germany 114–15; in the UK 116–18; in the US 113–14; types 120–1
ENI 130 241; *see also Bonny Island* scheme
Enron scandal 45
espionage, Chinese economic 3, 248
EU: agencies 104, 223; competition law 102; directive 49; extraterritoriality 4, 246; non-financial reporting 211; privacy laws 221
EU Commission 230–3
EU regulatory model 230–4
Eurojust 224; guidelines 223; *see also* Europol
Europol 224, 225; *see also* Eurojust
exchange of tax information 237
expertise 4, 231, 238, 243
external governance 191, 230, 249–50; *see also* governance
extradition 44, 98, 100
extraterritoriality 1, 9; alleviates the lack of enforcement *31*; and collective action 30–4; and OECD regime 215–26; clarity problems *34*; the effectiveness of 195–213; *see also* jurisdiction

facilitation payments 22, 45, 77–9
failure to prevent bribery 55, 66, 117
Fair Competition Act of 1998 52
FATF Recommendations 236–7
FBI 88
FCPA 2; bribe 76–78; compliance standard 242; corruptly 63; definition of briber 60; early legislative activities 42–3; foreign bribery definition 41–2; foreign public official 73; indirect bribery 63–4; jurisdiction *83*; matters 197, 200; opinion procedure 90; scope 52
FCPA Digest 113
Ferguson, G. 17, 69, 99, 104
Ferguson, W. D. 14, 17, 18, 29
FIFA 152–5; MLA 175; *see also* Racketeer Influenced and Corrupt Organization Act (RICO)
Financial Action Task Force (FATF) 235–6
Financial Conduct Authority (FCA) 88, 117
financial intelligence units 236–8
Financial Services Authority (FSA) 118
foreign bribery 40–6; investigation and prosecution 87–9; the offense of 59
foreign direct investment 7
foreign public official 70–3, 159; German law 74; UK law 73; US law 73
France 179–81; MNCs under US law **198**; multijurisdicitonal settlements 184
freezing and confiscation of assets 98, 175, 237
functional equivalence: methodological tool 50–1; minimum standard approach 51–52; principle 46–50, 86, 210; *see also* heterogeinity
future research 251

G20 Anti-Corruption Working Group (ACWG) 235
Germany: briber 60; complicity and conspiracy 69; enforcement authorities 114; enforcement system 88–9; foreign public official 74; indirect bribery 65; jurisdiction 84 5; law 53–4; MNCs under US law **198**; settlement procedures 94–5; Siemens **124**
Gesetz über Ordnungswidrigkeiten (OWiG) 54, 60, 64, 65, 95, 123
Getz, K. A. 28, 192, 193
Gibbons, R. 17, 27, 28, 194
gifts 6, 19; *see also* bribery
Global Network of Law Enforcement Practitioners against Corruption 218
global problems 4, 7, 246
global resolution *see* settlement, global
globalization 20, 150
governance: alternatives 243; economic 5, 6, 14, 16; good 4, 78; mechanism 17, 195, 217; *see also* external governance
Greif, A. 16, 240
Grundgesetz 91
guilty plea *see* settlement

Hadfield, G. K. 17, 29
Halliburton 2, *133*; *see also Bonny Island* scheme
harmonization 47, 216, 236
Henderson, R. 27, 28, 193
heterogeneity: collective action 59, 105–6; desirable and undesirable 215–17; enforcement 86; external governance 249–50; functional equivalence *see*

functional equivalence; implementation 52, 60; of national approaches 39, 55; of national measures 210
Hewlett Packard 22
Hewlett-Packard: Russia buy back scheme *21*
human rights 4, 227, 228

ICBC 117, 179
ICSID129
identification doctrine 66, 116, 157
Innospec 116, 179
IntBestG 53
Intermediary, liability for 61
internal controls: charges 157, 162, 171; provisions 126, 127, 135; violation 125, 164; *see also* books and records
internal market 231, 233, 251
international bribery scheme *22*, 19–22
international comity 99–101, 222
International Criminal Court (ICC) 10, 29, 227; model 228
International Traffic in Arms Regulation (ITAR) 142
issuer: accounting provisions 165–7; foreign 150–1; jurisdiction 126–7, 135–8; US law 81–3

JGC 131; *see also Bonny Island* scheme
Johnson & Johnson 168
joint investigation team 102, 103, 195, 224; *see also* parallel investigation
jurisdiction **83**; analytical framework 119; and conspiracy charges 170–4; appropriate 56, 98, 101, 212, 225; German law 85; limit 32; nationality principle 81, 119; overlap 33; reach 33; territorial 10, 79–80, 119; territorial basis 5; UK law 84; universal 29; US law 83; US territorial jurisdiction in practice 149; *see also* extraterritoriality
jurisdictional conflict 33, 106; and appropriate jurisdiction 220–5; coordination 97, 98–9; *see also* credibility problem; clarity problem

KBR 2, 130, *132*; *see also Bonny Island* scheme
Kennedy, D. 6, 25
Keohane, R. O. 5, 16, 193, 195
kickbacks 153, 185, 238; *see also* bribery
Kiobel 155
Koehler, M. 7, 70

Lambsdorff, J. G. 23
Landa, J. 16
law enforcement 24, 86, 235
legality and opportunity, principles 90–2
legitimacy 7, 23, 243
liability of legal persons 44, 47, 60, 64, 91
local law exception 76–7; *see also* bribe
Lockheed bribery scandals 41
Lord, N. 89, 90, 91, 220

Magyar Telekom 149, 163
market failure 14, 17, 18
Marubeni 131, 133, 145, 172; *see also Bonny Island* scheme
merger and acquisition 161, 168, 199
Milgrom, P. 16, 240
MLA: assistance mechanism for cooperation 97–8; BAE 143; Bonny Island 138; cooperation before the final resolution 174–5; effectiveness of enforcement 195; OECD Convention 44
MLA Convention: EU Convention on Mutual Legal Assistance 103; *see also* MLA
MNCs 4; accountability 197; hide 79, 196, 208; leave markets 207; power of 5
money laundering 44, 46, 84, 89, 112, 153; and direct cooperation 236–7
Money Laundering Control Act 1986 156
monitoring process, OECD 49–50, 72, 75, 78, 210
moral imperialism 6
Morrison 155
Munich Public Prosecutor's Office 115, 122; MLA 128

Nabisco 154; *see also* Racketeer Influenced and Corrupt Organization Act (RICO)
nationality of MNCs 81, **198**
ne bis in idem 100, 102; *see also* double jeopardy
Netherlands 179–81; MNCs under US law **198**
nexus: interstate commerce 82, 83, 126, 150; territorial 85, 106, 135, 137, 148, 165
Nexus Technologies 155
Nigeria: Panalpina 169; Siemens 125, 129; *see also Bonny Island* scheme
Nigerian National Petroleum Corporation (NNPC) 131
Nichols, P. M. 25, 42, 199, 228, 229

non-prosecution agreement *see* settlement
North, D. C. 17, 18
NRAs (national regulatory authorities) 231–2
NYSE 20, 121, 201

Odebrecht/Braskem 179, 185, 186
Oduor, J. 93, 94, 102, 110, 111, 126, 129, 174
OECD anti-bribery regime *see* regime, OECD anti-bribery enforcement
OECD Convention 1, 5; and national laws 52–5, 58; beyond 45–6; functional equivalence 46–52; towards 42–5
OECD monitoring mechanism *see* monitoring process, OECD
OECD Working Group on Bribery (WGB) 43, 48, 52, 219, 235
Oil-For-Food program 122
Olson, M. 8, 14, 15, 16
Openbaar Ministerie 181
Organization of American States (OAS) 26
Ostrom, E. 13, 16, 192

Panalpina 169–70
parallel investigation 98, 102, 128, 174, 188; *see also* joint investigation team
parent-subsidiary liability 161–5; *see also* subsidiary
Patriot Act 156
Petrobras: coordination challenges 187; protection of US investors 201
Pieth, M. 43–5, 50–1, 62, 71, 75, 77, 80–1, 87, 164
Poland 207; *see also Hewlett Packard;* Hewlett-Packard: Russia buy back scheme
policing 242, 252
political will 4, 13
politically exposed persons 89
price-fixing 157
Proceeds of Crime Act 2002 134, 158
Prüfer, J. 17
public procurement 21, 69, 71, 157, 173

quid pro quo 19, *see also* bribery; kickback

Racketeer Influenced and Corrupt Organization Act (RICO) 152–5, 159; *see also* conspiracy; FIFA
recovery of stolen assets 13, 46, 194
regime: decentralized 29; effectiveness 194–5; international 16–18; multilateral 29, 191–5, 203–5; transition 191, 203–6; unilateral 32–3, 193–203
regime, OECD anti-bribery enforcement 9, 28–30, 32, 213, 215–25
reporting, non-financial 211
resolution: coordinated 182; formal and functional understanding 110–11; of collective action problems 15–17; of foreign bribery cases 93–6; see also case; enforcement scheme; settlement
Resource Guide 68, 91, 148
Rolls-Royce 117, 118, 182–3
Roman law 101
Rose, C. 3, 43, 46
Rose-Ackerman, S. 22, 24, 25, 26, 247
rule of law 5, 13, 91, 183, 210, 250–1
Russia: Hewlett-Packard 19–22; MTS 3; Siemens 122; Teva 172; *see also* trade war

Saipem 130, 139, 241; *see also Bonny Island* scheme
sanctions, foreign bribery 92–3
Sandler, T. 13, 16, 17
SBM Offshore 181, 185–7, 206
secure jurisdictions 5, 30, 79, 196, *see also tax havens*
Securities and Exchange Commission (SEC): agency principle 64; *Bonny Island* scheme **136**; enforcement polic 90–1; Siemens **124**
self-regulation 188, 199, 239, 242
self-reporting 91, 157, 241, 252
Serious Fraud Office (SFO) 88, 116; MKWL 134; MLA 143
settlement: deferred prosecution agreement 94; definition 110; guilty plea 93; in Germany 94–5; in the UK 94–5; in the US 93–4
settlement, global 120, 179, 187
settlement, multijurisdictional 182–7, **184**, 206
Sherman Act 157
Shleifer, A. 4, 23
Siemens case 111, 115, 120, 121–30, 164; as the standard of global resolution 177
Slaughter, A-M. 29, 234
Snamprogetti 130, 133, 138, 165, 241; *see also Bonny Island* scheme
Snidal, D. 28, 193, 228, 229

soft law 30, 224, 225
Spahn, E. K. 34, 250
Spalding, A. B. 7, 41, 228, 229
statutory defenses 77; *see also* bribe
Strafgesetzbuch (StGB) 53–4, 64–5, 69, 74, 85, 122, 159–60
subsidiary: issuer 127, 138; responsibility of a parent 62; Siemens 125
successor's liability *see* merger and acquisition
Switzerland 201; bank transparency 177–79; MNCs under US law 198; multijurisdictional settlements **184**; *see also* banks, Swiss

Tarullo, D. K. 32, 43
tax evasion 84, 112
tax fraud 110, 209, 219, 236
tax havens 30, 196, 247, *see also* secure jurisdictions
tax regulation 237–39
Technip 130, 133; *see also Bonny Island* scheme
terrorism: combating 223; financing 236; international 16, 219; legislation 45
terrorist attacks 9/11 45, 195, 196
Teva 172–3
Total 171, 180
trade war 247
transgovernmental network 234–39
Travel Act 151, 153, 155, 156
Trump's administration 2, 248
TSKJ joint venture 130, 172, 241; *see also Bonny Island* scheme
Turk, M. C. 34, 250

UK: BAE 140–4; briber 60; complicity and conspiracy 69; enforcement system 88–9; foreign public official 73; indirect bribery 66; jurisdiction 83–4; law 54–5; settlement procedures 94–5
UN Convention against Transnational Organized Crime 104
UNCAC 46, 98, 101, 104
undue advantage *see* bribe
US: briber 61; complicity and conspiracy 68–9; enforcement system 87–8; foreign public official 73; indirect bribery 63–4; jurisdiction 81–3; law 52–3; settlement procedures 93–4
US Department of State (DOS) 141, 142
US Government Accountability Office (GAO) 90

victims 7, 223
VimpelCom 178, 181
Vishny, R. W. 4, 23

Watergate scandal 41, 195
Weingast, B. R. 16, 17, 29, 217, 240
whistleblowing 45, 211
willful blindness 62, 63
wire fraud 153, 154, 248
wire transfer 138, 149
World Bank 24, 125, 126, 129
WTO model 230

Young, O. R. 192, 193

Zerk, J. A. 4, 79, 80